Secret Tibet

Fosco Maraini

Secret Tibet

Translated from the Italian by
Eric Mosbacher and Guido Waldman

With an Introductory Letter by
Bernard Berenson

THE HARVILL PRESS
LONDON

First published in Italy in 1951 with the title *Segreto Tibet* by
Leonardo da Vinci, Bari, and in Great Britain in 1952 by Hutchinson, London

This revised, augmented edition first published in Italy in 1998 by Corbaccio, Milan,
and in Great Britain in 2000 by
The Harvill Press
2 Aztec Row, Berners Road
London N1 0PW

www.harvill.com

1 3 5 7 9 8 6 4 2

A CIP catalogue record for this book
is available from the British Library

ISBN 1 86046 693 1

Designed and typeset in Sabon
at Libanus Press, Marlborough, Wiltshire

Printed and bound in Great Britain by Butler & Tanner Ltd
at Selwood Printing, Burgess Hill

In thankful memory of the great Master
Giuseppe Tucci

With affection to the memory of my companions
Regolo Moise and Piero Mele

CONTENTS

LIST OF ILLUSTRATIONS

All photographs are taken by the author except where otherwise marked.

I Tatti
Settignano
Florence

March 23rd, 1950

Dear Fosco,
I have just finished your book on the journey to Tibet. I have read many travellers who have written about the top of the world and its forbidding approaches of mountain or desert. Even my favourites, the French Abbé Huc of a hundred years ago and the more recent Japanese Ekai Kawaguchi, have not succeeded as you have in making me forget that I actually was not with you. Only Doughty's *Arabia Deserta*, Freya Stark's *Valley of the Assassins* and Mildred Cable's *Gobi Desert* have taken me along with them as you did while I was reading you. I have been drenched to the skin, frozen stiff, disgusted with smells, nauseated with food, have been dropping with fatigue, refreshed by the ozone-laden morning air and gladdened by the warmth of a summer day. Above all I was there with you when you talked to Tibetans, lay and ecclesiastical, mystics, scholars, theologians, minstrels, shopkeepers, beggars, artisans and artists, proletarian priests and monks, peasants and shepherds. Like you, after getting used to their gorgeous raiment, their dirt, their rags, their bad smell, I encountered fellow-men singularly like ourselves. Culturally this is the best recommendation for travelling. It is so difficult to get over the deep-rooted conviction, amounting to an axiom, that we only and alone are rational human beings and that no foreigner, not even another Westerner, is quite that. It takes really sympathetic and continuous contact to bring it home to us that there are folk as good and true and intelligent as without questioning we assume that we are.

To achieve as much we must travel as wanderers in the way you have while in Tibet, and not, as more and more we are doing now, transported like letters in well-sealed post-bags, by so-called *rapides* or, worse still, by air, neither seeing nor hearing anything beside the clatter and whizz of the vehicle that is despatching us from one business or amorous engagement to another in a fake sameness, a sameness calculated to ignore, if not to repel, spiritual interest or mere curiosity of any kind.

One would be tempted to expect travelling in the old sense of the word to be coming to an end but for the young of the impoverished heirs to culture, who walk and hike as "enchanted Wanderers", sleeping in hostels or in the open, and looking and seeing, and enjoying and listening and learning.

How well you write! How you succeed in conveying every kind of information and sensation and evocation! You have managed to make me eager to flirt with the young Sikkim princess, half Westernized yet longing for Lhasa, not as for a sort of *Graaltempel*, as it is for us Europeans, but as a fashionable and pleasure-loving Paris. And your return flight from India to Italy, from Calcutta to Rome – what evocations, the names of the places you pass!

Hitherto distance has lent enchantment to names of countries and cities, has evoked longing – *dahin*, thither – for the far away, the almost unreachable, unattainable, that would demand courage and skill and ample means and luck as well as cunning to realize. And time – the Siva, the preserver, the destroyer of all that is – now more and more and still more ignored, all but abolished by modern transport.

Italo Balbo descended from his aeroplane at Gadames and asked the sheikhs, who had gathered to do him homage, how long it took them to go to Tripoli. "Twenty-eight days." "I have come here in three hours." "Then what do you do during the other twenty-seven days?" They lived while they travelled. He only flew.

There perhaps is a vital difference between past and present. In the past one lived whatever one did. Now one lives, not as a condition independent of deliberate activities, but only, if ever, in the interstices of action.

This is not your case as a traveller; and let me thank you beside congratulating you yet once again, for all the fascinating observations and suggestions your book has given me.

Sincerely yours,

BERNARD BERENSON

Author's Note

Anyone writing about Tibet is confronted with the problem of transcribing place-names and the names of gods, saints and other persons, as also a certain number of words, into the Western alphabet. The problem crops up in every Eastern language and often leads to unforeseen complications to say nothing of fierce quarrels among scholars. You have only to think of what happens with Chinese, where the proponents of the Wade-Giles system and those of the now officially adopted Pinyin confront each other disdainfully. Is one to write of the Ch'ing dynasty or of the Qing? It's no different with Japanese: Mount Fuji or Mount Huzi? Geysha or geisya? Chikatetsu (underground) or tikateku?

With Tibetan it becomes the very devil of a problem. Various systems of transcription do exist, true, but it ought to be possible to come to some agreement. The fact is that, once this first hurdle is overcome, a second and far more irksome one presents itself. Written Tibetan first appeared in the seventh century, employing a syllabic system said to have been invented by Thonmi Sambhota, an erudite minister; this was based on the Indian writing systems of the time. And yet Tibetan is fundamentally different from the north Indian dialects, which belong to the Indo-European family whereas Tibetan belongs with the Chinese family; it rests on a very complex foundation of consonants and vowels. Moreover, Thonmi Sambhota was evidently a perfectionist: his aim was to record the most fleeting modulations in pronunciation with the highest degree of precision.

Thus far the situation might not have been beyond hope. But there now cropped up a fact of history that proceeded to muddy the waters irremediably: ever since the eighth century, pronunciation has undergone a radical change. While the written language has remained just as it was, the pronunciation of names and words has been subject to simplifications of quite an acrobatic nature. In this respect Tibetan is like English, only worse. Everybody knows that comb, tomb and bomb are all written the same way but pronounced differently, as also cough and enough – for sufficiently noted historical reasons.

Much the same has happened in Tibetan, and names written down today as Rva sgrengs or 'Bras spungs are pronounced Reting and D(r)epung. The serious difficulty is that no general agreement exists as to how these modern pronunciations – which in any case vary, often a great deal, between one part of Tibet and the next – are to be recorded in the Latin alphabet. It might have been hoped that the dialect spoken in the capital, Lhasa, as happens in other instances (Tokyo for Japanese) might serve as the "official" pronunciation, but no, it does not. The Tibetologists, who for one reason and another gravitate towards a small sect of scholars deeply jealous of their arcane science, reject or dismiss any transliteration that fails to be "scientific" and complete. Thus Ngawang Lobsang Gyatso (the name of the Fifth Dalai Lama) is out, only Ngag dhang blo bzang rgyamtsho will do; the Lhasa region Ü is out, only dBus will do; sGrolma (woman's name) yes, D(r)olma, no.

From a certain viewpoint they cannot be blamed. "When different authors adopt simplified 'phonetic' transliterations for Western readers," one of the leading experts in this field, David Snellgrove, observes despairingly, "it becomes impossible to adhere to a generally accepted norm." Perfectly true. And yet it is simply not possible to present the poor Western reader of moderate, or even of first-rate education, with a name that features on the page as Khri srong de brtsan, and expect him to read it as Tisong-detsen after the Tibetan fashion. Quite impossible. Anybody who writes about Tibet and its civilization, unless he is addressing the small group of specialists, is at some point bound to grasp this nettle; he has to give his reader the names of places, people and local idioms in some pronounceable manner that does not leave him stubbing his toes at every second line.

All very well, Mr Maraini, but what has been your solution? "The best I could manage is all I can say. Indeed on occasions falling short even then." With the aim of facilitating reading and committing to memory (which is not to be overlooked by anyone wishing to hoist in a brief outline of Tibetan history) I have generally gone for the simplest phonetic transcriptions, for instance those adopted in the writings of R. A. Stein, Charles Bell, W. D. Shakabpa (listed in Bibliography I) – who frequently differ among themselves.

To venture too far into the minutiae would bring us up against a further singularity: Go ahead and transcribe Tibetan names and words as best you may, fair enough, but is this to be done according to Italian phonetics, determining the hard and the soft g by the addition of an h, for instance? Fair enough, but what happens if the reader wants to pursue his study into reading lists which, perforce, will generally involve British or American authors? Or if he wants to consult more or less international maps. Would it not be as well to try so far as possible to conform to a uniform transcription valid for the whole of Western writing on the Orient? The broadest approach to uniformity may be obtained by following a very simple old rule: "Italian vowels, English consonants". It is not perfect, nor is it the least bit scientific, but it does work. Thus we shall find *Gelug-pa* (hard g), Gyantse (hard g), and *geshe* (also hard g).

As if this were not enough, the matter is complicated yet further in these last years with the arrival of the Chinese, and the addition of another filter to the presentation of Tibetan, which is of singular importance in place-names. Thus we come across certain names that have reached us by an additional phonetic and graphical circuit. Such names emigrate to China, with conspicuous distortions in the process, and from Chinese they reappear in the Latin alphabet under the Pinyin system, looking like more or less unrecognizable apparitions. For instance the city of Shigatse is represented as Xigaze, while the neighbouring monastery known in all Tibetan literature under the name of Tashilhumpo reemerges as Zhaxilhumbo.

It's a problem that we might ignore were it not that the Chinese were enchantingly aggressive in this matter, as in others, and attempt to impose this "revised Tibet" of theirs on every conceivable occasion. Never mind what happens when we pass to an examination of the ideograms used to rename places up on the plateau: there are times when meanings are stood on their head. Gyantse, which means "the King's summit" or "the royal summit" in Tibetan, is represented ideographically as "Flourishing Harbour". The name Lhasa is written with two ideograms reproduced phonetically; but a close examination will lead you to a meaning that is far from enticing: "Buddha dragged off" for example. On the other hand the name for Tibet itself (Xizang or Hsi-tsang, to use the Pinyin and Wade-Giles transliterations) is entirely positive and of good augury: Hsi is West, tsang basically conveys a "depot or warehouse", but can also carry the sense of "treasury", as also of "possession". Thus Tibet or Hsi-tsang can mean "the West's depository or the West's treasury" or "the West's possession" depending on how you look at it.

To pass to a different topic, since many of the names of gods are known in their Sanskrit and in their Tibetan form, in the interests of simplicity, when I give the two alternatives I give them together, separated just by an oblique stroke, as in the case of Avalokitesvara/Chen-re-zi. I have adopted the same system in those instances where I have given Chinese names in the two principal transcriptions, Wade-Giles and Pinyin.

Sanskrit names and words are written without diacritics, save for an indication of long vowels.

1 *The name Tibet written (upper line) in Chinese ideograms:* Xizang *(in Pinyin) or* Hsi-tsang *(in Wade-Giles);* Sei-zō *(Japanese); (lower line)* Pö-yul *in Tibetan*

Then and Now (1937/1948 and 1998)

This book was originally published in 1951 as an account of journeys made to Tibet in 1937 and 1948 in the company of Giuseppe Tucci and, part of the time, Regolo Moise and Piero Mele. I have left the text as it was, save for the tiniest modifications and for the addition of certain diary extracts previously omitted. I expect the reader to keep well in mind that the conditions here described are those prevailing in Tibet before the Chinese occupation with all the social upheavals and local changes that have resulted. When the reader comes across a phrase like "Tibet is a feudal state" let it be obvious to him that we are talking of a world that has utterly vanished. I have avoided loading the text with constant notes by way of updating; my hope is that these lines will serve to set the whole volume in context.

The accompanying illustrations are as in the earlier editions, but enriched with many new photographs. The bibliography is of course entirely revised.

The first Italian editions and the foreign editions contained a dedication to "my master" Giuseppe Tucci; this dedication must now perforce be to the *memory* of Giuseppe Tucci, for the great authority on Tibet died in April 1984.

Years ago the professor was not pleased with this dedication of mine, because I had never been his "pupil" in any official sense; I was sorry then and am sorry now. And yet, I repeat, I consider him – along with the Hellenist Giorgio Pasquali – to be indubitably my teacher, and a highly respected one. Not that even Giorgio Pasquali was ever my teacher in any academic sense; but from him, as from Giuseppe Tucci, I learned the most precious and important things that a young man can learn about knowledge: it was not so much a question of notions as of an attitude to man in the framework of time and place; less a question of objects in a heap than of ways of looking at things; less a matter of lists and chronologies than of colours, scents, audible guidelines, those invisible conducting threads that give us a bearing on the whole panorama of the world, a whole life in the world.

I should like now not only to confirm my dedication to Giuseppe Tucci but to underline it and so to speak to insist upon it. Were it not for his guidance I might never have gone, during those happy and impressionable years of my youth, to Tibet, I might never have set eyes on a world which enchanted me, captivated me, and above all I should have understood all too little of what I saw. Those months of living with the master were an unorthodox degree course; they lay outside any programme, maybe they were heretical, but they were immensely fertile in seeding mind and spirit at every level. There were no lecture schedules, no reading-lists, no teachers' podium. Whenever Tucci got up in the morning in a genial frame of mind, whenever he made some discovery that left him satisfied, or often for no apparent reason, he would carry on with his course. It was a way of thinking out loud. He would scatter the golden sparks of his wisdom hither and yon in generous handfuls. He would paint sudden eye-catching frescoes in which Asia resided no longer in maps or in learned tomes but appeared as a pulsating mass of living people, tempestuous flashes of ideas, thoughts, powers, conceptions of the world, styles of art and of life. What unforgettable hours those were! What a rare privilege!

A great part of Tibet as described in this book is referred to in intensive studies[1] by Tucci published in 1941 that are not easy to come by and which are (be it confessed) not easy to read. Let me refer those readers to them if they want further or more detailed information, though they must bear in mind that all too little, perhaps virtually nothing, of what was then studied and described has survived the brutal destruction wrought by the "Cultural Revolution" of 1966–76.

At the time of our visits Tibet was for all practical purposes an independent country that supported an unusual form of government, at once theocratic and feudal. From many viewpoints Tibet then constituted the most conspicuous living fossil of a society that we might vaguely term mediaeval. There were no roads or railways, no cars or airstrips, and anyone who wanted to travel had to do so on foot or on horseback. There were no sources of energy beyond those provided by the muscles of men or beasts. Medicine was beautifully traditional, towns were few, castles and abbeys were plentiful. A prosperous artisan class existed, but to speak of industries would be euphemistic. Most of the population lived off its herds, agriculture, commerce. The positions of authority were divided between the aristocracy and the religious. Every aspect of life was dominated by religious faith, a particular form of Buddhism organized into a Church, the head of which was the Dalai Lama. Art, caught in the same Byzantine mould as that practised by the monks of Mount Athos, perpetuated changeless Buddhist icons with remarkable bravura and innocent inspiration.

For various reasons now generally well known, we are so wedded to the notion that happiness depends upon a tough, vigorous application of the verb to possess (perhaps I can here refer to Fromm), that a world described above would strike us as "dismal", "barbarous", "loathsome". There is no doubt that up there the verb to possess was reduced to a minimum, a faint glow. Even the famous nobles and the few rich men would, by our standards, have seemed petit bourgeois of very modest wealth, simply very small landowners. How did this undeniable poverty in the matter of to have, how did it reflect on the corresponding verb to be? I shall revert to this highly complex subject later on; but I should like to bear solid, explicit witness right from the start to what seemed to me then, and still seems to me, beyond doubt: the Tibetans struck me as in the vast majority a serene and happy nation many of the photographs in this volume will bear me out. You met this not only in the smiling faces, in the welcome you received, practically always warm and festive, from men and women, young and old of every class; you sensed it, too, as it were physically, in the air, which constantly resounded with song – especially where there were people working. The women would sing as they pounded the clay that then dried out to provide roofs to their houses, the peasants sang as they ploughed, the nomads sang as they drove their herds of yaks, the artisans sang as they planed, wove, painted, the merchants sang, so did the mothers with their babies on their backs. If ever there was a touch of reserve, some hint of a frown, some hardness in a gesture, you would meet it among the monks, particularly among those who counted for something.

I wrote in 1951 that Tibet stood as an exception in the world, on account of the integrity with which the various aspects of an ancient and singular culture had been maintained up there. And yet I had an instinct that this isolation from the rest of the world could not go on for much longer. In fact the changes – and what changes! – were just round the corner. Never, though, would I have imagined that what lay hidden in the future was to come to pass under such grim circumstances, in such a dramatic, painful, terrible way did it happen.

The Chinese occupation, which began in October 1950 and was completed a few months later to be ratified by the treaty of 24 May 1951, seemed to be contained within the limits of a reform programme, which undoubtedly was needed, and which was to be put through with a careful eye to the special circumstances, and then only gradually. For a few years these hopes were not entirely disappointed. But then the difficult and maybe utopian harmony was spoiled, the Tibetans rose up in revolt, the Dalai Lama fled to India in 1959 and Tibet was subject to years of repression and horror. The worst years for hideous brutality and bloodshed were 1966 to 1976 when the roof of the world – and China itself for that matter – was ravaged by what came to be called, with ringing irony, the "Cultural Revolution". In fact it was the "barbarian revolution", a savage regression into a past at its most ferociously destructive of human kind; vandalism, mindless desecration, mob-rule, violence, cruelty were the daily fruits of a blind and stupid fanaticism.

It is remarkable that the Thirteenth Dalai Lama, Thubten Gyatso (1880–1933), in a message he wrote shortly before his death, had had a glimpse of these grim possibilities for his country. "Those who work today for the state, be they monks or layfolk, will see a Tibet occupied by foreigners; their property will be confiscated and they will be forced to serve the enemy, or else to wander here and there like beggars. All will suffer untold miseries and live in constant fear. The days and nights will pass slowly amid suffering of every kind."

Later, under the new regime inaugurated by Deng Xiaoping, the situation appeared to be slightly improved, but the painful wounds inflicted on a naive and innocent people do not readily heal.

2 *Tibetan stamps (1930s and 1940s). Gyantse 1937 postmark*

1 G. Tucci: *Indo-Tibetica*, IV/1, 2, 3. See Bibliography IV

SECRET TIBET

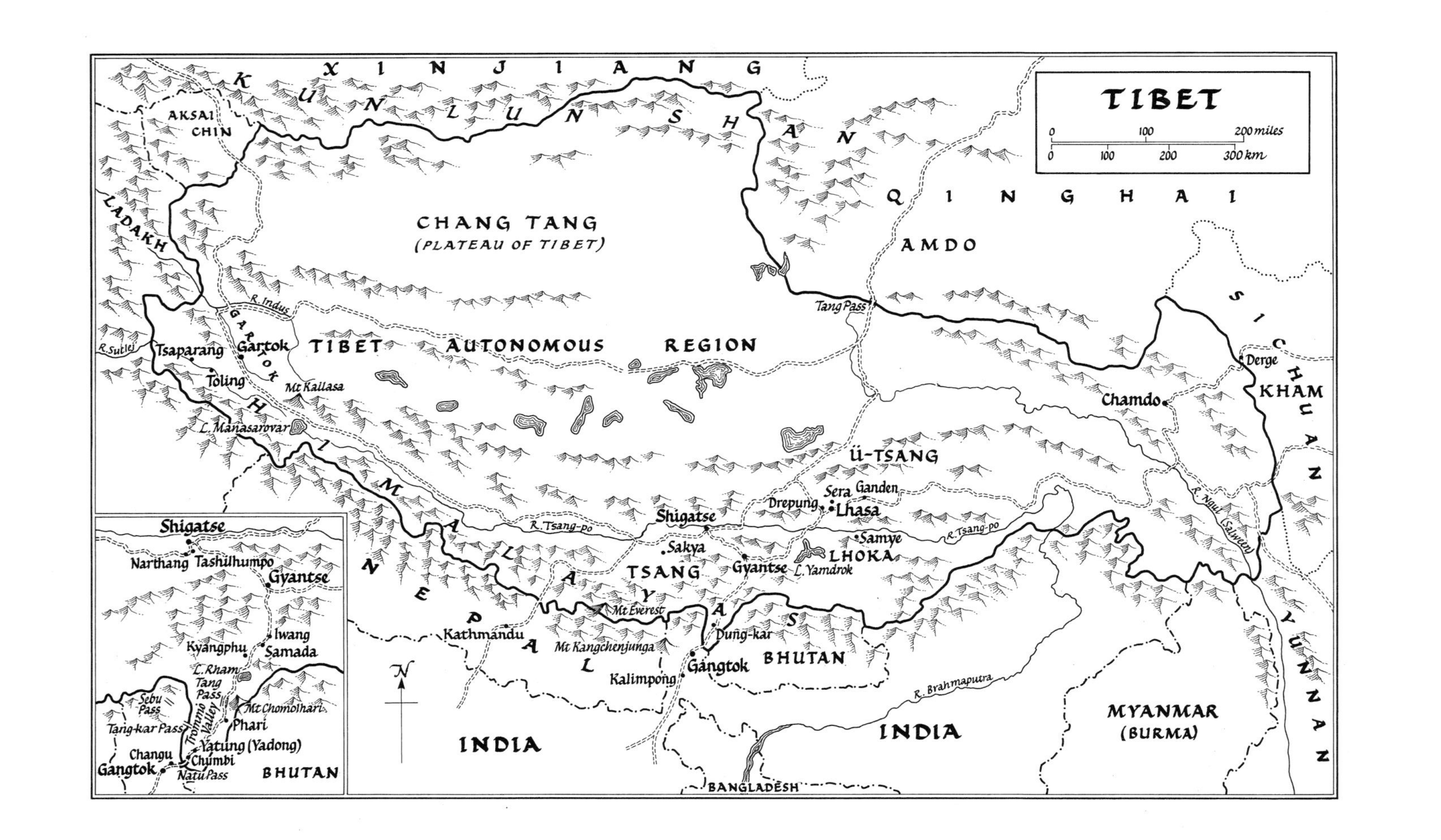
TIBET
0 100 200 miles
0 100 200 300 km
XINJIANG
KUNLUN SHAN
AKSAI CHIN
LADAKH
QINGHAI
AMDO
SICHUAN
KHAM
Derge
Chamdo
CHANG TANG
(PLATEAU OF TIBET)
TIBET AUTONOMOUS REGION
Tang Pass
R. Indus
GARTOK
Gartok
Tsaparang
Toling
R. Sutlej
Mt Kailasa
L. Manasarovar
HIMALAYAS
Ü-TSANG
Sera
Ganden
Drepung
Lhasa
Samye
LHOKA
L. Yamdrok
Shigatse
R. Tsang-po
Sakya
TSANG
Gyantse
R. Ngul (Salween)
NEPAL
Kathmandu
Mt Everest
Mt Kangchenjunga
Dung-kar
Gangtok
Kalimpong
BHUTAN
R. Brahmaputra
INDIA
MYANMAR
(BURMA)
YUNNAN
BANGLADESH
N
Shigatse
Narthang
Tashilhumpo
Gyantse
Iwang
Kyangphu
Samada
L. Rham
Tang Pass
Sebu Pass
Tromo Valley
Mt Chomolhari
Phari
Tang-kar Pass
Yatung (Yadong)
Changu
Chumbi
Gangtok
Natu Pass
BHUTAN

I

From Naples to Yoga

Naples harbour: ploughing through books

There is a great bustle on the quay, opposite the little ship.

A lorry with the expedition's baggage has arrived from, Rome, and packing cases, sacks and boxes are piled all over the place, all labelled "Professor Tucci's Expedition to Tibet". A crane hoists it all on board, while one of the professor's assistants, armed with spectacles, pencil and notebook, carefully checks it, with the air of one scrutinizing Tokharian verbs in some ancient manuscript or deciphering rare Chinese ideograms.

I arrived at the last moment, with my wife, in Piero Mele's car. Piero's mother said goodbye to him at the hotel. How sensible of her! Saying goodbye at a railway station is supportable, but quayside farewells can be appalling. When you are leaving people you love it is far better to say goodbye without waiting for the interminable departure of a ship. That was how I saw my mother for the last time, long ago in 1938, when I sailed from Brindisi for Japan, and left her standing on the quay. The last inquisitive onlookers went away, the last customs officials went back to their offices, but there she stayed, a dark little figure, as thin as could be, standing on the quayside. It grew nearly dark, and she was still there. I looked at her and looked at her, and then I couldn't see her any more. I never saw her again.

Meanwhile they are pulling up the gangway. All the baggage is on board. Giuseppe Tucci, the well-known Italian explorer, has a couple of moments to himself at last. He duly makes his appearance, says goodbye to his assistants, who have come from Rome to see him off, to his son, who waves his handkerchief, and to some Neapolitan friends, who have come down to the harbour for the occasion. He is a little man, half-way through the fifties, with a strange, philosopher's bead of hair, and side-whiskers. By rights he should dress in a style more reminiscent of the late nineteenth century, but he doesn't take much interest in his appearance. Under his arm he has the inevitable book. I am prepared to swear that within five minutes he will be curled up in some corner, reading it. Reading it? That's not the right word. To describe the process properly you'd need some such expression as "ploughing" through it. Yes, Tucci ploughs through books. I've often watched him. He sprinkles them with pencil notes, underlines passages, reads the paragraph headings aloud, grows furious if the author says anything stupid, or exclaims "*Perdinci!*" if a phrase meets with his wholehearted approval. Then, when the book has yielded all it can, like a field of wheat after a huge harvest, it falls worn and exhausted to the deck.

At sea: Vildo and the beginning of things

Vildo jumps up on me and licks my hands.

This Vildo is the kind of dog which, the uglier it is, the more you are called on to admire it. Of its colour, which is a kind of faded brownish-violet, the less said the better; of the abundant hair with which nature provided it all that has survived the shears is a tuft on its head, a brush on its tail and spats round its paws. The expression on its face is, in a way, pathetic; every now and then it seems to exclaim: "Why did they make me look like this?" But it doesn't take long to find out that Vildo is stupid. Now, a stupid dog, unless it is beautiful, is unforgivable. Vildo's master and mistress are two Americans, husband and wife, very rich and very reserved. They have on board a car as long as a battleship. They occupy the captain's cabin. They have the esoteric air of those who belong to the great world of fashion. They are going to India.

People keep on going into the bar, as happens in a ship soon after it has left port. Soon the bell will ring, the visitors will leave, and it will be quiet again. All the same, it's curious to note how well one can concentrate on the most recondite subjects – Tibetan, for instance – when there's movement going on all round one. I've just found a beautiful and profound expression, *kun-shi*, which means the primary origin, the first cause, of all. This is not, as one might expect, God, but soul, mind, the beginning of awareness. We of the West have always conceived of the mind as a kind of mirror of a kind of external world, while the Tibetans (the heirs of India) have from time immemorial been idealists *à l'outrance*. It is the self that creates the world, and any other proposition is preposterous. Away with mirrors, away with false illusions about an "external" world!

While I drink a whisky in the bar with Piero, who comes to keep me company, Vildo turns up again. With regard to this animal, let me state that I can accept almost anything as being a projection of my ego, but not Vildo. For me Vildo is an uncreated, eternal being, and I refuse to create such monstrosities even from the most unconscious depths of my unconscious. I return to the study of Tibetan. Passengers walk to and fro, and a number of boys run about noisily. There is a feeling of excitement in the air. Tibetan is a pleasing language; it has no singulars, plurals, genders or articles, to say nothing of other complications possessed by the grammars of more familiar languages. But Tibetan has its honorifics, its terrible honorifics. For instance, in speaking of an ordinary person, "to die" is *shak-pa*, but in the case of an important lama it is *ku-shing-la phep-pa*; while in the case of the Dalai Lama it is *ku-shing-la chip-gyu nang-wa*, which means "to ascend honourably with one's own body into paradise".

Here is Vildo for the third time. It appears that the derivation of the name is Deauville, turned back to front; Deauville, Villedeau, Vildo. No, Vildo, we shall never be friends; you're too ugly and too stupid. Or perhaps we shall be friends, just because you're such a wretched little beast?

We have definitely left Naples behind. Time has changed its rhythm. We saw Capri; then night fell. There's always a special feeling about a first night on board (who has not looked out to see the last light of evening over the steely sea?). *Partir, c'est un peu mourir*, etc. The new life hasn't started yet. On the other hand, when you're taking part in an "expedition", it's the first moment when you can sit back with a sigh and say to yourself, "well, at any rate it's started."

Still at sea: "how much on the water-measurer?"

During these first few days I've managed to find out one or two things. I've found out, for instance, who is the most important person on board – the person most worth cultivating, a Machiavellian would say. It's Vildo. The American couple are the king and queen of the ship, and attention is paid to every word they say; and Vildo is the king of the Americans, and the least of his desires is instantly fulfilled. When Vildo sleeps, there is universal quiet. When Vildo wants play or exercise, there is general commotion. Vildo dislikes fish, and fish is therefore not served. Vildo's frightened, keep still everybody please! Vildo's in a hurry, please get out of the way! Vildo, in short, is our king. When he plays, how human he is! When he runs, how swift! And when he stands still, how perfectly divine!

Meanwhile my Tibetan studies have yielded interesting results. For instance, "what is the time?" in Tibetan is *chu-tsö katsö*, the literal meaning of which is: "How much on the water-measurer?" – a reminder of the time when the clepsydra was used to mark the passage of the hours. At *druk-tang-cheka* – that is to say, at half-past six – the first gong sounds. I go down and change, and then return to the bar for the usual cocktail with the American lady and Piero.

The peculiar thing about Jane, Vildo's mistress, is that though her hair is white, she has a young face. Her complexion is fresh, her eyes bright, and her smile is both kind and malicious. She is certainly nearer fifty than forty, or perhaps her fiftieth birthday is a memory. The skin of her hands is certainly that of an old woman, but her cheeks and her expression are those of a girl. She is witty, has been round the world, admires Thornton Wilder, believes in the transmigration of souls, knows all the most fashionable Paris tailors and despises New York café society.

Her husband is Vildo's complete slave. Jane treats the dog as if it were a human being. She treats it affectionately, but never soppily. But Mr Millicent's behaviour to the dog is as soppy as could be. It is sufficient to mention the little beast in his presence to see him turn to treacle. He is a tall man, of Levantine appearance, with spindly fingers that look like slender asparagus. Am I mistaken, or does he wear a gold bracelet? Also he has long, thin, extremely white legs, with a few black hairs on them, large hips and false teeth, and he carries round an extraordinary number of ciné and ordinary cameras slung round his neck.

Alexandria: the Greek gnostic stays behind with the negroid prostitutes

At first they wouldn't let us disembark. "Italian passport? Certainly not!" said an Egyptian policeman, who was as rude as he was plump. But we were eventually allowed to set foot on *terra firma*, thanks to the intervention of the Italian authorities. [This was 1948, remember. Today Italians meet with no hostility in Egypt.]

Alexandria is a city which can truly be said to possess a frontage. Alexandria's frontage faces the sea and consists of the magnificent Queen Nazleh parade. The appearance of classical Alexandria, during the centuries when she claimed to be one of the chief cities of the world, was always, according to the archaeologists, distinctly Hellenic, and there is a fundamentally European look about the new Alexandria which has sprung up in the last hundred years, with its wide, traffic-filled streets, its big modern buildings, fine shops, and squares in which there is space to breathe. The tall Negro porters at the Hotel Cecil, with their white shirts and red fezzes, look as if they are there so that the good traveller may exclaim: "Here be lions!"

There are, however, no lions anywhere in the neighbourhood. The only exotic thing about Alexandria is the fez, which is worn by practically every male. It is a most becoming form of headgear, and must give a lot of poise and self-confidence to those who wear it. The real fez type is the plump, elegant, middle-aged Levantine *roué*, slightly sinister if you look only at his eyes, but amiable enough if you look at his lips and cheeks. The fez also sets off to advantage all the thin young men with a fanatical gleam in their eyes and the wise old men with beards and golden spectacles. The aesthetics of the fez are complicated and full of subtle *nuances*. Mr Millicent bought himself a fez immediately. Levantine as he is in appearance, it suits him admirably.

We dined last night at Pastroudis, a famous restaurant frequented by all the best people in Alexandria. The best people in Alexandria consisted of an extraordinary crowd of Nordic blondes, looking as sure of themselves as exclamation marks, accompanied by stout, elderly pashas. There were also people from the provinces who were just fat, and bourgeois families, the members of which devoured dainty morsels with greed. Jane was all of a quiver with excitement. "Just look at that girl's hat over there in the corner!" she exclaimed; or: "Have you seen Beauty and the Beast?" Meanwhile the meal was exquisite. The tournedos could not have been better.

Beauty and the Beast were sitting next to us. They were a couple of newly minted *nouveaux riches*. Their riches must have been so recent that hardly an hour could have elapsed since their acquisition. The man wore a dark blue suit and a pair of screaming yellow shoes, and the woman a greenish dress which had obviously been made for a person of normal proportions and not for one of her monumental bulges, which seemed to be attempting to escape simultaneously in every direction. She had pounds of lipstick on her lips and phalanxes of pearls on her neck and wrists. It must all have happened so suddenly that the couple had not yet had time to recover from the shock. They sat motionless and silent, in a kind of dazed happiness.

After dinner Jane, Piero and I set out to explore Alexandria. I don't know how, but a Greek, who spoke all languages terrifyingly quickly and terrifyingly badly, attached himself to us. He was an educated man, but he was dirty, dribbled continually, and picked his nose in a most shameless manner. As the evening progressed we went from respectable to less respectable places, and finally to very unrespectable places indeed. Meanwhile the Greek kept talking to me rapidly, in a low voice, like one hurriedly making a painful confession on the point of death. He talked about classical Alexandria and the library of the Ptolemies. Then he recited verses from Callimachus, and told stories showing a refinement of intelligence and imagination. Finally he ordered some green drinks.

As we descended down the path of evil, passing from streets which were simply dark to narrow alleys and stairways with stinking gullies running right down the middle of them, the Greek became more spiritual and transformed. First he assured me that the distance between the earth and the sun had been known at Alexandria two thousand years ago, and then he mounted to the empyreans of gnosticism. We went into a revolting den, where we were surrounded by horrible, negroid prostitutes – Jane explained that she wanted to see life unsterilized and in the raw, and things that were millions of years old – but the Greek seemed entirely unaware of his surroundings, so much was he carried away in talking about the Abyss.

"What imagination, what daring was possessed by the gnostic fathers, Basilides and Valentinus!" he exclaimed. "God, the origin of all things, the key to the universe, they called the Abyss! Here in Alexandria even the sand is sanctified by the great things of the spirit. *Madame*, *messieurs*, I am proud to declare myself a gnostic; my only wish is to be worthy of the glorious dust on which we tread, the dust of destroyed masterpieces, of crumbled papyri, of courtesans and scientists and martyrs, of queens and poets . . ."

Meanwhile two of the wretched women had started dancing, very badly indeed. They were naked, or nearly naked, and they danced to the sad and monotonous singing of a huge woman dressed in black, who beat a drum that she held on her knees. Nobody except this one-woman band seemed to take the slightest interest in the proceedings. Her monumental bosom heaved and quivered behind its covering of black cotton, and in her pig-like eyes, which were sunk like two pins in fat, there were gleams of an increasingly obscene frenzy. The Greek continued with his monologue as remorselessly as a gramophone record. He said such fine things that I felt compelled to go over to the window for a moment, to look at the stars and breathe the night air.

"The Abyss fertilizes the Eternal Silence, don't you see," he said, "and that is how everything is born. She, you, I, they, the old woman with the drum, even that creature who is dancing there, all of us are children of the Abyss and of Silence. The Abyss is our father and Silence our mother. It is to them that we shall return . . ."

A sinister-looking Negro flashed a knife, because he thought he had been inadequately tipped. Jane screamed, and we fled ignominiously. The Greek gnostic stayed behind with the negroid prostitutes.

Today Jane, her husband, Piero, Vildo and I all motored to Cairo. Where did that brand-new American car come from? It was not the car that Jane and her husband have on board, which is dark blue; this one was light grey. Jane and her husband are delightfully mysterious. I had never thought that Americans could be mysterious, because mystery is the sign of old civilizations. This, I feel, opens up new fields for thought and speculation.

After the usual squalid suburbs we emerged into the desert. There is no country round Alexandria. You pass straight from the built-up area into the desert, from crowds to solitude. Before us lay 120 miles or more of asphalt road, as black as a river of pitch, stretching straight across the yellow sand as far as the eye could see. At sunset we stopped for a moment and got out, to stretch our legs and take photographs. After several days on board ship and then in a crowded city, it was a precious moment alone with nature. Long, blue shadows lay across the orange-coloured sand, and there were green transparencies in the sky. The sun, a red ball of fire, was settling down on the horizon without a halo, without the slightest sign of haze.

Cairo: granite, sarcophagi, millenniums and garlic

We are at Cairo. Before I go on there is something I want to add. Last night, after the sun had set, when we got into the car again and went on our way, our Muslim driver turned on the wireless, because there were some prayers he wanted to hear, on I don't know what station. So we crossed the desert to the chanting of an astonishing, deep bass voice. We travelled for mile after mile listening to the Koran. Outside there was a thin, crescent moon.

But to continue. Today we saw the pyramids. It is always curious to see for the first time something with which you have been familiar in pictures since childhood. When I first arrived in Japan, for instance, I was astonished to find that Fujiyama, which looked such a smooth and kindly mountain in illustrations, was rugged, grim and rocky. The pyramids were also different from what I had expected. For one thing, they are coloured. Black and white photographs and the illustrations in school geography books give us an impression that they are greyish, which is completely false. Actually they are brown, the colour of baked clay, or actually tawny. When first seen in the distance they are as impressive as mountains, and the light plays bluish tricks between their summits.

Then they are not smooth; their sides are furrowed, so furrowed that when one is near them they look as if they were built like steps. That is because men and time have stripped them of their ancient outer covering. I climbed the steps to the top of the biggest pyramid (of Cheops) without any difficulty.

At the top I sat down and looked about me, as one looks at the panorama from a mountain-top. I saw the Nile, and other pyramids in the distance, a whole geology of pyramids. I didn't know whether to think about ancient kings or the mysterious forces of nature. But I was not on a mountain, but on a man-made pile of two million blocks of stone, each weighing two-and-a-half tons. A mountain can fill one with marvel, or terror at the subterranean forces that lifted it into the sky. The pyramids fill one with never-ceasing astonishment at the slow deliberation with which those gigantic edifices were erected by the hand of man; at the subtle, mathematical, astronomical, geomantic framework, like a hidden spider's web, which in its mute and enduring tracery invisibly supports the colossal weight; at the buried and forgotten suffering of which these blocks might tell if they could remember the days when the arms, chests and shoulders of slaves transported them, hoisted them and fixed them in the place which, after thousands of years, they still occupy today.

I was followed to the top by a filthy and importunate Arab, whose breath stank of garlic ("me guide pyramids, gentleman give baksheesh?"), and I couldn't shake him off. He followed me all the way down again, and into the chamber at the very heart of the pyramid which served as Pharaoh's tomb. We crept on hands and knees down dark tunnels until we reached the sepulchral chamber in the centre of the great edifice. The silence was terrifying. Granite, sarcophagi, millenniums and garlic.

The Red Sea: "I hate science, for instance!"

We embarked again at Port Said, and soon afterwards we were in the Suez Canal, another impressive piece of man's handiwork – endless expanses of sand on either side and this streak of blue water cutting straight across them.

Jane, sitting in a deck-chair, was combing Vildo. The conversation led to a comparison between the Suez and the Panama Canals.

"I prefer Suez," Jane said. "It's grander. You're aware of man's handiwork at every step. It's one long, continuous, breathless gash, tearing Asia and Africa apart. It's not a canal, but a wound made by a surgeon's knife."

"So the sea is the earth's blood, is it?" I exclaimed pompously, with a laugh.

"Yes. Is that a commonplace? Commonplaces are often great truths. Perhaps you're too young. In the second half of your life you go back to commonplaces with affection . . . Keep still, Vildo darling!"

Vildo was leaping about like a little dragon, trying to catch a fly in its mouth; every time it missed its teeth snapped together, sounding like the lid of an ivory box snapping shut.

"I agree about commonplaces," I answered. "But I prefer Panama. It has so many curves; you go through real forests. And then there are all those lakes and islands. In the Panama Canal it's worth staying on deck and watching, because the landscape keeps changing. Here, after five minutes, you know it's going to be exactly the same for the next hundred miles; in fact until next day!"

Next day we emerged into the Red Sea, the blueness of which was worthy of the Mediterranean. It was still relatively cool; the real heat would begin only in two days' time, when we neared Massawa.

I spent a long time this evening on deck, talking to Giuseppe Tucci. "I only like things that contain a mystery," he said to me, while a fierce, metallic sun rolled along the horizon. Mount Sinai was visible in the distance, a haunting, violet apparition, suggesting divine manifestations and infernal terrors in that land of hermits, relics, rocks and cypresses. "I'm interested in everything that is inexplicable, tangled, obscure," Tucci went on. Then he added, as if he feared he might have given himself away: "I hate certainty and clarity. I hate science, for instance!" and chuckled mischievously.

Giuseppe Tucci adores paradoxes; they make him happy. But they are a need of his intellect, not of his whole personality. If Giuseppe Tucci really hated science, he would not be Giuseppe Tucci, and he would not have left for posterity a row of standard works as a monument to his immense labour, study and researches. Perhaps he does not want to be believed when he talks; what enchants and stimulates him is the sound of his own voice, the linking of logical propositions into strange syllogisms, the drawing of the last conclusions from every premise.

To get to know Giuseppe Tucci properly, you have to see him as he is now, on a voyage. His cabin is transformed into a library, a study, a sanctum. The steward who makes his bed every morning has to move with special care to avoid disturbing his piles of books and papers. On top of the proofs of a book due to appear shortly there is probably to be found a Bengali treatise on logic or a German dissertation on ancient Chinese poetry; elsewhere sheets of typescript lie mixed with the thick, veined paper of a Tibetan work on yoga, while volumes of Valéry or a translation of Huizinga crown the pile.

Giuseppe Tucci is an almost unique example in our day of the new humanism in which Chinese philosophers like Chuang-tse, Tibetan poets like Milarepa, Japanese dramatists like Chikamatsu are not merely exotic ornaments of a distant civilization, but living voices in the mind, as Plato or Lucretius or Plautus have traditionally been through the centuries. In this Giuseppe Tucci is two or three centuries ahead of contemporary Europe.

"You believe in science," the professor concluded. "In other words, you're the victim of an illusion. Science postulates a self and a non-self linked in an immutable relationship. What a childish thing!"

The sun had disappeared behind the peaks of Jebel Garib. Tucci rubbed his hands and went on emptying all content from the non-self.

Massawa and Jibouti: "With no-one else eat like with Italians."

At Massawa there is the infernal heat normal in these parts. The heavy, humid sultriness of the tropics has now closed in on us. Here too we had difficulty before we were allowed to land. But, when we at last set foot on shore, we found ourselves in an entirely Italian town, with the usual advertisements for Fiat cars, Peroni beer and San Pellegrino orangeade, and people talking with the accents of Sicily, Piedmont or the Veneto.

Many Italians who travelled in our ship disembarked yesterday evening, and there are now very few passengers left on board – a few Swedes and Swiss, the American couple and ourselves. I spoke to a few inhabitants of the place. They talked sadly, as was natural, but I thought they also felt that their labour would not turn out to have been in vain, but that something would remain, was bound to remain, and that in any case they would pull through, with the patience and energy characteristic of the Italian countryside. The liking with which the natives spoke of the Italians was moving.

From Massawa we went on to Jibouti – a short journey, entirely devoid of interest. At Jibouti there was great excitement. We arrived about midday, and went ashore. When we returned to the ship for dinner we found everything – at any rate in the first-class accommodation – in a terrible state of commotion. What had happened, when I was able to reconstruct the facts, turned out to have been as follows. At about three o'clock in the afternoon Vildo had apparently left the cabin alone and gone wandering about the deck. The hold was open, and the little beast had fallen into it, nobody knew how, and broken a leg. When Mr Millicent came back from Jibouti and found Vildo apparently dead he was so overcome with emotion that he fainted. Complete panic seemed to have reigned for a good ten minutes. Nobody knew what to do first – whether to look after poor Vildo or to bring round his unfortunate master. Jane divided her efforts between blowing in her husband's face and taking the poor dog in her arms and cuddling it.

By the time we arrived the worst could be said to be over. Mr Millicent had almost completely recovered. "What a fright I had!" he exclaimed. "When I saw Vildo, I thought he was dead! Dead!" Jane had recovered her calm and her ready wit. Vildo, covered in bandages, seemed to be supremely happy.

Later in the evening Piero Mele and I went ashore again. We had an amusing conversation with a Somali, who talked to us at length about the time when "the Italians were here". "Then things very good," he said. "With no-one else eat like with Italians." He meant that when the Italians were here he had enough to eat, while now he was hungry, poor chap. Still, even if there was a grain of malice in his enigmatic remark, would it not pass even so for a tribute to the humanity of our Italian settlers?

Aden: miracles, Mexico, nomads, plaster

During the short crossing from Jibouti in Africa to Aden on the coast of Arabia the whole ship was mobilized on Vildo's behalf – the nurse for injections, the kitchen for special dishes, the dispensary for ice. Vildo, covered with bandages and with a supremely contented expression, sat enthroned in a desk chair, with all the majesty of a gouty old maharajah. At mealtimes Mr and Mrs Millicent took turns at staying with the precious little invalid. Jane had her meal first, swallowed it hurriedly, and then disappeared. A few moments later her husband arrived, wearing an expression of acute distress. At night they apparently took it in turns to sit up with Vildo. Even Jane seemed to be losing her usual sense of humour.

At cocktail time Piero proposed a toast. "Here's to Vildo's health!" he said.

"Yes, and to my defeat," remarked Jane. "Soon, perhaps, a small miracle will be needed!"

"Or a nurse?"

"My husband would never permit it. Trust Vildo to a nurse! Are you crazy?"

The word "miracle" started a conversation behind our backs. Every now and then we caught snatches of it.

"We know so little about things that I take the liberty of believing in miracles – real miracles, I mean, the suspension of the laws of nature, or things happening contrary to the laws of nature, or what you will."

"That's something I can't accept. It would mean the complete abdication of the intellect. The things we don't yet understand we call miracles. There are so many things that are miracles for primitive people but are no longer miracles for us – thunderbolts, earthquakes, epidemics or comets, for instance. In relation to a future, higher stage of humanity, we are still primitives. Our miracles will form part of their science."

Meanwhile Jane was talking to us about Mexico.

"It's a country you ought to visit," she said. "It's the only civilized country in the western hemisphere."

"Civilized because it's good at civil war?"

"Perhaps; or perhaps because the people have the courage to have faith; and also because it's like Alexandria, in the sense that your Greek friend talked about; full of the dust of artists, emperors, etc."

We reached Aden in the morning. At seven o'clock Mr Millicent was ready and waiting, dressed all in white, though he generally wore shorts all day long, until it was time to change for dinner. He ordered a motor-launch and went ashore to make arrangements for Vildo to be operated on by the best vet in the place. An hour later he came back to fetch Vildo and take him ashore. We learned later that he was not present at the operation. "I should have died to see him suffer," he said.

We went ashore too. The bazaar at Aden provides the most lively, the most kaleidoscopic spectacle of all the ports of the East. Shepherds, nomads and brigands from the Yemen and the Hadramaut come down to the city to see, to buy, to satisfy their curiosity and to enjoy themselves, and mingle with the crowd of Somalis, Hindus, Jews and Negroes. You often see tall, thin young men with extraordinarily fine features, with long hair, and garments of extraordinary colours covering their skin, which is the colour of old bronze; and carrying scimitars and daggers in their belts.

We were due to leave at midday, and we went back on board. The ship was ready, and everyone was waiting. Waiting for whom? For Vildo, of course. The operation must have been more complicated than had been expected. One o'clock came, and half-past one, and still no sign of Vildo. The captain was in a black mood. Eventually a motor-boat appeared, making the most appalling din. Mr Millicent was standing in the bow, with Vildo in his arms, and Jane sitting under a green sunshade in the stern.

As soon as all three of them were on board Jane saved the somewhat delicate international situation. With all the charm and naturalness in the world, she invited the captain and officers to cocktails. Who, in the circumstances, could nurse a grudge against a lady? Vildo was all covered up in plaster, and obviously felt more important than ever. Perhaps he did not notice the withering looks that were cast at him every now and then. Luckily for him, he's a stupid dog. An intelligent dog (they do exist) would have died of embarrassment.

At the gates of India: how to escape from maya

We are nearing Bombay. Up to Aden the distances between one port and the next were short; after Aden we spent several days crossing the Indian Ocean. At this time of year – it is March – the water is calm or barely ruffled, an expanse of blue under a clear sky; in a few months' time, in the monsoon season, it will be in a state of perpetual commotion, a horrible greenish or yellowish colour, under a low, white sky that is both stifling and dazzling.

Vildo is decidedly better; he runs about the deck, limping because of his plastered foot, and the Millicents eat their meals together again. I have struck up a friendship with a young Sicilian doctor, who is on his way to India to act as medical officer to a Catholic mission; but he tells me that his real object is to study yoga.

"You see," he concluded after a long tirade, "I have always been most interested in the fact that certain states of mind can influence the state of the body. How is it that the sick can be cured as the result of a psychological impulse? Yoga may be able to teach me many things."

Remarks that at home would appear wild or fantastic are already beginning to make sense. In fact the outline of the Ghat mountains, which rise behind Bombay, is already visible on the horizon; we are really at the gates of India. Nothing could express better than yoga the inner spirit of the country we are approaching. Yoga stands for India in all her philosophical profundity, her metaphysical flights, her moral daring, her perennial sense of man as an inseparable identity of mind and body, her self-assurance in the midst of the mysterious, the confidential terms she is on with death, and her admirable symbolism.

Yoga offers the sage a way of escape from *maya* (the illusion of transient things, designed to perish) into a fulness of being that transcends becoming. Long and sustained effort enables him to pass one by one through the eight stages that lead to liberation. During the process he can have no rest; there can be no truce for any part of his being. His body must slowly be trained by prolonged ascetic practices to become like a musical instrument, able to vibrate to the hidden impulses that govern the breath of the universe. His intellectual faculties must be purified by progressive renunciation of all false aspirations until it attains awareness of a life beyond forms and ideas; and his subconscious must undergo a prolonged education, until the thinking individual is able really to annihilate himself, disappear into the object of his thought, into the eternal, the infinite, the One.

Jane joined our group, with Vildo in her arms. We all observed with pleasure that there was in the dog's appearance a certain look of philosophical profundity. So, little beast, it does you good to suffer? At least you're human in that!

Bombay is now just visible, a white streak on the sun-beaten shore of India. In an hour we shall be in port.

Reconsideration, 1998

Above all an inevitable meditation on the vortex of technological changes in which we are involved. Three decades pass and voyages on a liner have practically vanished from the scene; when one speaks of them one seems to be evoking ancient history, as though one were talking of going from Milan to Rome by stagecoach. Few of today's young have experienced a long ocean-voyage. The airliner has practically entirely displaced the sea-voyage, with its many irritations and its few idle pleasures. Anyone wishing to reach India by sea today would need to pursue laborious researches at the appropriate agents' to track down a merchant vessel sailing for the Orient, then to fall in with the requirements of the shipping company as to the route and the dates of departure and arrival.

In contrast with this elemental fact that relates to the instruments for living and distinguishes the middle of the twentieth century from its end, human affairs enjoy a granitic permanence and stability. What applied to the Sumerians can to a great extent apply to us. From that angle, thirty or forty years are barely a second.

2

Indo-Gothic and Invisible Jungles

Bombay: knowing the world with one's nose

The British have always been very proud of Bombay, on the whole with good reason. It is still the Indian city in which one is most aware of Western influence. It has wide streets, tree-lined squares, parks, and walks along the seashore. Also it has certain features that movingly reveal the home-sickness for London felt by the Victorian architects who built the greater part of it.

Certainly it is a town without a history. From that point of view, compared with Delhi or Benares it is devoid of interest. In 1661 Charles II of England received the island on which the city now stands as part of the dowry of Catherine of Braganza. All it had to offer was a few huts, and perhaps one or two Portuguese trading stations. Bombay only sprang into prominence about a century ago, when British banks started opening branches there, and the first railway lines were built into the interior. The population quickly increased from 200,000 inhabitants to a million, and then to a million-and-a-half.

For a hundred years Bombay was the façade of the British Indian Empire. When you approach from the sea one of the first buildings you see is the Gateway of India, a kind of triumphal arch in which twenty different styles are unhappily united. Actually the whole of Bombay is ugly, but its ugliness is of a kind that may soon become interesting. It is not entirely improbable that a century hence tourists may seriously consider this city to be a gem of the fantastic Indo-Gothic style. Our generation is still too near that which created these hybrid monsters, born of a union between Rheims, Cologne and Uppsala on the one hand and Gwalior, Jodhpur and Tanjore on the other. But our grandchildren may contemplate the telephone and bank palaces, the Protestant churches, the stations and the hotels, all the temples of the Biblical-industrial-railway civilization of the nineteenth century, with the same sophisticated and slightly perverse pleasure with which we visit the Doric-baroque cathedral of Syracuse or the Tuscan-Moorish Panciatichi villa in the Val d'Arno.

We stayed at the Taj Mahal, the big hotel made famous by Louis Bromfield's novel *A Night in Bombay*. Calling an hotel by that name in India is rather like calling an Italian hotel the Cà d'Oro or the Villa d'Este. It recalls one of the most perfect architectural gems of India, the tomb that the Mogul Emperor Shah Jahan built at Agra for his beloved wife, Mumtaz Mahal. The architecture appears to have been due in great part to an Italian, Geronimo Veroneo. Colonel Moise, finding himself surrounded in a mere hotel with all these famous and romantic things, all these exotic words and moving and imperial memories, was most impressed, and he would talk of nothing else. When we went down to dinner we passed a Parsee lady of most uncommon beauty, draped like a goddess in a *lamé* dress, and the good, enchanted colonel kept on muttering: "Just like in a novel, just like in a novel!"

The meal is perforce not at all "as in a novel", but simply as in an English household; that is, terrifying. In India one eats badly, very badly (of course by that I am referring to European cuisine, or rather to the cuisine that Indians take to be European, because the various national cuisines offer some most appetizing dishes). The foreigner travelling in this country is presented with food that is skilfully cooked so as to deprive it of any taste; what appears on the plate is shapeless masses of indefinable hue, and in the bowl, washed-out broths of indefinable consistency, which need to be swallowed like a medicine, simply to survive. Italians – Falletti or Firpo, for instance – who have opened hotels and restaurants in these countries, have struck it rich, and it is not hard to see why.

The Taj Mahal is a vast edifice built to make an insupportable climate less insupportable. Not only is the climate of Bombay intensely hot, but it is extremely humid, and therefore debilitating. It used to be said that the life of a man in Bombay was two monsoons. That was when tropical diseases reigned unchecked. Nowadays, with improved methods of building and improved hygiene, the saying is no longer true. But the heat remains the same – oppressive to the point of prostration. That is why innumerable fans in the Taj Mahal continually stir the air in the spacious corridors. Everything is open and ventilated, so that the most fleeting draught may find encouragement to evaporate an extra milligram of moisture from the perspiring skin of its guests.

The ventilation also circulates perfumes, to say nothing of their poor relations, smells; and of course those olfactory outlaws, the stinks. Some of them are aggressive stenches, to which one is not accustomed; or else they are undefinable, as disturbing to the nose as oriental music is disturbing to the ear. I maintain that it is primarily through the nose that an alert sensibility is able to detect Bombay's greatness as a continental metropolis. It is outside the Taj Mahal, along Hornby Street, at the Boran bazaar, or in the bewildering alleys of Kamatipura, that you have a visual sense of this phenomenon. You find yourself surrounded by Afghans and Bengalis, peasants from the Deccan and mountain folk from the Himalayas, Parsees and Hindus, mysterious, small, dark Tamils and big, turbaned Sikhs, with long beards and a spirited look in their eyes. There too you are assaulted by smells – a confusing, overwhelming ocean of smells. But in the Taj Mahal it is different. Here, comfortably seated in an armchair, with half-shut eyes, you can detect in all their olfactory splendour ten different civilizations in half-an-hour, each one perfectly distinct, and you can study their characteristics and make subtle classifications.

A Pakistani girl passes in white trousers, wearing high heels and a sari. Her finger-nails are scarlet, and she carries a bag – European influence – and she leaves in her wake a scent of cheap eau-de-Cologne, with underneath it a suggestion of sandalwood and indefinable spices, and perhaps of garlic. Next there comes a tall and emaciated Hindu, a longitudinal caricature of Mr Nehru. He suggests pure spirit, refined by thousands of years of ablutions and vegetarian diet, but he too leaves something in his wake – a faint suggestion of cloves. For a time nothing else happens. Then a north European passes, identifiable by his cigar, his perspiration and a whiff of Atkinson's hair oil. Next comes a group of Muslim businessmen, with moustaches, pomaded hair, and a confident, potentially martial, crypto-aggressive air, but, strangely enough, with a sweetish, effeminate scent.

Still Bombay: making oneself understood

What real basis for unity can there be among four hundred million people [and up to seven hundred million by 1985], varying in race, culture and religion, some of them incredibly remote from one another? The sub-continent is a geographical unity, but there is no unity whatever about its population. For the overwhelming majority of its inhabitants the very idea of India is a relatively new thing. So fragile is it that when the "common enemy", the British, departed it promptly split into two, India and Pakistan.

The most serious problem is that of language. The fact that in India alone there are 50,000,000 people who speak Bengali – a highly developed language with a notable literature – 130,000,000 who speak Hindi, 20,000,000 who speak Marathi, 12,000,000 who speak Oriya, while more than 60,000,000 speak the Dravidian languages, gives a faint idea of the problem facing the Government.

A linguistic map of India gives the most significant clue to its age-long history. To the north there extends the compact group of languages associated with the latest invaders – Aryans, speaking languages akin to those spoken in Europe. While in the West Latin developed into Italian, French, Spanish, etc., in the East there developed out of Sanskrit, and parallel with Sanskrit, Hindi, Bengali, Gujarati, Pathani, and many other languages and dialects. For thousands of years this group has been expanding southwards at the expense of the southern languages belonging to the Dravidian group, which has nothing in common with the Indo-European group. That Dravidian languages were once spoken throughout India is proved by the fact that there are still people, such as the Brahui, for example, in isolated and backward areas in the north who speak Dravidian dialects.

In India men have always come down from the north. Successive waves have pushed on each other's heels at intervals of centuries. Hence the south represents the most ancient and indigenous level, the substratum underlying all the rest. The really autochthonous level, or the level older than all the rest, the Munda-Polynesian level, has been completely pulverized. First the Dravidian invasion and then the Aryan have left only small groups of people scattered about in the Deccan who still speak its dialects.

India claims in all more than two hundred more or less distinct languages; in Europe there are barely fifty. Also India is faced with a difficulty that Europe does not share. In addition to all these different languages, she has several different alphabets. The speakers of Urdu and the languages of the north-west use characters of Persian origin. Speakers of Hindi and the related group use Devanagari characters; and the languages of the south are written in the Tamil alphabet.

In Italian schools we are taught to admire the men of the Risorgimento who sought to unite our small peninsula; but think how admirable are men like Gandhi (leaving aside his universal significance) and Nehru, in their vast confidence and idealism, as they strove with all their strength to give cohesion to the boundless human ocean that is India!

Today I have been busy all day arranging for the unloading of the expedition's baggage and its transport to Calcutta. It consists of one hundred and sixty-eight separate pieces, including packing cases, boxes and packages of various sorts. Giuseppe Tucci's diplomatic technique is admirable. He knows exactly when to lift the thing to the national level and talk of "the Italian expedition" and when to reduce it to the level of a mere private scholar's journey in search of self-improvement and talk of "Professor Tucci's expedition to Tibet". It is worth pointing out, without implying any reproach, that one of the chief difficulties which have faced all explorers, from Marco Polo to Stanley, have been their relations with governments and other authorities, all jealous and suspicious of one another. In this respect the good explorer represents the triumph of individualism over the inevitable pettiness of the constituted powers. He is often the champion of science and humanity against superstition and reaction.

The Bombay stations are interesting places in which to observe Indian everyday life. People from all parts of the huge peninsula are to be seen in the bustle. To return to the language question. I noticed that clerks and travellers used English a great deal. At a certain level of education English has really become a *koiné*, a common language. At lower levels of education everyone gets along as best as he can by using his own language, eking it out, if necessary, with expressive gesticulations.

Elephanta: a face, the All

The sea is like the human body. It can be the most beautiful thing in the world, or the most dreadful. The Mediterranean, with its clear water, its rocky promontories plunging down from the blue sky to the blue, clear depths, reminds one of the bronzed flesh of young men or women used to the open air and the breath of the wind on their healthy bodies. But the sea of Bombay is an old sea, in a state of putrefaction, yellow, evil-smelling and covered with filth. The idea of falling into it is disgusting. It smells of refuse, drains and excrement.

Such was the septic stretch of water that we crossed, beneath a white and dazzling sky, in a broken-down old boat with a broken-down old engine, oozing oil from every pore, towards the island and caves of Elephanta. But an ugly beginning often enhances one's subsequent pleasure. When we landed on the wooded islet it at once struck us as very beautiful. We slowly climbed the stairs (it was very hot) and walked up an avenue of flowering trees. Many-coloured birds looked at us inquisitively from the branches. The hill became steeper and eventually precipitous. We had reached the caves.

These caves were carved with immense labour out of the living rock; it is impossible to contemplate them without astonishment. Superficially they can be compared with some of the *pietra serena* caves at Monte Ceceri, near Florence, or with the Cordari caves at Syracuse, but the caves of Elephanta are completely regular, far deeper, and much more mysterious. Moreover, they are not natural, but a man-made church of the spirit. For centuries they were used as a temple. Pilgrims still gather there every year in February; and the memorable sculptures that adorn the walls speak of great human things – myths, cosmologies, life, sacrifice, poetry, beauty and death.

We advanced between the monolithic columns towards the end of the biggest cave, where there stands a colossal bust of Siva, with three heads, feebly lit by distant reflection. The precise meaning of this magnificent statue of the Hindu god has been the subject of prolonged discussion. The face on the onlooker's left is probably intended to represent the god in his fierce aspect as a destroyer, that on the right his aspect as creator, while the middle one represents him as the Absolute. One thing is certain; no statue of such vast size anywhere in the world is infused with so much spiritual greatness. I think it was James Joyce who said that what mattered about a work of art was the depth from which it sprang. Contemplating this statue, you feel a depth that in our civilization only a few have attained (one of them was Leonardo). In its consummate beauty of outline, its deliberate, cosmic, slightly ironic tranquillity, as is appropriate, for the universe is primarily terrible – fire and ice, pain and destruction – it is an imaginative conception of the Absolute in the terms of his own features that has never been exceeded by the mind of man.

Still Elephanta: the world as cathedral and the world as womb

India is the Greece of Asia. India was for the East what Greece was for the West, for us; that is to say, the birthplace of all the philosophical ideas and all the influences in art and poetry which for thousands of years determined, and to an extent still determine, the intellectual life of millions of men. Moreover, India was something else as well. Greece did not give to Western civilization the religion that subsequently became its very life-blood, but with Buddhism India gave to Asia its most tremendous civilizing influence.

In connection with the parallel between Greece and India, and to underline the different character of the two civilizations, let me recall Grousset's phrase – *l'Inde, cette Grèce excessive*. In Greece everything tends to harmony. The Parthenon is a symbol for the arts, and the *Phaedo* and the Ptolemaic theory can be said to be the same for thought. Greek mathematics and geometry also concentrated on the finite and the measurable, shunning, as if it were intellectual sin, investigations that led in the direction of the infinite or the infinitesimal.

With India, *cette Grèce excessive*, it is different. Everything is immoderate, gigantic, teeming, sublime and terrible. Counterparts to the *Iliad* and the *Odyssey* are to be found in the form of poetic continents, with tens of thousands of verses, in the *Mahabharata* and the *Ramayana*. Indian architecture offers us Tanjore (the jungle in stone), Indian painting offers us the caves of Ajanta, Indian sculpture its wealth of fantastic symbolism. Indian philosophy with sublime madness investigates subjective universals, and Indian mathematics succumbs to a special fascination for the immensely big and the immensely small. In Greece the world is always brought back to the measure of man; the Greek tends to make of the universe a comfortable home – a warm, welcoming, reasonable, intelligible, human home; in India man strives to adapt himself to a phantasmagoria of universes fleeing away from him in spirals beyond the horizons of the mind, towards the mysterious horizons of the unconscious, with its unknown powers.

The cult of Siva is one of the most vivid and original products of the Indian mind. It fuses Aryan India, with its insistence on logic, system and light, with nocturnal, feminine, subterranean, Dravidian India, with its intuitions, its language of symbols, its fantasy, its magic and its sensuality. The cult of Siva presents us with the world as cathedral and the world as womb at the same time. We find in it simultaneously the crystalline, mineral vastness of a great stone nave, shaped subtly in accordance with mathematical lines of force, and the twilight of the alcove, the fertile, mysterious, warm, incomprehensible and desirable obscurity of the womb.

How can one briefly summarize the philosophy associated with Siva? In the world of our experience we are aware, on the one hand, of light, beauty, happiness – all that we mean by good; on the other there is darkness, ugliness, suffering and death – all that we mean by evil. Thus there are two aspects to life, and every religion and every philosophy is definable in terms of the position it takes up towards this dichotomy. The universe can, for example, be conceived of as an eternal struggle between the opposing principles of good and evil; alternatively it can be conceived of as being fundamentally good. If the latter position is adopted, a formidable problem arises – that of the origin of evil. Epicurus succinctly expressed the difficulty more than two thousand years ago. If, he said, God desires to overcome evil without being able to, He is impotent; if He is able to overcome evil and does not wish to, He is evil. Finally, if He has both the power and the wish to overcome evil, how is it that we can be aware of the existence of evil? The Indian school of thought of which we are speaking solves the problem by attributing to the Supreme Being (Siva) a total personality, not only beyond both good and evil, but intrinsically both good and evil. He is both Siva ("the Benevolent") and Bhava ("the Prosperous"), but he can also be Kala ("Time"), the great destroyer, or Bhairava, the personification of terror and death.

Siva thus represents the wild and untameable forces of nature, simultaneously pitiless and beautiful, destructive of life and fecund with life at the same time; he is the cruelty and ferocity of the laws that govern life, but at the same time he represents the indomitable impulse which causes life always to spring phoenix-like from the ashes and the ruins. Siva haunts cemeteries, the abode of death and dissolution, like an ungirdled ascetic, but wherever youth blossoms and flourishes he is also to be found. The *lingam*, the phallus, signifies his presence, as do a flower or a happy child. Destruction and creation, life and death, good and evil, extreme suffering, serenity and extreme pleasure, all find their final reconciliation in him. Every apparent contradiction is resolved in the compassionate and terrible, ferocious and loving, cruel and tender, but above all eternally mysterious, Absolute.

The words with which Siva is invoked in the *Harivamsa* express a profound inspiration: "I adore thee, father of this universe, through which thou wanderest along invisible paths, terrible god of thousands of eyes and a hundred armours. I implore thee, being of the various aspects, now perfect and just, now false and unjust. Protect me, thou only god, escorted by wild beasts, thou who art also delight, the past and the future . . . who owest thy birth to thyself alone, oh universal essence!"

The gigantic bust of Siva at Elephanta is the artistic expression of this philosophy. The three heads do not represent three persons, but the three diverse aspects of a single being; he appears sibylline and august as Siva (the Absolute); fierce and implacable as Bhairava (evil, destruction and death); serene and smiling as Vishnu (life, beauty, serenity, joy). The artistic catharsis is complete; the features of the separate faces convey their inner world of feeling by the barest suggestion.

Another notable piece of sculpture in these caves represents Siva in the dance of Tandava, the dance in which Indian thought has tried to symbolize the eternal process of the universe's creation, conservation and destruction. Alas! the great relief has been sadly mutilated; all that remains is a torso, and the sculptor's intention can barely be made out. It is sad to recall that the vandalism that damaged this and other sculptures at Elephanta was mainly the work of white men. The isle of caves is, alas! too near Bombay. Unlike other monuments of Indian art, discovered by the West in less troubled times, we have information about Elephanta from as early as the end of the sixteenth century, and only a few years later the Portuguese Diogo de Couto wrote his work, *Do muito notavel e espantoso Pagode do Elefante.*

The attitude of rude and bigoted European traders when confronted with these colossal monuments of a civilization profoundly different from their own is easy to imagine. Some must have felt contempt, others must have had a confused idea that they were carrying out an act of purification of some sort in destroying what they no doubt took to be idols. Others may have been moved by sheer whim. No doubt there were also other impulses that combined with these to impel them to smash and shatter these ancient stone figures. In any case there is no need to go so far back to find examples of fanatical shortsightedness. Up to a few years ago the official guide of the Victoria & Albert

Museum in London, speaking of Indian art, said: "the monstrous shapes of the Puranic deities are unsuitable for the higher forms of artistic representation."[1] Anyone with even the most superficial acquaintance with Indian art can see the incredible absurdity of such a statement.

On the other hand, one must admit that learning to appreciate the art of a civilization, when approaching it from a quite different one, is a long and difficult task. I had the opportunity for several years of observing the difficulties experienced by Japanese students in trying to understand Western painting and sculpture. Then I shared with them the opposite experience, gradually penetrating in my turn the atmosphere of a civilization different from my own. It is an experience for which one must prepare oneself with an open mind and with humility, and with confidence in the common essence of all mankind.

Besides, until a few decades ago it would have been practically impossible to penetrate beyond the outer forms into the minds of these peoples who created artistic idioms different from our own. All the elements for understanding were lacking. Little was known of their history or of the interior life expressed in their literatures, religions and songs. In three generations orientalists have quietly opened up whole continents for our edification, revealed whole realms of thought and aspiration, and demonstrated that European civilization is not the only civilization, aped by a variety of deviationist and exotic quasi-civilizations, as our fathers used complacently to believe, but only one civilization among many. It is now possible to approach arts different from our own from the inside, following the path taken by those who created them, and thus to arrive at any rate at a partial understanding of them.

In the future we shall perhaps attain a new, truly universal humanism, and talk of Assisi and Elephanta, Botticelli and Li Lung-mien, of the dance of Tandava and the Deposition, as of temples, personalities and motives all alike profoundly significant in the life of the human spirit.

In the train between Bombay and Calcutta: masculine trains and eunuch trains

According to the psychoanalysts, dreaming of speeding trains indicates an unconscious concern with virility. No great imaginative effort was required for this discovery. What could be more virile, more youthful and crazy than a train hurtling through stations and plunging through mountains in a headlong, exciting clatter of metal, with the sensation of irresistible power and will? The most virile railway journey in this sense is undoubtedly that along the Ligurian coast; the train, hurtling along the escarpments of the Apennines and the rocky seashore, massacres houses, hills, cliffs, bridges, walls, trees, roads, unexpected crowds, churches and markets, and the result is a sense of exhilaration bordering on intoxication.

But the least virile train I have ever travelled in is this one, transporting us across the plains of India. It moves slowly, pants, stops, and then ambles on again a little way, but the landscape is so vast, the world so huge, that you don't have the impression of any real movement. Meanwhile the compartment is filled with dust and smoke. Tucci manages to read, but he is a hero of the printed word, and is an exception. The three others, including myself, look out of the window in astonishment at an endless landscape of shrivelled trees, black rocks (the basalt covering of the Deccan), peasants' hovels and cows.

Calcutta: "Perhaps want boy, for massage?"

Bengal is two-thirds the size of Italy and has a bigger population. You get a vague impression of this immense mass of humanity, this dense population, on the train journey to Calcutta. Since early morning brushwood has given way to rice-fields. It is obvious at once that every square inch of land is exploited to the utmost, and supports the maximum possible population. The warm, humid air, the water flowing everywhere, guarantee that the only limitations to vitality and reproduction are those imposed by space.

As our train proceeds the whole life of the countryside is revealed before our eyes. We see work being started in one village and completed two or three villages further on. Here we see a man coming out of a house with two buffaloes; in the next village we see a man exactly like him, again with two buffaloes, on his way towards the rice-fields; in the third village a similar man has already started work. It's the same with the women going down to the canal to do their washing, with the boys with their fishing nets, the girls with their boxes, and the youths cycling along the canal banks. One great plain stretches all the way to the horizon, with endlessly repeated rice-fields, canals, villages and palm-trees; and so it continues beyond our horizon to the next, and so on for thousands of villages and thousands of miles. Humanity is like a close-knit tissue; life like sand; an anonymous thing. But if the train stopped and we got out and spent only a few days in the first village we came to, how many individualities we should discover, what stories and intrigues! (Meanwhile to the man at the plough looking at us we are a trainload of humanity, only one of many that pass every day – humanity flowing like a river, an anonymous river of faces.)

Calcutta was always the really serious thing about the British Indian Empire.

Englishmen went to Calcutta to make their pile. Bombay offered a quiet life to not excessively ambitious administrators, but Calcutta always had something dramatic up its sleeve. Moreover, the history of the two cities is entirely different. Bombay rose and flourished like a prosperous port, in which business thrived. Its only enemies were microscopic: bacilli and the viruses of tropical diseases. But Calcutta can be said to have been born as a fortress, was many times assaulted, sacked (in 1756) and recaptured, and had many bloodthirsty changes of fortune. "Calcutta was the true centre of government and Bengal the base from which the English between 1757 and 1859 expanded their dominion by wars with Indian powers," wrote the historian Dunbar. Calcutta has known plotting and treachery and corruption without end. Even the British, often cruel in their colonial wars and hard in their administration, but not given to double-dealing, succumbed to the influence of the place, and Clive prepared two different copies of his treaty with Mir Jafar, one true and one false, to use in his complicated intrigues with the local potentates.

Physically Calcutta came into existence gradually, emerging more or less concentrically from the marshes of the Ganges delta. In remote times the whole area must have been covered with tropical forest, a green tangle of rank vegetation battening on continual death and decomposition. A tree falls and rots; thousands of plants and animals immediately invest, assault and occupy it, prospering in their turn. The cycle is frantic, fierce, voracious, and it is infused with an all-pervading carnality expressed in the rich colour of animal life and the triumphant, magnificent, perverse luxuriance of fruit and flower. Today the jungle has disappeared, but it has not been conquered.

From the union of physical surroundings such as these with a people as intelligent, as sensitive to beauty and imagination, as sensual, speculative and versatile as the Bengalis there emerged the most baroque features of late Hinduism: the adoration of the feminine energies, the codification of magic and the occult in erotic forms, cruel sacrifices to the evil forces in the universe. Thus the ancient jungle, gradually eliminated by the hand of man, reappeared in an intangible but a thousand times more luxuriant form. I do not believe that there is any great city which is more of a jungle than Calcutta – the metropolis of tooth and claw, tyranny and blackmail, suffering, evil and asceticism. You feel it in the air, something intangible but very definite. The lianas, the orchids, the snakes, the forest with its blood-curdling screams and dripping green mysteries, survive invisibly under the wood, the concrete and the asphalt and between the railway lines.

This morning Piero and I went out to buy various things needed for the journey. The main entrance of the Great Eastern, the principal Calcutta hotel –

it's certainly very eastern, but it's not very great – leads out on to a dirty, crowded street, full of noisy trams and crowded with people of every type. No sooner were we outside than a boy approached us. We knew what he wanted to offer us, but there was no point in chasing him away, because another and more persistent one immediately attached himself to us. ("No want girl? Perhaps want boy, for massage?") The only way to get rid of him was to jump into a taxi driven by a venerable, bearded Sikh.

I don't know why, but all the taxi drivers in Calcutta are Sikhs. Even in the face of the phenomena of modern life, the various groups in India tend to keep together rather than to disperse. The Sikhs come from the Punjab, in north-west India. In the reeking jungle of Calcutta they are as solid and comforting as rocks. Unlike the Bengalis, they always wear turbans, often in delicate pastel shades *à la* Boucher or Marie Laurencin. As they look like Old Testament prophets or old men of the mountains, the pastel shades strike a curiously incongruous note. The Sikhs are forbidden to shave, and consequently have enormous beards, which are pitch-black in their youth but in old age turn perfectly white.

Our prophet took us to Kodaks, in Park Street. Park Street is a small, orderly oasis in the teeming metropolis. It has some fine shops, and you see nurses pushing white children in prams. There is a certain sense of spaciousness and wellbeing about Park Street, at any rate on the surface. But you only have to walk a few yards, towards the New Market, for instance, to plunge once more into the depths of the jungle. You see the most shameless riches side by side with the most abject poverty and squalor. Every few yards you come upon the victim of some horrible disease, or a beggar trying to attract the attention of passers-by in the most dramatic manner possible. This morning in Chowringee, the principal street, we saw a nearly naked, armless man, with legs which were presumably paralysed, rolling along the pavement, thus imprinting on his chest, stomach, legs and back the stains of the red spittle spat out by all the betel-chewers. From a distance this made him look as if he were lacerated and covered with blood. He was accompanied by a naked and indescribably dirty little girl of eight or nine, who followed or preceded him, carrying a tin for alms. The two were singing, or rather shouting, a kind of duet. The man sang one verse, and the girl the next. All the verses were the same, slow and inexorable. It was appalling music, not without a certain beauty of its own. Nobody took the slightest notice, of course. A tall, smartly-dressed, fair woman, carrying a painted wooden horse under her arm, suddenly emerged from a shop and nearly stumbled over the body of the man rolling on the pavement and singing.

In the midst of all this squalor and vice, wealth and destitution, orgiastic cults and cruel sacrifices, in the midst of this world of death, dances and epidemics, there survives, as is appropriate – I might even say inevitable – a fine tradition of learning. I shall not deal here with the museum (which is a real treasure house, and the Bengalis visit it as though it were a temple, stopping to pray in front of the statues and paintings), nor with the various universities, the hospitals and the botanical gardens. I shall mention only the lunch we had with Chatterji. Chatterji is a Bengali, an old friend of Tucci's, and he teaches philology at Calcutta University. He is a man of about fifty, of average height, sturdy without being stout, dark-skinned and dark-haired. He dresses in Indian style and wears spectacles. One is immediately struck by his wide forehead and intelligent eyes. He has the pleasing appearance of the scholar. He arrived at the hotel today while Tucci was out, so I received him; we sat in the lounge and talked.

Chatterji has an excellent knowledge of English. As often happens with men who have devoted their whole lives to humane studies, he started talking immediately, as if we were old friends, recalling persons, books, places and events.

"Yes, yes, Rome," Chatterji said. "I had a friend in Rome once; his wife was a Pole, I think, or something of the sort. He started a literary review called . . . I can't remember what it was called, but the name's of no importance . . . On the cover it had a star and a wave. I liked that very much. When I was in Rome I told my friend that they were very fine symbols indeed. The star reminded me of Emerson: 'Hitch your waggon to a star.' . . . There's a poem of Tagore's, you know – it moves me every time I read it – I can't remember at the moment what it's called, but the title's of no importance, but what it's about is this. It's a conversation between a star in the sky and a little oil lamp in an ordinary Indian house. 'You, little lamp, are the star of the house. I, little star, am a lamp in the sky,' and so on. That sort of thing may strike you as slightly rhetorical, but Indians find it very moving."

Beside us, sitting at the next table in the lounge, were some fat, suave, suspicious-looking individuals, with smiling faces and evasive eyes. They wore European clothes, and leaned forward in their armchairs when they spoke, to avoid being overheard. What were they? Foreign-exchange smugglers? White slave traffickers? Dope dealers?

"In every Indian home," Chatterji continued, "a lamp is lit by the woman of the house as soon as she awakens every morning. It's a beautiful rite, ancient and full of poetry. The lamp is taken into the family chapel, and is then used to light other lamps. It's an intimate little domestic ceremony that greatly appealed to my Italian friend . . . what was his name?. . . oh, well, it's of no importance . . . . I told him all about it in English, and he liked it so much that he said he would translate it into your language . . . ."

There was movement at the next table. An individual who seemed to be the gang-leader had arrived. He was a little man, getting on in life, very carefully dressed, and Chinese-looking. The fat men all got up when he appeared, and then sat down again. Nobody spoke. It seemed as if some sort of plot were being hatched. Finally one of the men produced a packet of photographs from his wallet and started passing them round.

"Symbols are a very important thing in life," Chatterji went on, wiping his spectacles with a corner of his dhoti. "The star and the wave! But man is more important than symbols, just as the living are more important than the dead. I remember a dinner-party to which I went once in Florence. I sat next to an American lady, who kept going into ecstasies about old Italian music and old Italian poetry. In the end a young man of your country said with a laugh: 'My dear lady, modern Italians exist as well!' I recalled that little incident some time ago when I was asked to go to Udaipur, in Rajputana, to give a lecture. Udaipur, you know, is rather like Florence, a city famous for its great artists and warriors, and for all the heroes who defended our country against the Muslim invaders five hundred years ago. At Udaipur there are sacred memories of memorable events at every step . . . ."

Our neighbours had lit cigarettes and ordered drinks (lemonade and soda, as today was one of the prohibition days). The photographs continued to circulate. The little Chinese-looking man seemed to be particularly interested in one photograph, which he kept looking at. Every now and then he murmured something into the ear of one of the others. The remainder of the gang kept whispering and plotting, looking around them and drinking lemonade and soda.

"My dear Chatterji!" said a well-known voice behind my back. It was Professor Tucci, who had arrived at last. After they had greeted each other, we sat down again and the conversation was resumed for several minutes. Then Colonel Moise and Piero arrived, and we could go in to lunch. Meanwhile our neighbours had departed. As we rose I noticed that they had dropped a photograph. I could not resist the temptation of picking it up and looking at it. It was the photograph of a model of a lady's shoe. (This evening I told Piero the story. "Don't be silly," he said. "They obviously dropped the photograph on purpose. It's an alibi!" On reconsidering the matter I decided to adopt the Mele interpretation as being in harmony with the spirit of the place.)

Our lunch, in the big, air-conditioned restaurant attached to the hotel, resolved itself, after a few minutes' general conversation, into a dialogue between the two lions of learning. It was an intellectual feast of the kind one rarely has the opportunity of attending, and I tried hard not to miss anything that was said. A remark about words in everyday use brought up the subject of the Munda languages, and from there it was but a step to the Dravidian languages. They mentioned works written by their colleagues .... "I agree with Schmidt, but only on general lines"... Tucci was the more scientific, in the German tradition, Chatterji more of a humanist, in the classical sense. When he recalled some colleague, he always produced some visible and picturesque image that made him vivid to the mind. "So-and-so passed through Calcutta two or three years ago," he would say. "He's a tall, fair, silent man, with a little round wife always dressed in white, just like a tennis-ball, bouncing round him all the time!" Then he would revert to quoting Kalidasa or the *Kangyur* in the course of comparing remote and present-day literatures and drawing conclusions that served to reconstruct the history of Asia.

The restaurant waiters numbered about fifty. They wore white, caliph-like uniforms, with a kind of little red fez turban perched on top of their heads. They moved silently, on bare feet. The whole thing was less like a meal than a ceremony – a coronation, or something of the sort. A solemn-looking doge, with a little white moustache, placed before me a tureen containing an almost invisible soup, in which there floated (or flew?) a small green leaf. At the next table was a party of Parsees, the women rather beautiful and the men rather fat. A few tables away sat a family of Europeans, all of them looking washed and dried out in the witches' cauldron of the monsoons. The husband, who seemed to be a decent professional man of about thirty-five, looked washed out; the wife, with her almost repellently whitish skin, looked washed out; so did their daughter, a little girl of six or seven. How sad white children look in this part of the world!

The lions of learning continued. Both of them were in magnificent form. They were terrific. From the Munda languages they passed to Tibet, the Uighurs, and the Nestorian Christianity of Central Asia. They mentioned Sir Aurel Stein, Marco Polo, and von Le Coq, made excursions into Bactria and Persia, taking in Manichaeism, ancient coinages and unpublished texts found in Himalayan monasteries. They followed Greek *motifs* across the steppes and oases along the Silk Road of Central Asia. They laid the whole of Asia bare before us, took it to pieces, dissected it and put it together again in space and time. They revealed links and affinities, unexpected relationships, facts that threw light on whole orders of other facts. They filled the map of Asia with life and movement, and turned history into a luminous fountain. With the eyes of gods, playing with ages and peoples like toys held in their omnipotent fingers, we watched the unrolling of the immense pageant of the past.

Chatterji traced the name of Rome in its passage across Asia. "In Syria," he told us, "it was known as Hrim. Chinese merchants, venturing to the extreme West of the Asian world, met merchants venturing to the extreme East of the Mediterranean world. They spoke of the empire of Hrim, but the Chinese could not pronounce the name correctly; the 'H' became 'Fu', and Hrim was transformed first into Fu-rim and then, undergoing still further adaptation to the Chinese mouth (which can pronounce 'l' but not 'r'), it became Fulin. That is the name the Chinese still use for Rome."

Chatterji was delightful. He talked and talked, forgot to eat, then hurried frantically to consume the invisible soup. Whenever anything fascinates him he becomes completely oblivious to his surroundings. But he is by no means blind. When the beautiful Parsee woman at the next table got up, he caressed her with the look of a connoisseur, and lost the thread of his argument. He's altogether simpler and more human than Tucci, but certainly no less learned. His intellectual equipment is of the first rank, and Tucci listened to him with great attention. Every now and then he produced from beneath his white cotton dhoti a copy of the *Acts of the Asiatic Society of Bengal* and noted in pencil on the cover the titles of books or articles quoted in the conversation. When he put the document back in its place again he revealed the primitive landscape of a vast, hairy belly just at the height of the ethereal soup.

Siliguri: at the foot of the Himalayas

We left Calcutta for Siliguri last night. We travelled all night on the Darjeeling Mail, the express to the north which runs with a great clatter of metal through innumerable stations. We crossed two frontiers: from India into Pakistan, and from Pakistan into India again. Now that the world is tending to unite, is not this division of the sub-continent a retrograde step? But it must be admitted that, accustomed as we are to seeing the world in political categories, we are not in a good position to judge peoples who still see the world almost exclusively in religious categories.

Reconsideration, 1998

India has changed very little, I mean the fundamental, basic, boundless and perennial Mother India, to use the title of a book by Mayo which was famous in its day. This is chiefly because the population has put on an impressive growth, cancelling out the advantages of independence and of every technical development in industry and agriculture; from the four hundred million souls in 1948 we have now passed the nine-hundred-million mark. In the towns this increase is all the more disturbing; if Bombay numbered one and a half million inhabitants in the 1950s, it is now up to eight million, while Calcutta is approaching ten million; but these figures are clearly below the actual totals, given the considerable and unquantifiable number of illegal immigrants who evade every check and census.

The political situation has evolved in important respects. During the years of the journeys here described, the English were a vigorous and determining presence everywhere, and India and Pakistan both belonged to the British Commonwealth.

For a great part of Asia the Second World War had resulted in an unprecedented political and social upheaval. The vast and powerful colonial empires formed in previous centuries had collapsed (apart from the Chinese), leaving room for the establishment of new and often dynamic independent organisms. South of the Himalayas the two great statesmen Mohandas Gandhi and Muhammad Ali Jinnah, representing the Hindu Congress and the Moslem League respectively, were unable to come to terms; on 15 August 1947, the day marking the devolution of power from the British Crown to the people of the sub-continent, there was coincidentally a partition of the territory and the birth of two new states: on the one hand India, that gathered together the vast majority of Hindus, on the other Pakistan, which united the Muslims. This distribution "was attended in the north of India by a terrifying explosion of popular anger against the minorities. About three hundred thousand Hindus and Muslims lost their lives, and more than ten million had to leave their homes in one of the largest and most tragic forced exchanges of population that history records."[2]

The centrifugal tendencies, ever present in the Indo-Pakistani region, given the extraordinary variety and multiplicity of human groups distinguished by race, religion, language, culture and lifestyle, produced sizeable convulsions in recent years, and it is easy to predict that they will continue to do so in the future. After the bloody events of December 1971 East Pakistan established its independence in March 1972 and now constitutes Bangladesh. Notable Indian minorities, the Sikhs for example, strain at the leash. The tragic assassination of Indira Gandhi was a political act for which the Sikhs loudly claimed the credit. Kashmir (where a Hindu minority rules over a Muslim majority), and Assam (settled by a people that is only partially Indian) constitute thorny political problems ever ready to explode. The people of Punjabi tongue seek a greater degree of autonomy, as do (peacefully for the present) the Tamil-speaking Indians and the Baluchi-speaking Pakistanis.

In general the message to be read in the panorama of these events in recent decades would seem to be this: what counts for most in relations between men, at least for the present and in large parts of Asia, are emotional responses, those that relate to the colour of the neighbours' skin, their religion, their tongue, their culture, their dress, their food – and not purely economic considerations that might lend themselves to a reasonable solution.

1 On Western prejudices concerning Indian arts, see the fascinating study by Partha Miller: *Much Maligned Monsters, A History of European Reactions to Indian Art*, Oxford, Clarendon Press, 1977

2 L. Petech: *Le Civiltà dell' Oriente*, Rome, Casini, 1956, vol. I, p. 737

3

From Fern to Glacier

Sikkim: from fern to glacier

We have arrived at Siliguri, and are now very near the Himalayas, which loom steeply and commandingly over the plains of Bengal. In a few days' marches, in less than a week, you can travel from a land of palms and tree-ferns to a land of snow and ice. In the pages that follow I have gathered together notes written at various times in the state of Sikkim, between India and Tibet, to give some idea of one of the most beautiful journeys in the world; from valleys sunk in mist and rain to mountain-tops glittering in brilliant sunshine.

Between Dikchu and Mangen

We are following the course of a tremendous ravine through which the Tista runs. In quality the Tista is a mountain torrent; in size it is a big river. Imagine the Adige or the Po in flood plunging through a twisting gorge, carrying uprooted tree-trunks and whirling them along as if they were twigs. We are several hundred feet above sea-level, and the heat is stifling. The air sweats and weeps; everything seems to be liquefying. But for the leeches and mosquitoes, we could walk naked, but because of them we have to keep well covered up, and our clothes stick to our skin. We are hemmed in all round by the green and dripping forest, and the mist dissolves everything we see – the slippery, rotting earth, the leaves, the tree-trunks, the trees, both near and distant – into a uniform, mysterious grey, which takes away the individuality of everything and suffuses a vague carnality over everything. Green tendrils and canopies, stretching up to the dense foliage of the trees, conceal sinister vegetable hollows, into which I look in the way a layman searches a wound with his eyes. Every now and then you come across masses of white orchids hanging from the boughs. They are beautiful but sinister – flowers with poisonous scent, the kind of flowers to send to an enemy. Then there are the snakes, which stop, and glide silently away, and pulpy fruits, which drop in the dripping silence with a squelch. The forest is alive; individually and collectively, it is alive. It is alive in the tree-trunks covered in lichen and moss and clothed with ferns; in the butterflies, in the constant squeaks and pipings, in every sudden and inexplicable rustle. You feel that the forest has its own personality, its own desires and whims, its own hates; its own hunger and weariness and languors, its own hidden eyes. Once you have penetrated into it, you cannot escape it. Its green tentacles enclose you in an agonizing embrace.

How shall one describe the strange excitement induced by the luxuriant vegetation, the monstrous tree-trunks covered with dripping lichen, the caress on one's hand of those huge, shiny leaves, the feel of the bark, the intoxication of the smells and perfumes? At the same time, how express the revulsion provoked by so much teeming, gliding, creeping, turgid vitality? Who could put into words the fear of death that lurks everywhere? Not of death because of any specific danger, but of death in a subtle, all-pervading sense. Nowhere else are

3 *Forests in Sikkim*

life and death so intimately united and intertwined. Here a fallen tree provides nourishment for the thousands of living things that batten on its decomposing fibre; a whole population of fungi, insects, worms, ferns, moss, lichens and moulds; there a snake glides noiselessly between carnivorous flowers; there a butterfly flies solemnly and capriciously, finally settling on the yellow carcass of an animal; here is an ambush, a trap-secret, stabbing, evil; here are both splendour and horror. Baudelaire would have been delighted by all these occult suggestions:

Serré, fourmillant, comme un million d'helminthes
Dans nos cerveaux ribote un peuple de Démons . . .

and he would at once have drawn the great parallel between the tropical forest and the heart of man.

Mangen

Glory and liberation this morning! For a moment the clouds lifted, and after many days we saw the blue sky again, and there, at an incredible height, nearly 24,000 feet above our heads, frighteningly far away and near at the same time, we saw that divinely pure and unsubstantial thing, consisting only of shape and light, the sparkling pyramid of Kanchenjunga (28,208ft).

Nearing Sing-hik

Yesterday's unforgettable vision lasted only for a moment. Then the mists closed down again, plunging us back into our stifling, subterranean world of green, drizzling semi-darkness, pregnant with the aggressive smells of the forest. Trees, trees, millions of trees. This evening, while day was slowly turning into night, I heard some blue pigeons singing in the distance. Their cooing is musical and exquisitely sad, with strange transpositions into a minor key of a motive that they repeat at long intervals in a delicate tone which would have delighted Debussy.

Between Sing-hik and Tong

The people that live in these valleys, the Lepchas, are small, furtive and silent. The excesses of nature in these parts – the terrifying rivers, the destroying, devouring forests, the ice-bound peaks vanishing into the sky – seem to have completely overwhelmed and subdued those who came to live here in ancient times. Or was it only by creeping, hiding, evading, that adaptation was possible? Today I heard a barely perceptible rustle behind my back, and two barefooted men emerged from the dense green undergrowth. One was aged about fifty; the other was his son. Both had long hair, as is still the custom in these parts, but neither had the trace of a beard. The boy, whose name was Gu-lung, was nineteen years old, but he behaved like a girl of thirteen or fourteen, full of shyness, timidity and blushes. The Lepchas now number only a few thousand, and most of them are to be found in the neighbourhood of Mangen, Sing-hik and along the valley of Talung.

The Government of Sikkim is in the hands of a small ruling class of Tibetans who invaded the territory from the north some centuries ago. On the whole they are vigorous, enterprising people. The majority of the population of Sikkim, however, consists of recently immigrated Nepalese. Like the Lepchas, they are little men, but they are extremely active, and spread all over the place like human ants. There is some resemblance between them and the Japanese. (Nepal, the Japan of India!) They are gradually spreading East and West. They work hard, co-operate with each other, organize themselves, multiply and always talk Nepalese. In the country they always go about armed with a curved blade called a *kukri.* I bought one yesterday from two Nepalese who looked at me unpleasantly. I thought that buying their weapon from them was the one means of enabling me to rest really peacefully. The *kukri*, complete with sheath, subsidiary dagger, flint and steel, etc., weighs about 5 lb.

Following our stony mule-track we come across Lepcha dwellings every now and then. They live in huts, of the kind typical of the whole of south-east Asia, built on piles of varying height. From Japan to Java, from Burma to Bengal the details vary, but the structure is the same. At one point we met some Tibetans by the side of a stream. They had erected a tent, had been bathing, and were eating and drinking. When I greeted them in Tibetan they insisted on my joining them to drink some *chang*. The differences in character between the human groups that inhabit these valleys are most marked. The Lepchas are small, shy, silent, childlike; they are always concealing themselves, and know all the secrets of the forest. The Nepalese are small and silent, too, but they are active and vigorous, continually bestirring themselves like ants. The Tibetans are big, noisy, expansive, the least oriental of orientals, men made to stride like giants over their endless plateaux, always ready to drink, sing, or believe in a miracle; merchants, bandits, monks and shepherds.

Near Tsungtang

The world seems to consist of nothing but water and vegetation. Stones and rocks are so completely covered by the forest that you never see them. Only where there is flowing water is the mountain rock laid bare. Today we had a little sunshine, and I went down to the Tista for a bathe. The air is still very hot, but the water, which comes straight down from the glaciers, is freezing. The strength of the current was frightening, and it was impossible to swim. All one could do was to take a dip between some huge boulders near the bank where the waters were less swift. Not far away a rope bridge, of the kind used in these parts, was suspended over the ravine. It danced about in an alarming manner, and only the Lepchas are able to use it with confidence. The abundance of water in the valleys of the eastern Himalayas is a terrifying thing. Everywhere there are waterfalls, torrents, whirlpools, springs. You have the distinct impression that these mountains are still fabulously young, that the levelling-out processes are still extremely active, that everything is moving, plunging, slipping and sliding downhill. Actually the water carries away fantastic quantities of earth and sand and rolls down masses of rock, thus destroying the colossal mountains bit by bit every day.

Lachung

The last mists and the first fir-trees. Suddenly we are in another, a more familiar world, in surroundings that recall the Alps, Italy, beautiful and distant Europe. Even the huts are no longer built on piles and covered with straw. But for some typical signs which show that we are in a Buddhist country, the cottages we see might be in the Bernese Oberland or the Val d'Aosta.

4 *Torrent in Sikkim, carving the rock face*

Beyond Lachung

Once more we are in the midst of a thick and apparently endless forest, but how different it is from the forest we were in only two or three days ago! We have reached a height of 9,000 feet, and instead of being surrounded by the alien and exotic, the stupendous and the horrifying, we are now among vegetation consisting of conifers and rhododendrons. The contrast could not be more complete. The only obstacle that confronts the teeming life in the never-ending heat and humidity down below is the lack of physical space. Every form of life has to make its way at the expense of other forms of life; life thrives on death, and the thief and the parasite, the blood-sucker and the crafty, fatten and multiply. Up here the struggle for life is different. It is less a struggle of the species among themselves than a struggle of all against the elements – wind, frost, rock, avalanches, storms. The consequence is that the essential character of the two forests is diametrically different. The forest we are in now is tall and dry. Here craft and cunning no longer count for anything, because what is needed for survival is strength, toughness, innate vigour. In human terms the forest down below was like a big city in which craft and racketeering prospered, but up here life is lived in the sun and the wind, the big things in the face of which it is useless to lie.

Up a lateral valley

The rhododendrons! In the Himalayas the rhododendrons are trees as tall as lime or walnut trees. Instead of being humble little plants, as in the Alps, they form thickets that cover whole mountainsides. From May to July they bear superb pink, pale violet or bright yellow flowers, flowers delicate almost to the point of decadence. This morning I left the mule-track, the paths, the last traces of the passage of man, and spent hours climbing a lateral valley lost in the forest. At this distance from any inhabited place nature is intact, wild and full of mystery. I had to climb over the trunks of some trees that had recently been struck down by a storm, and others that had been lying there for years, covered with lichen and moss. Every now and then a frightened bird emerged from the foliage and flew away. The dry leaves, the pine needles, the fallen branches, crackled when I walked on them. Finally, in these recesses of the primaeval forest, suitable for battles between bears and giants or for the yells of savages, I came upon whole gardens of sumptuous rhododendrons, rich, infinitely refined and languorous, having a texture that was something between flesh and silk, tinted with the delicate colours of the alcove – a festival that has been quietly prepared every year for ages, for nobody at all.

Beyond Yumtang

We are among the last trees, and the first snow is visible in the distance. This morning we set out at dawn. Strange lichens, pearly with dew in the early morning light, hung from the plants in the forest.

Nearing Samdong

The trees suddenly disappeared. Thickets of rhododendrons accompanied us for a time, and then we came to the open spaces, the high mountains. But who were those sulphur-coloured personages climbing up the mountainside? They looked like flamens on the way to a solemn reunion on some remote summit. They were *chu-kar*, strange plants belonging to the *Poligonaceae*, which grow in isolation up to incredible heights, up to fifteen thousand feet and more, in the moraines, beyond the last meagre pastures to which only grass, sedge and tiny alpines can stand up. The porters told me that the pith of the *chu-kar* could be eaten raw. I tried it, and found it tart and refreshing. Whoever brought you up here, superb, exotic plant worthy of a greenhouse? Perhaps you are a last greeting from India.

5 *Mt Chombu (20,800ft) in northern Sikkim*

Sebu-la (17,224ft)

Our first real meeting with Central Asia was with a yak, the great, hairy, tame, slow, abstemious and agreeable beast of burden of Tibet. It was grazing peacefully at the foot of a colossus of 21,000 feet, and was perfectly at home. Then we came to the first snow, and we camped for the first time in frost. We set out for the Sebu pass yesterday at dawn, and soon the sun was illuminating the ice palaces of Chombu, the last important mountain in these parts still unconquered by the foot of man, [although the 20,800ft peak was evidently climbed on 13 October 1961 by a small Indian expedition (*Himalayan Journal*, 23, p. 169 and 24, p. 157)]. Last night we camped beside a little lake, in the still waters of which unknown and unnamed peaks were beautifully reflected. It was strange that the lake did not freeze; perhaps it is fed from warm springs.

6 *Sikkim: snows and flowers*

At Samdong, not far away, there are several such lakes.

We are only a few miles from the valley of the Tista, which we spent the last few days climbing, but how infinitely remote seems the world that we left down below! There we were oppressed by the enormous overhanging mountains, the exuberance of the vegetation, the low ceiling of clouds that weighed down on us like a horrible penance. Here we breathe the open sky and see the giants of the eastern Himalayas – Kanchenjunga (28,208ft), Kangcherjhau (22,700ft), Pauhunri (23,180ft), Chomolhari (23,930ft), and, in the extreme distance, Everest (29,002ft), shining like sublime and brilliant islands in a boundless sea of space. We can turn round and say: There is Tibet, there is Nepal and over there is the huge expanse of India. We are on terms of intimacy with the breath of the continents.

7 *Crossing the Sebu pass*

The valleys down below were hot and wet, full of a voracious, imperious or cunning, aggressive or insinuating vitality. Up here we are in a realm of ice and clarity, of ultimate and primordial purity. Night and death are so very different here from what they are down below! Down below night is even more alive than day. Night turns the valley into a huge maw. You seem to be surrounded by strange secretions; you feel the touch of strange breath upon you; invisible desires and terrors entwine themselves into the dense tissue of branches, leaves and sod. But up here the night is nothing but light and space. Everything lies motionless in the great frost, with only the stars shining, or the moon gliding along channels of ice or sheets of blue brightness. Time and matter seem no longer to exist. Hence here death immediately suggests eternity. Down below death is decomposition, a minor, unimportant phase in the cycle of living; it is the state which permanently gives nourishment to the vortex of new lives. Up here night has the solemn, crystalline, dignity of the great truths; it is mind, God.

The porters accompanying us are Bhutias (Tibetans) from Lachung. They are strong, simple, cheerful fellows, perfectly attuned to these places. They face the climb without complaint; on the contrary, they regard the enterprise and its difficulties as a personal challenge, which they cheerfully accept. In the evening they sing round the camp fire, and they sing on the passes, loudly, in chorus. The valleys far below are buried in mists, which from above are seas of cloud.

8 *Gangtok: the main temple*

How sudden was the transition! A few days ago we could stop to admire the reflection of a ray of light on a butterfly's wing. This evening one of the porters picked up a handful of snow and let it drop bit by bit to the ground. The crystals flew lightly away, reflecting the light of the sun setting between the peaks in gleams of green, pink and gold.

Gangtok: dinner with the Maharajah

In this Himalayan landscape, with its dizzy extremes and excesses, it is appropriate that by way of contrast there should be a toy capital, with a toy bazaar, toy gardens and toy houses, set among tree-ferns and wild orchids on a hillside among the clouds. Such, indeed, is Gangtok, the capital of Sikkim. We reached Gangtok several days ago. It is connected with the rest of the world by telegraph, it is at the end of a motor-road (seventy miles from Siliguri), it has a post office, a hospital and the Maharajah's palace. All the same, you feel out of the world. The whole thing is a fairy-tale.

Yesterday we were invited to the palace. We were received without any formality, and it was a very agreeable occasion. This evening we were invited again,

9 *The Maharajah of Sikkim, 1948*

this time to dinner. We were twenty-six at table. I watched the Maharajah, small, thin and elderly, as delicate as a little bird and as noble as a coat of arms, draped magnificently in his brown silk Tibetan robe, bend over his plate, peering through his thick spectacles, and follow up – with notable ability, it cannot be denied – some peas which tried to escape the points of his fork.

All Gangtok was present at the dinner in honour of Professor Tucci and his companions: the Political Officer and his wife, the Maharajah's private secretary, and the heads of the various noble families who hold the reins of government of the tiny state of Sikkim. Every now and then the Maharajah turned and spoke to Mrs Hopkinson, the wife of the Political Officer of the Indian Government. I think the subject of their conversation was butterflies. The butterflies of Sikkim are extremely beautiful and incredibly varied. His Highness Sir Tashi Namgyal, Maharajah of Sikkim, though of Tibetan origin, like the whole ruling caste of Sikkim, is a perfect representative of the small, secretive type of humanity that peoples the valleys at the feet of the giants of the Himalayas. He loves fine things, rare stones, lacquer and jade, which he caresses with the thin fingers of a refined ascetic, and passes as quietly from room to room of his palace as if he moved by levitation. I could not take my eyes off him as he tackled his peas; it was an exquisite, microscopic struggle; something between a game of chess and the infinite pains of the miniaturist; something between a secret rite and a piece of court ceremonial. But now the struggle was over. The last pea, defeated and impaled on the fork, was raised to the royal lips, which opened delicately to receive it, as if about to give, or receive, a kiss.

The dining-room was a small one. The big, oval table and its twenty-six diners practically filled it. On the walls were Tibetan pictures on cloth (*tangka*), depicting scenes from the legend of the Buddha. They belonged to a series called the *Tse-pa chu-ni* ("The Twelve Scenes of the Life"), and were of notable, but not exceptional, beauty. The magnificent Tibetan sense of colour was reflected, not only in our hosts' pictures, but also in their clothes. The Maharajah, besides his brown silk robe, which was held round his waist by an orange sash, wore black velvet Mongolian slippers with green flourishes. The Princesses Pemà Chöki and Sönam Palden, to say nothing of the wife of the *Lachag* Taring, were dressed in Tibetan style and wore rich golden *kau* (boxes for amulets) on their necks. The men all wore silk robes of various colours, and all had red, orange or yellow silk sashes round their waists.

Among all this splendour and delight for the eye we Europeans looked like penguins. When will Western taste revert to expressing itself in the richness and colour of the people painted by a Bronzino or a Holbein? The black and white

10 *Pemà Chöki on the Natu pass*

evening clothes of the twentieth century are a grim and horrible thing. In the company of intelligent Asians who stick to their magnificent costumes one can only feel an acute sense of shame at our stupid abdication. It is said that colour is stupid and effeminate. One might as well say that love is effeminate.

Opposite the Maharajah was seated the Princess Pemà Chöki, his second daughter (the eldest is married to a high Tibetan functionary, and lives in Lhasa). As the Maharajah is separated from the Maharani, Pemà Chöki acted as hostess. She is twenty-two, her name means "lotus of the happy faith", and she is as pretty as her mythical name. She is intelligent, proud and highly strung. Her black hair, gathered into a plait in the Tibetan style, provides the frame for a slender, pale face, and eyes that are now intense and penetrating, now unexpectedly languorous. Her mouth is small and expressive, passing from smiles to disappointment, from the seriousness of a thoughtful moment to laughter at a misunderstanding, with the quick changes of mood of an alert and active mind.

Pemà Chöki was, of course, dressed in Tibetan style. Tibetan is the language of the palace, and to a large extent life is lived in the Tibetan manner. The title of Maharajah attributed to the Dren-jon-gi Gyal-po ("king of Sikkim" in Tibetan) is one of the few concessions to Indian usage. Lhasa, the Tibetan capital, is undoubtedly the local Paris from which fashion, etiquette and customs emanate. When dinner was over Pemà Chöki rose, and one noticed that she was small. But her Asian dress made her look taller. Besides, she is so well-proportioned that it is only when standing close to her that you can tell her real height. She wore a robe of violet silk, with a sash round her waist and an apron of brilliant, electric colours. Hanging from her neck was a golden *kau*, thickly studded with diamonds. Pemà Chöki's personality was tastefully expressed in a few innovations immediately perceptible to an experienced observer. Instead of the traditional *lhani* (coloured cloth slippers), for instance, she wore elegant black leather French sandals; and her finger-nails were painted red.

After dinner we went into the drawing-room, and I found myself next to Pemà Chöki, who talks excellent English. She knows about the West from books and study, but has never been outside Asia. At school she learned English stories and poems by heart (she went to school at Kalimpong), and now reads *Life, Vogue* and the *Reader's Digest*. She confused Colbert (Claudette) with Flaubert (Gustave) and Aristotle with Mephistopheles. But of Tibetan culture she knows every aspect. She adores Buddhist ceremonies, and has a special veneration for Milarepa.

"Just imagine," she said, as if talking about some catastrophe that had happened only yesterday, "Milarepa [who incidentally lived a thousand years ago] dwelt in a cave in the Himalayas, among snow and ice, winter and summer. I go into the mountains sometimes myself, but I shouldn't like to stay there always! Milarepa had one single possession: a pitcher for water. One day the pitcher fell, and broke into a hundred fragments. Instead of complaining or despairing, Milarepa sang. He said to the pitcher: 'You were the only thing that I had. Now that you're broken, you have become a lama and preached an admirable sermon on the impermanence of things!' . . . Rather divine, isn't it?"

A servant, dressed like a genie of the woods, passed with a tray. The princess invited me to take a drink and continued:

"In a few days' time there's going to be a wonderful ceremony at the monastery; you simply must come! A new lama has arrived from Tibet. He has such a beautiful voice! And then he's really handsome. Am I foolish if I suggest that a lama should be handsome, to help him lead our mind to faith?"

Pemà raised the glass containing the liqueur that we had brought with us as a gift from Italy, and laughed. She was well aware that her last remark had been delightfully frivolous. Without knowing it, she had repeated a question asked a thousand years before by Sei Shonagon in the journal she kept as a lady at the court of the Fujiwara in Japan.

The princess then talked about her visit to Lhasa two years ago – the gorgeous processions of lamaist archbishops and abbots, the singing, the incense and the music. "Imagine an important ceremony in a big temple," she said. "Imagine a gathering of all the highest dignitaries of the Church and all the principal families of Lhasa. Well, right in the middle of the blessing a servant came and fetched me, or rather I suddenly noticed him making signs to me from the other end of the temple. As I was sitting nearly in the front row, I almost died at the thought of getting up and treading on the feet of all the grandest ladies of Tibet. The wives of several *sha-pes* (Ministers) were there, and several relatives of the Dalai Lama. Terrible, wasn't it? Also I wasn't sure that my hair was tidy. But the servant kept on making urgent signs to me, and I thought that something terrible must be happening at home – perhaps the house was on fire, or thieves were trying to break in. Heaven knows what it might have been!"

"And what did it turn out to be?"

"All it turned out to be, after I had trampled on the toes of a large number of important people, was my puppy, which was bringing up all the rice she had been given an hour before. I expect there were dogfish fins in it, which she detests! What a predicament! All I could do was to shut her up in the only place available at the moment, the *gön-kang*!"

The word *gön-kang* struck me as a discordant note. As I listened to the princess's description I had been imagining the scene in the lamp-filled temple, with the gold brocade, the psalm-singing, the silk-robed lamas, the clouds of incense, the gilded statues, the crowd of dignitaries in all the splendour of ecclesiastical and feudal Tibet, the Tibet that still belongs to the Asia of Marco Polo.

A *gön-kang*, however, is a dark, crypt-chapel such as is to be found in every monastery; it is the abode of the *yi-dam*, the tutelary deities – a mysterious recess, where the stink of the rancid butter of the offerings on the altars is even more sickening than usual. At the entrance are hung the decomposing bodies of bears, wild dogs, yaks and snakes, stuffed with straw, to frighten away the evil spirits who might desire to pass the threshold. The carcasses fall to pieces, and are as disgusting as a space under a flight of stairs would be with us if it were full of rubbish covered with cobwebs, ancient umbrellas that belonged to great-grandfather, and fragments of bedraggled fur that had been worn by a dead aunt. On top of it, of course, there is the rancid butter. Pictures of the gods are painted on the walls. At first sight you would say they were demons, monsters, infernal beings. They are, however, good spirits, protectors, who assume these terrifying shapes to combat the invisible forces of evil.

The association of Pemà Chöki with a *gön-kang* struck me as a criminal offence. It was impossible to imagine anything lovelier than the princess at that moment, with her colour, her jewels and her youth, and impossible to imagine anything more revolting than a *gön-kang*, a dark, dusty pocket of stale air, stinking of rancid butter, containing skinless, greasy carcasses, with terrifying gods painted on the walls, riding monsters, wearing diadems of skulls and necklaces of human heads, and holding in their hands blood-filled skulls as cups.

The princess once more raised the transparent glass to her lips, sipped, smiled, and continued: "But you don't even know what a *gön-kang* is!" She then gave me a full description. She spoke of bones and dances, of *dri-dug*, the sacred knife, of *dorje*, the thunderbolt, of garlands of skulls, of sceptres of impaled men. In her was Tibet, the secret and untranslated Tibet; Tibet, the land of exaltation, beauty and horror, the land of open sky and stony wastes and fetid *gön-kang*s, of lofty peaks sparkling in the sun and of places where dead bodies are hacked to pieces to provide meals for the vultures; land of simplicity and cruelty, of purity and orgy.

Changu: Verlaine and the "wind-men"

Pemà Chöki and her brother, Prince Thondup, decided to accompany us towards Tibet to do some ski-ing in the mountains. Climbing up to Changu with Pemà Chöki was a continual process of discovery, both charming and exhilarating. She was no longer a fairy-tale princess in her toy palace, surrounded by Tibetan pictures painted on precious cloth, surrounded by jade and chairs in the worst English colonial taste. Now she was a simple and sturdy companion, breathing the thin air of 12,000 feet and laughing in the sun, her head covered with a fur cap of the kind worn in the high plateaux in winter. Who would have suspected that there was so much strength and determination in her pearl and porcelain body?

Today there was snow all the way up to the mountain-tops, from where the wind kept carrying away minute crystals that glistened in the sun; in the distance the giant peaks could be descried amid the blue glaciers. I was still haunted every now and then by the memory of the *gön-kang* and its monsters. How reconcile the divine purity and serenity of these mountains, the infinite sweetness of sky and space, with the stinking, bloodthirsty horror of the lamaist phantasmagoria? Yet both were Tibet. How reconcile those monstrous tutelary deities with the grace of Pemà Chöki? Perhaps the mystery of Pemà Chöki was to some extent the mystery of Tibet, and perhaps she could give me the clue to its solution.

This evening we spent hours round the camp fire sipping *chang*, the Sikkim beer brewed from millet, from tall bamboo cups, called *paip*. We talked of Verlaine, and Keats. I admired the princess's knowledge of Western culture, though laughing with her every now and then at some mistake. Is not a temple containing a Greek statue the same sort of thing to her that a Chinese pavilion, or a pagoda, is to us, namely the extreme of the exotic?

Next, I don't know how, Pemà Chöki started talking about things more truly her own; about *lung-pa*, for instance, the "wind-men" – monks who, after years of extreme asceticism and strenuous preparation, succeed in freeing themselves almost completely from the weight of the human frame and are therefore able to travel hundreds of miles in a single day.

"In fact, they can make a complete circuit of Tibet in a week," Pemà assured me.

She also told me how a storm arose if you threw a stone into certain lakes, and about a witch who was buried near a Lhasa monastery.

"Though she died such a long time ago," the princess said, "the top of her head sticks a little way out of the ground every day. No-one succeeds in forcing her down. Just imagine, she actually has fleas in her hair! The lamas exorcize her every day, but she is stronger than they!"

This, and not little temples with imitation Greek statues or cardboard-and-paste gardens painted by English governesses, is the soil in which Pemà Chöki's mind has its real roots; a soil honeycombed with ancient dead, where esoteric poems and thaumaturgic revelations can come to light any day, where there are gods who make love in the midst of fire.

It was natural that the conversation should come round to poisons. "Be careful on your travels," the princess said. "In Tibet you never know. There are poisons that kill without anybody's noticing them. In Tibet it is believed that poisoning a person who is fortunate or rich or powerful means that his fortune or wealth or power accrues to the poisoner. Sometimes poisoning is done for still more subtle reasons. People try to inherit sanctity that way. A great sage runs the risk that some madman may try to poison him in the hope of getting for himself the sage's priceless advantage over ordinary people – his superior position in the cycle of birth and death. Several attempts were made to poison my uncle for that reason!"

"What? The famous thaumaturge whom I've heard so much about?"

"Yes."

I poked the fire, and we drank more *chang*. Pemà Chöki continued:

"Poisons, you know, are almost living things. You smile? You don't believe it? Ah, but you don't know what strange things happen in these parts! I know a wizard who had prepared some poison to kill a rival. But, as it happened, this rival was taken ill and died a natural death just a day or two before the stars said the poison would be ready and effective. Well, there was no way out. When a poison is ready, it has to be used. The wizard had either to give the poison to somebody, or die of it himself. The poison was ready and waiting. It was hungry, don't you see? So the wizard gave it to his daughter. Poison is like a living thing. It's alive, and has a will of its own. Terrible? But everything's terrible in Tibet!"

Everything's terrible in Tibet! The phrase used by pretty Pemà Chöki awakened memories and echoes in my mind. It was true, true. The silence, the space, the temples crowded with gods, like ships crowded with crazy people stranded on a crazy coast . . . . But the mystery of Tibet now started taking on a new light. Because of this new friendship I started seeing things, no longer from the outside, but from within. I started to be able to feel them, and when one begins feeling, is one not nearer to understanding?

Pemà talked about her uncle again.

"He was the most extraordinary man I have ever met. I remember that when I was a little girl he lived in a completely empty room and flew . . ."

"Weren't you afraid? Did you actually see him?"

"Yes. He did what you would call exercises in levitation. I used to take him in a little rice. He would be motionless in mid-air. Every day he rose a little higher. In the end he rose so high that I found it difficult to hand the rice up to him. I was a little girl, and had to stand on tip-toe . . . There are certain things you don't forget!"

The *chowdikar* of the shelter had thrown a lot of wood on to the fire, which blazed up. Warm and still full of light, we all went out for a moment to breathe the night air. A huge, dazzling moon rode in the night sky. All round us was nothing but the starry silver of the snow. As we walked the ice on the path crackled beneath our feet. It seemed to be a scream in the silence.

Reconsideration, 1998

With regard to this particular chapter, any reconsideration, so many years after the events described, can only take the form of a brief and heartfelt letter to Dü-kor, the Indo-Tibetan personification of Time, sent in the spirit of those small children who write to Baby Jesus or Father Christmas.

"Venerable and mysterious being! It is well known that you scour the world unflaggingly and change its face. Tonight the moon is a slender sickle in a mother-of-pearl sky, before long it will be a full disc in a vast, inky black vault; some nights later it will rise yellow and hunched amid smoking chimneys or on the lonely waves of a sea already pink with dawn. In today's child tomorrow's elder is being made ready, and the bare bones of the skeleton and skull are being prepared in secret, with care and finesse, for the day after tomorrow. Mighty, sibylline, tremendous Dü-kor! When you are at peace you model the world with ruthless but deceptively gentle fingers: you do not see the tree grow, you do not see the married couple grow old if you are with them every day. Then suddenly you are shaken by itches, tantrums, rages. Then it is not enough for you to make changes; you want to break, smash, destroy. You are not satisfied with growth, evolution; you must have catastrophes. Death is a flower in your garden. You mix pearls and agonies in your sacrilegious goblets. Where were you, you incomprehensible demon, on 6 August 1945? At Hiroshima, of course. And on 9th? At Nagasaki, naturally. You jump and mandala-cities appear! No creation without destruction, that is written on your banners. Seldom, though, do such epoch-making feasts come your way. Usually you must rest content with a modest harvest, with echoes confined to a single province, indeed to a parish. During a certain period of your destructive languors you deigned to give your attention even to that little corner of the world that seemed outside the world, and thus secure, untouchable, that cloister of fables and flowers that was once Sikkim. How you enjoyed yourself turning Gangtok from a toy capital of a dream kingdom into an ugly, disorderly military frontier-post full of shiftless, loutish sergeants and haughty two-faced policemen! Thanks to you, Sikkim no longer exists as a semi-independent little state; it is nothing today but a tongue of provincial Indian land on the border with China. The Maharajah, "as delicate as a little bird and as noble as a coat of arms", died some years ago; so also did the enchanting princess Pemà-Chöki – she died young. Her elder brother Thondup, robust and well-intentioned, succeeded his father in

1963 and attempted the difficult and exacting operation of modernizing his tiny country with paternal hand; and for some years he seemed to be attended by success. That same year Thondup married Hope Cooke, a young American woman of the New York upper bourgeoisie. The marriage caused a worldwide sensation and was eagerly written up and photographed in the press of every continent. The best testimony, and the most accessible, is still the article by L. E. Battaglia, [in "The Wedding of Two Worlds" with many illustrations, in the *National Geographic Magazine* of November 1963].

"But you, venerable, mysterious, tremendous Dü-kor, with things in this happy state, you felt at a loss, didn't you? You were overcome with an urge to create avalanches that sweep mountains clear, that drag everything to the ground on their precipitous path. You had a savage appetite for emptiness, for your hidden plans of new developments to come. Strange to relate, the alluring Miss Hope possessed to perfection the physique du role to play the little queen in a small oriental Buddhist court. A horsey, aggressive American woman? Not remotely so! She was petite, gentle, sinuous, she spoke little, loved ritual. Nonetheless you contrived to insinuate yourself into the rosy nuptials, created jealousies and poisons, dreamed up polite humiliations (and thus all the less bearable for a sensitive person), so much so that Hope forsook husband and throne to return to the less demanding horizons of Manhattan with all its comforts. Politically too, things took a dangerous turn for the worse. Thondup suffered ostracism, even violence. He was deposed. Eventually he perished, victim not of terrorists but of some disease that knew no cure. As ever, Master, you were the winner! You had destroyed, buried, obliterated. Rereading today the account of those festivities at the "palace" of Gangtok, those days and evenings up at the mountain refuge of Changu, is a little like running through the lines of an age-old saga, almost indecipherable, practically forgotten. But did those people really exist, did those things really happen? And I, what was I? Could it all be a play of reflections of the karma between one life and the next, of the samsaric garland of deaths and rebirths experienced as in a dream?

"Greetings and adoration, ruthless divinity Dü-kor!"

4

Natu-la: Entrance to Tibet

Ro-lang, standing corpses

One of the passes by which one can gain entry to Tibet is the Natu-la (14,200ft), a few miles from Changu. It takes you across a grim, stony saddle surrounded by gloomy, ragged mountains. At the top of the pass is a big cairn, some stakes, and hundreds of little coloured flags on which Buddhist prayers are printed by woodcut. When a caravan goes by everyone adds a new stone to the pile, crying: "*So-ya-la-so!*"

When we reached the cairn the sky had brightened a little and sunset was approaching. Pink and brown snatches of cloud floated above us, as in seventeenth-century paintings. The air was cold. Ahead, in the direction of Tibet, was the clear sky normal in those parts, now distant from Bengal; it is the wind coming up from India that brings damp, clouds, rain and snow to these mountains. Piero Mele had reached the top before me, and was already putting on his skis. It was April, there was still snow about, and we wanted to make our entrance into Central Asia in a solemn and sporting manner. Before going on I turned for a moment to look back on the valleys from which we had come. They were already hidden by the violet mists of evening. "Goodbye, Sikkim! Goodbye, pretty Pemà Chöki!"

I cannot say I enjoyed the descent. I was suffering from an attack of mountain sickness, and every now and then I had to stop. Piero kept making fun of me, but as soon as the snow came to an end he helped me by carrying my skis. We walked for a good stretch along the muddy, stony mule-track, and then it grew dark. The first small thickets were succeeded by bigger ones, and then we came upon the black outlines of some fir-trees; we were down to tree-level again. We reached Chubitang, our destination for the night, very late. Tucci and Colonel Moise were there already, warming themselves by a magnificent fire of dried branches.

Every time I cross the Natu-la I think of Paljor and his standing corpses, an incident that served as such an appropriate first introduction to these remote parts of Asia. It happened several years ago now. We had reached the pass in a thick mist. The air was full of obscure menace. The contorted, weather-worn rocks loomed out of the grey mists like the shapes of mysterious beings who had stopped and were waiting for us. It was most disagreeable.

"They look like *ro-lang*," said Paljor, who was carrying the sack containing my cameras. He smiled knowingly, wanting me to believe that he did not really believe in *ro-lang*, but I'm sure that at heart he did believe in them. *Ro-lang* are "standing corpses" – a horrible idea, a characteristic product of the diseased and sinister Tibetan imagination, which revels in bones, blood and death – all the pleasures of the slaughterhouse. Nothing pleases it more than the thought of troops of demons engaged in liturgical rites among dismembered parts of the human body, skeletons and entrails, disporting themselves in lakes of blood, using skulls as sacred symbols. The Tibetan imagination enjoys the macabre, delights in the revolting, intoxicates itself with tortures described with voluptuous relish and realism. In a way the *ro-lang* incident was an appropriate welcome extended to us by secret Tibet.

On the other hand, how surprising and unexpected all this was! And how illogical! Travelling in Tibet, over those wind-swept plateaux, where the sun, with his escort of light and happy clouds, is the lord of space, where everything is clear, limpid and crystalline, where there are no mysterious forests or long-drawn-out northern twilights, you would expect to find a people whose interior world was in more apparent harmony with their natural surroundings. You would expect to find the serene reasoning of the Greeks, a cult of beauty of Doric simplicity, a courageous spirit of luminous analysis, southern, sunny empyreans, mythologies in which gods as august as the Himalayas revelled in metaphysical harmonies the essence of which was extreme abstraction. You would expect Tibet to generate in the human mind the daring of the highest flights of Western mathematics.

There is a theory, as ancient as man's first reasoning about his own environment, according to which a country's landscape and climate in some way explain, not only its inhabitants' physical appearance, but also their character, philosophy, religion and art. From Hippocrates [*Perì áeron, ùdaton kai tópon*] to Rätzel, from Polybius to Taine, it has been regarded as a self-evident proposition, not even worthy of discussion.

That man must be influenced by his environment is undeniable, but to define its influence is another matter. "*Une vie d'analyse pour une heure de synthèse!*" exclaimed Fustel de Coulanges. The time for synthesis is still a long way off, though no-one seems to be aware of it. I open a volume of history at random and find the phrase: "It seems reasonable to say that the Parthenon could have arisen only on the soil and beneath the sky of Attica." (H. Berr) The proposition could be interpreted as follows: Given a people of great intelligence, living in a country of clear skies and brilliant sunshine and a much-indented coast, a climate in which everything appears in sharp outline, where everything is clean-cut and the whole atmosphere encourages objectivity and discourages vague dreaminess and the unbridled flow of the imagination, the natural result is the Parthenon. The Parthenon is the result of the spontaneous flowering of a civilization guided by clear and luminous ideas to harmonious and simple goals. Should we not expect from the same environment a cult of the rational in philosophy, of the nude in art, of the measurable in geometry? And as for the gods, it is only natural that they should be comprehensible, reasonable, anthropomorphous . . . The argument is perfect, too perfect.

The difficulty is that the whole argument could be applied to Tibet. Tibet is a vast, rocky country, a kingdom of the sky and the sun, where the wind blows for days with no obstacle other than the ice-bound, deserted crests of the *kang-ri*, the "snow mountains", where rain is rare, and mist exceptional, where there are no forests, where everything seems a glorious symbol of the most crystalline rationality, of serene and harmonious thought. Will not the interior life of the inhabitants of such a country resemble the nature that surrounds them? . . . Ingenious and deluded theorist, your logical castles in the air will receive blow after blow from each successive contact with the Tibetan soul, and will end by being mercilessly demolished.

"How do you become a *ro-lang*? And who becomes a *ro-lang*?" I asked Paljor.

"If you are struck by lightning and killed, sometimes you become a *ro-lang*," the young man replied. "Your body stands upright, with its eyes closed, and walks. It walks straight ahead, and nobody can stop it, or make it change direction. In any case anyone who touches a *ro-lang* falls sick and dies. *Ro-lang* wander about the mountains. They only stop if someone throws a shoe at them . . ."

This last remark broke the tension, and I laughed heartily. But that too was characteristic of the country. The sudden transition to the comic from the macabre, the grotesque, the obscene, the sudden burst of laughter, was something essentially Tibetan. Paljor, however, remained serious. For him the throwing of the shoe was a magical act, an act of exorcism, a rite, and not a ridiculous anticlimax as it seems to us.

At Chubitang: implication and explanation

At every stage along the caravan route to Lhasa you find a visitors' book. At Chubitang, when I turned over the pages, I found the names of many people I had met in Tibet or Sikkim – Granger, for instance, a huge Englishman, as vast as a peninsula. I met him ten years ago at Gyantse, where he was in command of the company of Indian soldiers which the British Government obtained the right to station there in 1904 to guard the caravan route. (The right passed to the Indian Government on August 15th, 1947.) I made his acquaintance one morning, and at about three o'clock the same afternoon I found two horses outside my house. One of the horses was ridden by an impressive, black-bearded Sikh, wearing a violet turban (just like the prophets who drive the Calcutta taxi-cabs); the other horse was for me. "Captain Granger say you come play polo." Play polo? I had never done such a thing in my life. Naturally I plunged headlong into this new experience. True, at 12,000 feet even horses start panting quickly, and we had to have frequent rests. But it was an exhilarating game.

Granger had been overcome with a sudden and immense admiration for Giuseppe Tucci. "That professor of yours, he's rather formidable, isn't he?" he exclaimed. He had spent two years in Tibet without taking any interest in the country, but he now suddenly developed a passionate interest in Buddhism. In the middle of a game of polo, whenever our horses brought us close together, he would shout questions at me. "I say, what is a *Bodhisattva*, old boy?" or "Hullo! How much would a copy of the *Kangyur* cost?"

The *Kangyur* is the scripture of Tibetan Buddhism, and normally consists of 108 volumes. The *Tangyur*, which is the commentary on the scriptures, comprises 225 volumes. The two together represent a small cartload of printed matter. That reminds me of the occasion, ten years ago, when Professor Tucci and I climbed the Natu pass with I don't remember how many mules loaded with learning. The poor beasts, used to carrying wool, tamely climbed the hill with all those stories of myriads of gods, magic formulae for initiates, subtle disquisitions and visions of fire and bloodshed on their backs. The *Tangyur*, after being buried for some time in the belly of a ship, between boxes of spices and bales of cotton, eventually arrived in Rome. Who of the million inhabitants of the capital of Italy knows that there lies, mute and dumb in the heart of their city, this fantastic universe of unexampled imaginative wealth? But what is a book which hardly anyone ever reads? Paper – the beautiful, fascinating, primitive paper of Tibet, with irregular fibres as big as veins.

Mr and Mrs Nalanda must have passed this way a few days ago. What a strange couple! He is a ceremonious German Jew, getting on in years, who came to the East about twenty years ago. He adopted a Buddhist name and the Buddhist faith, and he wears a kind of generalized Indo-Tibetan robe, very distinctly yellow in colour. He wears a rosary on his wrist, and his grey hair is slightly wild, suggesting a modest music master who had not allowed himself to be entirely subdued by convention. His wife is much younger than he; she is by no means unattractive, and sometimes actually rather pretty, with a white skin and black eyes and hair, just like the Parsees of Bombay. She too dresses in Tibetan style. They wander from monastery to monastery, copying pictures and living on roasted barley flour. They are rather heroic, rather ridiculous and rather extraordinary. They do not seek excessive publicity for themselves, which means they are sincere, but fundamentally they are disloyal to the West, which is sad.

Studying the East and loving it does not involve conversion to it and renouncing one's own civilization. The glory of the West is science, not just science in the ordinary meaning of the word, but in a deeper sense – knowledge of the world that surrounds us. It is right that the West should dissect the East, as it dissects the concepts of right, good and time, or phanerogams and dicotyledons and the chemistry of the stars, and in doing these things it is perfectly loyal to and consistent with itself. But when the West seeks to shift the angle of vision and scrutinize the universe through eyes other than its own, that is a betrayal. Europe is Leonardo, Descartes, Leibnitz, Bach – the world as thought and cathedral; it is Cervantes, Titian, Shakespeare – the world as activity, colour and passion. But in all its aspects the Western world is a world of explanation, while the Eastern world is that of implication. The West is centrifugal, living in an unstable, dynamic equilibrium; the East is centripetal, drawing into itself. It will therefore probably survive us for a long time. But the true European should not leave his place in his own civilization, in the crazy, meteoric course to which it is committed.

A year ago Pemà Chöki passed this way, through Chubitang, on her way back from Lhasa. She travelled alone, with five servants. What a tiny caravan! She told me about her journey the other night, sitting by the fire, in the Changu refuge. It would have been delightful to have met her for the first time in real Tibet, on the Tang-pun-sum, for example, that endless plateau exposed like a great bowl to the sky at the foot of Chomolhari, its greenish peaks of ice standing out against the bright purple of the rocks. First I should have seen the caravan like tiny dots in the distance; gradually the dots would have transformed themselves into men, horses and yaks. Then I should have heard the animals' bells and the servants' voices; finally I should have seen Pemà Chöki, Lotus of the Happy Faith, for the first time, riding a horse, her eyes fixed on the distance, her head in the sun; beautiful, strong, and as fragile as jade. Then she would have disappeared into the immensity of the plain. Last of all I should have heard the voices of the men, for whom she was a delicate and precious thing to protect and defend and guide over the Himalayas.

The Kar-gyu monastery: the symbolism of chortens

Coming down from the Natu pass into Tibet, we descended upon the Kar-gyu monastery. This monastery, also known as Kajü-gompá (*gompá* = convent) belongs to the *Kargyu-pa* sect (*see* Glossary). It is also known under the name *Trommo-me* (Monastery) "Inferior of the Trommo"; this is to distinguish it from the monastery of Dung-kar (which we shall be discussing shortly), which lies one day's hike to the north. The Dung-kar monastery belongs to monks of the Yellow Sect (*Gelug-pa*), and is also called *Trommo-tö*, (Convent) "Superior of the Trommo". "Descended upon" is the right expression. The track suddenly grew steep, and, coming round a spur of the mountain, we saw, many hundreds of feet below us, the monastery roof, crowned by its gilded pavilion (*kenchira*), sparkling in the sun. Still farther below we saw the Amo-chu, a huge Himalayan torrent, flowing swiftly and white with foam.

It is a lovely spot, in its Alpine fashion – different from the sad, misty solitude of the first outposts of the Himalayas, and different again from the yellow, sunny, heroic Tibet of the high plateaux. We are here in the Trommò valley, the "valley of buckwheat', which, like many similar spots in Bhutan, Upper Sikkim and Nepal, is a delightful reminder of the Italian Alps. You see torrents winding their way between steep, wooded mountainsides, and every now and then the ground is broken by precipices on which an experienced eye can detect the traces left by the passage of ancient glaciers. But we are not in the Alps. Even in its minor outposts the proportions of the Himalayan world are on a fantastic scale. There is something primordial, fabulous and excessive even about this ordinary, fir-covered slope. One is aware, as if it were whispered or suggested, of the close presence of giants of 24,000 feet.

A little way above the monastery there are some *chortens* which give a typically Tibetan aspect to the place. *Chorten* is the name given to the walled towers, anything from six to fifty feet high, which are as typical of Tibet as *torii* are of Japan or big crucifixes are of many Alpine valleys. All three are of religious origin and poetical significance. Small and insignificant though they may be in the face of the grandiose nature which surrounds them, they suffice to give form and atmosphere to a whole landscape.

In the Alps in Christian Europe a crucifix where two paths meet gives a meaning to the mountains and serves to place them in history. The crucifix speaks for a whole vision of life; it recalls the cosmic drama on which the West has been nurtured for 2,000 years – the drama of God's creation of man, man's rebellion and fall, God's sacrifice of His Son to redeem His creatures by suffering.

Similarly a *torii*, the simple structure of wood and stone that stands over

11 *Traditional* chorten *high up on the plateau*

the entrance of a *jinja* park, a Japanese Shinto shrine, suffices with its few rough-hewn beams and its stone columns to give a poetic note to what would otherwise be no more than a clump of trees in the plain or a small wood in the mountains. A *torii* suggests by implication and remote association the vague and mysterious world, ill-defined to the intellect but full of emotional content, of the *Kami*, the Higher Ones; it also recalls the world of ancestors (who are Higher Ones too). It stands for continuity, union with the invisible, the archaic, the remote, with myth and the very soul of the world, which is revealed above all in trees, in the lofty foliage of the cryptomerias, where the wind murmurs secrets and the stars stop at night.

Similarly in Tibet a *chorten* gives life to a whole mountainside, to a recess in the rocks, or to a waste at the foot of an ice-covered peak, swept by the winds that blow at an altitude of 15,000 feet. Very exceptionally a *chorten* is the last resting-place of a venerated lama, sometimes it contains ashes and bones, but generally its contents are sacred pictures or writings. To Tibetans the *chorten*s that they pass on their travels (they are always careful to pass them on the left) stand for their religion itself. It reminds them of another grandiose cosmic drama, so different from the Christian one – the drama of myriads of beings who, passing through the cycle of birth and rebirth, travelling down the tormented and troublesome river of life and death, turn their steps, first doubtfully and hesitantly, groping in the dark, and then consciously and deliberately in the direction of enlightenment, the state of Buddhahood. The *chorten* is primarily a symbol, something that fills a valley with serenity, as the presence of a loved person spiritually illumines a house.

In Tibet you find *chorten*s of every age; new ones still freshly white-washed, and old ones falling to pieces, ravaged and worn by the passage of centuries. An old, wind-worn *chorten*, rising against the endless background of ochre, yellow and red mountains fading away into the blue distances and sparkling with snow, is a thing of pure poetry. In these Himalayan valleys the *chorten*s have a special charm that they do not possess in the sterile climate of the high plateaux. With the passing of the years they are covered with plants and flowers; a bush often finds a home between the stones. They thus become delightfully romantic places, worthy of an Asian Piranesi, endowed with the subtle vein of melancholy always found when the work of man is being silently taken over again by nature.

But what exactly is a *chorten*? The Tibetan word means literally "receptacle for offerings"; it is the Tibetan equivalent of the Sanskrit *dhatugarbha* (which was corrupted to *dagaba*, from which our own word "pagoda" derives). Thus its origin, like the origin of practically every spiritual *motif* in Tibetan civilization, is to be sought in India. It was the custom in India from time immemorial to bury the bodies of particularly venerated Buddhists, or important relics, in stone mausoleums called *stupas*. In Tibet the *stupa* underwent a process of lengthening, and gradually assumed its characteristic shape. Its purpose and its meaning also underwent a transformation. It became less of a tomb or reliquary and more of a cenotaph, and was built "to recall some special fact, or for the salvation of him who erected it or of his relatives, or as a votive offering or expression of gratitude".[1] In addition to that a *chorten* is a symbolic structure accurately representing in miniature the whole lamaist cosmology. Each part of it represents one of the elements of which everything consists, and into which bodies are resolved again after death. The base of the structure represents earth, the tower water, and so on. At the top are two objects that look like a sun and a crescent moon, but the crescent moon stands for air, the atmosphere (the inverted vault of heaven), and the sun is a flame, symbolizing space, the ether, the last and most subtle of the elements.

The oriental love of symbolism – or rather the indispensable oriental need

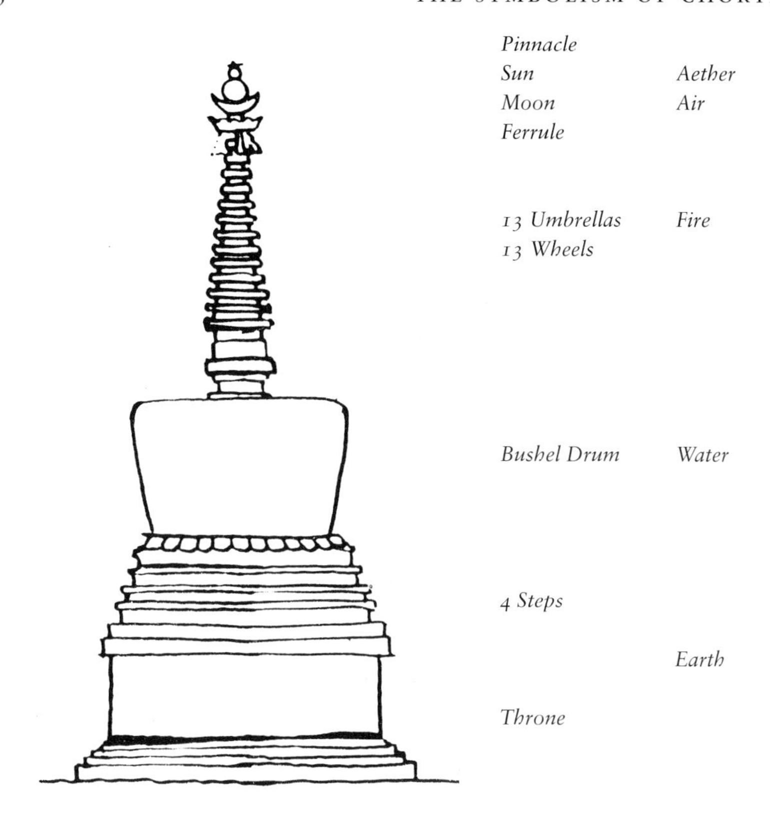

12 *Plan of a* chorten.
There are eight principal types of chorten. *Here is a simplified plan of one of the commonest. (See Tucci:* Indo-Tibetica *I, p. 16.)*

of symbolism – means that other things can be, and often have to be, read into a *chorten*. It is thus not just a straightforward ideogram, but an esoteric one, from which knowledge is to be derived in the form of mystery and rite, an abstruse process transmitted from master to disciple within a restricted circle of privileged initiates. Moreover, interpretations vary according to the different schools, and there is always the possibility of still more difficult and recondite interpretations; the esoteric of the esoteric. What one mind has conceived (or has received by revelation) is passed on to a few adepts, a few chosen disciples, in the course of centuries. Such is the East; a world which is a constellation of secluded and exquisite gardens for the *élite*; an *élite* that lives on a few roots or a handful of flour roasted in a cup formed of the hollow of a skull; an *élite* covered in rags, living in freezing cells, surrounded by perilous mountains and grim precipices.

13 *Plan of possible relationships between the Indian* stupa, *the Tibetan* chorten, *and the pagodas of Nepal, China and Japan*

The plan shows some of the many structures scattered about eastern Asia and derived from a common inspiration: to preserve sacred relics and celebrate the Buddhist faith. The specialists are not in agreement as to how the more flamboyant transformations have taken place. (Note that the illustrations are not all to the same scale.) Illustrated by S. Pannuti under the author's guidance.

1. *The great* stupa *of Sanchi (2nd/1st century* BC*).* 2. *Rock-carved* stupa *at Karli (2nd century* AD*).* 3. Stupa *inside the 19th cave at Ajanta (4th–7th century* AD*).* 4. *A* stupa *at Nalanda (9th century* AD*).* 5. *Ceylonese* dagoba *or* stupa *at Anuradhapura (1st century* BC*).* 6. *The world's biggest* stupa *at Borobudur, Java (8th century* AD*).* 7. *A small* pagoda *with thatched roof; Bali (contemporary).* 8. *The Mingalazedi* stupa *at Pagan, Burma (14th century).* 9. *Ruins of Ayudhya, a* prachedi *or* stupa *in Siam (14th–18th century).* 10. *The Shwe Dagon* pagoda *in Rangoon, Burma (contemporary).* 11. *Model of a* stupa *at Gandhara, from the Jaulian excavations (1st–3rd century* AD*).* 12. *Tibetan* chorten *from Lhasa (15th–19th century).* 13. *The Kum-Bum at Gyantse, Tibet (15th century).* 14. *The small* stupa *at Bodnath, Kathmandu, Nepal (9th century).* 15. *Small Buddhist shrine at Patan, Nepal.* 16. *Twelve-sided* pagoda *at Sung-yüeh monastery, Honan, China (6th century* AD*).* 17. *Ta-yen-t'a* pagoda, *Hsian-fu, Shensi, China (7th century* AD*).* 18. *"Iron-coloured"* pagoda *at K'ai-feng, Honan, China (11th century).* 19. Pagoda *"of the relics", Wu-tai-shan, Shansi, China.* 20. *Wooden* pagoda *at monastery of Fo-kung, Ying-hsien, Shansi, China (11th century).* 21. Pagoda *on Mount Fang (12th century).* 22. *The "white"* pagoda, *Ch'ing-chou, Jehol, China (11th–12th century).* 23. *Pei-chen* pagoda, *Chin-hsien, Manchuria (11th century).* 24. Pagoda *at Ch'üan-chou, Fukien, China (13th century).* 25. *Small* pagoda *in park at Seoul, Korea (14th century).* 26. *Hry-ji* pagoda, *Nara, Japan (7th century).* 27. *Yakushi-ji* pagoda, *Nara, Japan (8th century).* 28. *Yasaka* pagoda, *Kyoto, Japan, (rebuilt 1618).* 29. *Small* taht-*type* pagoda *at Ishiyama-dera, Otsu, Japan (11th century).*

Reconsideration, 1998

Nowadays the Natu pass (14,000 feet) is crossed by a trunk road, one of the vast network of roads built by Beijing after 1951. All the great caravan routes of long ago have been turned into roads, often involving major engineering works. For the moment the access from India is closed, but assuredly the day will come – and maybe soon – when it will be possible to reach Gyantse and Lhasa by minibus, car or perhaps even motorcycle from Gangtok. A complete liberation would make it possible to cross a great part of Asia without much difficulty, from Calcutta to Beijing via Lhasa – a route offering all manner of splendid views. The roads exist. Unfortunately a policy based on suspicion and fear keeps most of them closed to the ordinary traveller. We were among the last to travel those ancient tracks on foot – they were not unlike the mule paths in our own mountains – ways that had been trodden for thousands of years by merchants, pilgrims, bandits, abbots, caravans of horses, of mules, of sheep (with small sacks of salt on their backs), and of course scattered, disorganized herds of those useful, strong, patient, endearing but capricious creatures – the yak.

As for the monastery of Kar-gyu, described in the next chapter, it was barbarically destroyed during the Cultural Revolution. The building was not all that ancient, nor did it contain any works of art that stood out for aesthetic or historical value. But why so much gratuitous violence here, as elsewhere in hundreds of shrines, temples, and chapels? Evidently the monks from this sanctuary suffered a savage persecution.

It is said that today the monastery is being rebuilt, at least partially, by the local people.

1. For the various types of *chorten* and their symbolism, see: G. Tucci, *Indo-Tibetica*, I, "*Mc'od rten* and *Ts'a ts'a*" in *Tibet indiano ed occidentale*, Rome, Accademia d'Italia, 1932, p. 24ff.

5

Rancid Butter and the Exotic in Reverse

The Kar-gyu monastery: what did Lama Ton-gye see?

I should like at this point to describe the Kar-gyu *gompá*, or monastery. It is neither very big, nor very old, nor is it a celebrated goal of pilgrims, nor is its abbot politically important (there are monasteries in Tibet whose abbots are politically important). But the fact that it is an ordinary, average monastery, just like hundreds of others in Tibet, perhaps makes it the more interesting. About sixty monks live in it, including about thirty student-monks. It is not very rich, though it enjoys various sources of income (investments, flocks, donations); and the walls of its temples and chapels are adorned with frescoes or carvings of about two hundred and eighty different divinities.

The Kar-gyu *gompá* consists of a number of buildings built in a small, level area in the slope of the mountainside. A few leafy trees grow there, the residue of a wood which must once have covered the place. The spot has been sacred for centuries, but the monastery is recent.

14 *Kar-gyu monastery seen on the approach from the Natu pass, in 1948*

Opposite the entrance is a fountain, where the animals stop to drink. It should be remembered that in the Buddhist universe animals are "living beings" (*sem-chan*) just as much as man, and that there is no categorical distinction between the animal and human World. All are capable of eventual salvation; all are potential saints. An animal is simply a more limited being than man, a less individualized being, entirely taken up with the elementary, brutish necessities of feeding, sleeping and reproducing itself. But the spark, the essence, that today sleeps in an ox or a mule will shine tomorrow in a man, or shed light on the whole universe in a Buddha. The Buddhist world is thus fundamentally an optimistic one. There is no final distinction between the elect and the rejected, and there is no trace of Calvinist predestination; or rather there is predestination, but only in the sense that in the long run, after thousands and thousands of years, all beings will attain enlightenment, will be Buddha and will be dissolved into the Absolute.

The running water of the fountain turns a prayer-wheel, and every revolution of the prayer-wheel rings a little bell; it has a sharp and cheerful note. The "wheel" consists of a drum half-a-yard high, on which Sanskrit letters are painted in gold. Inside it are innumerable, tightly-rolled pieces of paper, with thousands of phrases printed on them by woodcut. The commonest is the celebrated *Om mani padme hum*, which is usually translated *Om* (Hail!) *mani* (oh jewel) *padme* (in the flower of the lotus) *hum* (hail!). The jewel, according to the current interpretation, represents Chen-re-zi, or the Dalai Lama. It is as if at every turn of the wheel the phrases were repeated aloud as many times as they are written within. As the prayer-wheel works by water-power for twenty-four hours a day, one could work out for oneself how many pious ejaculations were "uttered" in the course of a month or a year.

Ingenious applications of this principle of mechanical prayer are to be found throughout Tibet. Before laughing at it, one should bear in mind that it is a minor, popular manifestation of lamaism. Every religion that makes a deep impression among men and women relatively unaccustomed to thinking and analysing necessarily has aspects like this. Should we condemn Christianity because of the prayer put up to St. Anthony by an Italian peasant woman, beseeching the saint's aid in finding her lost needle?

At the entrance to the monastery we were met by a well-nourished lama, who looked like the manager of a thriving Tuscan estate. He was Yul-gye ("Victorious over the country"), the *om-tse*, or rector, and he had obviously been waiting for us. He was a tall, strong, energetic and rather crude individual, aged about fifty. When he laughed he was jovial, and when he moved he looked as if he were about to scale a mountain or seize a demon by the throat. He

15 "Om Mani Padme Hum"

"Hail, Jewel in the Lotus Flower!", the most popular mantra in Tibetan Buddhism – it may be seen inscribed in three-foot-high letters on a rock overlooking the Chumbi, or Trommò, valley. The Jewel refers to the Bodhisattva *Avalokitesvara (Chen-re-zi in Tibetan), who is considered to be reincarnated in the Dalai Lama. The Lotus Flower is symbol of purity, for it grows in delicate splendour out of the bog-waters, and symbol of immortality, for it recalls the Buddhas and* Bodhisattvas *who rise heavenwards above the vortex of passion and illusion, above birth, death and suffering. The formula lends itself to a number of other interpretations at differing levels of esotericism. Frequently it is interpreted in sexual terms: the Jewel in the Lotus Flower gives poetic expression to the union of male and female. Hence a complete metaphysical symbolism similar to the one implied in the figures of Tantric gods locked in mystic embrace* (yab-yum) *with their* shaktis, *the female personifications of psychic and spiritual energy.*

was certainly a terror to the seminarists, the pupils at the monastery. He smiled at me, because I was a foreigner with rupees in my pocket. (Fearing that his benevolence might cease, did I not promptly hand him a silver coin? It would seem that fundamentally one ought to be tough like him in life.) When I caught sight of him when he thought I was not looking at him I saw that his features hardened, and made a mental note of the resemblance between his square jaw and his great, knotty fist. The boy pupils at the monastery must instinctively have noted it too. Meanwhile they were hovering about, not knowing whether to yield to their fear of the *om-tse* and go away, or to their desire to approach and observe the white man more closely.

Some European writers seem to create the impression that lamas are a class consisting exclusively of more or less fabulous sages or ascetics, all capable of the most extraordinary supernatural feats. Nothing could be more false. The ecclesiastical world of Tibet is alive and various, rich in personalities of every calibre, strength and colour. It is, in fact, so much like the Roman Catholic ecclesiastical world that the missionary Abbé Huc was struck by the resemblance as long ago as 1845. True, you find the ascetic who has mortified his body until it has become a subtle instrument of hidden psychic forces, almost a sensitive, living human tentacle stretched out into the superhuman and supernatural. But you also find the acute, well-nourished abbot who will solve you a psychological or economic problem in the twinkling of an eye, the acid, disagreeable disciplinarian, the good-natured simpleton, the learned doctor who knows the *Kangyur* and the *Tangyur* by heart, though lacking the slightest interior spark; and you find, too, the blessed of God who gets drunk, sings, plays, makes love and yet has wisdom in his folly. But is it not a thousand times better that this should be so? Who can take an interest in abstractions when there are men of flesh and blood to get to know? The lamas are not what we should like them to be, they are not museum pieces, unreal figures painted on ivory or parchment, but human beings, with their defects and qualities, each with his own distinct individuality, coloured by the subtly different light of a civilization based on premises different from ours. An Anatole France might well write a new *Orme du Mail*, with scenes laid not in Europe, but in Lhasa or at Tashilhumpo.

We passed under the arch of the entrance gate and found ourselves in a sunlit courtyard, with green grass growing among a few irregularly placed stones. It was full of a delightful sense of peace, the kind of peace that belongs to such ancient, venerable places. A large number of *trapas* (a *trapa* is an ordinary monk, as distinct from a *lama* – "master" – who has to have studied and passed certain examinations) appeared at the entrance to the kitchen – an immense, smoky, sooty place, with fantastic cauldrons worthy of a mock-heroic epic, and huge, perfectly black beams disappearing into the darkness of the roof. Other *trapas* appeared on the steps. They all smiled, most of them shyly, waiting for me to say something or make a friendly sign. The Tibetans are really xenophobes of a most curious kind. Their xenophobia is exclusively abstract and theoretical. They close their country to foreigners, and the most rigorous laws are issued from Lhasa to keep them out, but when a white man arrives in their midst they greet him with enthusiasm and make a tremendous fuss of him.

To the Tibetans a white man represents a world of fascinating mysteries. To them we represent the exotic in reverse – the exotic of aeroplanes, cameras, clocks, penicillin, a world of controllable, repeatable miracles. (A lama can learn to suspend himself in mid-air by levitation, but only after years and years of preparation and the severest ascetic ordeals, and even then he may not succeed. But anybody can fly in an aeroplane.) Our exotic characteristic in Tibetan eyes is our magical mastery of the elements. We are a mythical people, in alliance with super-terrestrial and subterranean demons, who give us superhuman powers as part of heaven knows what sort of diabolical pact. The *om-tse* left us for a moment, no doubt to warn the father superior of our arrival. The seminarists immediately swarmed round us, all wanting to see and hoping to touch my camera. I was hardly able to make headway through the throng. Meanwhile I breathed lungsful of *foetor tibeticus*.

Foetor tibeticus consists of various ingredients, the basis of which is the extreme dirtiness of the Tibetan person and Tibetan clothing. The universal smell of rancid butter gives it a finishing, lyrical touch. The dirt is ancient, stupendous and three-dimensional. Tibetan arms, thighs, feet and backs are ingrained and encrusted with the filth of months and years. Each individual's covering of dirt seems to be lovingly cultivated, perhaps for the purpose of creating a more lasting monument of the body, or of studying the geology of dirt in its slowly acquired and complicated stratifications. In the end the dirt must acquire an individuality, a personality of its own; you must feel that there are two of you inside the outer covering; and that a time will come when it, the thing, the crust, will constitute a shape, a negative, from behind which you will creep secretly one night, leaving it leaning against the wall, as ugly and buttery as a *ro-lang*.

Butter (like bones and silence) constitutes one of the most characteristic features of Tibet. It seems impossible that the thin females of the yak, grazing among stones and sand, should produce such an enormous flow of butter. But Tibet is full of it. It is on sale in the most remote villages; it is used for offerings to the gods in every temple and private chapel; it is carved in masterly fashion into statues and complicated ornamental patterns, and then coloured with extraordinary delicacy; it is burned in lamps, and taxes are paid with it; women spread it on their hair, and often on their faces; it is always an acceptable gift; it is mixed with *tsampa* for food and with tea for drink. In Tibet there is butter, butter everywhere. It is used all the time, for every conceivable purpose, and you can never get away from it.

Bones are as universal in Tibet as butter. Many more animals die or are killed in other countries than in Tibet; but nowhere else in the world, so far as I know, do you see so many carcasses, skulls, thigh-bones, vertebrae and ribs scattered along the roads, outside the houses, along the mountain passes. There is no reason whatever in the nature of things why this should be so; it is just a curious cultural trait. The bones of animals are not buried, or hidden from sight, or destroyed; they are just left, like stones on the road outside the doorstep. Children play with them, or throw them at one another. I suggest that there must be an active side to this apparent passivity; the Tibetans must positively like having bones lying about. They must regard them as a kind of

16 *Dung-kar monastery: ornamental sculpture in yak butter*

flower, a decoration, a comfort, a pleasure. Are they perhaps a reminder of the illusory nature of the temporal world, from which man must escape if he desires salvation? Who knows?

The third characteristic feature of Tibet, after the butter and the bones, is the tremendous silence. Modern physics talks of a four-dimensional space-time continuum. Tibet consists of a four-dimensional space-silence continuum. There is the yellow, ochre silence of the rocks; the blue-green silence of the ice-peaks; the silence of the valleys over which hawks wheel high in the sun; and there is the silence that purifies everything, dries the butter, pulverizes the bones and leaves in the mind an inexpressible, dreamy sweetness, as if one had attained some ancient fatherland lost since the very beginning of history.

The *om-tse* appeared on a balcony and called out: "*Kushog-sahib*! The Great Precious is waiting for you!"

On hearing his voice the seminarists, who had been excitedly crowding round

17 *Bones, lake, mountains: a yak's skeleton by Lake Rham*

me to look in the view-finder of my Leica, disappeared in a flash. Guided by the *om-tse*, and escorted by various other monks, I finally reached the room where the Rimpoche ("Great Precious") Nge-drup Dorje ("Blessed Thunderbolt") was due shortly to appear. Actually he was not the real head of the monastery. Its real head was a personage of the name of Thupden Öden ("Perpetual Light of the Doctrine of Buddha"), who lived about a hundred years ago. His terrestrial career was distinguished by so much sanctity, so much penetrating wisdom, so many conspicuous signs of approaching final illumination, that after his death he was considered to be a *Bodhisattva*. It is a great and glorious thing for a monastery to have a real *Bodhisattva* as its head! It is like giving hospitality to an ambassador of the Absolute, or having one's own personal representative in the adamantine halls of the cosmos – a sure and comforting link with the indubitable and the permanent.

In what way did Thupden Öden return among mankind? Not long after his death he was reincarnated in another body, that of a child. His rebirth, his presence in a new terrestrial guise, was revealed by a series of miraculous events. The child grew, and was educated with special care at the monastery and at Lhasa. He reached manhood, controlled the destinies of the community for many years, and eventually died.

Not many years ago, in 1937, Thupden Öden was reincarnated for a third time, once more appearing in the person of a child. There was, of course, no question of birth and death in our sense of the word, but only of the passage of the same spiritual essence, the same *Bodhisattva*, Thupden Öden, from one garment of flesh and blood to another. So he now looks at the world through the eyes of a slender, thoughtful boy of nine. Until he reaches his majority the temporal direction of the community remains in the hands of the regent, the Rimpoche Nge-drup Dorje. Later we shall see how all this is repeated, on an incomparably vaster and more magnificent scale, in the case of the Dalai Lama and the government of Tibet itself.

While we waited for the Great Precious a young lama named Ton-gye ("High Goal") showed me the various chapels. I have rarely in Tibet seen such a perfect incarnation of the ideal of monastic beauty as Ton-gye. He was handsome and impressive, and wore his long, black hair carefully gathered behind his head. His beardless features had a serene, mythological beauty, somehow suggesting the South Seas. He was shy and solemn, embarrassed and august. His toga-like monk's robe fell round his body in classic curves.

We returned to the room. Next door there was to be heard the hurried footsteps, the agitated rustle of robes and soutanes, the brief, pregnant silences that foreshadow the approach of an important and long-awaited ecclesiastical personage. The *om-tse* came in, told me to stay where I was, and to have my sash ready. In Tibet it is the custom, when you pay a visit to an important person, to present him with a white silk sash (*kata*). He presents you with a similar sash in return. The exchange is accompanied by many bows and smiles, and the studied and carefully graduated signs of deference that orientals so much love.

A few moments later I heard the slow footsteps of an aged man, wearing sandals, and the Great Precious appeared in the doorway. He was a vigorous giant of eighty-four, a real human oak-tree, whose vitality and intact faculties shone through his lively, acute, penetrating eyes. He was robed in undyed, canvas-coloured Bhutan cloth, with simple, coloured stripes, a cloth of great,

18 *Kar-gyu monastery: Lama Ton-gye*

archaic beauty, and he wore a turban of artificial hair, as is worn by the monks of the Kar-gyu sect.

After pausing for a moment at the threshold, to allow time for the full effect of his presence to make itself felt, the Great Precious advanced solemnly towards me. I realized at once that I was confronted with a consummate master of choreography, and in offering him my sash I tried to play my part to the best of my ability. But evidently I committed some gross error of etiquette, because everybody burst out laughing. To save the situation I recited a greeting in the most highly honorific terms, and this seemed to satisfy the old man, who muttered something and went and sat in his own lacquered chair. A horrible European chair, reminiscent of a cheap café, and a small table, both of which clashed dreadfully with the Tibetan atmosphere of the place, had been prepared for me. How sad it is that the West is always represented in Asia by the cheap, the ugly and the trivial!

"Where do you come from?" the Great Precious asked me.

"From a country named Italy, *Italia-yul*."

"That is good, because if you come from *Italia-yul* I shall be able to talk to you freely in our language!"

It is amazing how news spreads about these valleys. Europeans and white men in general are so rarely seen here that they are the object of much curious attention. They are mysterious beings, representatives of a still more mysterious and remote outside world, populated with magical, terrible and at the same time desirable things. The white man in Tibet is therefore closely observed and studied, even in his most intimate and irrelevant characteristics. People in distant villages, where you have never set foot, know how old you are, what you like to eat, whether you are rude or polite, mean or generous, equable or bad-tempered, whether you like sleeping, whether you read a lot, whether you like the local girls, whether you go shooting, and whether you give good tips. Thanks to Professor Tucci, Italians now enjoy the reputation in Tibet of being students and connoisseurs of every aspect of Tibetan civilization, and they naturally conclude that all Italians talk Tibetan as excellently as the illustrious *geshe* (doctor) from Rome. However, the Great Precious had excessive confidence in my grasp of Tibetan grammar and vocabulary, and I had to ask him to speak more slowly and simply.

"But where exactly is *Italia-yul*?"

While sipping my cup of Tibetan tea I did my best to explain to the Great Precious the position of Italy in relation to other, better-known places in the world. It was a difficult task, because his knowledge of geography was majestically vague.

"But where is America?" he exclaimed, after I had given him a long explanatory dissertation, eked out with gestures and illustrations, using a cup to show where India was and the tea-pot to show the position of the British Isles.

"America is in another direction," I explained.

"So Italy is near *Ripin* (Japan)?"

"No, Rimpoche, it's here, much nearer England."

"In any case it's a very long way away, a very strange place."

There came to my mind the Tibetan treatise on geography called *Dzamling Gyeshe Melong* ("Mirror of a Complete Description of the World") which was still used in schools until not so very long ago. It contains this curious passage about Sicily. In Sicily "there is a high mountain; from among its rocks a big fire comes out. This goes to the ocean and returns to the rocks. It does not burn grass or trees; but burns gold, silver, copper and human beings. And there is a certain kind of grass, which grows in no other place. If a man eats it, he dies of laughter." Could this be a distant echo, not only of Etna, but of the vines cultivated with such excellent results at its feet?

There was a pause in the conversation, and out of courtesy to my hosts I felt it my duty to eat one of the oily, buttery biscuits, covered with fur and dust, which I was offered. They must have been standing on some shelf in the monastery for months, and I found them unspeakably disgusting. I tried not to think about them (though one or two pieces I had to send down by force), and meanwhile I watched the Rimpoche's face. What character there was in his eyes! He was certainly not the ascetic type of lama, superior to the things of the world, but a successful prelate, drawing contentedly to the close of a brilliant career, a connoisseur of men, their weaknesses and their secret motivations.

Meanwhile a monk entered the room with a letter. The mail from India had just called at the monastery and gone onwards on its way to the north and to Lhasa. The letter bore an Indian stamp, and the address had obviously been written by a European. The Great Precious, after examining the outside of the envelope for a long time and then opening it with a hand that was extraordinarily firm for his eighty-four years, saw that the letter was covered with writing that he was unable to decipher; he therefore turned to me and asked me to read and translate it. It was from those old acquaintances, the Nalandas. They had spent a few weeks at the monastery some months previously, and now they wrote saying that they were well, and that they had left Calcutta for western Tibet. They asked for news of the Lama so-and-so and the *trapa* so-and-so, and how was the Great Precious, and the little living *Bodhisattva*? Everyone in the room seemed delighted at the letter, and the names mentioned in it were immediately on everybody's lips.

Raising my eyes at this point, I noticed that the young lama Ton-gye was looking extremely agitated, almost beside himself. As I picked up the envelope to put the letter back in it, two or three photographs which I had not noticed fell from it, face downwards on the table. The lama Ton-gye pounced on them like a flash, picked them up, hurriedly glanced at them, hid them in the folds of his robe and left the room. The others smiled. I never found out what those photographs were. Were they photographs of Ton-gye taken by Mrs Nalanda, or were they portraits of the dark, sibylline, Tantric Devi Nalanda, with her half-quizzical, half-sad smile?

When my visit to the Great Precious was over I was taken by the *om-tse* to see Thupden Öden, the little living *Bodhisattva*, for a moment. Opposite the monastery was another, smaller building in which the boy, his instructors, and the seminarists lived. I was received by a big, youngish, Chinese-looking lama, who was vigorously chewing betel. It made his whole mouth look red, as if he were spitting blood. This vice, the results of which are so horrible to look at, though they are completely harmless, is spreading rapidly among the Tibetans who live along the caravan route from India to Lhasa. The big lama courteously invited me to drink a cup of tea with him in his room. It was an extremely agreeable room, obviously the sanctum of a scholar.

Big square cushions (*den*) about nine inches thick, which the Tibetans use for chairs, lay along one wall. Perhaps the lama slept on them at night. In the daytime he sat on them cross-legged. At the end of the room near the window was the place where he generally worked – a small, low, square table, with many books and papers, an inkpot and pens. Tibetan books are long and narrow, and are hand-printed. The pages are wrapped in a piece of cloth and "bound" between two wooden boards. Many more books were piled on another table in the corner. There was also a little shrine, with offerings of rice and butter. On the walls were a number of *tangka* (pictures on cloth), of which one was very beautiful – the terrifying form of Palden Lha-mo, vividly painted in gold against a black background. It was superbly done; a masterpiece of diabolical metaphysics expressed in symbols. (Palden Lha-mo is the only female divinity among the group of Eight Guardians of the Faith.)

Talking to the lama, I discovered at once that he was a man of learning, a real mine of information. It was a pity to be in a hurry, and to have to leave. Also the room was so delightful. You felt in it the serene, detached-from-the-world atmosphere characteristic of rooms lived in by men who live for knowledge and study. It reminded me of similar rooms I have known in other parts of the world; of Giorgio Pasquali's, the Greek scholar's, "den" on the Lungarno at Florence; and Hiromichi Takeda's little home at Kyoto. Hiromichi was twenty-four years old, a philosophy graduate, and an assistant at the university. He had only recently married, and he lived with his wife, Namiko, in two rooms. One of them was filled to the ceiling with books, and books had started invading the other; only the tiny kitchen was still free of them. I spent whole afternoons with Hiromichi, talking about everything under the sun, in a mixture of Japanese, French and German. We agreed to collaborate in writing a life of Leonardo da Vinci for the Japanese. Then the war came.

The dictators who believe that such untidy places, crowded with books and papers, are the breeding-ground of the worst crimes against their tyranny are perfectly right. It is in such places that there germinate the first seeds of new ideas, which by way of books establish contacts and sympathies beyond the narrow limits of nations. He who has lived quietly among his books often emerges from the four walls of his study with more inner strength than he who has spent his youth shouting in the market-place; and it is in such places that one is perhaps more aware than anywhere else of a universal solidarity among men, even if they belong to remote civilizations.

"*Kushog*, shall we go up and see the little Great Precious now?"

We walked through a few rooms in silence. The child had not been forewarned (or had the whole thing, perhaps, been carefully stage-managed?).

We found him in a square room, bare of furniture, but containing many golden ornaments. He was seated on a cushion in front of a tiny, carved wooden table, painted in many colours, reading the huge pages of an ancient book. He was a thin, slightly-built child, pale, not handsome, and rather sad-looking, simply clothed in his reddish-brown monk's robe. I don't know why, but I felt infinitely sorry for him.

19 *The young living Bodhisattva, Trommò Geshe (or Domo Geshe)*

"He's barely nine years old," the lama said as we went downstairs again, "but he's already incredibly learned. He certainly knows more than I, who am his teacher, and more than many monks who have spent all their lives in study. Don't you think that's an additional proof that he's the Great Precious Thupden Öden returned among us once more?" The smile of the humanist and expounder of the scriptures was subtly ironic, and his resemblance to the classical type of Chinese scholar leapt more clearly than ever to the eye.

"Be careful, the stairs are steep," he went on. I had in fact ceased for a moment to look where I was going, and had been trying to look him in the eyes.

We descended once more to the courtyard. A strange noise came to my ears, like the creaking and grinding of an old mill-wheel. At every turn, keeping time with the sighing and groaning of the wood, a bell rang. I went towards the little chapel built in the corner of the courtyard, entered, and saw that the sound came from a huge wooden drum, at least nine feet high and obviously very heavy, which a poor old blind woman, sitting on the ground, was turning by rhythmically pulling two cords.

The *om-tse* came and joined us. He told me that the drum contained a *mantra* (magic ejaculatory prayer) written out millions and millions of times. "It is the *mantra* of Dorje Sem-pa," he said. "The words are *Oma-siva-sato-hum*. The meaning? No-one knows exactly, but repeating it does good. Every time it turns, it's as if it were repeated an almost infinite number of times. It does good

20 *Children look admiringly at Trommò Geshe*

all round here; and the old woman earns herself a supper in the kitchen, ha! ha! . . . Are you tired, old woman? . . . She works all right . . . The *trapas* will look after you all right at supper this evening, old woman!"

With his huge, bony hands the *om-tse* gave two vigorous pushes to the drum, which for a moment moved faster. The old woman moved backwards, straightening her back. She smiled into the void, as the blind do.

My visit to the Kar-gyu *gompá* happened to coincide with one of the big Buddhist festivals. In the big temple, on the ground floor, I found two rows of seminarists (*tsun-chung*), sitting cross-legged on their high cushions. Lamas stood at the end of each row, one with a drum, the other with a trumpet; there was even a prefect (*u-cho*) to direct the singing and reading in chorus. It was all very austere and very solemn. There was a complete lack of the slovenly, casual reading often to be observed in other monasteries – the presence of the *om-tse* had been noticed at once. As soon as he appeared the boys became models of perfect behaviour.

The *om-tse* walked slowly up and down the temple with his great hands behind his back. There was revived within me the fear with which a not dissimilar father of a teaching order, one Novelli, known as "the vintner", used to inspire me and my companions when I was a boy in Florence. Poor little chaps, taken away from their mothers and forced to act the thaumaturge, among terrifying symbols and diabolical miniatures made of butter! I stayed for a long time watching them, as if I were one of them.

The reading went on rhythmically. The prefect intoned a few phrases solo, in a low, sonorous voice, and the others intoned the responses. At moments one might almost have been in a Catholic church. Then, without warning, a lama sounded the *gyaling* (silver trumpet), and one of the students sounded the *kangling* (trumpet made from the thigh-bone of a sixteen-year-old virgin), and the universe collapsed into a thousand pieces, among the craziest dissonance.

Reconsideration, 1998

The hapless Kar-gyu monastery, as we have seen, has been one of the many victims of the barbaric violence to which the Chinese fanatics and their young Tibetan hangers-on devoted themselves between 1966 and 1976. Therefore whatever is mentioned in the text concerning for instance the number of monks in the community, and about the 280 different gods seen represented in sculpture and painting, must be taken as referring to the past, and in particular to the period prior to the 1960s. I have not touched the text because it seems to me right that it should stand as a record of a vanished Tibetan world.

21 *Yatung: Lama of the* Kargyu-pa *sect performs a ritual*

Possibly some time in the future, if circumstances allow, that world will be re-established, at least to some extent; but it will never be exactly as it was. There will be no more living in a genuine mediaeval world remote from the rest of the world, as Tibet was in 1937. However genuine may be the feeling for and desire for a return to the past, it will be impossible to recapture it, except in an artificial, gimcrack form – too much has changed thanks to the new ease of communications, the spread of broadcasting, the imitation of foreign fashions, the arrival of electricity, petrol, plastics, liquid gas, the influence of Communist propaganda and Chinese cultural indoctrination. It may be possible to introduce the monastic life afresh in these places, maybe even purified and raised to a higher level of consciousness – as is the case with certain Christian monastic communities in the United States today, or in other equally developed countries – but we (or rather our grandchildren) will be living in quite a different world.

Even the great, imposing monastery of Dung-kar halfway between Yatung/Yadong and Phari/Pari, was set ablaze and savagely destroyed. By a miracle its abbot, considered to be an incarnation of a *Bodhisattva*, Ngawang Lobsang, succeeded in escaping. It is a moving tale that affects me. One day in 1995 I received a letter in Florence sent to me by an American lady (I think she was of German origin) asking if I would send her a copy of my photograph of the young living *Bodhisattva* (see photo 19) as she wanted to make a gift of it to Lama Ngawang Lobsang, who evidently was teaching Tibetan in the United States, and who was about to turn sixty. I was touched by the news – at least one of the people who were at Yatung in 1948 was safe and sound – and I sent the photograph at once, one to the American lady, another copy to the Lama himself. This small beginning led to a delightful correspondence between the Lama, who was known abroad as Domo Geshe Rimpoche, and the author of these pages.

In 1959 I was at Lhasa, [he wrote] and the Chinese Communists put me in prison for about two and a half years. Fortunately I was set free and went to India. Then I travelled a great deal . . . In 1969 I visited Rome and called on Professor Tucci. Finally, since 1976 I have settled in the Catskills, in New York State. I have been able to divide my time between the United States and India, moving from one country to the other once a year . . . Seeing your photographs has given me enormous pleasure. Alas the monastery of Dung-kar was completely destroyed, they did not even leave the foundations! But my people are very strong. It is already some years since they rebuilt the monastery and given it new statues and everything necessary. I do hope to revisit Dung-kar, but I don't know when this will be possible. It would be lovely if you could come here for a few days' rest. We are in a most beautiful and peaceful forest. Meanwhile take care of yourself and may you know inner peace. With all good wishes,

Ngawang
(Domo Geshe Rimpoche)

[In April 1999 I met the Lama in New York. Though little past sixty, he looked very weak; evidently he had suffered severely when in the hands of the Chinese.]

6

Guests in a Tibetan Village

Two ways of travelling

There are two ways of travelling. One is to cover a long distance in a short time, taking in the general outline of mountain and valley and the most obvious characteristics of the people. The other is to stop, go deeper, strike root to some extent, and try to imbibe from the soil the invisible spiritual sap which nourishes the inhabitants of the place. Both are perfectly legitimate, both can be sources of pleasure, and both can lead to useful knowledge and useful comparisons.

We have just arrived at Yatung (which the local people call Shasima, possibly a name of Lepcha origin). It seems that we shall stay here for some time. Does this mean an opportunity for travel of the second kind? Yatung is situated nearly 10,000 feet above sea-level, at a point where the valley of the Amo-chu, up which the caravan route climbs in the direction of Lhasa, divides into two. It is an ugly village, without any special character, but the surrounding country is rich in unsuspected beauties, and many other villages, higher up or lower down, can truthfully be called ancient centres of a secluded, static, mountain-valley civilization of a kind often to be found in the Alps.

A noisy torrent runs along the bottom of the valley. Its source is not far away – the glaciers of Pauhunri (23,180ft) – and it is swollen by several tributaries. The valley is narrow, enclosed between tremendous cliffs, reaching to 13,000 feet – well below the permanent snow-line. The outlook is Alpine. There are firs, pines, pastures and rhododendrons. The climate is on the whole damp. For several months of the year (the summer monsoon) there is a great deal of rain, but even then the sun shines brilliantly every now and then in the clear sky of these high altitudes.

As is normal in villages of the Buddhist Himalayas, a row of *tarchos* stands at the entrance to Yatung. A *tarcho* is a long pole to which there is nailed a cotton pennant on which innumerable sacred phrases are printed by woodcut. The wind moves them, "utters" them and fills the air with good. The idea of the quasi-physical spreading of a spiritual aura is a beautiful one, and the *tarchos* are themselves very beautiful. They stand tall, white and glorious in the sun,

22 *Yatung , some 10,000 feet up in the Himalayas, on the R. Amo-chu*

and the gay whistling of the wind through them is cheering and refreshing to the traveller.

A man who wishes to set up a *tarcho* starts by buying the material for the flag. Cotton is rationed, and the other materials are rather dear. He then takes it to a monastery, where a lama prepares one of the wooden matrices which are invariably to be found in monasteries, inks it, and prints the required prayers on the customer's material in return for a small fee. The next step is to procure a pole and erect it, or have it erected, in the desired place, with a lama officiating. All this takes time and money; it is a "sacrifice", and "sacrifices" are required by all religions. A *tarcho* can be erected as a votive offering, to ask a grace or out of religious fervour. All the inhabitants usually contribute to the maintenance of the long row of *tarchos* at the entrance to a village.

At first sight Yatung seems to present no features of interest. It consists of four rows of half-timbered cottages, roofed with shingles, flanking two longitudinal streets, of which the bigger, with its little shops, constitutes the bazaar, the market. The goods on sale are few and of poor quality, except for the Tibetan paper, which is a fascinating tissue of vegetable fibre. As for antiquities, the

23 *Yatung: prayer flags at the entrance to the village*

24 *A* lung-ta *"wind-horse", a banner printed with invocations*

The lung-ta *is a printed cotton banner that is tied to twigs stuck between stones up on the mountain passes, atop houses, in the fields. The horse with a jewel, or carrying a jewel on its back, symbolizes a gift of one's chattels to the gods. The text reads:*
"Om! Protect us, o great, holy, saintly one [Buddha]!
Om! And you, god of supreme wisdom [Manjusri] whose word is all-powerful!
Om! And you, god of mercy [Avalokitesvara], keeper of the Lotus and the Jewel!
Om! And you, omnipotent god [Vajrapani], lord of the thunderbolt!
Om! And you, goddess of longevity, grant us days without end, grant us victory, grant us the nectar of immortality!
Om! And you, goddess of holy works, redeemer from evil, protect us!"
Below is written: "As the new moon rises in the heavens, so does the lung-ta, *wind-horse of good omen, carry up on high, from peak to peak, the fortunes of a whole people, its destiny, its riches, its children!"*

time has passed when one could buy for a few rupees good pictures and statues, brought secretly to the market by unscrupulous monks.

Tibet is a completely feudal country; there is a hereditary caste which shares political and economic power with the lamas. But at Yatung the elegant world of the feudal nobility of Lhasa, Shigatse, Gyantse and Gangtok is practically unrepresented. Apart from a few retired officials, the inhabitants (there are about 450 of them) are small traders, artisans, shopkeepers, mule-drivers; and there are a number of peasants and woodmen. Thus we have an opportunity here of studying the everyday life of the Tibetan common people.

The ex-official Lobsang: pride and prejudice

But there is no doubt that we are in Tibet. Not only the *tarchos*, but the smaller flags (*lung-ta*) waving in the wind outside all the doors and houses, strike the eye immediately, giving something of a festive air to the squalid little village. No house has more flags and pennants than the house of Lobsang, whose flags are more brightly coloured and better kept than anybody else's.

We have now been here for three weeks. Every now and then I go and see Lobsang. He is a curious type.

"Good morning, good morning!"

Lobsang, seated on his bed-sofa, continues placidly and attentively turning his little prayer-wheel. He and I have known each other for a long time; we first met ten years ago. The last time I saw him he was an important intermediary between the British and the Tibetans; he was working as an interpreter, and all important "international" affairs passed through his hands. But now he has retired from public life, and bought this cottage and a little land on which to live. I don't know if he is married; he seems to have no family. With the years he has become exaggeratedly pious; he spends half the day in prayers, in edifying reading and in murmuring ejaculatories.

"Good morning, Lobsang, how are you? How many thousands of millions of prayers this morning?"

Lobsang laughs, and continues almost defiantly to turn his prayer-wheel, which consists of a small brass drum decorated with the Eight Glorious Emblems (*thrashi te-gye*); that is to say, the Golden Fish, the Umbrella, the Conch-shell Trumpet of Victory, the Lucky Diagram, the Victorious Banner, the Vase of Ambrosia, the Lotus of Immortality and the Wheel of Law. Inside it there is a long, tightly-rolled scroll of paper on which Lobsang himself wrote out 10,000 times (with a fountain-pen!) the sacred formula *Om mani padme hum*. The little drum serves the same purpose as the much bigger ones to be found in the monasteries.

"Well, how is Lobsang?"

"So-so, so-so! How would you expect a poor old man to be?" Then he livens up. "Tomorrow an incarnated One, the Doctor of Trommò, is passing through Yatung – a fortunate event for our little village, lost among the mountains!"

25 *Prayer-wheel* (mani-khorlo) *and the "Eight Signs of Good Fortune"*

*The Eight Glorious Emblems (*ashtamangala *in Sanskrit,* thrashi-te-gye *in Tibetan) are, from top left to bottom right: goldfish, the royal baldaquin, the trumpet of victory, the monogram of good fortune, the banner of victory, the vase of ambrosia, the lotus of immortality, the wheel of the law.*
The eight glorious emblems are frequently featured on Tibetan household objects, whether embroidered, depicted, cast in metal, nielloed, or whatever else.

"We shall go and see him together, Lobsang. Meanwhile I've brought you some photographs that I took ten years ago."

"Oh, thank you! I'll fetch my spectacles . . . You took your time, didn't you!"

We both laugh. Lobsang is small and thin, rather worn-looking and extremely Mongolian in appearance. He wears his long, silver-streaked hair in two plaits around his head. He might be a retired secondary schoolmaster, or stationmaster, or minor official of some kind; a man who has worked hard all his life, been reasonably successful, grown old, and has now started asking questions. Why are we alive and why do we suffer? But it is too late. He will never set out now on the enterprise of trying to find out. Papers, documents, officialdom have exhausted his strength. All that is left is the rosary and an inarticulate faith. Besides, Lobsang always was a pessimist. Now he shakes his head, and repeats in a voice that has grown greyer than ever his discouraging views about absolutely everything.

"What do you think, Lobsang? Shall we get to Lhasa?"

"The ways of the Tibetan Government are involved and intricate. At Lhasa they have special fears and antipathies that nobody understands. Don't be too hopeful, my friend! Much gold for little ink, much ink for little gold. It all depends. That's what governments are like! On the other hand, don't you see how attachment to things leads to unhappiness? The more you think of Lhasa, the unhappier you become. Mark my words, it's all illusion. Don't allow yourself to become the slave of anything!"

Lobsang, while giving his personal interpretation of the Buddhist Four Noble Truths, puts down his prayer-wheel and starts combing his long hair with the nicety of an official scrutinizing a document.

"I wash my hair once a week!" he announces with a certain pride. Having been in contact with the British for so long, he has acquired unusual habits of cleanliness. He now looks like a village old maid dressing up for the fair. His face is invisible, being completely covered by his hair, which falls forward like a waterfall on to his knees while he continues meticulously combing it. When he considers that he has combed it enough, that is to say when every single hair is perpendicular and parallel, he divides it into two with his hands, and his face reappears in between, like someone coming out of a tent.

Then, with the conciliatory smile of the Mongolian who wants something, he asks:

"But after all, why do you come to these parts? Why do you spend so much money and put up with so much discomfort? Why?"

How often have I been asked that question! To humble folk it suffices to answer: "A pilgrimage"; to the educated one can explain the real reasons; one can talk of studying art, ethnography or philology. But what is one to say to a man such as Lobsang, who has lost his primitive innocence but has not acquired enough education to understand? People of his type always suspect espionage, secret deals, international intrigue.

The door opens and Sönam appears. Sönam is a village lad, aged about twenty, who cooks and cleans for Lobsang. As Sönam enters he makes a hurried movement, trying to hide something. But it is too late, we saw. It was a cigarette-end that he threw into the street. Lobsang blazes up.

"Haven't I told you a hundred times not to smoke? The next time I catch you smoking you'll get the sack! You know you're not to smoke! What does our holy religion say, to say nothing of your health? . . . Don't you know you're spoiling your chances of a satisfactory rebirth? . . . Rebirth? You'll end up as a *yi-dag* or worse, you'll go to hell!"

Sönam scuttles into the kitchen like a scalded cat, while Lobsang continues to unburden his feelings to me on the abominable vice of smoking. It's strange that the Tibetans should be so hostile to the cigarette, while the little Chinese pipe, though not positively favoured, is nevertheless largely tolerated for laymen. The very word *shikre* (as the Tibetans pronounce "cigarette") is said to be ill-omened. *Shik* means to demolish and *re* to tear, and it is thus a combination of very sinister ideas, indicating that the thing concerned will bring evil and ruin to the country.

"It is also known that smoke is displeasing to the spirits, and that is really serious," Lobsang continues, completing his right-hand plait and starting on the other one.

Moreover there are the unambiguous words of a famous book, the *Lohi Chö-jung* ("Religious History of the South"):

"There is one evil custom," it states, "which is the forerunner of the Tempter himself. It is spreading among the general population as well as among the garrison forces . . . It is the unceasing use of the evil, stinking, poisonous weed named tobacco. The smoke from this drug defiles the sacred objects of worship, the Images, the Books, the Relics. It weakens the Gods above, causes fighting among the Spirits of the Middle Air, and injures the Serpent Spirits below. From this cause arises an endless cycle of epidemics, wars, and famines in the human world."

Lobsang is unable to reconcile himself to Sönam's desire to smoke.

"You know," he says, "Padma Sambhava foresaw smoking a thousand years ago and more. In his great foresight he knew that men would one day succumb to that extreme and incomparably stupid vice . . . Smoke, smoke . . . He spoke of it in a *termá* . . . "

Meanwhile Lobsang's toilet has been advancing steadily towards its completion. One plait is finished, and the second nearly so. When three-quarters of the work is done, Lobsang's deft and agile fingers insert into the hair a number of silk ribbons, coloured pink, cobalt green and sky blue. The ribbons on each plait end in a long, many-coloured tassel, and this makes the final effect very decorative when he winds the plaits round his head.

"*Termá*?" Lobsang continues, noticing my puzzled expression. "*Termá*s are books, thoughts, works, which the great sages of the past wrote for the illumination of future ages . . . Sönam! Hi! Sönam! Is tea ready? . . . Would you like Tibetan or Indian tea?"

"If it is all the same, I should prefer Tibetan!"

"Sönam! Sönam! *Pö-cha kesho*! (Bring Tibetan tea!) . . . The great men of the past foresaw everything. Every century has its vices, so they wrote books adapted to every century. They wrote books in which they gave remedies for all the vices of man, and buried them in the mountains, underneath rivers, among the ice-peaks. When the time comes, somebody discovers them. Thus we know what to think about all new things!"

Lobsang has reached the consummation of his labours and has started winding the plaits round his head. He rises, fetches a little mirror, and resumes his seat. He holds the mirror on his knees and starts fixing the plaits in place round his head with hairpins.

"When I was young," he says, "I would not believe in these things. But now I am convinced of them. We are all surrounded by mysterious events. Our ancestors knew better than we, so why should we not follow them?"

"What happens if a *termá* is discovered before its time?" I ask.

"That is terrible, terrible!"

Lobsang now has a hairpin between his lips and is holding his arms behind his head, putting the finishing touches to the meticulous labours of the last half-hour. As soon as he is able to remove the hairpin from his mouth and put it in his hair, to keep the last piece of multi-coloured silk in place, he goes on:

"Do you know the story of the Abbot Ken-rab?"

Meanwhile Sönam brings me a jade cup with a cover shaped like a pagoda and a curious silver, lotus-shaped saucer. I open it, and the boy pours the brew that Tibetans call tea from an elaborate brass pot.

"The Abbot Ken-rab," Lobsang continues, "dreamed that he heard a voice saying: 'Go to such-and-such a mountain and walk a hundred paces beyond the first waterfall. There you will find a revelation.' The Abbot Ken-rab at first took no notice. Then the voice became more insistent, and finally the abbot decided to obey. He climbed the *kang-ri* (snow mountain), walked a hundred paces beyond the waterfall and found a smooth, flat stone, which looked as if it had been shaped by man, in a place where certainly no-one had ever been before. His monks raised it, and underneath they saw an ancient wooden box. They opened it, and found a book . . . Once upon a time I did not believe in these things – drink your tea, it'll get cold – but now I'm convinced of them. Just when the Abbot Ken-rab was about to turn the pages of the book terrifying screams were heard, and green fire started issuing from the hole in the ground, threatening to burn them all alive . . ."

I sip the tea brew – made of butter, soda, salt, boiling water and tea prepared in a bamboo drum – and accept an oily, fur-covered biscuit, which I swallow with difficulty.

"But I don't understand," I say to Lobsang. "Why did the Abbot Ken-rab have the dream?"

"Exactly," says Lobsang. "That is the point."

He rises and puts the mirror back in its place. His hair is now in perfect order, and he can proceed with the no less elaborate ceremony of putting on his Tibetan clothes, which he wears with the solemn dignity of a Chinese scholar.

"Zat is ze point," he continues, in his bad but fluent English, while he puts on a fine silk robe over his shining white shirt and trousers, and ties it round his waist with a silk sash.

"The question was studied for a long time," he continues eventually. "Many lamas were consulted, and many well-known oracles, and eventually it was discovered – just imagine it! – that one of the monks had been stealing offerings, and that the tutelary deity of the monastery had therefore been deprived for a long time of the altar offerings which were his due. To avenge himself the tutelary deity had therefore caused the abbot to dream of the ill-omened discovery of a future *termá*. Tutelary deities are very malicious sometimes!"

As he says this, Lobsang carefully smooths out with his hand part of the edge of his *chuba* in which there seems to be the suggestion of a crease. Then he sits down again.

"So that nobody ever knew what was in the book?"

"No! There are certain things that one must not know. Would you like some more tea? Even you strangers ought to have great respect for the gods, you can never tell what will happen. Do you know the story of Williamson?"

"The Political Officer who died at Lhasa in 1936?"

"Yes. You think he died because he had a weak heart and an altitude of 10,800 feet was too much for him? Nonsense, my dear sir! He died because he had photographed the gods in a *gön-kang*, a shrine of the tutelary deities. You may not believe it, but it's a fact known to everybody in Lhasa and Tibet . . . Please help yourself to another biscuit, they're fresh. Sönam baked them; he's a good lad . . . A few hours before Williamson died a perfectly black figure entered his room and snatched his soul . . . Won't you have some more tea? No? Once upon a time I used not to believe in these things, but gradually I became convinced, there were too many facts for me to do otherwise.

Well, shall we go out? Let us walk down to the bridge, if you agree."

Lobsang is now ready for the calm and devoted day of a Buddhist personage in retirement. He has little to do with the people of Yatung. He is aware, and rightly aware, of being one of the few civilized persons in a small community consisting of people of every sort except the right sort. He stays at home, or walks about his garden. Once a day as regularly as clockwork he walks down to the bridge, saying his prayers on the way, with his rosary of stones held in his hands behind his back. After eleven o'clock in the morning he is always as ready and prepared as if the Regent of Tibet, or the representative of a foreign power, or one of the five or six most important lamas in the whole of Central Asia, were about to pay a ceremonial visit to his house.

The living Bodhisattva

Lobsang told me yesterday that an Incarnated One was coming. The importance of the event was immediately made clear to me this morning by the extraordinary fact that the whole population turned out to clean up the village. The Incarnated One was coming! The Great Doctor!

From early afternoon all Yatung was in the street. The air was cool and the sun shone brightly in an Alpine sky. All the boys were happy and excited, and ran about more vigorously than usual, and the girls all wore aprons (*pang-den*) of electric colours. Two rows of white stones had been laid along the street, to help to keep evil influences away. Branches of cypress were burning in braziers outside every door, filling the air with scented and amazingly blue smoke.

The famous personage was thus received under a smoke-filled sky. He was preceded by a long procession of monks on horseback, servants with rifles and bandoliers, well-nourished abbots, and beasts of burden carrying sacks of *tsampa* (roasted barley flour); others carried books, shrines, sacred pictures. The yellow robes, the crimson silk hats, the brown and black fur hoods, stood out in explosions of colour against the heavily-scented blue smoke, which hung over the village almost as if there had been a fire of cigarettes.

Suddenly there were shouts of, "There he is! There he is!" The boys rushed forward to see, the women went down on their knees, the men bowed, wheels whirled giddily. The Great Doctor, wearing an ample, yellow silk robe and a hat of gilded metal, appeared out of the blue haze, riding a little white horse. He was twelve years old. He was enchanting.

Visit to the living Bodhisattva

I paid my respects officially to the living *Bodhisattva*. The famous little doctor sat cross-legged on a kind of throne, covered with silks and Chinese brocades, in the middle of a temple. In front of him were offerings, as well as the double drum (*nga-chung*), the ceremonial bell (*tril-bu*) and the bronze thunderbolt (*dorje*). The temple was dark, deep, mysterious. People passed the little doctor in silence, bowed and received a blessing. Those who made a sufficient offering received in return a white silk sash (*kata*). The child laid his hands on everybody's head. On the walls you caught glimpses of the frescoes of Buddhas, meditating serenely in their hieratic attitudes, and of terrifying gods dancing in lakes of blood, drinking ambrosia from human skulls made into cups.

The doctor's full name was Ngawang Lobsang Gyalden Jigme Chöki Wangchuk. He was the son of the Enche Kasi of Gangtok. Soon he would be going to complete his education in one of the big monasteries of Lhasa.

I offered a few rupees to one of the monks, and received a sash from the hands of the little living god. There was not a trace of uncertainty, not a shadow of doubt, in the child's handsome, bright eyes. He knew he was one of the elect. He had never thought otherwise.

The headman Mingyur: why not export coral?

Mingyur, the *gong-thu* (headman) of the village of Yatung, cannot stand the ex-interpreter Lobsang. I have never found out how the antagonism between them originally arose. But the retired official's way of life, his living apart and aloof, like an offended king in exile, might have been specially designed to irritate the representative of authority in any little community anywhere in the world. Lobsang's manner does not suggest pride or superiority; he does not put on airs of any kind; but his behaviour subtly suggests dissatisfaction, the dissatisfaction of a man who has looked about him and seen that everything is beneath his notice, so much beneath his notice that there is no need even to show it. On the other hand the people of the village have allowed themselves gradually to be impressed, both by Lobsang's retired life and the ever more conspicuous manifestations of his piety. Mingyur's authority has suffered in consequence. An argument often ends by somebody's suggesting that they go and see what Lobsang has to say about it.

"But who is this Lobsang?" Mingyur then shouts, losing his temper. "He's done nothing but cause trouble and confusion all his life, and now, just because he plays the holy man, you all bow down and worship him!"

"Lobsang is Lobsang," the people reply. This statement, however stupid and unreasonable, is incontrovertible and final.

Mingyur is a wizened old man in his sixties, but he is much better preserved than Lobsang. He is generally regarded as a fool, but I suspect that the truth is that he is the only really honest man among all the traffickers and smugglers along the caravan route. He is to be seen going about his affairs every day; his own and those of the community. He is always dressed in Tibetan style, the style worn by the country-folk: a woollen *chuba*, an unbleached cotton shirt and leather boots. He wears his hair short. He is what is known as a moderate and sensible man – he is a traditionalist without going to extremes; religious, but not to excess; a drinker, but in moderation, etc., etc. He is certainly less educated, less curious, less subtle, less everything than Lobsang, but he is simpler and more human.

Now and again I go to his house for a chat. Mingyur's family consists of an exceedingly ugly but extremely devoted and attentive wife, and an apparently endless number of children. There must be at least nine or ten of them, but I don't know; in any case a very large number for a by no means prolific country such as Tibet. The two eldest girls – Pemà Chödrön and Pemà Sandup – who are about fifteen or sixteen, would be very nice girls if their heads had not been turned by the fact of being the headman's daughters.

The Mingyurs' house is more or less typical of those of the relatively prosperous inhabitants of Yatung. You first enter a room used as a store-room, full of saddles, tools, sacks of merchandise, all the things characteristic of the romantic, feudal life of this country. You then enter the kitchen, a dark, sooty place, with the Eight Glorious Emblems crudely painted in white on the wall; and finally you reach Mingyur's own room, which also serves as parlour and chapel. In its capacity as parlour a number of the thick cushions which the Tibetans use for chairs are arranged around the walls, as well as a few small lacquered tables for tea and biscuits. In its capacity as chapel it has a beautiful little carved and gilded wooden altar, with a few statuettes (Padma Sambhava, Chen-re-zi, Sakya-Thupa); and on the wall there are two or three *tangka* (pictures painted on cloth), and some photographs of lamas and celebrated temples, as well as a view of Lhasa. His chapel is every Tibetan's pride. The chapel in the house of a feudal lord often rivals those of the temples in richness of decoration, number of statues, pictures, books, precious cups and wealth of offerings.

Mingyur sees in me, as a European, primarily a mechanical wizard. Every time I go and see him he asks me to repair either an old alarm-clock that won't ring, or an old padlock that won't open, or an old electric light bulb that won't light. In spite of my many protests and failures, he is never discouraged. He always wants me to try again. Also he always has a list of English words which he doesn't know how to pronounce, and he always and invariably makes the same mistakes in trying to pronounce them. Yesterday I finally managed to repair the alarm-clock, whereupon Mingyur invited me to dinner.

I insisted that the meal should be in Tibetan style; that is to say, that it should consist, not of the dishes that the rich cause to be served on special occasions, which are practically the same as Chinese, but of what ordinary Tibetans eat on ordinary occasions. Mingyur and I ate in the parlour-chapel. Every now and then his wife came in to serve us, stayed a few moments to exchange a few words, and then vanished into the kitchen again; the children stood in the corridor, peeping round the door. They enjoyed themselves hugely, laughing outright at all the errors of etiquette that a foreigner inevitably makes at meals.

"Go away! Go away!" Mingyur would shout, and silence would reign in the corridor for a few moments. But then the door would imperceptibly open again, and the face of a child of three would appear in the opening, with an expression of infinite curiosity in its eyes. Mingyur taught me to pour tea into *tsampa*.

"You wanted to see how we Tibetans eat, didn't you? This is an ordinary, everyday meal. A poor thing, isn't it? You westerners are all rich, but we are all poor!"

I tried to convince him that this was not so, but it is the general belief, and there is little one can do about it.

Tsampa is simply roasted barley flour. Every Tibetan family keeps a stock of it, and Tibetan travellers always have a small sack of it in their baggage. You take a small handful, put it in your bowl, and pour over it the requisite amount of hot tea; you then mix it with your fingers into a dough of the consistency of fresh marzipan; and you then, of course, add butter, again mixing it with your fingers. Finally you eat it in small mouthfuls. Does it sound revolting? It's a thousand times better than the tragic messes with high-sounding French names served in Indian restaurants. True, you need a certain amount of appetite, and a certain capacity for adaptation. But if you travel you don't lack the former, and if you lack the latter you don't travel.

Mingyur likes talking business. Like all Tibetans, he is full of sound commercial ideas.

"Why don't you export coral from your country?" he asked. "They say Italian coral is the best in the world. At Lhasa they're crazy about coral. You could sell it at very high prices!"

"That's certainly an idea."

"You could take turquoises in exchange. Here they're very cheap. Isn't there a demand for them in your country?"

Mingyur's eyes shone with pleasure. A good business deal gives almost physical pleasure to a true Tibetan.

Mingyur's wife brought us a dish of yak meat, roasted and cut in pieces. Yak meat, mutton or goat, salted, smoked and dried in the sun in the sterile air of 12,000 feet, is one of the principal foods of the Tibetan people. In a country where cattle-rearing is so widespread and agriculture often so difficult, because of the cold and the dryness and the poverty of the soil, it is natural that meat should be an important, if not exclusive, article of diet.

But for centuries this has confronted the Tibetans with a grave moral conflict. The first commandment for all Buddhists is: Thou shalt not take life. How, then, can a Buddhist reconcile himself to the taking of animal life, even if it be to feed his own children or parents? All monks, incidentally, claim to be vegetarians, and, within certain limits, that is what they are. But laymen make no pretence to be vegetarians, and for most of them meat is an important article of diet. Clearly custom is the practically unalterable foundation on which the characteristics of a civilization are based. Buddhism did not make the Japanese less warlike, and Christianity did not make the Latins less sensual. Similarly lamaism was able only partially to modify the Tibetans' taste for meat.

Certain fundamental rules and fictions are nevertheless observed. Butchers constitute a kind of caste apart; they live in a state of inferiority, and are considered in various ways to be "impure". But, fortunately for them, the sin, the bad *karma* accumulated as the result of their activities, is considered to be shared by the whole community. Being divided among so many heads, each individual's share is small, infinitesimal – practically nil. In the Wa-pa-ling quarter of Lhasa Mohammedan butchers (of Chinese descent) are employed. For these people slaughtering animals is no sin.

This always reminds me of the Japanese monks who called wild boar *yama-kujira* ("mountain whale"); this enabled them to eat it as if it were a creature of the sea. Other abbots and monks used to engage in long religious ceremonies aimed at securing the rebirth of slaughtered animals at a higher evolutionary level, thus enabling them to claim that slaughter actually benefited the beasts. Another Japanese memory is of the big religious ceremony, conducted at the expense of the Imperial University, which used to take place every year at Sapporo, near Hokkaido, in one of the biggest temples of the city, when the monks prayed for all the animals killed for experimental or other purposes in the medical and scientific departments of the university. I used to accompany Professor Kodama (whose assistant I was), and we attended the service with much solemnity and ceremony, dressed in black, and prayed for the frogs slain by our colleague the physiologist and for the guinea-pigs slaughtered by our colleague the pathologist.

To return to Tibet, here is a proverb, quoted by Sir Charles Bell in *The People of Tibet*, that reflects the general way of thinking in regard to these problems: *Sha-di nying-je-chen kyi sa, nying-je chang-chup lam ne dren.* (If its flesh be eaten by one of merciful mind, it will be led on the road of pure and perfect mercy.)

Human nature inevitably won the battle, and to justify itself appealed to the noblest part of itself, generosity. Dinner with Mingyur came to an end. I forgot to mention that we should really have eaten with our fingers, but the mistress of the house insisted on providing us with those foreign inventions, knives and forks.

Afternoon at the torrent

The surroundings of Yatung are as beautiful as the village itself is ugly. The valley is like any Alpine valley. The same steep mountainsides climb up towards the sky, with the same woods of fir, larch and pine, the same flower-filled meadows, the same torrents, the same rocky crests standing out in the sun. But, as you get to know the place better, you discover that there is also something different. Perhaps it is the latitude (we are on the same latitude as the Fezzan, in Libya); when the sky is clear there is much more light than in the Alps – more fire in the air. Also, everything is more grandiose and primitive. The woods are more like the primaeval forests that must have covered Europe in the Magdalenian age; huge torrents dash wildly and noisily downhill; and the silence, the distance and the heights are all on a heroic scale.

Spring is over, and with it the mythological flowering of the rhododendrons. Summer has started now, and the wild roses are out. The roses grow in tall, dense thickets, covered with petals of delicate colours, creamy-white or a pale pinkish-red. You see them everywhere, but particularly along the river. And down below, among the grass, there are millions of strawberries.

The Kar-gyu lama: fingers like a corps-de-ballet

Tibetan men normally wear their hair long. The only men with short hair are the monks of the Yellow Sect, as well as a few "modernists" along the caravan route. The monks of the Kar-gyu sect, in addition to their own long hair, wear a kind of turban of artificial hair.

A few days ago a tall, smooth, clean-shaven, mysterious lama belonging to that sect appeared at Yatung. He spends his time going from village to village. A long way away, in eastern Tibet, he has a wife and five children, a fact which greatly scandalizes a friend of ours, a lama of the Yellow Sect, the *Gelug-pa*, the "Virtuous", who fulminates against the slackness and immorality of the Kar-gyu sect, whom he calls cheap magicians. The newcomer is undoubtedly a wizard, as is asserted by popular repute and confirmed by something indefinably serpentine and faun-like which he constantly betrays in his person. Also, there are his hands. They are long, supple hands, the hands of a sorcerer or alchemist, and no effort is required to imagine them in the act of transmuting metals or summoning up demons from the bowels of the earth. His whole art consists of charms and exorcisms, in the power he is said to exercise over the obscure forces of evil by which every Tibetan feels himself surrounded. He goes from house to house offering his services. He knows how to ingratiate himself with the women, walks barefooted, keeps on appearing suddenly out of nowhere, and you never know what he is thinking.

Today he conducted the *barche-serwa* ceremony, which is always observed before starting on a journey. For lack of a temple of his sect in the village, he used the house of an acquaintance, Sandhup. Sandhup, however, was not present; he suffers from rheumatism, and had gone up to Phari Dzong for the sake of the hot baths, and his wife therefore did the honours. The parlour served as chapel; a medium-sized room, containing many hard cushions for sitting on, a cupboard and an altar, as well as a number of brass tea-pots, photographs (the Thirteenth Dalai Lama, the Regent, the temple of Bodh-gaya), and a number of rifles, saddles and sacks of grain. There was a feeling of age-old silence about the room, and it stank of butter. The ceremony lasted for hours and hours. Every now and then the endless chanting was interrupted by strokes on a drum. The lama formed offerings, consisting of *tsampa* dough and butter, into strange shapes with his fingers. Some were placed on the altar, others thrown out into the street to placate the spirits.

Two things struck me with an almost terrifying vividness, which I shall never forget. One was the deep, cavernous, subterranean voice with which the lama read his invocation to the terrifying gods; the other was the play of his hands in the various mystic positions in which he placed them according to the deities being invoked. His fingers were now snakes, now members of a *corps-de-ballet*. The rest of the man was forgotten, absent, left outside in the dark, but those hands of his lived a life of their own in the centre of an immense, deserted Tibet, as infinite as space and as deep as the jungle.

The tailor Tob-chen: the privilege of initiates

Tob-chen is the tailor of Yatung. He is also an antique dealer, a doctor, a smuggler, the happy father of a family, a forger, a pillar of the whole neighbourhood, a corrupter of youth and a patron of the local monasteries. Sometimes he makes a *chuba* (coat) or an *onju* (shirt), but the widespread ramifications of his affairs keep him constantly on the move up and down the valley. If you want meat, butter, petrol, cigarettes, Tob-chen is your man. If you want a statue, a picture, a carved mask or some jade cups, Tob-chen is your man. If you want a piece of forest, a monastery, a girl, a rare book, pearls or a martyr's bones, Tob-chen is your man. I don't believe there's anything in the world he couldn't get for you, naturally in return for a suitable fee. Woe to him who falls into Tob-chen's bad books! He is as ingratiating, humble and charming to his superiors – rich men, lamas, or those who have lent him money – as he is haughty, rude, overbearing and unpleasant to the poor, to strangers and to those who owe him money. He is less than forty, fat without being flabby, has drooping moustaches, and can pass instantaneously from his ingratiating smile to Jesuitical demureness or the icy reserve of an offended statesman. He lives in a house near the bridge. His wife is ugly, gentle and kind-hearted. Some people like him, a few fear him and perhaps nobody hates him. But nobody trusts him.

If Lobsang to some extent represents the upper classes, at any rate in his manners and because of a certain breadth of view, and if Mingyur can be said to belong to the petty bourgeoisie, Tob-chen belongs frankly to the people; not to the labouring, honest people of the countryside or the mountains, but the people of the seaports, the bazaars and the caravan route. I met him today in the street. He was advancing solemnly with a companion, with his usual air of one basking in the prosperity, peace and serenity of the righteous. He was dressed in what he takes to be European style; that is to say, he wore a shrieking pair of American yellow shoes, violet socks, green trousers coming to below his knees, a violet pull-over and a filthy white shirt. Planted comically on the top of his head was a yellowish soft hat, from under which there descended an untidy, dusty pigtail, which had not been attended to for months.

As he approached his smile expanded from the broad to the ineffable. With a low bow he then said to me:

"Why not come along and see me this evening about that little matter?"

Talking to a foreigner in the presence of a third party and hinting at "little matters" and other mystifications is all part of a complicated behaviour-pattern intended to put him on a pedestal in relation to his fellow-villagers.

Tob-chen's house is typical of the houses of the people in this part of Tibet.

We are still in the Himalayas, and there is no lack of timber. The walls are of stone, but the roof, the stairs, the balconies, the floors and the fixtures are all of wood. I went up a few steps, passed through the so-called shop, where from time to time Tob-chen makes a coat, singing as he works, walked down a long dark corridor crowded with sacks, saddles, tools, odd pieces of furniture, skins full of butter, old rifles and boxes containing heaven knows what, and eventually reached the kitchen.

"Come in! Come in! No, don't come into the kitchen, it's dirty! Come upstairs! You'll excuse my humble home, won't you, I'm only a poor man!"

But I stopped, enchanted. The kitchen belonged to a world of fairy-tales and witches. It was black and sooty, with enormous pots, pans and sinks. On the smoky walls someone had crudely but effectively drawn the Eight Glorious Emblems. A whining child came up to me and said something that at first I could not catch. But then I made it out very distinctly. It was the word "Baksheesh!"

I went upstairs and entered Tob-chen's sanctum; his sitting-room, chapel, den, office, antique-dealer's shop, food-store and opium parlour. I sat down on one of the big cushions that are to be found in all Tibetan houses. Tob-chen started rummaging in his sheepskin-covered boxes. His wife brought up the inevitable tea and biscuits. A blue *Bodhisattva* looked at me from an altar of carved, lacquered and gilded wood. I think the *Bodhisattva* was Tse-pa-me ("Life without Limits"). He had a sly expression, of a kind rarely found in Tibetan sculpture; it made him a suitable accomplice for Tob-chen.

As soon as his wife had gone, Tob-chen started producing silk handkerchiefs from a package. Finally he produced a statuette of Chen-re-zi, the *Bodhisattva* of mercy, who is incarnated in the Dalai Lama. I had seen it a few days before and recognized it at once.

"But, Tob-chen," I exclaimed, "I saw that statue at the . . . monastery!"

Tob-chen indicated by signs that I should talk more quietly.

"I'm sure you will appreciate," he said, "that every now and then the poor monks need to have a beam or a wall repaired, and haven't got the money."

"Of course! But I always thought it was forbidden to sell things belonging to a monastery."

"Certainly it is. That is to say, it's forbidden to fools to sell them. *We* know secret ways."

How much technical, professional competence there was in that "we"!

"But what about the gods?"

"They'll shut one eye. After all, we've all got to live! Don't you know the Tibetan proverb? *Lha dre mi cho-nang chig* ('Gods, devils and men all behave in the same way'). Do you mean to say that they won't understand and forgive?"

Tob-chen rose and lit a number of little butter lamps in front of the statuette of Tse-pa-me.

Visit to a hermitage: serenity of a meal in a skull

In a rugged valley high up in the rocky fastnesses above Yatung, in the shade of clumps of fir-trees which cling like birds'-nests to the mountainside, are the hut-cells of a hermitage, the *ri-trö* of Chumbi.

I went there this evening; only the tree-tops were still lit by the golden gleam of sunset; the high mountain on the other side of the valley was already plunged in shadow. The place seemed to be deserted. The path climbed through grass and between tree-trunks. Every now and then I saw a little hut-cell. Was it empty, or inhabited by a silent hermit? Suddenly I heard a voice, and saw just above me a man's face peering out of the window of a tiny hut that seemed to be practically hanging from the wall of rock.

"*Kushog-sahib*!" ("Sir-sahib!"), he called out. "Come up here! Rest for a moment, there's no hurry; and there's no-one in the *ri-trö*."

I climbed a few more yards, and found waiting for me at the entrance of the hut a young-looking lama, short of stature, whose manners and appearance were immediately pleasing. His hut was really minute. It was no more than a wooden box, one end of which rested on piles while the other rested on a ledge of rock. I almost feared that my extra weight might topple it over.

Lama Gedul belonged to one of the non-reformed sects, and therefore wore his hair long. He was preparing a modest supper – boiled herbs and a little *tsampa* which he would later eat out of a skull. The skull was there, shaped into a bowl. It was smooth and clean, looking like old ivory. There were also a few books, a few liturgical objects and two or three paintings. Through the window there was a view of distant, snow-capped peaks.

Mrs Yishe: mechanical wizards and pharmaceutical saints

Let us return to the high society of Yatung. The male pillar of this society is, as we have seen, Lobsang, and Mrs Yishe is his female counterpart. She is the widow of a man who played a big part in relations between Tibetans and foreigners; he was actually Lobsang's superior. His widow, a majestic, matronly figure, is now the supreme and undisputed social arbiter of the village. Unlike Lobsang, who shuts himself up in his embittered old age, Mrs Yishe is a cheerful and sociable lady, and she is therefore generally popular.

Mingyur, the village headman, cultivates Europeans in their capacity as mechanical miracle-workers (repairers of rusty and gangrenous alarm-clocks, locks, padlocks and fountain-pens); but for Mrs Yishe Europeans are primarily purveyors of the miracles of the chemist's shop (pills, powders, injections, creams and lotions). Most Asians, in fact, tend to vary between Mingyur's view of us and Mrs Yishe's. We are not more civilized, or more profound, or even more industrious than they. But we are more surprising, more diabolical, more fortunate. We are alchemists; we have found the philosopher's stone, and have bound ourselves by secret pacts to the serpentine spirits of the lower regions. Kings and ministers of state are perfectly willing to applaud from their ring-side seats at the circus acrobatic feats which they could not possibly emulate. But, when the performance is over, the kings and ministers remain kings and ministers, while the poor acrobat, when he leaves the ring, is nobody at all. From the point of view of the inner recesses of the oriental mind, we are the poor acrobats and they are the kings and ministers. Dante, Bach, the Roman Empire, the Renaissance, Shakespeare, Leonardo, the Gothic cathedrals and St. Francis make little impression on them. But a Kodak – what a prodigious thing!

The fault is ours. Adventurers, soldiers, merchants, administrators have been to Asia – men who were either ignorant, or bigoted, or intent only on gain, or alternatively kept to themselves with little concern for "the natives". The only ones who concerned themselves with these were the missionaries; but their work – carried out, it is true, with great self-sacrifice and often with supreme heroism – was to teach a universal religion, not to present a picture of European civilization. The only nation to which we owe something in this field is the French.

One of the few Europeans who have realized the existence of this problem is Marco Pallis, who is writing a book on this subject at Kalimpong which will be invaluable to the Tibetans. Marco Pallis is Greek by origin, English by education, and speaks excellent French. He is, therefore, a European in the sense the word will have when the so-called nations of today are reduced, as they ought to be reduced, to the status of provinces in a greater, continental unity. Marco Pallis first got to know Tibet in the course of a climbing expedition a few years ago. He promptly fell in love with it, and since that time has dedicated himself exclusively to studying it. A book of his, *Peaks and Lamas*, was very successful; and he is now writing a little book, to be translated by a lama, intended to introduce the essence of European civilization to the Tibetans, whose knowledge of it is restricted to arms, the wireless, films and pills. Who else has tried to do so much for Europe in Asia? Very few. This sense of lay mission is extremely important for the mutual understanding of the peoples and for world peace; it is as important as a religious mission. So long as East and West fundamentally consider each other to be barbarians, there can be no basis for the most elementary understanding.

As for Mrs Yishe, she has no real need for any kind of pill or medicine. Her big, well-nourished frame was built to take her through the years to a healthy and dignified old age with a minimum of trouble. But to her pills are as important as a sacred rite; something both simple and mysterious, belonging partly to the world of magic (like exorcism), partly to the world of scientific wonders (like matches). If there is no illness, it is necessary to invent it. Pills and powders must be taken, and injections are absolutely essential.

Mrs Yishe, being grateful for her examination by our doctor, Colonel Moise, and for all the medicines with which the expedition has provided her, came to see us today in all her splendour as a former lady of high society in Lhasa, a city a long way from Yatung and as fabulous as Paris could possibly be from Chivasso or Rome from Piazza Armerina. Her jet-black, Mongol hair was held up and displayed by a *patruk*, a support made of wood, velvet and coral, and round her neck was an infinity of jewels. Gold and turquoises provided the keynote. The turquoises in her big earrings (*elkor*) were the colour of Alpine blue; they were bright, alive, stupendous. Her box for relics and benedictions (*ser-kau*) was of gold, studded with precious stones and turquoises. The equipment corresponding to the contents of a European woman's handbag was suspended from her left shoulder – a number of tiny, silver cosmetic appliances. Mrs Yishe had about her a value equivalent to several thousand pounds, and was naturally very proud of it.

Conversation was difficult at first, and there were a number of those painful pauses which are usual between Asians and Europeans on formal occasions, but then a happy subject was found, and it brightened. The subject was horoscopes. The Tibetan mind is continually occupied with horoscopes, which give them endless joy, hope and fear. Horoscopes are, of course, by no means an alien or unusual thing with us. I know a number of perfectly intelligent and well-informed people who frequently consult astrologers and the like before making difficult decisions. (The reader, if he considers for a moment, will find that he knows a number of believers in astrology himself.) There is a universal need to lean on something outside ourselves and to relieve the mind of the supreme burden of decision. But in Tibet it is all much simpler and more natural, and no-one is ashamed of it. Talking about horoscopes is like talking about the latest fashions or the latest film or yesterday's football match.

In working out a Western horoscope the fundamental thing is the date of birth. This establishes which constellation was then in the ascendant, and what were the relations between it and the planets. In Asia horoscopes are worked out on a different principle. (This might be the subject of a fascinating comparative study!) To understand the Asian system, it is necessary to explain that in Tibet, as in China, Japan, Korea and other Eastern countries, the calendar is divided into a sixty-year cycle. Each year of the cycle is designated by associating one of the "twelve animals" with one of the "five elements". Here is an example:

Part of the 17th Sixty-year Cycle 1987–2046

1990	Iron – horse	2001	Iron – snake
1991	Iron – sheep	2002	Water – horse
1992	Water – monkey	2003	Water – sheep
1993	Water – cock	2004	Wood – monkey
1994	Wood – dog	2005	Wood – cock
1995	Wood – boar	2006	Fire – dog
1996	Fire – rat	2007	Fire – boar
1997	Fire – ox	2008	Earth – rat
1998	Earth – tiger	2009	Earth – ox
1999	Earth – hare	2010	Iron – tiger
2000	Iron – dragon	2011	Iron – hare

A realistic significance is given to the various animals and elements, and proportions are worked out which serve as data for working out the horoscope.

There are antagonisms between certain animals, for example between the rat and the horse, the hare and the cock, the snake and the boar; and there are certain affinities among the elements. There is, for example, a "maternal" affinity between water and wood, because wood does not grow without water, which is therefore its "mother"; there are also "filial" affinities (the opposite of the preceding); "friendly" affinities (fire is the "friend" of water, because fire warms water); and "hostile" affinities (earth is the enemy of water, because earth confines water), and so on.

Other factors that have to be taken into account include time factors (the day and the hour), because there are favourable and unfavourable times. The 2nd, 14th, 18th, 20th and 26th days are always days of ill-omen, and the 9th is a good day on which to undertake a long journey, but not a short one. There also have to be taken into account certain combinations to be obtained with the 54 hexagrams (of Chinese origin), to say nothing of the influence of the constellations and the planets and the attitude of certain well-known evil spirits. Finally the *me-wa* (magic square) has to be consulted, the age reversed is calculated, and data connected with the "celestial rope" and the "terrestrial dagger" are taken into account. The whole is, of course, considered under five separate headings: life, body, power, fortune and intelligence. As the final result depends on so many variables, a Tibetan horoscope is obviously a matter of extreme complication, and naturally the lamas insist on being very well paid for it.

The Pak-jan monastery: the Six Good Things, and the little girl with the hare-lip

One of the characteristics of ancient, settled civilizations which have had a long development, and have reached – at any rate relatively – a kind of final stability, is the special significance attributed to certain numbers. In the West the classical world invented and handed down to us the Seven Wise Men, the Three Graces, the Seven Wonders of the World, the Nine Muses, and so on; Christianity added the Ten Commandments, the Four Evangelists, the seven deadly sins and four cardinal virtues, to quote only a few. In the East, Chinese civilization presents us with a whole universe as tidily and permanently arranged as the goods in a chemist's shop, with its Two Principles, Four Forms, Eight Trigrams, Four Books, Five Canons, Three Kingdoms, eight classes of spirits, six dynasties, and so on.

But we live in a world of continual change and evolution. Everything is dying and being reborn. We have, perhaps, acquired a Bergsonian sense of time and becoming, but we have certainly lost the Parmenidean sense of being and eternity. Such numbers have therefore lost their meaning for us, and there is no basis for fresh ones to establish themselves. From this point of view we read Dante with a purely archaeological interest. The only real, modern number of this kind that belongs entirely to ourselves is the ninety-two elements, but these are undergoing too much modification on the part of physicists to assume the final, rock-like stability in the mind that other spiritual or material numbers had in former centuries.

Tibetan civilization (perhaps the only civilization of another age to have survived intact into our own time) is naturally permeated with such numbers and similar symbols. I have already referred to the Eight Glorious Emblems (*thrashi te-gye*), the Twelve Animals and the Five Elements. Other important signs and symbols are the Three Gems (*Kon-chok sum*); *Senge*, *Chö*, *Gedun* (Buddha, the Law and the Community); to say nothing of the Seven Gems, the Wheel (representing the symmetry and completeness of the Law); the jewel (which procures every good thing desired); the Jasper-girl (who fans the air so that her prince may sleep and remains beside him with the constancy of a slave);

the Gem of a Minister (who ingeniously administers the affairs of the realm); the White Elephant (symbol of the sovereign power); the Horse (which perhaps symbolizes the coach of the sun, *i.e.* "a dominion over which the sun never sets"); and the Gem of a General, who throws back the forces of the enemy. Then there are the Seven Personal Gems, the Eight Glorious Offerings, the Five Sensuous Qualities, the Five Good Fortunes, the Sixteen Disciples of the Buddha, the Ten Directions of Space, the Twelve Episodes in the Life of the Buddha, the Four Truths, the Five *Dhyani* Buddhas, with which are associated the Five Colours, the Five Symbols. and the Five Vowels; you never come to the end of them.

In this, as in other cases, a student who went to the heart of the matter would find elements of Indian origin closely linked with elements of Chinese origin. Tibet, that high, remote country, lying at the heart of the biggest continent, is a living museum, and there lies its great fascination. Visiting Tibet, getting to know it, means travelling in time as well as space. It means for a brief while living as a contemporary of Dante or Boccaccio, Charles d'Orléans or Jean de Meung; breathing the air of another age, and learning by direct experience how our ancestors of twenty or twenty-five generations ago thought, lived and loved.

Today, when I visited the Pak-jan monastery, near Yatung, I discovered the existence of a number which I did not know; that of the Six Good Things – nutmeg, cloves, saffron, cardamom, camphor and sandalwood. An old lama of the monastery happened to mention them while I was sipping a cup of Tibetan tea, which always tastes abominably of smoke.

Pak-jan is very near Yatung – barely a quarter-of-an-hour away. First you go northwards, mounting the caravan route, and then cross a little bridge, passing over a torrent and a tiny pond full of magnificently green water-plants; then you climb a steep slope and see above you, on a small piece of level ground, the group of houses of which the so-called "monastery" consists. It was so unlike what such places in Tibet are supposed to be like that it is worth while describing.

At first sight you would think you had come to a farmhouse. The stones in the yard had been worn by generations of footsteps and threshing; there were goats and sheep, and cows going to and coming from the grazing. Rakes, shovels, stakes were leaning against the wall. A big Tibetan dog, which was chained, kept on barking, till one of the family came out and told it to be quiet.

Yes, one of the family. The monastery belongs to the *Nima-pa* sect ("the Ancient Ones") and is inhabited only by an old lama, his wife – a little woman who is all bows and smiles – and five or six sons and daughters who work in the fields and take the beasts to pasture. There is always something moving about the combination of husbandry and religion. Is not the raising of plants and animals the continuation of God's work? That may be true in the abstract, but the impression made on the visitor to Pak-jan by the lama of the place was far less elevating.

I do not say he was a bad man, but his lined, discontented face betrayed a long-standing, bitter grudge against life. Perhaps he had had a vocation and lost it; or perhaps he had never had a vocation, but became a lama just as one might become a trader or a clerk. Perhaps he had ambition, and now felt himself a failure in this remote and inaccessible spot. I do not know. On my first visit he received me coldly, but after I gave him a tip he became servile.

He must have been about sixty, and he was tall, dirty, slovenly and clumsy, with long, rapacious hands and long, filthy finger-nails. His woollen robe was greasy, worn, and covered with stains, and he kept a whole store of things between the folds of the material and his chest. His expression was that of a suffering cab-horse which still had enough spirit left to bite. Strangely enough, however, his family was immediately likeable. The eldest son, who was aged about twenty, was a strong-looking lad, almost clean-looking, with a high forehead and intelligent eyes, and the eldest daughter was pretty. There was a whole series of other boys and girls, down to a little girl of three, who had a pronounced hare-lip, which completely spoiled her face. Every now and then the old man picked up the poor little thing and cuddled her. A look of unexpected tenderness then came into his dead-looking eyes.

"Can one visit the *lha-kang* (the house of the god, the temple)?" I asked.

"Certainly, certainly, come this way."

The old man led the way. We mounted two steps, went through a gateway and entered a dark, damp little yard on to which the kitchen opened. The lama disappeared and returned a moment later with some very beautiful Tibetan keys in one hand and a handful of roasted seeds in the other. He offered me the supposed delicacy.

"Take some," he said. "They're good for you!"

They may have been good for me, but they stank of staleness and rancid butter. I had no alternative but to accept some from that grimy hand, the slightest lines of which were ingrained with black.

The temple was a big room next to the kitchen. The heavy wooden door, which creaked when it opened, might have been the door of a granary or of a storeroom in which fruit was put to ripen or demijohns of olive oil were kept. But when the lama lit a tiny lamp there glimmered at the other extremity of the great, cavernous hall the gold of a dusty statue, covered with ceremonial shawls which were all falling to pieces. It was a statue of Padma Sambhava, the sage who introduced Buddhism into Tibet in the eighth century and is an object of particular veneration to the "ancient" sects. Beside it were other statues, and there were big frescoes on the walls, representing ascetics with tigers on the leash and esoteric gods engaged in mystic embraces. From the ceiling there hung masks, sashes and pictures painted on silk.

Everything in the place was old, smelling of rancid butter and space that had been enclosed for ages. It was all falling slowly to pieces and turning to fine dust, which went up one's nose and mouth and subtly made one cough. The pictures, barely lit by the priest's tiny candle, took the mind into the fantastic metaphysical empyreans of lamaism, so remote in one sense from the farmyard outside, the kitchen next door, the cows, the farming implements, the ordinary, simple, everyday things outside, the children playing and chasing each other (I could hear their voices) between a pile of turnips and the sheafs of straw. But there they were, the last, over-ripe fruit of thousands of years of subtle intellectual labour; Dorje Sem-pa ("Whose essence is lightning"), the personification of the Original Principle of the Universe, sitting erect and rigid in the ritual position of meditation, while his own Female Energy, holding in her left hand a skull full of blood, clothed in fluttering, precious robes and glittering with gold and jewels, abandoned herself with an infinite, divine voluptuousness to his arms, which were active as if in dance . . .

"Papa! Papa!" whined a small child who had crept noiselessly into the temple on bare feet. "Mama says she can't find the key for the flour. Have you got it on your ring? Mama wants it!"

The tired old lama, with an expression of unspeakable boredom, searched for a long time between his robe and his chest. Then he found the key and gave it to the child, who disappeared.

On either side of the mystic pair of cosmic lovers were a number of supremely Tantric representations of Padma Sambhava, in the form of ascetics surrounded by flames, engaged in meditation or escorted by wild beasts. They were fine pictures, having a strange, intoxicating force; they were among the best in the valley.

"Can I take a photograph?" I asked.

The lama immediately realized that I had admitted his prerogative in the matter, and that he was therefore in a position to ask me for something in return. His eyes brightened, and his long, filthy fingers became animated.

"All right," he said, "but leave something . . . *shomé* . . . for the lamps."

The magnesium flash startled him violently. After a moment's terrified silence, he unexpectedly turned on me in a towering rage.

"Get outside!" he shouted. "Go away from here! Don't you realize you've been disrespectful to the saints? The sudden light must have terrified them, and they'll revenge themselves! And on whom? Not on you, because you'll be a long way away! They'll revenge themselves on us, don't you understand . . ."

The tone of his voice was already dropping and turning into a whine.

"They'll revenge themselves on us, I tell you, and we'll have to pay because of you, all because of your imprudence . . ."

His voice had dropped completely and become abject.

"Give me another two rupees because of the flame photograph!" he finished up.

The whole *gompá*, the lama's house, the temple, the apartments of honour, must have known much better times. Perhaps that accounted for the lama's mean, grasping: behaviour. Nothing is more humiliating and degrading than continued lack of money. Any man subjected to it for a long time, condemned to impotence in the face of the slow disintegration of things, ends by degenerating and becoming brutalized. We went up to the first floor, where there were a number of chapels and the apartments of honour. The Maharajah of Sikkim was the patron of the place, and everything up here was pretty well looked after. While I sipped a cup of tea from a jade cup the lama disappeared. He reappeared soon afterwards with something hidden under his robe. With an air of great secrecy he produced a carved wooden mask, painted in bright colours. It was ugly, and in any case he asked me a crazy price, so I didn't even consider it.

We went on talking for a while. From the ornaments on a silver vase we jumped to the Seven Gems, and from there to the Six Good Things. I could tell that the old lama was pondering other ways and means of extracting a little money from me. Nets of that kind can be spread with style and dignity, but he had neither the one nor the other, and besides he was dirty, slovenly, ugly and depressing.

The door opened and the little girl with the hare-lip came in, with her thumb in her mouth and a green apple in her hand. The old man picked her up and held her to his chest, and his eyes moistened.

"Haven't you got a medicine, you who have so many medicines, for her mouth?" he said. "Now you hardly notice it, but when she's older no-one will want to marry her, and she'll be very unhappy . . . It's sad, sad!"

We went downstairs again. As we passed through the temple door the lama took me aside and whispered in my ear:

"If you give me a little more money, you can take another photograph with the flame!"

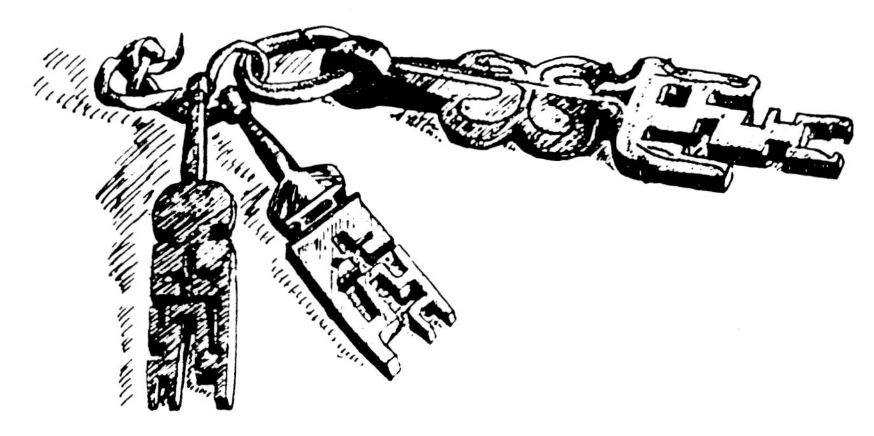

26 *Tibetan wrought-iron keys (shown full-size)*

Reconsideration, 1998

Let us start with the little which we are sure of. Yatung (today Yadong) has become a major military post on China's border with India. The village is now a proper town with a greatly increased population: the Chinese presence, which used to be negligible, is now huge. Communication with Gangtok and Kalimpong in India may be exceedingly difficult for obvious political reasons, but in purely technical terms it is well established thanks to bold new roads that cross the Natu and the Jelep passes (both around 14,000 feet). A major road that follows the old caravan route now connects Yatung with Gyantse/Jangzi via Phari/Pari, the Tang pass (about 15,000 feet) and Kangma(r); turning east from Gyantse the road makes for Lhasa; turning west, it goes to Shigatse. It appears that recently another road has been built, supporting a line of defence, as it were, that gives Yatung a direct connection with Shigatse via Khampa (Dzong); it first runs along the valley at the foot of the 23,000ft Mount Pauhunri. This massive human input will have profoundly affected the landscape with cuttings and embankments and hairpin bends, given the notable relief features to be tackled. It will no longer be the cries of the drovers urging on their yaks and mules, that break the age old silence but the rumble and thud of engines, and the pure air of times past will now be blessed with the equivocal stenches and acid odours of "civilization".

As for the inhabitants in whose patriarchal company we had spent so many carefree weeks, the question arises: how will they have fared in the great storm? Will they have found some refuge, or will they have been caught up in the fury of the elements? When a Communist regime takes power in your own country it is attended by a social upheaval that inevitably, for some at any rate, must mean penury, fear and danger. But when it is a foreign invasion that brings in the change of regime, and when that invasion is resisted, everything becomes enormously more complicated and, as may well be understood, infinitely more painful. The battle arising out of economic and ideological factors is overlaid, compounded by primitive and often frightening emotions and resentments that arise out of ethnic, racial, religious and linguistic frictions, the clash of often conflicting views of life, hatreds exacerbated by history, reciprocal scorn and mistrust. So what surges up is not simply a new economic system but all the ingredients of civil war. In the case of Tibet the clash was (and to some extent continues to be) all the more savage and ugly on account of the fanatical hatred that always boils up when people are fighting for and against a religion, when the destruction acquires the perverse flavour of desecration, and the slaying of an adversary unconsciously meshes with secret ancestral rites involving a sacrifice offered to one's god.

Among the great number of ghastly news stories that keep filtering out via refugees, there is this one too: those condemned to death for whatever form of resistance to the Chinese (and in this respect Tibetan nationalism may have nothing whatever to do with Communism) had their vocal chords severed to prevent them at the last moment shouting out phrases in honour of some ideal.[1]

In a framework such as this nothing can be predicted: wealth or influence is no protection against stumbling into arbitrary responses, into violence, rage, vengeance; the most dire fate can befall the sorriest wretch, one who never took advantage of anything or anyone, while the man who really did have his just deserts coming to him gets away scot free or even gets a leg up. If I were told that Mrs Yishe and Lobsang had escaped to safety in Bhutan or Sikkim at the first whiff of an ill wind, I should not be the least surprised. Tob-chen will assuredly have kept the world at bay. But good old Mingyur and Lama Ngawang will have been trapped and destroyed. How I should like to reconnect those tenuous threads of human contact with the good old days! But obviously this is impossible.[2]

If it is true, as the Central Office of the Dalai Lama advises from Dharamsala, that in the thirty-three years of the Chinese occupation (1950–1983) as many as 1,278,387 Tibetans died[3] either by violence or from privations, and even assuming that the figure is exaggerated (chiefly through the duplication of accounts given by refugees) and the number were halved to 600,000, we are still looking at some ten per cent of the population of Tibet, a fearful hecatomb.

It would be much as if five or six million Italians had been wiped out in a great, disastrous, protracted social upheaval. In a country like Tibet, in which the nobles, the rich, the prelates made up barely some tens of thousands in the population, what this means is – as is evident from research among the 100,000 and more refugees in India, Nepal and elsewhere – that virtually the entire population of Tibet, at one time or another, was persecuted, hounded and subjected to the most barbarous and savage treatment.

It is well known that poor woodcutters, herdsmen, peasants, even penniless labourers were beaten mercilessly if they were found in possession of religious images, if they showed respect towards the lamas, if they did anything to celebrate the feasts of the Buddhist calendar.[4] Not everyone succeeded in controlling himself in such circumstances, the less so when it was a foreigner who abused his power. One might now and then have got away with reacting, but usually it meant being targeted, suffering reprisals, being interned in one of the concentration camps in which many were to spend fifteen or twenty years before being freed.

It was lucky for the Chinese that all this happened in remote valleys and sparsely populated plateaux, protected and cushioned by boundless space, and the victims were people who had no experience of contact with the outside world. It took years to make even the roughest sketch of the vast tragedy undergone by the people of Tibet, especially in the decade 1966–1976.

1 *Tibetan Review*, January 1985

2 See on page 82 what was said about the fortuitous new contact with the living *Bodhisattva* Lama Ngawang Lobsang, whom I knew in 1948 as a nine-year-old boy (page 79) and met again as a man approaching sixty in the USA in 1999!

3 *Tibetan Review*, March 1984, p. 7. The total breaks down as:

died in prison or labour camps	174,138
executions	156,758
died in battle	432,607
died of starvation	413,151
died under torture	92,731
suicides	9,002
	1,278,387

4 See for instance the many cases recorded in *Le Tibet et la République populaire de Chine*, Commission internationale de juristes, Geneva, 1960.

7

Metaphysics and Politics in Upper Asia

The Dung-kar monastery: "Who is your protective deity?"

Champa is a young *trapa* (monk) and is studying theology. He lives in the Dung-kar ("White Conch") monastery, a little way to the north of Yatung.[1] He is about twenty years old, he is tall and thin, and, as he belongs to the Yellow Sect, the *Gelug-pa* ("The Virtuous"), he keeps the hair of his head closely shaven. His skin is naturally encrusted with the perennial and universal Tibetan dirt. He is delicate in health, takes an interest in many things, was born in Sikkim, talks a little English, and in his youth was a Christian – I do not know whether Protestant or not. He reminds me a great deal of some of the Japanese students with whom I lived for so long. He has the same pathetic good will, the same tragic lack of direction and personality, the same emotional and intellectual extravagances, the same reverential fear in the face of any kind of superior.

Champa comes to see me every now and then with books. We translate Tibetan songs together, he explains Tibetan phrases and expressions to me, tells me about his life and, above all, asks me questions about the outside world, about which he is shyly but intelligently inquisitive. He doesn't confine himself to questions such as "What do you eat?" or "What are your houses like?" Yesterday he asked me: "Are the people of your country more fortunate and happy (*thrashi-pa*), or are the people here?"

It is a difficult question to answer. Happiness obviously does not depend on greater technical complications, and obviously one can be happy with very little and wretched in the midst of abundance. Each civilization must have its own typical, average man, however hard it may be to define him, and on that basis it should be possible to make comparisons. I should say without hesitation that the Tibetans of the Trommò valley have a thousand reasons to consider themselves more fortunate and happy than the poorer inhabitants of the big cities of Europe. They are not rich, but neither are they poor. They have no newspapers, wireless or cinemas, but they have professional story-tellers, wandering minstrels and a popular theatre, and in the fine season they can go for excursions along the rivers, drink *chang* and sing until late at night. Finally they live in a profoundly stable society, in which relations between individuals, between individuals and the community, between man and the universe, are a solid reality, which nobody either doubts or insists on.

The other day Champa suddenly asked me: "Who is your *yi-dam*?" ("Who is your protective deity?") In Tibet not only does every sect, every order, every monastery, have one protective deity or more, but every individual lives under the constant protection of his own personal protective deity. He may have chosen his *yi-dam* for himself, but more probably his *yi-dam* will have been indicated to him by his *guru*, or spiritual director. (*Guru* is a Sanskrit word, possibly related to the same root as the Latin *gravis*.) Champa's question struck me for two reasons. In the first place, I have no particular *yi-dam* (though, if I had to choose, I think my choice would fall upon Dü-kor, "the Wheel of Time"; because what is more mysterious than time? Eternity is intelligible, I should say obvious, as is being. But the really insoluble puzzles are time and becoming, the world, the multiple and the finite). In the second place the question interested me because it reflected Champa's conception of life.

A man is in the first place the universe that he carries about inside him. Every one of us has, or rather is, such a universe; whether big or small, simple or complicated, childish and imaginative or mature and analytical, no-one is without one. Our inner universe takes shape slowly in childhood, in the course of our upbringing and education, and is permeated through and through, to its profoundest depths, by the civilization which nourishes us. There is no such thing as "natural" man; there is only "civilized" man. We are Europeans, not only because we use concepts such as right, romanticism or parliament, or because of our reactions when confronted with the naked human form or the doctrine of the transmigration of souls, but because we walk like Europeans, make love like Europeans, hail a friend on the other side of the street like Europeans. For a time, believing that Champa and I, because we used the same vocabulary, spoke the same language, I was led astray, but this question was like a sudden ray of light illuminating an otherwise invisible abyss.

Champa has often invited me to visit the Dung-kar monastery, and today I decided to spend the day there, and eat with the lamas. It is a big monastery, fairly recently built, and rises over the untidy stones of an ancient moraine that blocks the valley of Trommò. Above the moraine there must once have been a lake, but this has completely disappeared, leaving a long, green plain (*Ling-ma-tang*), which serves as pasture for herds of yak. Steep bare mountains rise all round, and in the distance you see snow peaks gleaming in the sun. It is, in short, a place of great romantic beauty, where the mind can be profoundly moved.

Ling-ma-tang: who shall speak to us of the inner life of the secret?

When I was within a quarter of an hour of the monastery I came upon a number of young monks gathering strawberries; Champa was among them. I don't know why, but he always looks slightly out of place in the company of other young men. He was gathering strawberries with the air of one construing a difficult text.

"Bravo!" he said when he greeted me. "You have done well to come at last. But we are not at the *gompá*; we are staying down here for a week's holiday. The Rimpoche (the little living *Bodhisattva*) is here too, and wants to see you. Have you brought the medicines? There are many who want them!"

Where the Ling-ma plain began we found a whole encampment, consisting of those little white tents of Chinese origin, with big blue flourishes on them for ornament, in which the Tibetans delight in spending the fine summer weather in contact with nature, resting, eating, drinking and singing. If they are monks, they also set aside hours for reading and meditation; if laymen, they dance and flirt, while the children run about or squabble for biscuits. Does this love of camping represent the survival of a custom among a people who were nomads up to not so many centuries ago? Very probably it does. Thousands of years have to pass before a characteristic propensity of a civilization finally disappears. The peoples of the Mediterranean have been cultivators and town-dwellers for many more centuries than the peoples of northern Europe. That is why the natural centre of life in south European countries is the *agora*, the market-place, while in the north the need to have frequent contacts with nature is still so very much alive.

As soon as we reached the camp I was made to sit down in a tent, open at one side, in the place allotted to guests. Soon afterwards the father superior arrived, with his three assistants – the father superior who would direct the monastery until the little Incarnated One reached the age of eighteen. After the usual greetings, tea was brought in. The father superior was an elderly man, inclined to stoutness. He was bald, and had small, sharp eyes. The lower part of his face clearly indicated strong will and practical sense. He was no mystic, but a conscientious administrator and an efficient upholder of monastic discipline.

One of his assistants immediately struck me because of his un-Mongolian features. As soon as the conversation permitted, I asked him where he came from. "From Ladak," he replied. In other words, he came from western Tibet. He had a distinctly Caucasian caste of countenance, so to speak; he might have been a south Italian peasant. He was tall, dark-haired, olive-skinned, with a big nose and big eyes and, so far as I could judge, a dolichocephalic skull. The fundamental difference between the Mongolian and the Western face is that in the former the flesh is modelled compactly on the bones, while the skin of the latter is slacker, forms folds, hollows, valleys. An aged Mongol can be very lined, but the lines are creases in, not undulations of, his facial landscape.

The father superior suffered from rheumatism, and described his symptoms in detail. Fortunately Colonel Moise had examined him several days previously, and I had brought with me the medicines he had prescribed. A week of camp life in a meadow which was damp by day and dripping wet at night was not likely to help him, and I told him so. But he said he couldn't help it. "We are on holiday, you see." Other monks with other complaints asked permission to come in. They complained of indigestion or toothache, and one had an infected spot on his knee in short their complaints were mostly trivial. Colonel Moise says that on the whole the health of the inhabitants of the valley is excellent. The only disease that works havoc every now and then is smallpox. The Tibetans are very much afraid of it, but are only just beginning to be vaccinated.

Champa, who had disappeared for a time, returned to the tent and announced that the Rimpoche was ready to see me. We went out. The little *Bodhisattva* was seated outside a tent, on a small throne of cushions. In front of him was a carved and gilded wooden table, with a jade tea-cup, a *dorje* (bronze thunder-bolt) and various other liturgical objects. The abbot sat beside him. He too had a throne of cushions and a little table, but both were slightly lower than those of the Rimpoche. The height at which one sits has enormous importance in Tibet. No-one, for instance, is allowed to sit higher than the Dalai Lama. Only when the Dalai Lama is a minor is his theological instructor allowed on certain occasions to occupy a seat higher than his. I offered a silk sash to the little Precious One, and then squatted to one side.

Some pilgrims had arrived from the country and the mountains, to pay homage to the Incarnated One, bearing gifts. Men and women prostrated themselves before the little throne, then crept forward, rose, without looking the little god in the face, and placed their offering – generally money or butter – in his hands. The child immediately handed it to the abbot.

There really was something divine about Ngawang Lobsang Choden, though in a sense different from that which there might have been for the nomads or shepherds who prostrated themselves before him. It was the divinity of the dawn, of newly-opened flowers, of all the things that contain the beauty and mystery of burgeoning life. I watched him for several minutes. The thing that so movingly illumined his child's face, the look in his eyes, was his unquestioned awareness of being a god, his complete faith in the myth, his absolutely certain knowledge of having come down to earth on a mission of mercy, the continuous joy of playing a part in a just and marvellous fairy-tale. He did not make a movement that was vulgar or ostentatious. There was no flicker of doubt or hesitation in anything he did. It was all completely and perfectly natural.

How much I should have liked to have been able to follow the child's inner development, to find out about the first doubts that were bound one day to cast a shadow over his mind, to share the pain that must inevitably accompany the collapse of that delightful fiction! How would it happen? Would it come as a single, heart-breaking blow, from the love of a girl, an illness, the reading of a book? Or would it be a slow, inexorable process? And then what would happen? What would be left? Opportunism, perhaps. ("Life has given me this enviable position; let me take advantage of it.") Or perhaps a truly religious feeling. ("It is not for me to judge, but no matter, I can do good.")

The pilgrims went away. The little *Bodhisattva* covered his head with a tall hat of yellow silk, lined with many-coloured Chinese brocade, and I took some photographs. Then, with complete naturalness, he removed his hat and handed it to a monk, who took it with signs of almost exaggerated reverence, descended from his little throne, removed his ceremonial garments, called a companion of his own age, and had himself brought a ball.

"Come," he said to me. "Would you like to play? Teach me how to play ball!"

I was a stranger, I did not count, he need have no inhibitions in front of me. So we played ball. Ngawang Lobsang Choden who, sitting on his throne a few minutes earlier, had been thousands of years old, with an infinity of lives behind him, who had renounced *nirvana* and had deliberately returned to be reincarnated on earth for the good of mankind, had turned into a happy, high-spirited boy, red-cheeked and out of breath from running about.

The Dung-kar monastery: monstrous couplings protect the meditating doctor

My intended visit to the Dung-kar monastery the other day stopped short at the Ling-ma-tang, but the "summer holiday" of the little *Bodhisattva* of Trommò is now over, and the monks have all gone back to the *gompá*, the monastery. I was assured of the fact by Champa, who came to fetch me, so at eight o'clock this morning we set out from Yatung, talking busily.

The road followed the bottom of the valley, and all along the torrent thickets of roses were in glorious bloom. Every now and then we came upon a *tarcho* singing in the wind, or saw a *chorten* or a *mendang*. *Mendangs* are sacred walls, containing the ashes of dead lamas, liturgical objects, relics of various kinds, or the scriptures. On top of them stand long rows of stones, crudely carved to represent the most popular divinities – the Buddha Amitābha or the Buddha Akshobhya, the *Bodhisattva* Avalokitesvara or the *Bodhisattva* Manjusri, the *Manushi* Buddha Sakya-Muni or Maitreya, besides terrifying male or female figures, among whom Vajrapani is the most common and Vajravarahi is frequently to be met.

For a while the road continued between vertical walls of rock, on which there were sacred carvings (the biggest represented Padma Sambhava). *Om mani padme hum* was also painted hundreds of times in vivid colours. You can never get away from signs of religion in Tibet. Nearly every caravan driver whom we met had his *kau* (for relics) with him, and wore a small talisman round his neck, even if he were brazenly smoking a cigarette. Many caravans were to be seen on their way down to India with loads of wool. Wool is the chief Tibetan export. It provides the Government with a certain amount of dollars, which it uses for the purpose of slowly (and for the time being wisely) modernizing the country. Lhasa already has a power station, a hospital is projected and bridges are being built. The only thing they draw the line at is proper road-building and the introduction of power-driven vehicles. If these were admitted, they say, what would happen to the mule-drivers? The truth of the matter is that the Tibetans prefer isolation and independence to communications and inevitable subjection. Given the world as it is today, it is difficult to blame them.

We came across the ruins of the old Chinese military station, which fell into decay after 1904, when the British military expedition led by Colonel Younghusband penetrated to Lhasa. China seems infinitely remote from here, but every good Chinese still considers that these villages are part of China. [Alas, all too prophetic, considering what was to happen in 1951!]

We left the caravan-route on our right and went down to the little village of Galigang, consisting of about forty houses, lying among well-kept barley fields. There are many variations in the local architecture, which is pleasing in its rustic style. The walls are built of stone and earth, with a huge wooden roof and big, wooden-framed windows. The walls are whitewashed, and the timber of the architraves, the roofs, the windows and the doors acquires a good, honest, brown patina in the course of time.

From Galigang we continued our descent to the stream, and then started climbing again up a steep path that wound its way between rocks and thickets. There were endless strawberries, and roses in bloom. Champa climbed slowly; his health is poor, and he has to avoid fatigue. Every now and then we stopped, looked down at the valley, and exchanged a few words. A frightened horse, its ears erect, dashed past us downhill, and disappeared. Then a boy carrying a stick appeared, very out of breath. "Your horse is down there!" Champa shouted.

When we finally reached the monastery we were met with a furious barking of dogs. Tibetan watch-dogs are enormous, ferocious beasts; fortunately they are chained in the daytime. We went down an entrance passage and came to a big courtyard surrounded by wooden cloisters. The entrances to all the temples are in the courtyard, which also serves as a threshing-floor. A monk was unloading sacks of grain from a horse, and a number of farming implements were lying about. The monastery, like all those of the Yellow Sect, receives big subsidies from Lhasa, mostly in kind, and it possesses land of its own, which the monks either cultivate themselves or lease to farmers.

Two lay craftsmen were working at the entrance of the biggest temple. One was stamping out clay statues of various divinities; these, after being dried and painted, were to be sold to the faithful. The other was a painter, who was engaged in touching up the frescoes. In one corner of the courtyard some carpenters were noisily sawing and hammering at some tables. Clouds of blue smoke were pouring through the kitchen door. A young monk, wearing a big, shiny black apron of indescribable filthiness, appeared at the door with a huge saucepan, which he hung on the wall in the sun.

Champa had disappeared, having gone to fetch the custodian. While I waited a number of students surrounded me and started excitedly shouting: "*Par! Par!*" ("Photograph! Photograph!") Champa returned with the custodian, and we mounted a few steps to the portico to be found outside every Tibetan temple. The walls were completely covered with frescoes. I recognized the Four Kings of the Directions of Space, as well as the Two Protectors, Vajrapani (Chanadorje) and Hayagriva (Tamdrin) in their terrifying form, next to the door – see Glossary under *Lokapala*. The Four Kings (Gyal-chen de-shi) are mythical figures who are to be found associated with the Buddha legend in the earliest known documents. Paintings of them in India, in the great *stupa* of Sanchi, date back to the second century B.C. The Tibetans like painting them as warriors, following models from Central Asia, each one of them in his own colours and with his own symbols. Kuvera (the north) is yellow, holds a banner in his right hand and a mongoose in his left. Virudhaka (the south) is either green or blue; his symbol is a sword, and on his head, instead of a helmet, he wears an elephant's head. Dhritarashtra (the East) is white, and plays the lute, and Virupaksha (the West) is red, and carries a little *chorten* in his hand. These figures rarely have any individuality; they are generally lost in a maze of colour, ornament, and symbols, having a most lively decorative effect, like tapestry.

Every style is a language, and every language has to be learnt. When, in the course of time, one has grown accustomed to this idiom of lines and colours, the finest examples of the paintings in which the Four Kings appear strike one as the expression of a tumultuous joy in the lovely, rich, transient things of the world. Generally, of course, these paintings have a mere decorative purpose (similar to those of the king, queen and jack in a pack of cards), or succumb to the grotesque (an ever-present danger to Tibetan art). But when the artist takes fullest advantage of the traditional pattern, the Four Kings present him with a notable opportunity for celebrating the glorious but relatively commonplace themes of life as strength, achievement, abundance, and of avoiding the two Tibetan poles of horror on the one hand and ascetic mysticism on the other. The Four Kings, clad in shining armour, sit in their flowery gardens, among flags, musical instruments, arms, gifts, jewels, corals, silks, precious stuffs, heraldic animals and symbolic ribbons, making music with lutes, flying banners, playing with exotic animals, secure lords of a distant, golden age.

All the dreams of Tibetan merchants and brigands are expressed on these walls – wealth and the pleasures of this world, which Buddhist teaching condemns as vain, harmful and sinful. It is interesting to note that the Japanese, who resemble the Tibetans in many ways, but are more martial, have always emphasized the sculptural (in form) and threatening (in character) side of the Four Kings (whom they call Shi-tenno). In other words, they emphasize strength and action rather than colour and abundance.

The inside of the temple is enormous and, as usual, dark, mysterious, impressive; a place of secret, perhaps obscene, perhaps cruel and bloodthirsty, rites. But there was nothing of all that now. Three boys were running about between the long benches. One had a biscuit and the others were noisily trying to get it away from him. The custodian, a wizened man of about fifty, his face marked by smallpox, called out: "Quiet!" and the boys ran away in terror. At the end of the temple were some huge gilded statues. In the centre stood Maitreya (Champa), the Buddha of the future, the apostle of the fifth *kalpa*, and next to him was Tsongkhapa (1357–1419), the founder of the Yellow Sect. There were several lesser statues, among them one of the Trommò *Geshe* (the doctor of Trommò), who had been reincarnated ten years ago in the person of our little friend Ngawang Lobsang Choden.

It is very obvious that the Yellow Sect (*Gelug-pa*) is the most powerful religious institution in Central Asia. Its temples are better tended, their fabric is kept in better repair, their pictures are (only too often) not only retouched, but completely repainted, and all the liturgical objects are of great richness. Here, for example, were enormous, solid silver cup-lamps for burning butter in, and there was one that certainly weighed several pounds. Tibetan goldsmiths' work

27 *Temple at Galigang, Trommò valley: statue of Buddha displaying* vitarka mudra, *the "gesture of the exposition of the Law"*

is beautiful, barbaric, slightly opaque, with reddish gleams in it; it is gold worthy of Agamemnon's treasure or Theodoric's breastplate. It has nothing in common with the cold, scientific, gleaming golden ornaments worn by ladies in Europe. You really feel that it is the sacred treasure of the earth, and you understand at once why the extraction of gold is forbidden in Tibet. "The fields lose their fertility – if the gold is extracted," they say. Next to the principal temple, in a chapel which was lighter than usual – it was a new one – lay the body of the Doctor of Trommò, embalmed and buried in a high *chorten* completely enclosed in silver. The paintings round the walls were not yet finished. The general effect was pompous, macabre and rather vulgar.

The paintings in the principal temple were modern too, but they were the work of a painter who was at least occasionally inspired. When you talk about Tibetan painting in Europe, people generally turn up their noses if you mention anything more recent than the eighteenth century. That is a mistake. The old artistic tradition is very much alive in Tibet; the cultural context on which pictorial expression is nourished is robust and vigorous. In the West the Romantic movement has led us into a cult of personality, an often absurd worship of personality, and we therefore view with suspicion the phenomenon of artists who use, not a specially created individual idiom, but an idiom that has been breathed in and assimilated with century-old traditions. This is a prejudice on our part, and it is this prejudice that we should suspect, rather than the capacity of living artists to express themselves and create works of value in an anonymous grammar and syntax.

Two of these frescoes were particularly striking. The first is to be found on the great wall of the Chö-kyong ("Protectors of the Faith") series; these are monstrous and terrifying champions of religion and virtue, surrounded by blood and fire in their perennial struggle with evil. It represents the two Shin-kyong skeletons engaged in an orgiastic embrace. The *motif* of the mystic embrace is here applied to the two skeleton companions of Yama, the king of death and the infernal regions; a tremendous invention in which lamaism has perhaps reached the extreme limits of its macabre fantasy. The artist put the ferocity of a jaguar and the sensuality of a Bacchante into his conception of the theme. But he possessed a strength superior to the fable with which he was dealing, for he treated it with detachment, with a clear, scientific line, as if he were composing a design with acanthuses and lilies instead of with bones and lust.

Champa, and the seminarists – who had crept back quietly into the temple – followed me while I took my photographs. I tried to find out whether these pictures raised any emotion in them, and, if so, what kind of emotion, but it was a difficult task. They seemed completely indifferent. The boys were absorbed in examination of my camera, a far more mysterious thing to them than Tantric emanations. Champa explained the meaning of the pictures to me, but in the tone of a guide saying: "On the right is St. John with the eagle, and underneath St. Catherine with her wheel and martyr's palm." Perhaps they see with eyes very different from ours. I always remember how struck I was by the remark of a Japanese friend, who one day said to me: "What a bloodthirsty, violent religion yours must be, with that tortured man suspended from two pieces of wood on every altar!" Europeans and Americans, born in a Christian environment and brought up to accept it as a religion of love, have been inoculated by centuries of familiarity against the cruel first impression made by the crucifix, and a reaction such as that of my Japanese Buddhist friend, whose conception of the divine was contemplative serenity, takes us completely by surprise. But to hear such a startlingly different point of view is a valuable and important experience.

Another notable item among these paintings is that part of them which contains a stylized and idealized portrait of the Doctor of Trommò, who died little more than ten years ago. The sage, wearing his brownish robe and yellow mitre and holding in his hands two heraldic lotuses, out of which there grew a sword and a book, was sitting absorbed in profound meditation, while in a nimbus all round him Tantric deities in their terrifying aspect danced, clasping their *shakti*s in orgiastic embraces and copulating with the perfection of a metaphysical rite, adorned with jewels, wearing the skins of wild beasts over their shoulders and with snakes round their waists and holding in their hands scimitars, skulls, blood-covered corpses, thunderbolts, hearts newly plucked from living bodies, lightning flashes, hangmen's nooses, sceptres, rosaries and flowers.

These were the Dharmapala, the Chyö-kyong, the "Protectors of the Faith" of the *Gelug-pa* sect. On the left there was a dark-blue Dü-kor ("Wheel of Time") with twenty-four arms and three heads. His *shakti*, who had eight arms was coloured yellow. She too was standing, abandoning herself to him with head thrown backwards. The pair of mystic lovers were trampling on dead bodies symbolizing conquered passions, in their dance. To their right, also standing and painted in blue, was Dem-chog ("Renowned Felicity"), with twelve arms. His *shakti* was nude, but adorned with innumerable jewels, and in her hands she held a ritual dagger and a skull. Still farther to the right, but lower down, was Dorje Chi-che ("Terrifying Lightning"), the martial aspect of Manjusri (the divine substance of wisdom) and lamaism's supreme effort in monstrosity. He was represented with sixteen legs, thirty-four arms and nine heads, trampling on animals, while he drew to himself a *shakti* who held in her left hand a bloodfilled skull-cup. In the middle of his forest of arms, his liturgical objects, necklaces of skulls, legs, animals, jewels, sexual organs and skins of wild beasts, there stood out, clear, grotesque and monstrous, his central bull's head, with flames for hair, with the third eye of mystic wisdom, and above his head, as a crest, the small head of Manjusri. The Divine Doctor, protected by these and other champions of the faith in terrifying splendour and horrific glory, meditated angelically, crowned by a halo of little white clouds and rainbows.

"*Kushog*," a student came and said to me, drawing me aside by the arm, "the abbot has rheumatism. He wants you to come and give him the medicine you promised. Besides, tea is ready. Come quickly!"

I asked Champa why *Bodhisattva*s and celestial Buddhas in their terrifying aspect were painted thus, in intimate union with their own *shakti*s; I was curious to hear what the popular interpretation of the deep and complicated Tantric symbolism might be.

28 *Yamantaka (Dorje-chi-che in Tibetan), the annihilator, the conqueror of Yama, "the Lord of Death". Here he is shown in terrifying aspect, in a mystic embrace* (yab-yum) *with his* shakti.

"They are more effective if worshipped so," he replied in his curious English.

"More effective because they are happier like that?"

"Yes, that is the reason."

I wanted to go to the rheumatic abbot straight away, but Champa insisted on my first visiting the smaller temple on the other side of the courtyard. "There's no hurry," he said. "He won't get rid of his pains at once anyway, he always has them." This temple had interesting genealogies of lamas painted on the walls, but the most notable thing in it, from one point of view, was a lacquered, polished, wooden statue of the new divinity, Namka-bazin, in his terrifying aspect. The history of this new and entirely local divinity gives some idea of how alive and creative Tibetan Buddhism still is, even in its less elevated, popular, superstitious forms. In 1920 or thereabouts a lama, after receiving his fee for teaching in Sikkim, set out to return to Tibet with the money. But in a gorge near Phari he was waylaid by an evil acquaintance of his who knew about the money and tried to wrest it from him. The lama refused to surrender it, and the result was a struggle, in which the unfortunate lama was killed. When a just man is killed, according to Tibetan superstition, he acquires extraordinary evil powers, and he has to be continually propitiated. In a few years the cult of this lama spread throughout the valley of Trommò, and statues and pictures of him are frequently to be found. He also appears as one of the principal characters in masked dances at various places, at Kirimtse, for instance.

"Aren't you coming, *kushog*?" the seminarist kept whining, dragging me by the arm. "The abbot's got rheumatism!"

"You've still got to see the butter carvings," Champa said to me. "Go away, you little nuisance!" he said to the seminarist. "Go and tell the abbot we're just coming!"

We mounted a creaking staircase to the *gön-kang*, the chapel of the tutelary deities of the place. Among skinless, decaying carcasses, shining statues of terrifying gods consumed with metaphysical rage, cryptic, symbolical frescoes, old armour, masks, liturgical instruments and rancid relics, in the still, silent, stuffy atmosphere, was a cupboard containing the butter carvings – butter worked into complicated patterns, filigrees of tall flames, landscapes, empyreans, groups of saints, all of them coloured.

"But don't you realize the abbot's got rheumatism?" the seminarist wailed. I had no alternative but to go with him. We went up to the apartment of honour, where the abbot was waiting. When the visit was over ("You see, when I bend it hurts here . . . at night I feel pains there . . . if I turn over my neck creaks . . ."), we went to the suite of the little Great Precious. But today he was engaged in meditation, and was not to be seen. So the seminarists took me up to their quarters, to the "class-room", where several boys were reading aloud a treatise on Dorje Chi-che ("*Dorje-chi-che-gyi choga chatsang . . .*"). The master, a dusty, tired-looking monk of about thirty, slowly read out a phrase, and then the pupils repeated it after him in chorus; and so it went on for hours. This was their lesson.

The "class-room" was a room with very big windows, and it must have been infernally cold in winter. The pupils sat cross-legged on the floor, each with his own book in front of him. The light was poor, and everything seemed to be intended to mortify the senses. All round the walls were shelves with hundreds of statues of Tsongkhapa, all alike, all ugly, all gilded and all dusty. In the middle, in the place of honour, in an altar-cupboard enclosed in glass, was a big statue of Tsongkhapa.

"It's a miraculous statue," the bored master assured me, his eyes brightening a little as he spoke. "Do you see its head? Every year it grows a little. The yellow hat has had to be enlarged three times. We don't know what it means, but it's a great miracle!"

The boys, delighted at the interruption of their lesson, enjoyed watching that extraordinary, exotic creature, a foreigner, and seeing me drink Tibetan tea amused them immensely. Their life must be very hard. They get up at dawn, and an hour's lesson follows. They then go down to the temple, where they drink tea, eat a little *tsampa* and say prayers for about two hours, sitting on the long, cold benches. After this there are three hours of reading "in class", with the master intoning the text while the boys follow him in chorus – a primitive and stupid way of teaching, but one which in the long run produces a certain effect. At midday they drink tea again and have another light meal, after which they rest in the courtyard. In the afternoon there is more reading, and at last, about six o'clock, it is time for dinner.

It was just six o'clock, and I was able to be present at the meal. I felt very sorry for the poor boys. They sat in rows on the ground in a cold, dark corridor. Each had two wooden bowls before him, one for *tsampa* and tea, the other for a dish of vegetables – boiled vegetables prepared without any condiments. There were no spoons or chopsticks; they ate with their fingers. A draught of cold, damp, stale air came up from below; the smallest boys – they were eight or nine years old – drew their robes round their shoulders. Each boy helped himself to *tsampa* from his own little bag. One boy's bag – he evidently came from a poor family was nearly empty, and another, who evidently came from a richer family, passed him a handful of his own *tsampa*. It was a moving little incident; it was over in a second, and nobody noticed it.

The meal only took a few minutes. It was a barbarous, stoical, excessively ascetic experience. All the same, the boys did not seem unhappy. They devoured the vegetable course greedily. Then, after putting their bowls away, they dashed down to play in the courtyard, shouting. I was left alone with the master. He told me he had syphilis. Could I get him some injections?

Succession by means of reincarnation

Ngawang Lobsang Choden, *Trul-ku* ("Phantom Body") of the Dung-kar monastery, offers a particular instance of a system that is unique in the world, whereby the succession and continuity of an institution may be assured. According to recent researches, the idea that an eminent person may, after his death, be reincarnated in a young boy in order to continue his beneficent labour of guidance could go back to the thirteenth century. It seems that the first lamaist schools to put the system into effect were those of the *Karma-pa* and the *Drikung-pa*. The idea gradually achieved enormous success and was adopted by nearly every Buddhist school in Tibet, including the most important, that of the *Gelug-pa*. Their leaders, who are in fact the Dalai Lamas, adopted the system in the fifteenth century. It is said that in 1959 there were some five hundred *trul-ku* in Tibet; every monastery, no matter how small, wanted to have one, if only for the prestige it conferred.

It could be interesting to take a look for a moment at the way in which certain specific recent successions of some significance have taken place, these being well documented. "We are very fond of this system," Lobsang once explained to me. "It combines the advantages of the hereditary principle with those of elections. It has all the advantages. of the hereditary principle, in that it guarantees social stability. It has all the advantages of an electoral system, as with every Dalai Lama a fresh start is made, and there is no question of becoming the slave of a class. And consider the profound sense of unity that the system has ended by giving our country! The Precious Protector (the Dalai Lama) may be born in the house of any citizen, rich or poor, townsman or countryman. Potentially we all take part in the system. It is nobody's privilege. We thus combine popular democracy with metaphysical monarchy. The father of the Great Fifth, for example, was a humble peasant of Chung-gye." This is true: the system neatly combines the "hereditary line" with "elections". Strictly speaking there have not been fourteen Dalai Lamas governing first the Yellow Sect and later Tibet – there have simply been fourteen successive apparitions of the same human beings identified with the identical spiritual entity, the *Bodhisattva* Avalokitesvara/Chen-re-zi, the personification of Compassion and Benevolence. The actual human frames are essentially no more than garments that are put on and taken off, thrown out when no longer of use.

With us it is commonly believed that when a Dalai Lama dies – the expression that the Tibetans use on such an occasion is that he honourably ascends to paradise with his own body – the spirit of Avalokitesvara immediately reappears on earth in the body of a new-born child. This is by no means correct. The maximum period envisaged for the reincarnation of ordinary persons after their death is forty-nine days. In the case of a *Bodhisattva* the period can be much longer; it is often as much as two years.

However, the difficult task of finding the baby in whom the *Bodhisattva*, "he whose essence is enlightenment", has gone to reside eventually presents itself; and at this point there comes into play one of the most typically Tibetan institutions, linked by direct descent to those of the ancient shamans, who were the priests of Tibet before the advent of Buddhism. I refer to the institution of the oracle. Upon the Dalai Lama's death the most important lamas in the country meet in solemn conclave, and the first thing they do is to consult the oracles. There is actually an official, state oracle at the Nechung monastery, less than four miles from Lhasa, whose pronouncements have a supreme value. However, when the state oracle has been consulted the search is still only in its earliest stages; it is a long and arduous process, and may last for years. It is interesting to note that it varies from occasion to occasion, and that there are always miraculous natural signs of various kinds which have to be taken into account. The search by no means consists of the pedestrian application of a stereotyped formula; it is rather the expression of a living spiritual reality which in every new situation embodies itself in different outer forms.

In the case of the Thirteenth Dalai Lama, that is to say in or after 1878, the Nechung oracle fell into a trance, as is usual in such cases, and actually revealed the names of the baby's father and mother. But in Tibet names do not help very much. Except in the case of noble families, surnames do not exist, and there are thousands of Dorjes and Drolmás. At this point the oracle of Samye (one of the oldest Tibetan monasteries, traditionally founded by Padma Sambhava in the eighth century), declared that "the mountain near the house of the reborn Precious Protector has the shape of an elephant". For the removal of doubt, however, more precise information was required. As always happens in human affairs, any power – whether that of money, prestige or arms – causes various parties to arise who try to obtain control of it. Thus some (the pro-Chinese) declared that the reborn *Bodhisattva* would be found to the East. Others (the anti-Chinese) maintained that he would be found to the West. A third group felt confident that the most likely place was Tak-po, in southern Tibet. The Nechung oracle was consulted again, and actually mentioned Tak-po by name. However, it was just as well to obtain some less general clue.

In southern Tibet there is a lake called Lhamoi Latso in which it is said to be possible to foresee future events. A Tibetan gave to Sir Charles Bell (reproduced in his *Portrait of the Dalai Lama*) the following description of the visions to be seen in it. "The water of the lake is blue. You watch it from the hillside. A wind arises, and turns the blue water into white. A hole then forms in this white water; the hole is blue-black. Clouds form above this hole and below the clouds you see images showing future events."

It was thus that the important Lama of Gyu (one of the Lhasa monasteries) was called upon, with various doctors of theology, to scrutinize the lake. At first the committee seems to have been disappointed; the lake was frozen, and there was nothing to be seen. Fortunately, however, a wind soon arose and swept the snow from the ice. The ice shone like a mirror, and presented the vision of a house and a flowering peach-tree. That same night the Lama of Gyu had a dream. He dreamed that he saw a mother with a child of about two years old in her arms. A few days later the lama, travelling along the lake-side, saw a peach-tree in bloom (an extraordinary thing at that time of the year), and next to it a house. Inside it he found the mother and the child of whom he had dreamed.

In other words the new Dalai Lama had been found. But, to make sure, a careful examination of the child was necessary; there were some special signs that he must have on his body. The *Bodhisattva* Avalokitesvara is always represented with four arms, and the child, if he really is an incarnation of the divinity, must have fleshy protuberances on his shoulders or shoulder-blades. Sure enough, the child had such protuberances. Also his ears must be longer than the average, for such ears are a sign of wisdom. Sure enough, the child had long ears. Then the palms of his hands must have tiny imprints in the shape of a shell. This sign was also not lacking. The child, having passed the first examination, had then to be subjected to the second and final one. He must distinguish correctly between personal possessions that had belonged to him in his previous life – his rosary (*threng-wa*), his small liturgical drum (*nga-chung*), his bell (*tril-bu*), his bronze thunderbolt (*dorje*), a handkerchief, a tea-cup, etc., etc., and exact duplicates of them. Only after the child had passed all these tests, and after the Nechung oracle had confirmed the fact, could the discovery of the new pontiff be announced, and only then could his solemn installation take place.

The search for and discovery of the Fourteenth Dalai Lama was quite different. In 1935, two years after the Thirteenth Dalai Lama's death, the Regent, after a long period of vain searching, visited the Lhamoi Latso lake in the hope of seeing a vision that might be of assistance. The results were strange. The Regent distinctly read in the lake the three syllables A-Ka-Ma. Next he saw a three-storey monastery, with a gilded roof and turquoise tiles. He also saw to the east of the monastery a winding road leading towards a bare, pagoda-shaped hill. Facing the hill he saw a little house with caves of a type unknown to him. The meaning of this vision was discussed for a long time by the most learned theologians of Tibet, and it was finally decided that it indicated, but only vaguely, the probability that the new incarnation had taken place to the east of Lhasa. Meanwhile consultations both of the state oracle and of other, minor oracles (which are held sometimes to be more effective) actively continued.

At this point a miracle of the kind to which Tibetans attach great importance occurred. It should be noted that, while the bodies of ordinary mortals in Tibet are normally hacked to pieces on special mortuary hills, so that birds and animals can feed on them, the bodies of Dalai Lamas and a few other personages of exceptional importance are embalmed. Pending the completion of a special mausoleum, the body of the Thirteenth Dalai Lama had been placed on a throne in a hall of the Potala, where the thousands of pilgrims who always gather in Lhasa could do homage to what for fifty-nine years had been the terrestrial garment of Avalokitesvara. Now it happened that on several mornings the monks who watched over him found that the dead Dalai Lama's head and body, which normally faced the south, were facing East. The theory that the new Dalai Lama would appear to the East of Lhasa immediately gained great favour.

The appearance of other signs that pointed in the same direction led in the spring of 1937 to the despatch of various groups of lamas to search the eastern regions of Tibet. Each party took with it objects that had belonged to the previous Dalai Lama, as well as exact duplicates of them with which to make the requisite tests. The child-candidates were finally reduced to three. One died before he could be examined; another fled, weeping in terror at the sight of the lamas – a very bad augury indeed – and this left only one. The leader of the deputations, the *Trul-ku* ("Phantom Body") Kyi-tsang, realized as soon as he approached the house where the child lived that he had reached his goal. He actually saw the three-storey monastery which the Regent had seen in his vision at the lake several years before. He saw the gilded roof and the turquoise-coloured tiles, the winding road and the house with the unusual roof; and, when he was told that the monastery was dedicated to the sage Kama-pa, he realized the meaning of the two syllables *ka* and *ma* that the Regent had read in the Lhamoi Latso lake.

Before entering the home of the presumed new Dalai Lama the *Trul-ku* Kyi-tsang disguised himself as a servant. When he approached the door he found a child playing there. The child at once rose and ran towards him, crying: "Lama! Lama!", and seized a necklace which had belonged to the Thirteenth Dalai Lama. Presumption was now approaching certainty, but the *Trul-ku* Kyi-tsang, desiring absolutely final proof, still said nothing. He summoned the members of the deputations, and in their presence caused to be presented to the child, who must have been about three years old, the various objects that had belonged to the Thirteenth Dalai Lama and their facsimiles. The child chose the right one every time. Finally there remained only a walking stick and its copy to choose from. To the general consternation the child chose the wrong one, but then shook his head and dropped it. He then seized the right walking stick, from which he refused to be parted. The usual signs of good omen were naturally detected on his body. The Fourteenth Dalai Lama had been found.

For various reasons the important news was kept strictly secret, and it was not announced in Lhasa until September, 1939, when the little god was on the point of arriving in the capital and it was too late for any dissident political faction to put forward any rival candidate. The meeting between the emissaries of the Lhasa Government and the caravan with whom the child was travelling took place to the north of Nagchuka before dawn on September 20th. The small group of monks, Ministers, secretaries and soldiers who came from Lhasa found the child sleeping in a litter, accompanied by his parents and escorted by a group of Chinese Muslim pilgrims on the way to Mecca by way of Lhasa.

The *sha-pe* (Minister) Bhondong placed a ceremonial white sash in the hands of the *Trul-ku* Kyi-tsang, so that he might offer it to the little Dalai. Even a Tibetan Minister is not allowed to offer a sash directly to the supreme pontiff. Near Nagchuka the caravan found an encampment and a throne prepared. The child, soon after he was awakened, was placed upon the throne with great ceremony. The Minister Bhondong prostrated himself three times before him, and presented to him a letter from the Regent recognizing him as the Dalai Lama, and offered him symbolic gifts appropriate to the occasion. The little living god continued his journey to Lhasa in the gilded palanquin of the Dalai Lama, greeted at every village on the way by crowds of the faithful prostrating themselves. The journey was made as quickly as possible, in order to arrive at Lhasa before the eighth month (Tibetan style) which, in that year of the Earth-Hare, was considered to be extremely ill-omened.

From the day of his installation in the Potala an entirely new life begins for this child selected by fortune. Instead of the humble country cottage, the kitchen, the farmyard, the fields and the flowers, the games with little friends of the same age, he now occupies a whole suite in the vast complex of palaces, temples, mausoleums, dungeons, halls, passages, libraries and kitchens of which the Potala consists. His parents are also given a suite in which to live, and his father is honoured with the title of *kung*, or duke, but after the first few months both he and the child's mother see less and less of their offspring. The new Dalai Lama, like every other monk, must die completely out of civil life; even his name is changed. The Fourteenth Dalai Lama's name at birth was Lhamo Dhondup, but that humble appellation was replaced by a long series of magnificent epithets, such as the Holy One, the Tender Glory, Mighty in Speech, of Excellent Intellect, Absolute Wisdom, Holding the Doctrine, the Ocean (of Wisdom), etc.

The first important ceremony in which the new Dalai takes part is that of the reoccupation of the throne left vacant by his predecessor. The ceremony is called the "Prayer for the Power of the Golden Throne". It is worthy of note that during the interregnum the usual meals are served every day on the little table beside the throne; as a way of recalling and emphasizing that the pontiff is not dead but absent, and that nothing of him has changed, except that transient and unimportant thing, his body. The essence of the ceremony is the lamas' appeal to the Dalai to reoccupy "his" throne, which he had left a few years earlier.

The Ceremony, as is usual on great occasions in Tibet, where the early hours of the day are held to be the most propitious, begins before dawn. The various personages start filing into the hall of the Golden Throne. All round there gleam the gold and the carved wood of the altars; sound is muffled by the silk pictures and cushions and the woollen carpets. Gradually the hall fills. There are the Ministers (the *sha-pes* – three laymen and one lama), there is the Regent (the *Poi-gyalpo*, "King of Tibet"), there are the abbots of the great monasteries – thin ascetics with flaming eyes, plump, self-satisfied dignitaries, lean disciplinarians – the heads of the principal noble families, and the foreign delegations. Finally silence is imposed, and the holy child, arrayed in his ceremonial vestments, is brought into the hall, lifted on high and placed on "his" throne with affectionate solicitude. Everyone prostrates himself; Tibet has now officially consecrated her new Dalai Lama. Sir Basil Gould, who was head of the British delegation at the Prayer for the Power of the Golden Throne in 1940, relates that the child's composure and gravity during the endless hours of the individual blessings were really moving. It must be remembered that the little pontiff was then barely four-and-a-half years old.

After the discovery and installation of the new Dalai his education begins. This is a very severe process, and every detail is rigidly prescribed. Henceforward, apart from his little brothers, who are seminarists too, he is surrounded only by monks. He plays, of course, as every healthy, normal child must do, but he has to get used to long hours of study, penitences and public ceremonies. He is attended by a Chamberlain, a Master of the Household, who tastes all the food set before him, a Court Chaplain, who makes offerings to the gods on his behalf, a Controller of the Kitchen, a Chief Physician, a Librarian – in short, a whole court with a very rigid and elaborate etiquette, from which women are completely excluded.

The young Dalai learns reading, writing and the elements of arithmetic. Soon the time comes when he has to spend his first periods of retreat in the company of an instructor in theology. As soon as he is old enough, he starts receiving instruction in the theory and practice of State administration, but above all he reads, rereads, interprets and comments on religious books, from the innumerable volumes of the *Kangyur* to the writings of Tsongkhapa. He often attends the theological disputations which take place either in the Potala or in the big monasteries of Lhasa. Before attaining his majority at eighteen he must pay a visit to one of the sacred lakes of Tibet, to receive a vision concerning the future events of his "reign".

The principle of succession by reincarnation seems to have been adopted in Tibet in the thirteenth century. The *Gelug-pa* sect applied it from 1476, for the Second Dalai Lama. From 1663 on it was applied also to the abbots of the monastery of Tashilhumpo, that is to say to the Panchen Lama. The Panchen Lama is, after the Dalai Lama, the most important figure in the spiritual life of Tibet. The two pontiffs are linked in a metaphysical interdependence, which explains many things about their mutual relations. While the Dalai Lama is the incarnation of the *Bodhisattva* Avalokitesvara, the Panchen Lama is the incarnation of the *Dhyani* Buddha Amitābha. But, if we refer to Chapter 15, "The Metaphysical Adventures of Prince Gautama", it will be seen that the spiritual prestige of the Dalai Lama is less than that of the Panchen Lama, on whom he is spiritually dependent, because in the last resort Avalokitesvara is only an emanation of Amitābha.

The fundamental distinction between Buddha and *Bodhisattva* must also be remembered. The former lives on the plane of the Logos, that of pure thought; the latter represents the dynamic moment of creation, contact with "the vortex of life". The same distinction has been held to apply to the functions of the Dalai Lama and the Panchen Lama on earth. The Dalai Lamas, as is only natural, have been quick to seize on the point. "You, O Panchen Lama, are my spiritual superior," the Dalai Lama says in effect. "That is perfectly true, and is universally admitted. But your function is to remain in the sacred, silent field of the invisible. Remain therefore at Tashilhumpo, and enjoy your ineffable beatitude. Leave to me, who am a mere emanation of yours, the affairs of the world, which are too low, too transient, too insignificant to be worthy of your attention." The Panchen Lama, particularly after the Dalai Lama succeeded in getting rid of the Chinese in 1912 and becoming really independent, was naturally unable to accept such a situation.

The consequence was that the relations between the two pontiffs gradually became strained to breaking point. In the course of time the Dalai Lama became identified with pro-British policies and the Panchen Lama with pro-Chinese policies. In 1923 the Panchen Lama actually had to leave Tibet and take refuge at Kum-Bum in Mongolia. In 1935 he died, to reappear not long afterwards in a new "phantom body", the seventh of the series, who is today (1948) represented by a boy of eleven.

It is a grave misfortune for a country to harbour two powers of equal or similar influence. A time comes when there is a schism, the people are faced with conflicting loyalties, and the result is chaos. Just as in the nineteenth century white men played on the rivalry between Shogun and Emperor in Japan in order to force the country to open itself to international trade, so is it foreseeable that, when a foreign Power wishes to enter Tibet, it will start by using as a lever the rivalries existing between the two supreme pontiffs, the Dalai Lama in Lhasa and the Panchen Lama at Tashilhumpo. [This prediction has alas been borne out by events. The seventh Panchen Lama died in February 1989.]

Apart from these two supreme luminaries in the Tibetan firmament, there are many other living *Bodhisattvas*. In the past two centuries the system of succession by reincarnation has spread amazingly. At the present day every monastery of any importance has its own Incarnated One, its own "phantom body". There must be several hundreds of them. There is also a woman living *Bodhisattva*, Palden Lha-mo ("the Glorious Goddess"), who lives in a monastery on the shore of Lake Yamdrok. When the young Dalai Lama goes to the Lake Lhamoi Latso to receive his vision, he stays at the monastery of Palden Lha-mo.

Palden Lha-mo as a divinity is one of the "Eight Terrible Ones". She is considered to be a special protector of the Dalai Lama and the Panchen Lama. The Sanskrit name signifies "The Adamantine Whore". She is always represented in her terrifying aspect, as a frenzied enemy of the forces of evil. She sits sideways on a white mule wading through a sea of blood. She is hideously ugly, is frantic with rage, and is coloured blue. She wears garlands of skulls and crowns of bones, carries a fan of peacock's feathers, two dice with which to play for human lives, a number of snakes, many jewels, a tiger-skin, a sceptre, and a skull carved into a cup, which is full to the brim with blood and smoking entrails; she holds it in front of her mouth, which is distorted into a savage grin. Her present terrestrial incarnation is, however, said to be a pretty, pale and rather sad-looking girl. She is rarely visible, but only in the distance, in the mysterious darkness of the temple.

One can imagine that few encounters can take place in the world stranger, and in some ways more moving, than the brief, single, ceremonial meeting between the Dalai and the incarnation of Yamdrok-tso – two adolescents, both the prisoners of rigid monastic conventions, each the prisoner of a different myth. One of these myths is vast, beautiful and noble, the latter terrifying, nocturnal and primitive. Each is a mere symbol, an incident, a "phantom body" in an incredible metaphysical phantasmagoria, a crazy game of symbols. Each is the gilded prisoner of the ceremonial and the etiquette of courts and monasteries. But they are also two human beings, and they are young. What must their feelings be during their brief encounter?

Chumbi: shall we be put in prison?

Yatung is an entirely modern village; Chumbi, which lies a few miles lower down the valley, and is nowadays a far less flourishing place, is the poor but dignified seat of the ancient local nobility. It is only a village, a modest little village, but it has five or six fine, solidly-built, patriarchal houses. The type of building is the same as elsewhere in the valley; sturdy walls, sloping slightly inwards, with a huge and complicated wooden roof, and broad windows with rectangular wooden patterns, painted in many colours, running round them. They immediately call to mind the old, well maintained chalets in the Aldo Adige.

The residence of the *tsong-chi*, the local representative of the Tibetan Government, is outside Chumbi, beyond a wooden bridge that spans the torrent. It is a kind of long, low, small fortress. Elsewhere in Tibet it would be the residence of the *dzong-pön*, the "fortress captains". There are always two of these, the captain of the East and the captain of the West. The Tibetan theory is that they keep an eye on each another. Here, however, in view of the special position of the Trommò valley and its relations with India, the position is occupied by a *tsong-chi*, a commercial agent. The commercial agent is now away – he is, of all places, in America. Some enterprising young men belonging to the Lhasa nobility, acting on the initiative of the merchant Pangda-tsang, succeeded in persuading the Tibetan Government of the advantages that might accrue from sending an economic mission to the United States, and the mission left at the beginning of 1948. Each of its members was provided with an enormous sheet of paper, bearing the Regent's red seals, to serve as passport. A Mr Tob-wang was left behind at Chumbi as the commercial agent's deputy.

Mr Tob-wang sent for us – not, that is to say, for Professor Tucci, but for Colonel Moise, Mele and myself. Our position is ambiguous and undefined. They have refused to let us go to Lhasa. Professor Tucci, being a Buddhist, is the only one who has received a permit. The rest of us, though we have made repeated applications for permission to accompany him, have not even been granted a regular permit to remain on Tibetan soil. We could not imagine what Tob-wang might want of us. When we went to see him he might even throw us in prison.

"You don't know anything about orientals," I told Piero Mele, to frighten him. "They invite you to tea, talk to you for half-an-hour about art and poetry, and then signal with their eyebrows to their retainers and tell you you're under arrest."

"Rubbish!" Piero replied. "You'll see that all he wants is to have a fountain-pen or a padlock repaired."

"That's what you think! Well, you may be right. But I can't help remembering what happened to me in Kyoto in 1943. After being confined to our house for a whole month, under continual police supervision, one fine morning towards the end of October Mr Iwami, the chief of the aliens department, came to see us with six or seven unpleasant-looking companions. 'Good morning, Mr Maraini, how are you?' he said to me very politely. 'Can we drop in for a moment?' I let them in, and they all sat down in the drawing-room. We talked about one thing and another for a few minutes, and Mr Iwami noticed that the gramophone was open, and that there were some records lying about; we had been listening to some music the evening before. He picked up one of the records, and said: 'Do you like Mozart? . . . I am very fond of him indeed,' he went on, without waiting for an answer. 'Unfortunately my pay permits me few luxuries, but whenever I manage to lay a little money aside I buy records of Western classical music. I like Beethoven too. Do you know the Sixth Symphony?' Meanwhile my wife, who had heard the voices – Japanese houses are built of wood, and you can hear everything – got up and came downstairs to see who the visitors were. Iwami greeted her in the most florid Japanese, with all the ritual *gozaimasu*, and went on talking about music. The maid came in and served tea, and the conversation continued – it was conversation of a kind more usual at five o'clock in the afternoon than at eight o'clock in the morning. 'You see,' Iwami remarked, 'Beethoven in the Sixth Symphony reminds me of our great painter Kano Eitoku,' and he went on talking about art, nature and serenity. He emptied his tea-cup, but saw that we had not quite emptied ours, so he waited for a moment. Then, not suddenly, but quite slowly and firmly, and completely changing his tone of voice, he said: 'Get up!' He now used the familiar *kimi* instead of the more respectful *anata* in addressing us. We got up, and he went on: 'From this moment you are no longer dependent on your embassy [foreigners in Japan are always 'dependent on their embassy'], because we do not recognize your Government. You are now dependent on the Imperial Japanese Government, and you must take orders from us. Get ready to leave, with your children, and as little baggage as possible.' Then he turned to two members of his tough-looking escort and said: 'You stay here! Watch them; they are enemies!'"

Meanwhile, as I told this story, we had reached Chumbi. We immediately started noticing all sorts of ominous signs. An untidy-looking soldier who had been squatting at the entrance to the village got up when he saw us and hurried off.

"D'you see?" I said to Piero. "He's gone to warn them that we're coming. They're getting ready!"

"Nonsense!" replied Piero. "He's gone to fetch a broken alarm-clock or an aunt who's got rheumatics!"

We crossed the bridge, crossed a wide space where about a dozen desperadoes were cleaning arms, shoeing horses or sitting and smoking in the sun, and entered the courtyard. A big gate, with a huge and complicated lock, slammed behind us. Two louts came forward to meet us.

"The *ku-tsab* is expecting you. Come along!" they said.

We mounted several steps, passed through a big gateway with many-coloured decorations and entered a secondary courtyard, where the *ku-tsab's* rooms were. Another servant showed us into a room, where chairs had been prepared for us; a high one for Colonel Moise and two lower ones for Piero and myself. We were in a living-room typical of the Tibetan lesser nobility or bourgeoisie, with sofas built up of cushions, low tables beside the window, cupboards against the walls, a few pictures painted on cloth, a little altar and small pieces of furniture of carved and gilded wood. In one corner we noticed a rack containing about twenty rifles; there were also some big pistols, and some swords and daggers.

"Mark my words," I said. "They've got everything laid on! They'll talk to us about flowers and poetry for half-an-hour, and then they'll throw us into prison. Did you bring a file?"

Piero shook his head and started getting really annoyed. He looked at Colonel Moise, who, however, was completely calm, as usual. Eventually we heard footsteps and the *ku-tsab* Tob-wang made his appearance. He greeted us cordially and took his seat in his own place near the window. He was a tall, strong man of about forty, with a serious and, if you like, ambiguous expression. He was dressed in Tibetan style, with long hair, and on his left ear he wore the gold and turquoise earring which denotes the Tibetan official. Conversation was difficult, and there were a number of awkward pauses.

"How do you find Yatung?" Tob-wang asked. "It's a poor village; there's nothing there. It's a real shame that they won't allow you to go to Lhasa. There you'd see the finest things that our country has to offer."

I looked at Piero. This was a bad beginning; these compliments were exceedingly inauspicious.

Colonel Moise asked me to explain that we, for our part, had the liveliest desire to go to Lhasa, but that a great deal depended on him, Mr Tob-wang, and the reports on us that he might send to his Government. Tob-wang assured us that he had already sent most favourable reports about us to his Government.

The conversation continued in the same way for some time. Two boys poured out tea and offered us Indian biscuits, which are considered a great luxury. Then Tob-wang opened a box and produced a padlock.

"For some time I have been entirely unable to open it," he said. "Would you be capable of performing the miracle?"

Piero looked at me with a triumphant smile.

One after another we examined the obstinate padlock. While this was going on I noticed that several of the desperadoes whom we had seen in the open

29 *Chumbi: the* ku-tsab *Tob-wang*

space outside were quietly filing in and gathering at the dark end of the room. Tob-wang kept on talking. He must have thought that my Tibetan was much better than it is, because, after the first few phrases, which he pronounced slowly and distinctly, he started talking rapidly, and I had difficulty in following him. He kept a little way away from us, but did not assume any air of particular importance. He kept harping on the same theme. "If it depended only on me, you'd be in the Potala already, paying homage to the Regent." Piero passed the padlock to Colonel Moise. As he turned to do so he too saw the men obstructing the exit. He looked at me, and I replied with a nod of my head, as if to say: "I told you so." That, after all, was the oriental procedure, and something disagreeable might well be in store for us. Tob-wang suddenly turned towards the band of cut-throats.

"Let those who have some illness to cure step forward," he said. "The *amchi-sahib* (doctor-sahib) will examine them!"

When I translated the phrase Piero looked at me in triumph over the top of the tea-cup he was holding to his lips. Padlocks and rheumatism! He had been perfectly right and had every reason to gloat over me.

Yatung: a feudal lord on the bridge

Last night a messenger from Mingyur, the headman of the village, came hurrying to see us, with the news that the *lachag* Jigme Taring was going to pass this way today. So this morning Piero and I went down to the bridge to wait for the *lachag*'s caravan and take some colour photographs. The weather has been perfect all day, with a deep blue sky and small, cheerful clouds in their perennial course from peak to peak of the Himalayas.

Jigme Sumchen Wang-po Namgyal Taring is aged thirty-seven and is a nephew of the Maharajah of Sikkim, but he belongs to the Tibetan branch of the family, and lives in Lhasa. He has not yet reached very high rank (he belongs to the fourth of the seven grades of Tibetan officialdom), but he is a member of one of the most important Tibetan families and moves in the highest society. His father, Taring senior, the Maharajah of Sikkim's elder brother, died some years ago. I remember him at Gyantse in 1937. I was invited to visit him at Taring (the Tibetan nobility nearly always draw their names from one of their estates), on the way to Lhasa. I rode for hours across the deserted plain, 12,000 feet high, before seeing fields in the distance, and then a low palace-fortress, surrounded by many other low houses. This was Taring. Meanwhile the weather had deteriorated, and a big storm came on. The Tibetans fear hail as one of the greatest scourges, because it sometimes completely destroys their wretched crops. A peasant was standing on the roof of his house, desperately blowing, like a Triton, into a big white shell, "to drive the storm away". But the storm did not seem to be intimidated by this procedure, and soon thunder and lightning started, and a terrific downpour, but no hail.

I entered Taring as the first drops were falling. A servant took my horse, and another led me through various courtyards which betrayed all the signs of flourishing agricultural life-sacks, saddles, farming implements. We climbed the usual steep, Tibetan wooden steps (they are just like Japanese steps), walked down a long verandah, where a number of women were working at their looms (they greeted me by putting out their tongue, as is still the country custom), and finally I was introduced into the "prince's" apartments. So far I might have been on a farm, but when I crossed the threshold I found myself in a suite of Tibetan drawing-rooms, the baroque richness of the decoration of which reminded me of eighteenth-century Palermo drawing-rooms. The ceilings were supported on columns and entablatures painted in the vivid, joyous colours of Tibet (blue, green, orange, yellow); innumerable pictures painted on cloth, some of them of notable beauty, were on the walls; the furniture was carved and gilded, decorated with Chinese *motifs* (dragons and peonies) and Indian *motifs* (the lotus, the Eight Glorious Emblems); and cup-lamps of massive silver for burning butter stood in front of the small, gilded altars.

The Tibetan style of furnishing is elaborate and luxurious; it can easily degenerate into heaviness, clumsiness and over-elaboration. But when it is carried out with taste it has a bold, barbaric fascination that can hardly be excelled. It is a style which seems natural to a country of boundless plateaux, to a people who set out on 2,000-mile journeys on horseback as if it were the most natural thing in the world, who are used to violent gales and extreme cold, who pass with ease from the rigours of asceticism to hearty enjoyment of life, who laugh, play, fight, drink, make love, kill, repent, believe in miracles and are, in short, full of an inexhaustible vitality. A great deal of the merit of the Tibetan style is due to the taste of Tibetan craftsmen; their liking for ornamentation on the one hand and their feeling for colour, materials, surfaces, on the other. Tibetan tea-pots, for instance, look like fantastic little round fortresses of brass and silver, with dragons entwined round the spout or handle; they are always a symphony of various metals; and the same applies to the coffee-pots, beer jars, cups, travelling flasks, waterjugs, trumpets, boxes for amulets, and a hundred other articles of everyday use. Their painting and sculpture are in Indian or sometimes Chinese style, partially Tibetanized, but in their furnishings the Tibetan spirit expresses itself with much greater freedom.

30 *Tibetan copper tea-pot, with decorations in pewter. Tea-cup and saucer with metal lid (from Gyantse, author's collection)*

31 *Tibetan beer* (chang) *jug in copper with decorations in brass; and a typical Tibetan pewter jug, decorated in brass (from Gyantse, author's collection)*

I remember little of old Taring's conversation during my visit, which was very brief. The storm passed over us, and we sipped tea and ate biscuits and dried fruit to the accompaniment of flashes of lightning. Then I left for Gyantse, and went through another tremendous downpour on the way.

But to return to the bridge at Yatung. At eleven o'clock a boy came running along, shouting: "They're coming!" Sure enough, a cloud of dust appeared along the road towards Chumbi, and soon we could make out the individual horsemen; the caravan was coming. The cloud of dust grew nearer, and through it we could soon make out the people's faces. "There they are! There they are!" The little boys all round us jumped with excitement and clapped their hands with glee. When Jigme Taring passed he greeted us. He was dressed in Tibetan style, though, as usual, he wore a European felt hat. He was followed by his wife and a niece about twenty years old (a very pretty girl), and by two guards, each with a rifle and a big metal-work *kau* (box for relics) slung round his neck. There were also various other servants, a number of mules with baggage – big trunks and boxes covered with skins, sacks and shrines.

That is how a Tibetan lord travels; in a slow, solemn, brilliant, fairy-tale caravan, reminding one of the three Magi, Benozzo Gozzoli, Carpaccio. I stood among the boulders of the dry river-bed, with the bridge high above me. Against the clouds and sun the passing figures were explosions of colour. I reflected sadly that within a few decades these same people would be passing this way in motor cars, in horrible clothes not designed for them, and that all that I was seeing and admiring would be nothing but a memory.

In India, China and Japan customs, habits, local peculiarities, are subject to the continual impact of all the alien things – railways, ready-made clothes, mechanical toys, illustrated papers – which modern industry pours upon the world. These things have a bewildering, disintegrating effect on their ancient cultures, causing them rapidly to decay. The world is in a state of continual flux, and the foundations have been swept away. True, there is abundant vitality, but there is also abundant confusion and ugliness. Ours is an unhappy age of transition. Everywhere the world is passing from age-old equilibriums, in which moral and aesthetic standards had been slowly evolved, to other, future equilibriums that cannot be foreseen. They too will ultimately find their centre and acquire their own ideals and standards. But by then we shall have been dead for a long time. Meanwhile Tibet is an exception. How much longer will it be able to endure?

Note on the Tibetan Government [2]

In Europe Tibet is always thought of as a strange country, exclusively populated by mysterious sages, who pass their time performing incredible miracles in endless, rocky wildernesses inhabited by rare blue poppies. It is thought of as a country of monks governed by monks. It should, however, be remembered that only a tenth of the population – a high proportion, it is true – is professionally associated with the various religious bodies, and that, though the Dalai Lama is the head of the state and the government and the Panchen Lama and the *trul-ku* ("phantom bodies") have a voice in every important decision, there are laymen who occupy places of great importance in the public life of the country.

The ultimate control of all ecclesiastical as well as civil affairs lies in the hands of the Dalai Lama. Immediately under him are the two principal organs of government, the Ecclesiastical Council (*yik-tsang*), consisting of four clerical members, and the Council of Ministers (*kashag*), consisting of four members (*sha-pe*), of whom three are laymen and one clerical. Two Prime Ministers act as intermediaries between the two councils and the Dalai Lama – an Ecclesiastical Prime Minister (*chi-kyap chempo*) for religious affairs and a Prime Minister of State (*lön-chen*) for civil affairs. These two officials are, however, less important than might appear; the real seat of power is in the two councils. The Ministers (*sha-pe*) of the lay council (*kashag*) do not have separate portfolios, but exercise general control over all political, judicial and fiscal affairs. A Ministry of Foreign Affairs, under the control of the *chigye lön-chen*, is a relatively recent creation, but it appears to have advisory functions only. Foreign affairs have always been under the direct control of the Dalai Lama, or the Regent.

Finally there is a National Assembly (*tsong-du*), which meets only to deal with exceptionally grave and important matters. It has about fifty members, who include many of the most important personages in Lhasa. It should not be forgotten that the abbots of the great monasteries – Sera, Depung, Galden – being able to count on the complete loyalty of several thousand monks, constitute a formidable political force. Sera, indeed, showed such independence that in 1947, at the time of the death of the Regent Reting, the Government had to undertake a regular siege of the monastery in order to restore discipline. It was machine-gunned and finally subjected to an artillery bombardment. In the last resort, however, the functions of the National Assembly are advisory. After the resolutions presented to it by the *kashag* have been discussed, they are submitted to the Dalai or the Regent for final decision. Power is thus extremely centralized.

The country is divided into five provinces – U-Tsang (Lhasa and Shigatse), Gartok (western Tibet), Kham, (Chiamdo, eastern Tibet), Chang (Nagchuka, northern Tibet), Lhoka (Lho-dzong, southern Tibet) – and in each the representative of the Government is a *chi-kyap*. The *dzong-pöns* (captains of the fortresses) are subordinate to the *chi-kyaps*. The functions of a *dzong-pön* are on the one hand to maintain order and on the other to see that the taxes (generally paid in kind) are duly paid into the Treasury. The *dzong-pöns* enjoy great independence; also all the revenue that they succeed in collecting over and above the amount due to the Government is their own personal property. The position is therefore sold by auction to the highest bidder. I have already mentioned that important posts in places distant from Lhasa are always doubled, the intention being that one official should keep his eye on the other.

Apart from the monks, the most important class is that of the landowners (*gyerpá*), who constitute the great and small nobility. It is interesting to note that their ownership of the soil is theoretically not absolute. The primary condition is that the family must regularly supply one or more of its members to enter the Government service. Young nobles are sent for a few years to a special school in Lhasa to complete their education, and they are then admitted to one of the Ministries. They enter as officials of the seventh, or lowest, grade, but, if a young man has the necessary ability, he may rise rapidly to the higher grades (*de-pon*, *sha-pe*, *chi-kyap*, etc.). There has been only one case in Tibetan history of a layman's becoming Regent for a brief period. A boy belonging to the humbler classes – the peasants or artisans – who wants to make a career in the world can always enter the church. If he enters a monastery and distinguishes himself he may be sent to a special school in Lhasa for ecclesiastical officials. Government officials, except the *dzong-pöns*, receive a small annual salary, say about £50 or £75 a year. It is assumed that the rest is supplied by his family, or that alternately he supplements his income by accepting gifts, which are normal, indeed obligatory, in dealing with Tibetan officials.

The leading nobility in Tibet consists of a very few families. One very ancient and exclusive group consists of descendants of the ancient Tibetan kings (sixth and seventh centuries, A.D.). The Lhagyari, Rakashar and a few other families belong to it. The heads of these families are accorded religious and civil honours. There are also noble families founded by men of humble origin who at various times rendered special services to the state and were rewarded by lands and titles. Some of these are of quite recent origin. As an example, let me tell the story of Tsarong Dzasa. He was born in 1885 of a humble family and entered the service of the Dalai as an ordinary servant. He promptly attracted attention because of his exceptional gifts of intelligence and character, and he accompanied the Dalai to Mongolia in 1903. His great hour came in 1913, when the Dalai was fleeing to India, pursued by Chinese troops. With a handful of soldiers and monks he succeeded in holding up the Chinese at the Chaksam ferry, thus giving the Dalai time to reach a place of safety. A year later, when the Dalai returned from India, he was appointed Dzasa and commander-in-chief of the Tibetan army. Two years later he was appointed a Minister (*sha-pe*). After 1925 he fell out of favour for a while, but he has always remained one of the most influential figures in Tibetan political life. He is distinctly progressive in outlook, speaks English, is always friendly to foreign travellers, and favours a policy of slow modernization.

A third group consists of descendants of the families of successive Dalai Lamas. The Potrang family, for instance, is descended from the brother of the seventh Dalai (1708–1758), and the Punkang family from the brother of the tenth (1819–1837); one of the most influential families, the Lhalus, are descended from the union of two branches, one descended from the family of the eighth and the other descended from the family of the twelfth Dalai. So far the Pangda-tsang family is the only one to have received *gyerpá* (landowner) privileges because of the important position they have come to occupy in commerce. The Pangda-tsang can well be called the bankers of Tibet. The recent economic mission to the United States was the result of the initiative of the present head of the family, and the thriving woollen export trade is to a great extent in the family's hands.

Once a noble family has established itself, there is no reason why it should ever disappear. When there are no sons to carry on the line the daughters, even after marriage, can retain their father's name. In such cases the son-in-law is adopted into his father-in-law's house, as is also sometimes the custom in Japan. That is what happened in the case of Tsarong Dzasa, whom we mentioned above; his original name was Namyang Dazang Damdu, but he assumed the name and rank of the Tsarong family when he married the eldest daughter of Tsarong-*sha-pe*, an important official.

Tibetan life, viewed as a whole, is typically mediaeval. It is mediaeval in its social organization – the predominance of the church and the nobility – and its economic basis is agriculture and stock-breeding. It has the colour and incredible superstition of France and Burgundy, the two most perfect examples of European mediaevalism; it has a mediaeval faith; a mediaeval vision of the universe as a tremendous drama in which terrestrial alternate with celestial events; a mediaeval hierarchy culminating in one man and then passing into the invisible and the metaphysical, like an enormous tree with its roots among the stones and its leaves lost in the blue of heaven; mediaeval feasts and ceremonies, mediaeval filth and jewels, mediaeval professional story-tellers and tortures, tourneys and cavalcades, princesses and pilgrims, brigands and hermits, nobles and lepers; mediaeval renunciations, divine frenzies, minstrels and prophets.

I must add that to me the Tibetans seem to be really happy people – so far as people can be happy on this earth. Happiness does not necessarily depend on social structure or system of government, as our contemporaries seem to think. To me it seems to be primarily a question of equilibrium between the world by which man is surrounded and the world which he carries in his heart. We live in an age of terrifying disequilibriums, and should be equally unhappy under kings, presidents, Popes or tribunes of the people, whether organized in republics or empires, soviets or theocracies. Our science offers us one picture of the universe; our traditional religion another. Physics and chemistry have advanced a thousand years ahead of the social sciences and the education of the will. Europe *caput mundi* is living through the agony of a noble decline. Ideals and standards are in a state of continual flux; professional standards and

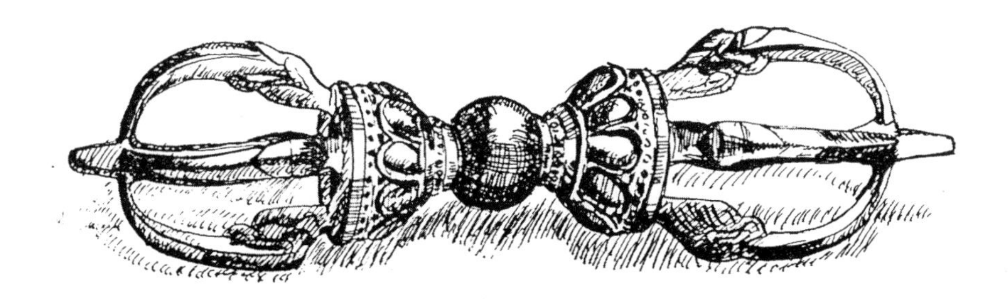

32 Dorje, *an artefact symbolizing a thunderbolt and endowed with magic powers (shown full-size)*

ideals, sexual standards, class ambitions, the kind of life that people aim for at different ages – all important elements in a stable society – are subjected to constant criticism and revision; everything is changing, becoming, perpetually fluid. New equilibriums unknown to us are perhaps on the way, in which future generations may perhaps find greater peace. But we are caught up in the grinding of the gears. Some of us succeed in extricating ourselves, but the majority are crushed.

1 The name "derives from the shape of the rock that towers above the convent; it is covered in strange spirals that from a distance look like the whorls on a shell. The conch or shell is well known to be a good-luck symbol among the Indo-Tibetans." Tucci, *Indo-Tibetica*, IV/1, p. 8.

2 I have left these brief notes as they were in the 1951 edition. Obviously everything has changed, but they may stand as a record of an archaic world that survived until 1959.

8

The Prince Gives his Eyes to the Beggar

Yatung: a village holiday

This morning there was a festive air about Yatung, because a play was going to be performed. But the "stage" and the players were not yet ready; preparations were still in full swing. When I crossed the bridge I saw three men running towards me. They were Losel, Paljor and Sönam. They had obviously been drinking, particularly Losel. They were singing at the top of their voices the current popular song: *Chang tung arak tung* . . . ("Drinking *chang* and drinking arak . . .")

"*Kushog-sahib*!" Losel shouted. "We've come to fetch you! It's Kenrab's birthday. He says he met you ten years ago, when you first came this way, and he wants to see you again. We're drinking and singing. Look what a lovely, sunny day it is! Won't you come? Yes, I knew you'd come! I told you the *kushog-sahib* would come!"

We walked for half-a-mile along the river. It was a perfect Tibetan summer morning, luminous and serene. Light, pearly galleons were navigating in the sky. Not only the village, but the whole universe seemed to be on holiday; you felt it in the air. Near the stream we came upon two tents (you can't have any kind of celebration in Tibet without tents) and a whole gathering of men and women, boys and girls, children and old women. It was a regular village outing – a side of Tibetan life that few Europeans know or imagine exists. It was neither sublime, nor thaumaturgic, nor hieratic, but simply gay, pagan and innocent.

"Sahib, here, come and sit down, make yourself at home!" They laid a carpet for the guest. "What would you like? Do you drink *chang*?" Of course I drink *chang*. It's a light, milky beer, refreshing and very mildly intoxicating. "No, thank you, no arak for me." Arak is strong, but has a flavour of petrol and leaves you with a headache. "Hallo, Kenrab, how are you? No, you don't look a day older! What? Oh yes, let's hope to meet like this every ten years, another ten times, *lho gya-tampa*, a hundred years of friendship! . . ."

The girls had taken off their *lhams* (Tibetan coloured-cloth slippers) and were paddling up to their thighs in the icy water of the river. They started singing a song at the top of their voices, but after a few verses they stopped, burst out laughing and started splashing one another. The men protested, but the girls took no notice. Tibetan women are independent and have minds of their own. Eventually one of the girls fell and was pulled out of the water, wet through. She took off her bright green vest and remained bare-breasted in the sun. This caused an uproar, and laughter that seemed as if it were never going to end.

A meal was spread on the grass. The men went on talking, and the women sat down and started to eat, calling their husbands, brothers and fiancés. The men eventually allowed their attention to be attracted, and squatted on the grass too, each taking a bowl and helping himself to food and drink contained in about fifty receptacles of various kinds, all tiny – bowls, cups, plates and pots – which were spread on a kind of tablecloth. It was a real Tibetan feast. There were Chinese noodles, rice, meat-balls, meat cut into crescents, squares, slices, many kinds of vegetables, boiled and fried, *tsampa* (roasted barley flour), butter (the everlasting butter), as well as arak, *chang* and tea.

We ate and drank. A monstrously filthy beggar approached, his face twisted into a grotesque, inexpressive smile. He was covered in rags and sores, carried a saucepan, a rosary and a prayer-wheel, and had a worn-out American soldier's cap on his head. He made innumerable jerky little bows, putting out his tongue and making gestures with his thumbs. An old woman filled her bowl with scraps and gave it to him. He thanked her, but then whined something. He wasn't hungry, he was thirsty; he wanted *chang*. This made Kenrab angry, and he sent the man away, but the old woman sent a child after him with a bottle of *chang*.

By this time everyone had drunk a little too much. The girls had started chasing one another about among the thickets of wild roses, laughing and shrieking, making an infernal din. Babies cried and their mothers suckled them. The men lay supine on the grass, looking like wine-skins put out to dry. The old women spread scraps of butter left on the plates on their hair.

Suddenly someone remembered that today was *ache-lhamo* day. Someone else called out: "*Gyok-po! Gyok-po!*" ("Hurry! Hurry!")

At first nobody moved, but then everybody got up, as if a magic word of command had suddenly penetrated into their stupefied minds. In a few moments they were all hurrying back to the village. Kenrab, who had woken up too, took me by the arm and said: "*Kushog-sahib*, you must come to the *ache-lhamo* too. Come along! Come along!" The whole valley was swaying, the mountains were collapsing and the forests were green flames. I ate millions of strawberries and dipped my head in the river. When we got back to the bridge we all felt a little better.

Yatung: the legend of Thrimikunden

In Tibet theatrical performances take place in the open air. The sacred mystery plays (*cham*) are performed in the courtyards of the monasteries and the profane plays (*ache-lhamo*) are performed in the public square. The distinction between the two categories is by no means well defined, and the plot always comes from Buddhist hagiography. Sacred plays are always acted and danced by monks, but profane plays are often given by wandering players, who go from village to village. They are also often performed by the villagers themselves. Once or twice a year they stop work, close their shops or drop their spades against the wall and act, sing or dance.

The actors of Yatung, though amateurs, are very good ones. Needless to say the chief actor, master of ceremonies and leader of the chorus was Tob-chen, the tailor. The play started at eleven o'clock this morning and was not due to finish till six o'clock this evening and when we arrived Tob-chen, though he had already been acting for three hours, showed no sign of fatigue. Every now and

33 *Yatung: Tob-chen, master of ceremonies in the ache-lhamo theatricals*

then he stopped, called to a child to bring him some *chang*, swallowed a cupful, and then went on again. The whole population of Yatung was present, as well as many people from the surrounding valleys, to say nothing of a number of chance spectators, travellers from Lhasa, Shigatse or Gangtok, who happened to be passing through. Some spectators sat on the ground on mats, and others on carpets. Many watched from the roof-tops and windows. The seats of honour on these occasions are generally those in tents, erected, I think, by the municipality. The orchestra consisted of one drum and a pair of plates for cymbals.

Spectators came, stayed a while, drifted away, came back, ate, drank and slept. Many brought low tables with them, on which they put tea-pots and cups. Women knitted and suckled their babies and old men smoked and chatted. The shepherds from the mountains looked on in fascinated astonishment, and the local, fashionable young men talked, laughed and argued, to show how used they were to theatrical entertainments. Everyone naturally knew the play by heart. Every now and then an actor would say a few lines with particular

34 *Yatung: theatricals – mask of an old man, the King of Betha*

35 & 36 *Yatung: spectators at the theatricals*

spirit, or sing particularly well, or dance with special fire and virtuosity, whereupon there would be applause or laughter. There was an atmosphere of complete rest, of delightful and total relaxation, such as could only be the result of customs that had been alive for centuries. The conventions of the whole thing had become part and parcel of the social organism, had become people's reflexes and instincts.

I asked Kenrab to tell me the story of the play, but he was too drunk, and had gone to sleep; so Mingyur Dondup, who speaks a little English, explained to me in detail all that was going on.

The hero of the play was the pious Prince Thrimikunden, the scene was laid in India, and the time was immemorial antiquity. Even the female parts were played by men. They all wore handsome silk costumes, and some wore masks. The audience's imagination had to make up for the complete lack of scenery; there was not even a placard, as there might have been in Elizabethan England, to indicate that we were supposed to be in India.

Thrimikunden ("the Immaculate") was destined to be the son of the King of Betha, but when the play opened he was still unborn. Meanwhile the King, though a fortunate and powerful monarch ("he has five hundred wives of noble lineage, five hundred wives of great wealth, five hundred wives of perfect beauty, while his wants are attended to by three thousand servants and he reigns over sixty vassals and possesses the *gö-dö-chung-jom*, the jewel which fulfills all desires") was in despair because he had failed to become the father of a son. The oracles whom he consulted advised him to invoke the Three Precious Things, Senge, Chö and Gedun (the Buddha, the Faith and the Community), and to sacrifice to the eight classes of demons and give many alms. One happy day the Queen Gedun-tsangmo ("Virtuous and Good") had a premonitory dream, after which she announced that

> The pure and vast palace of my body
> Shall be the receptacle of a son having infinite wisdom . . .

Thus Thrimikunden was born. No sooner was he born than he exclaimed: "*Om mani padme hum.*" At the age of five he already knew the scriptures, understood astronomy and delivered inspired discourses on the transient nature of human affairs and the universal reality of suffering:

> Alas! I live again the infinite sufferings
> Of the whole abyss of transmigrations.
> I suffer for the creatures who are led astray
> By the deceptive thirst for gold . . .

> I commiserate with him who does not know how to free himself
> From his self-centredness
> In the flaming city of desires . . .
> I am afflicted with the sorrow of husbands and wives
> Deceived by the hope of remaining together for ever.
> I pity those whom self-love
> Binds to their country;
> For their country is only
> A temporary camp in a stony waste.

But little Thrimikunden was not satisfied with merely proclaiming in verse the sublime truths of Buddhist philosophy. He wanted to act, to help his fellow-men, and he therefore ardently implored his father to allow him to give away as alms to the poor and needy all the wealth contained in the state treasury, which was sterile and useless so long as it lay idly locked up in strong-boxes. The old man was much moved by his son's words, and gave him *carte blanche* to do as he liked. However, the wicked Minister Taradze intervened, reminding the King that, though alms-giving might seem a very fine thing, his son's proposals were fundamentally harmful, because they would result in the impoverishment of the state. Might it not be advisable instead to find the young prince a wife?

> When he is married
> He will be attached to wealth . . . .

However, Princess Mende-tsangmo, who was chosen to be his bride, though she was extremely beautiful

> White in colour and of sweet odour . . . .

was as devout as Thrimikunden himself. Far from encouraging him to practise economy, she encouraged his charitable ways. Very soon three children were born to the happy couple – two boys, Leden ("Virtuous") and Lepel ("Good and Noble"), and a girl, Lendzema ("Good and Beautiful"). The little family was the ornament of the whole kingdom.

Where there was so much happiness, it was natural that evil should be lurking. The neighbouring King Ching-thri-tsangpo, jealous of Betha's power, started scheming to obtain "the jewel that carries out every desire". Having heard of Thrimikunden's unlimited generosity, he decided to take advantage of it; accordingly he sent a brahmin to ask him for the jewel. The brahmin travelled over mountain and plain and finally presented himself to Thrimikunden and made his request. After some hesitation, the prince gave him the jewel.

When the King, his father, heard of this, his rage knew no bounds. Thrimikunden was handed over to the royal torturers, who dragged him round the city, whipping him, as well as the pious Mende-tsangmo and her children who came behind, weeping. Meanwhile the Ministers gathered at the palace and discussed whether the guilty prince should be skinned, whether his heart should be torn out, or whether he should be cut in pieces bit by bit. But the good Minister Dewa-tsang-po, rose to speak; he persuaded the King to forgive his son and give him some milder punishment. The result was that the prince was condemned to twelve years' exile on the Duri-hashang mountain, a wild, savage spot, populated by demons. Thrimikunden prepared to depart, and bade a moving farewell to his aged mother.

When Kenrab and the rest of us reached the little open space by the bridge where the performance was in progress Thrimikunden and his family were in the hands of the torturers. The five unfortunates, bound to one another, were making their way bent and shamefaced round the square, while the torturers pushed them and went through the motions of whipping them. It was curious to see an important oriental judicial principle in action – that is, making his whole family pay for a crime committed by the head of a household.

The action developed extremely slowly. That is why the play lasted for eight hours. The actors began every one of the innumerable scenes by formally presenting themselves to the audience. They then walked once or twice round the open space, keeping time with the drum and plates. Finally, the leader of the chorus – our old friend Tob-chen – intoned a long running commentary which described in full what was going on, while the actors acted in a kind of pantomime a scene which took the action forward by one step. Then there was another dance, the actors presented themselves all over again, there was another pantomime accompanied by a running commentary, and so on until sunset.

The scene changed slowly from the kingdom of Betha to the demon-haunted mountain. The spectators' imagination had to supply the deep, wooded valleys, where the silence was broken only by the howling of wild beasts, the tall, snow-covered peaks, the huge rivers dashing over precipices, or the glades where nature grew milder for a moment and the caravan halted for the night.

Thrimikunden left his father's kingdom with a large escort, but very soon he met people who begged for alms. He started by giving away all the wealth that he had brought with him, and when it was exhausted he gave away his horses and elephants as well. The royal exiles were reduced to advancing through the mournful, desolate mountains on foot. Mende-tsangmo had a moment of dismay, but recovered from it, and when Thrimikunden decided to send her home she refused to leave him. When they reached a glade with lotus flowers in bloom Mende-tsangmo went into ecstasies:

> You who rise out of the mud untouched by the mud
> Smile with delight, lotuses adorned with stamens . . .

This peaceful interlude did not, however, last long. Thrimikunden's generosity was like an inescapable doom. "Only thus do merits acquired in past lives rise up to bear their final fruit." More beggars appeared in the forest, and the Prince, having nothing else left to give away, gave away his children. However absurd this incident may seem to us, the fact that the author meant it, and that it was in harmony with the Buddhist outlook, was shown by the intensity of the feeling which he put into the mouths of his characters. The grief of this father, who sought to find peace in the repetition of religious truths ("no union can last for ever"), was vividly portrayed; so, too, was the children's horror at being handed over as slaves to unknown men; and so was the mother's anguish. She turned on her husband like a wounded animal and cursed him for his utter devotion to a superhuman ideal. But then she asked his forgiveness and sought consolation in accepting the sacrifice.

The audience had grown most attentive; I saw dozens of rapt faces. Dondup explained every phase of the action to me with admirable clarity. I don't know whether I was more moved by the play or by its reflection in the eyes of the children, shepherds, women and old men. All this part of the story, which grappled with immense, eternal human themes, was full of the most exquisite and profound poetry. Above all, it dealt with the great theme of the conflict between celestial and terrestrial love. Generous deeds were done and agonizing farewells spoken in an atmosphere of continuous miracles and superhuman phenomena. The limitations of nature were broken through; birds talked, rivers brought tidings, flowers understood, the wind gave counsel. Finally the Tibetan imagination gave rein to one of its favourite themes – monstrous, terrifying demons – and masked dancers leapt screaming and pirouetting about the square, while terrified children clung shrieking to their mother's necks.

Kenrab woke for a moment from his heavy sleep and looked at the demons. "*Kushog* won't believe me," he said, "but *kang-chen ri la*, on the big ice-mountains, demons dance just like that. I've seen them with my own eyes!"

Then he fell asleep again. I'm quite convinced that Kenrab had seen demons. Who does not project his own interior universe into the outside world?

Finally the grand ladies of the neighbourhood arrived: the postmaster's wife – a little Nepalese woman covered with golden necklaces and bracelets, with a gold disc appended to her nose – Mrs Yishe and the headman's daughters. It is considered smart to make one's appearance in the middle of the afternoon, when the sun is not too hot and some of the most stirring scenes in the play are just coming on, and you can say: "But, my dear, you should have seen last year's performance at Shigatse!" or "But this is absurd! Now, in Lhasa . . ." Women had their babies slung round their shoulders (just as in Japan), and when the babies woke they rocked them gently without stopping talking (just as in Japan). Tob-chen, the "king", not of the plot but of the production, grew tired at last. Every now and then he sat down, had a drink of *chang*, and said his lines holding his hat in his hand, like an old man saying his prayers in church while thinking about something else.

The drama neared its end. Thrimikunden's sufferings were by no means ended, but now at last he was on his way home again. But at this stage he was faced with his hardest, his most sublime, ordeal. Coming down the Hashang mountain he met a beggar, and all he had left to give him was his eyes. (The dance of the beggar with his eye-trophies in his hands was unforgettable.) Then miracles started happening. Thrimikunden reacquired his sight and found his children again. The wicked King Ching-thri-tsangpo repented and returned the jewel to the King of Betha, and everything ended in glory.

The last lines were sung after the sun had disappeared behind the fir-trees on the mountainside. The actors, exhausted after eight hours of poetry and dancing, took off their costumes and removed their masks, and the boys were at last able to run across the square, shouting and laughing.

9

The Mysterious Bon-Po

Pemogang: the original Tibetan religion

Writings on the walls reveal the soul of a country. It is natural that Italy, a country of excessive individualism, should present the traveller with the sight of walls painted all over with the letter W standing for *Viva* (long live) so-and-so, and the letter M standing for *Morte* (death) to so-and-so, and that the Ws should be frequently turned into Ms and *vice versa*, the whole frequently ending up in an indecipherable scrawl. It is natural that in certain northern countries much addicted to discipline the traveller should find inscriptions in the parks with the word *schön* (beautiful) and an arrow; and it is equally natural that in India, where faith in the purifying power of words is an age-old tradition, slogans such as the following should be written up in the stations: "Be well-behaved, because only thus will you be able to gain the confidence of others."

In Tibet you see inscriptions of all kinds, chalked on the walls, painted on the doors, formed of rows of white pebbles on the mountainsides and carved in the walls of rock. But they are always religious: *Om mani padme hum* ("Hail, O jewel in the flower of the lotus"), or: "Long life to our Precious Protector (the Dalai Lama)," or: "Honour the Three Precious Things (*Senge, Chö, Gedun* – Buddha, the Faith and the Community)." Swastikas, whether pointing right or left, are also often to be seen. The swastika is a very ancient symbol, which the Germans took from the East; in China, Tibet and Japan it is everywhere associated with Buddhism. The swastika pointing to the right is used by the Yellow Sect (the *Gelug-pa*); the "unreformed" sects generally use a swastika pointing the other way.

Sometimes, however, you see the left-pointing swastika in villages or on the doors of houses that do not belong to any of the lamaist sects. In such cases, instead of the familiar *Om mani padme hum*, you find the variation *Om matri salei du*. There will be the same *mendang*s, the same *chorten*s, the same *tarcho*s, and you may even find a small monastery in the neighbourhood, but you will certainly be in an area where the ancient, original cult of Tibet, the Bon cult, has survived.

Everything connected with the Bons is extremely interesting. After centuries and centuries Buddhism has succeeded in extensively modifying it (and undergoing its influence in turn). Buddhism has eliminated it altogether from vast areas and circumscribed it in others, but it has not succeeded in doing away with it completely. Here and there you still find families which are Bon by tradition, and districts or villages which are exclusively Bon. Pemogang ("Knee Hill"), not far from Yatung, is predominantly inhabited by Bon-po, adherents of the Bon religion. I went to it this morning. From Yatung I followed the caravan route for a little way, left it at the bottom of the valley, and clambered for hours up a stony mule-track that wound its way between dried-up shrubs and past rocky precipices. Down below me the valley opened up in a manner that grew more grandiose every minute, while the roar of the torrent faded into a deep, continuous but indistinct murmur. The peaks across the valley seemed simultaneously to rise and acquire ever more magnificent proportions. In the distance was Kundugang, covered with snow and ice. I came to a wood of fir-trees, and emerged on to a plateau at the foot of some high mountains. Here, among fields of barley and grazing cattle, were three villages: Kirimtse, Gangku and Pemogang. Kirimtse and Gangku are normal Tibetan villages, with their little Buddhist *lhakangs* (houses of god, temples). But Pemogang is an exception; it is a refuge of the Bon-po.

As the morning advanced the weather, which had been magnificent at first, gradually deteriorated, and when I reached Gangku ("The Nine Ridges") the sky was overcast. The landscape was grim. Pemogang was visible in the distance, at the other end of the plateau. It is a village of about twenty houses, and all its inhabitants are peasants. I approached it by a path that wound its way among thickets of wild roses and fields of barley, but it still seemed incredibly remote.

Anyone who tries to search out the hidden soul of the places through which he travels knows how profoundly a place is inhabited by its gods. True, God created man, but men also create God. Indeed, the supreme and final goal of every civilization is the creation of God. Poets' visions are sublimated in His person, cathedrals of thought are erected about Him, and. the most sublime and consummate expressions of beauty are directed towards representing Him. Finally God returns among mankind, filling the valleys, the seas, the forests and the cities with life and aspiration.

Perhaps because Buddhism is a religion of such vast and profound significance, perhaps because Buddhist, like Christian, art has conferred upon humanity some of the most memorable testimonials of the heights to which inspiration can mount, perhaps because of the number of great men who have endowed it with space, light and metaphysical pride, perhaps for these as well as other reasons of which I may be unaware, I have always found something familiar and likeable about the villages of Tibet, almost as if I had been born and bred there instead of in Florence. But as I approached Pemogang I felt it to be a small stronghold of an unknown universe, possibly a hostile universe, possibly a stupid or mean or evil one. The little I knew about the Bon-po, was not encouraging. In ancient times they practised human sacrifice. There were strange links between them and the Manichees and shamanism. Their world was populated by good and evil forces, engaged in an eternal struggle. According to popular repute, they were necromancers and exorcists, snake-breeders and experts in the preparation of poisons. They were the occult, demonological Etruscans of Asia.

A few years ago I had similar feelings when for the first time I approached an Ainu village, in Hokkaido, in northern Japan. I knew about those primitive aborigines' cult of certain vague personifications of fire, the sea, mountains, water, various illnesses, the huts in which they live; and finally of the cult of the bear which is carefully reared in every Ainu village and is then killed and eaten at a ceremonial feast as a way of establishing communion with the invisible – a wild and barbarous form of theophagy. But then I got to know the Ainu better, and grew familiar with their legends and their world, and gradually the valleys and mountains of Hokkaido started talking to me with their own voices. They

37 *Pemogang, near Yatung: temple guardians of the Bon-po sect*

were no longer just a place, an area on a map, and my sense of the unknown, my suspicions, diminished. The Karnui, the Ainu gods, turned out, like the Ainu themselves, to be simple, impulsive and adventurous, playful or ferocious, but quick to forgive, and in any case entirely irrational. They were brothers of the wind playing among the leaves in summer, of the noise of the torrents in spring, of the roar of the avalanches in winter; vague personifications of nature, of ancestral memories, of primitive philosophical intuitions, at the centre of which there was the idea of *ramat* (spirit), the secret link between the heart of man and things.

But here was Pemogang. Life here was no different from what it was in Gangku or Kirimtse. Women were working in the fields. As soon as they saw me they called out: "*Par! Par!*" ("Photograph! Photograph!") A white man in these parts is primarily *homo photographans*. There were two noisy old women – as noisy as all old women are in Tibet – and a girl of fifteen or sixteen all covered in rags, which were tied round her waist with a piece of string; every movement revealed her fresh and healthy, but horrifyingly dirty, body. Soon there arrived the usual horde of Tibetan children, who do not know the meaning of shyness. They jump on you, snatch things from your hands, drag you by the clothes, out of pure high spirits and cheerfulness.

The houses of Pemogang were poor. The path connecting them consisted of nothing but mud, stones and cow-dung. The village had the characteristic smell of small Alpine villages. There were some broken-down *chorten*s and many stones with *Om matri salei du* written on them. Eventually I met a man. He looked like a peasant, but there was a certain stiffness about the way in which he approached me, and he looked at me as if to say: What is this intruder doing here? I asked him where the village temple was, and he suddenly became smiling and servile, but his manner was not inwardly servile; it seemed to be adopted in the hope of doing a stroke of business. He spoke to me with an air of patronizing superiority, of ill-concealed contempt, a state of mind which I rarely came across among the lamas.

There was nothing to distinguish the outside of the temple from any of the lamaist temples. It was a square building, with a big timber roof, with a small gilded pavilion (*kenchira*) on top. The entrance was under a portico, and there were the usual decorative wall paintings. I noticed at once the Four Kings (*Gyalchen-de-shi*), similar in every way to the lamaist Four Kings, and four female divinities who preside over the seasons, the blue Yagi-gyerno (queen of summer), the yellow Gungi-gyerno (queen of winter), the green Tongi-gyemo (queen of autumn) and the red Chigi-gyemo (queen of spring). These four queens seem to have a special importance in the Bon religion, but they are painted to look exactly like the lamaist female divinities; that is to say, their appearance is ultimately based on that of Indian divinities. I had hoped, vaguely, it is true, and without any justification from anything that I had read or been told, that the Bon religion might have developed at least some elementary independent artistic expression of its own, but I was completely disappointed.

Actually it was completely unreasonable to have expected anything else. Only a very few supreme civilizations have been able to create truly independent, artistic idioms of their own. Practically nothing has been produced, for instance, by the pre-Buddhist Japanese spiritual world and the world of Shintoism (the native cult of the Japanese archipelago). The nation's artistic efforts were from the first directed to the celebration of Buddhism. The matter is more important than one might suppose. Unless a principle is adopted, as in the case of Islam, to avoid any form of iconography, the common people, the great mass of believers, if not the philosophers, require their divinity to have a form. The choice and adoption of that form by a civilization is a process of incalculable consequence.

As soon as I set foot in the temple I saw that every detail of the architecture, iconography and sacred furnishings had been taken from lamaism; I believe that the liturgy is also very much the same. There were the same drums, the same trumpets formed of human thigh-bones (which when possible have to be the thigh-bones of a sixteen-year-old virgin), the same lamps for burning butter, the same little throne for the chief lama, the same white shells for use as trumpets, the same benches for the celebrants, the same wooden masks for dances; everything, in fact, was the same. If I had not known I was in a Bon temple, I should have had difficulty in believing it. There was even a big, glass-fronted book-case full of books, exactly like those in which the Buddhist *Kangyur* is kept. This book-case, however, contained the mysterious scriptures of the Bon-po, which Giuseppe Tucci will be one of the first to investigate.

My companion told me that he was the Lama Yulgye – even the term *lama* ("master") is taken from the rival religion – and he gave me long explanations in a sing-song voice, rather as if he were repeating verses which he had learned by heart and only imperfectly understood. Pemogang must be very remote from the world, because he looked at my camera with great apprehension. He knew what it was, but seemed very uncertain whether to allow me to photograph his gods or not. At last my eyes got used to the darkness, and I saw that the walls were completely covered with frescoes, and that at the end of the temple there were some large gilded statues.

As I started seeing better I noticed some differences between these and the paintings and statues usual in Buddhist temples. The names were all different too. The figure that appeared most often was that of Tömba-Shenrab (or Shenrab-mibo), the master and revealer of the Bon doctrines. His place in this religion corresponds to that of Gautama Buddha in lamaism. In one big fresco to the left of the entrance he was actually shown with sixteen disciples in a group which exactly followed the celebrated and frequent *motif* of the Buddha with his sixteen *arhat*s.

Against the bottom wall of the temple were some huge statues, standing in a big, gilded shrine. On the left was Tömba-Shenrab again, looking like Buddha. Next to him was a still bigger and more impressive statue, of notable ugliness and clumsiness, representing Pema-chung-ne ("Emerged from the Lotus"). It was covered with gilt, and stood half in and half out of the shrine.

"Tömba-Shenrab is exactly like Buddha," I remarked.

"Certainly," replied the "lama" Yulgye. "All our gods have a Buddhist counterpart."

Actually he did not use the word "Buddhist", a word which does not exist in Tibetan. The word they use is *chö*, faith, religion. Yulgye referred to Buddhism

38 *Pemogang: Pema-chung-ne, a Bon-po deity in gilded wood in the Bon temple*

as "the faith of the *Gelug-pa*". I don't know whether the Bon-po always refer to Buddhism in this way, or whether Yulgye did so to make his meaning clear to me.

"Pema-chung-ne, for instance, is the same as Padma Sambhava, the Guru Rimpoche of the *Gelug-pa*," he went on.

"But Bon is one thing and Buddhism another, isn't that so, Lama Yulgye?"

"Yes," he answered. "We were here first." He said this as if it were a fact well known to everybody. "Ours is the real religion of Tibet," he went on. "Buddhism came from India. In any case, we all aim at the same goal. It's as if I went to Lhasa by way of Phari and you went by way of Kampa. The route is different, but the destination is the same."

This was a very fine parable, but, if one's first impressions are to be trusted, I do not like the Bon religion. There's something uncanny about it, though that's only an impression, I repeat. Perhaps it's the feeling that it's a primitive religion, which only came to have proper temples, scriptures, ceremonial and art because of contact with its Buddhist neighbour. Finally there is the fact that no great human spirit has expressed himself in it – a sure sign of inferiority. Its spaces have never been illuminated – they have always been gloomy and nocturnal.

We have only limited information about the ancient Bons, mostly contained in the *Kesar* of Ling, an enormously long, war-like, chivalrous poem dating from the first millennium of our era. It is certain that cruel human sacrifices were practised, and the spirit of the age seems to have been, not just robustly barbarous, but savage in the extreme. There is continual talk of eyes being torn out, of blood being drunk from skulls, of tortured enemies, of trophies consisting of parts of the human anatomy offered as gifts to victorious kings, and so on. When a Ling soldier captures a Hor spy he gloats over the tortures he is about to inflict on him and, in Bell's translation:

> The blood of the liver will escape from the mouth.
> Though we do not injure the skin,
> We will take out all the entrails through the mouth.
> The man will be alive, though his heart will come to his mouth.

When Buddhism at last came to the country and modified the customs of the wild mountaineers and introduced the light of Indian civilization, the Bons were obliged to abandon their human and animal sacrifices and instead use *torma*, little statues made of dough, consisting of barley flour, butter and water. This very much resembles what happened in the third century A.D., in Japan, when terracotta statues (*haniwa*) were substituted for the men and women who used to be buried alive when the Japanese sovereign died.

The struggle between the two demiurges of good and evil is fundamental to the Bon conception of the universe. Their theogony is thus definitely derived from Iranian and Manichaean sources. It is not for nothing that the Bon-po agree in attributing the origin of their faith to western Tibet. Their cosmogony and their rites, however, go back to the primitive and undifferentiated cults of central and northern Asia known under the generic name of shamanism. For the Bon-po, as for the shamans, the heavens are an entity of supreme importance. The heavens are wisdom and power, the visible aspect of divinity. From the heavens – that is to say, from one of the nine heavens – there descends to earth a rope (*mu-tag*) along which exchanges between this and the next world take place; the dead mount it to their ultra-terrestrial destination.

The Bon mythology is exceedingly complicated; it enumerates an endless number of occult spirits or divinities, nearly all hostile to man; these spirits are jealous of their possession – lands, trees, rivers – and it is necessary to propitiate them by continual sacrifices. For this reason, among others, Bon priests have always been exorcists and necromancers, easily falling into trances, which are understood to be possession by or communion with the divine spirits. Perhaps the Tibetan love of masks is of shamanistic origin. In many places, outside as well as inside Tibet, the shaman, when possessed by a spirit or a god, covers his face with a mask as a symbol of the total alteration of personality that takes place in him.

On my way out I noticed on the walls near the entrance a series of four terrifying divinities (the lama could not tell me their names). My first reaction was to say that the differentiation of the gods into terrifying and pacific categories had also been copied from lamaism. But on reflection it occurred to me that it was the reverse that was probably true. In fact, ancient Tibetan legends say that when Padma Sambhava preached Buddhism in Tibet he converted not only men but also a large number of local genii and demons, who were thereupon accepted into the faith, maintaining their terrifying aspect as its champions and defenders. All that contains profound elements of truth; it means, in other words, that Buddhism did not replace the pre-existing religion overnight, but instead absorbed many of its features. This provides an explanation for a great deal of the savage, bloodthirsty, barbarous, satanic spirit of Tibetan art, which represents the survival of an ancient Asian substratum, of which the Bon religion is an important element. Thus, considering these pictures a second time, they can be considered to be the only really autochthonous feature, perfectly attuned to the secret spirit of a grim, sinister religion, all snakes, exorcism and magic spells.

We went outside. The sun was shining again. Little red and yellow wild flowers were growing in the spaces between the big stones that paved the village square. It was a liberation. In the distance the icy summit of Kundugang gleamed for a moment in a clear sky, and then heavy midday clouds covered it again. The women working in the fields were singing.

IO

The Visions of the Dead

Lama Ngawang: "At bottom you are civilized people like us."

Kirimtse is a tiny village lying on the same plateau as Pemogang ("Knee Hill"). But, while Pemogang has a Bon temple, at Kirimtse there is a fine Buddhist temple, belonging to the *Nima-pa* sect ("the Ancient Ones"). One might have expected a certain rivalry between the two villages, but I could find no trace of such a thing, at any rate on the surface. The people of Kirimtse say that the people of Pemogang are Bon-po just as casually as the people of an Italian village might say of those of the next village that they were water-diviners or were good at grafting, or some such thing. In other words, they talk of them as a group of neighbours who happen to have special characteristics but are fundamentally the same as themselves.

Only one person made a slight grimace when I told him I was going to Pemogang; he was Lama Ngawang, of Kirimtse. But Lama Ngawang is a rather special individual, and a law unto himself He is an old grumbler, with an incredible number of years on his head and incredibly few hairs in what might be described as his beard. His opinions are always ready, clear and precise, and he always states them in very outright fashion.

I shall not easily forget our first encounter. I came down from the mountains that enclose Kirimtse on the West. The weather that afternoon from bad had become appalling. I remember the clouds growing greyer and greyer, the mountain that rose interminably until it vanished into the clouds, and finally the rain which came down and laid a grey mist over the whole landscape. Eventually I felt I had lost my way. Fortunately I came upon a *chorten*. I stopped, heard voices, and found I was just outside the village. I went straight to the monastery-temple. It was a big, solid, white-washed building, with high walls enclosing a courtyard, which one entered by passing through a wooden doorway; the door squealed open. The courtyard was deserted. I was wet, cold, hungry and tired. I called out. An old woman appeared on a wooden balcony.

"Come in!" she said. "There's a fire alight!"

I went up the creaking stairs and found myself in a smoky room, half kitchen and half sacristy. An old lama was sitting in the corner near the window. His spectacles were perched on the tip of his nose and he was reading prayers aloud. Every now and then he broke off to sip a little tea, but his attention was not distracted, and he did not so much as look at me.

"Lama Ngawang is reading the scriptures," the old woman whispered, with great and obvious reverence. "Don't disturb him! Sit here near the fire and dry yourself. But where do you come from? What have you been doing in the mountains at this time of day? Don't you know there are *rii-gompo* (mountain demons) who suck one's life out and leave one empty? Drink a little tea! The lama won't be long."

Her lama-husband (it is normal for the lamas of the *Nima-pa* sect to marry) continued reading impassively. My clothes steamed and started getting dry, and I felt better every minute. It was getting dark and the kitchen-sacristy filled with shadows. It was an irregular-shaped room, blackened with soot. Against one wall were pots and pans, flour sacks, a pile of logs, bowls, saddles, Tibetan slippers, cups, and packets of tea; on the other were books, a few pictures on cloth, statuettes, a little drum, lamps, peacock quill-pens, offerings of butter, a bronze thunderbolt – in short everything needed by a pious lama in the exercise of his duties.

Soon afterwards, while I was holding a cup of tea between my fingers to warm them, I felt a hand on my shoulder and heard a low, almost cavernous, voice.

"*Oé! Oé!* And where do you come from?"

It was Lama Ngawang, who had got up and walked barefooted over to the fireplace. Later I found out that he started practically every sentence with "*Oé! Oé!*", in the tone of voice of one saying: "My boy, just you listen to me!" The first time I heard it it struck me as rude, and it made me take a momentary dislike to him. But I soon discovered I was mistaken; the lama was an enchanting old gentleman. He was one of those persons of great faith and great directness of speech, who know exactly what they want, and want it because it reflects their unshakeable idea of what is good and right.

The next time I went to see him the weather was fine. The temple courtyard was flooded with warm, bright sunshine. All round I saw flowers growing in rusty old petrol tins. Who knows how they had got there? The courtyard naturally served also as a threshing-floor, and herbs and beans had been laid out to dry in the sun.

I went upstairs to Lama Ngawang. He greeted me with a broad smile, the kind that comes from the heart. He had not believed me when I had said I would come back. But here I was. He was delighted.

"Will you have some tea? *Oé! Oé!* Drolmá! Bring some tea for the *chiling-pa* (foreigner). But you were really crazy to come up here so late the other day, and in the rain too! Who knows what you might have met on the mountains at night! Did you say *Om mani*?"

The lama looked hard at me.

"Yes, yes, of course I did."

It would have been impossible to have answered no. Who would have had the heart to disappoint an old man with such a firm and impregnable faith? To Lama Ngawang everything was obvious, clear, beyond dispute. Soon afterwards he asked me about my country.

"Are there monasteries where you come from?" he asked. "*Oé! Oé!* You don't come from a barbarous country, do you?"

"No, I do not come from a barbarous country, Lama Ngawang," I answered. "In my country there are many monasteries."

"And many lamas?"

"Many lamas."

"And you read the scriptures?"

"We read the scriptures."

"Bravo, bravo, then you're like us, you're a civilized people too! *Oé!* Drolmá! Did you hear? They're like us! They're civilized people too!"

I suppose I should have explained the difference between the two countries in religion and in so many other things too, but I lacked the courage. The lama's happiness at what I said filled his face with light and warmth. I thought of how Christians of former ages must have looked when merchants from Central Asia told them of scattered communities of faithful Nestorians in the empire of the Mongols. Lama Ngawang is a straightforward, simple man, who has lived in an isolated village in the mountains for seventy years and more, and to have undeceived him would have been useless and cruel.

Then we went down to see the temple. On the steps we were stopped by an old village woman, who was accompanied by a little girl. The old woman spoke rapidly to the lama. When she had finished he turned to me.

"*Oé!* The little girl is ill, you must cure her," he said.

I tried to explain that it was impossible, because I was not a doctor.

"What? You're not a doctor? But you *chiling-pa* are all doctors! When needs be, we are all doctors too . . . And you have so many extraordinary medicines! *Oé! Oé!* Have a look at the girl, and prescribe her a good medicine."

I had to give in, and try to find out in my own way what was wrong with the girl. Alas! No very great medical knowledge was required. She was thin, pale, flushed, and said she had pains in her chest. I made her spit on a piece of paper, and she spat blood, bright, purple blood. Poor little girl! What could anyone do for her? Air better than that of Kirimtse would be hard to find, I said she must rest and eat well.

"I know what is the matter with her," Lama Ngawang announced. "There is some devil who wishes her ill. I shall exorcize him. Drolmá! *Oé!* Drolmá! Bring me the *damaru* (the little drum)!"

The exorcism lasted for some time. When the old woman and the girl had gone Lama Ngawang stood at the temple door with his feet apart, looking like an ancient tree that had survived appalling tempests. With a threatening gesture he said something about the "accursed demons who never leave us in peace". The effect of his words was that it must be clear to all, in heaven and on earth, that he, Lama Ngawang, and they, the demons, were irreconcilable enemies.

The Visions of the Dead

In the little temple of Kirimtse, as in all other Tibetan temples, there are many frescoes. Two are of special interest. One shows the Great Paradise of Padma Sambhava; the other shows the Visions of the Dead (*shi-trö*). Let us for a moment contemplate the painting of the Visions of the Dead, and consider what are the effects on a civilization of adopting a belief in a single mortal life, and compare it with the effects of a belief in successive incarnations.

Belief in only one life – the Western belief – leads to a strained, tense, hectic outlook. Time presses, and our single, never-to-be-repeated youth runs through our fingers like pearls dropped irremediably into an abyss. Loves and hates swell to the size of irremovable mountains. Virtue adorns the soul like a flashing sword and sin weighs it down like a lump of granite. Everything is unique, final, immense: an interjection in the biography of the ego, set for chorus and orchestra. Finally death presents itself, not as a stage in a journey, but as the end; an event of outstanding, terrifying importance.

The career of the individual is thus simple, but full of care and responsibility. Creation is followed by life in time. There is freedom of action, and one's deeds can be salutary or harmful, or actually fatal to the eternal Principle within. Finally death cuts short the process of becoming, and henceforward the past is congealed and irremediable. Sin inexorably demands its punishment. Earthly life is followed by the judgment, and beyond that there is eternity. We have made our single appearance on the stage of life, to which there is no return. "You only live once," as popular wisdom puts it. You only die once too.

But a belief in reincarnation, in a succession of lives, leads to an outlook both more grandiose and less dramatic, to a broader but cooler picture of the universe; a calming, analgesic picture, full of time and patience. In such a universe there are certain cruel questions which lose their sting, including the cruellest of all questions – why should innocent children suffer? In such a universe the suffering of children enters into the order of things; it is the consequence, the punishment, of evil done in previous lives. The whole picture is more serene and more logical. Life is not so much an episode as a state; true, it is theoretically a provisional state, but a provisional state that lasts for an untold number of centuries. The cosmic life of man could, as a theoretical minimum, consist of one terrestrial life only, but in ordinary cases it consists of innumerable successive lives. Death is therefore not a tragic, supreme culmination, a single, fearful event, a crucial moment from which there is no return, but is, like life, an experience that is repeated at certain intervals, a normal transition to which one must become accustomed, a process as natural as sunset at the end of day. Hence Buddhists have always been great thanatologists, great students of death. Preoccupied as they are with the problem of escaping from the flux of becoming in order to attain the ineffable serenity of being, they have been able to study death with the simplicity and detachment of an industrialist studying a phase of production. To them death is not a mystery, but a problem.

The results of their long and profound labours in this field of intellect and intuition were collected as early as the fourteenth century in a book that is of cardinal importance in the spiritual life of Tibet. This is the *Bardo Tö-döl* ("The Book that Leads to the Salvation of the Intermediary Life by the Sole Fact of Hearing it Read"). Like a *Baedeker* of the world beyond, it gives astonishingly detailed descriptions of the visions that appear in the mind of the dead, from the first until the forty-ninth day after it has left the body; that is to say, until the moment when it is on the point of entering a new bodily envelope. These visions constitute a synthesis of the lamaist conceptions of reality and of the universe. From the purity of the undifferentiated Absolute, of which gleams are obtained in the first stages of this temporary life after death, there is, as time passes, a gradual transition to ideal thought, then to individuated thought, and finally to matter. Just as the West, considering life from the biological aspect, sees the development of the species repeated in the development of the individual, so does lamaism, looking at life from the cosmic aspect, see in this intermediary state of life after death (*bardo*) a repetition of the evolution of reality from the Absolute (Buddha) to illusion (*samsara*).

Let us try to be more specific. After death, as we have mentioned, the conscious principle enters upon an intermediary stage of being, which lasts for forty-nine days. From this it can either emerge into liberation (*nirvana*) or return to *samsara*, the vortex of life. The *Bardo Tö-döl* tries to set it on the path of esoteric knowledge of the fundamental Buddhist truths, enabling it to experience "an immediate revulsion from the phenomenal plane of existence and an impulse towards the sphere of the absolute". (Tucci.) The fundamental truth of Buddhism is that *samsara*, "the vortex of life", is nothing but empty appearance and illusion, that only the Absolute really exists, and that it is only by identifying oneself with it (becoming Buddha) that one can be liberated from *samsara*.

The crucial phase in the cosmic history of the individual occurs in the first days after death. The conscious principle becomes aware of a pure, colourless luminosity. He who recognizes the Absolute in this and is able to fuse himself with it is saved, and has ended his cycle of lives. The alternative is descending a step towards the multiple, towards becoming, illusion and suffering. In the days that follow, the whole cosmic evolutionary process is represented in vast, symbolical visions which the conscious principle gradually experiences as it detaches itself from the body. The possibilities open to it present themselves in successive dichotomies, alternatives of liberation and enslavement. Understanding the first means re-entering the cycle of rebirths at a higher level; being bound to the second means being dragged lower because of the operation of *karma*.

On the walls of the temple of Kirimtse are large-scale paintings of the terrifying gods, terrifying to the conscious principle of him who is still bound to the illusions of life and believes he really sees them, but mere shadows to him who has reached a sufficient stage of maturity to understand their essential vacuity. These paintings show a stupendous population of fantastic forms, not creatures of the artist's imagination, but painted according to meticulous instructions set forth in the scriptures. Above all there are the Heruka, the terrifying manifestations of the *Dhyani* Buddhas, dancing in union with their own *shakti*s. Around them is unleashed a maelstrom of witches, with the heads of crows, tigers, scorpions, dogs, and other fantastic, raging animals.

The Lama Ngawang raised his lamp (the temple was very dark) and threw light on the picture. In the uncertain, tremulous light the monstrous figures seemed to come to life.

"*Oé! Oé!* Examine them well!" the lama said to me, turning and looking at me over his spectacles. "Examine them well, because one day you too will see them. When that happens, you mustn't be afraid. *Oé!* They are nothing but imagination, shadows, fantasies. If you remain perfectly calm and don't get frightened, it means salvation."

"But at bottom I'm afraid of death, Lama Ngawang."

Oé! You are foolish, *kuk-pa du.*" He looked at me severely again over his spectacles. "Everything dies, it's nothing to be afraid of! Who knows how many times you have died already! You must always be ready. If you die here, I'll read the *Bardo tö-döl* in your ear, and you'll see that it'll help you. *Oé!* Look well at the figures, they are void, nothing, illusion!"

The Lama Ngawang went to the end of the temple, took a piece of incense, lit the end of it from the lamp he held in his hand, put it in front of a statue to Padma Sambhava, bowed, and we went out.

The masks

Not far from the temple of Kirimtse there is a little *gön-kang* where the masks for the sacred dances are kept. When I mentioned the place (which I had heard about from a peasant to whom I talked on the way) Lama Ngawang turned out to be entirely opposed to the idea that I should visit it.

"What? You want to go to the *gön-kang?* No, no, it would be an act of madness! *Oé! Oé!* The gods there dislike being disturbed. Good heavens! The *gön-kang*? What are you thinking of? Besides, you would be running a grave risk; you don't know what might happen to you. You might become ill, you might even die. *Oé!* the gods of the *gön-kang* are very touchy; even a trifle can upset them!"

I knew that it was useless to tempt him with money. Lama Ngawang is incorruptibility personified. The first time I saw him I noticed a fine painting on cloth in the apartment of honour behind the kitchen, a portrait of a lama to whom some monks were bringing offerings. I asked the Lama Ngawang if by any chance he would be willing to sell it, but I found myself up against a brick wall.

"*Oé!* Where are we? What? Sell a saint?"

Today, after a great deal of insistence, I succeeded in getting him to agree to let me enter the *gön-kang* to see the masks and pictures. I hoped to be able to photograph them. Should I succeed? Lama Ngawang gave the keys to a peasant who accompanied me.

"No, no, I shan't come with you," he said firmly at the monastery gate. "I shall have nothing whatever to do with it! *Oé!* The gods there are very easily angered. Don't they have tutelary deities in your country? Well, then . . ."

The peasant opened the big locks of the *gön-kang* door. Behind it was another door, on which there was an extremely effective painting of the face of one of the terrifying deities. We went inside. The place was small, dark, ancient, low-ceilinged, and full of old armour and the carcasses of animals. On the walls were frescoes of local demons, painted with a fine vigour, and in a corner was a gilded pavilion with some statues. The masks, about thirty of them, hung from the ceiling, carefully wrapped in cotton handkerchiefs. I asked the peasant, as if it were the most natural thing in the world, to take some of them down, because I wanted to photograph them. The young man grumbled, but obeyed.

As the dirty, greyish cotton handkerchiefs were removed those fantastic personages with the soul of the wind and the look of wood came alive in the darkness of the temple. There were the terrifying gods, there was Namka-bazin (the murdered and deified monk), there were masks representing the *shi-trö*

39 *Kirimtse:* Cham *ritual dance in the little* Nima-pa *temple*

40 *Kirimtse:* Cham *ritual dance of the skeleton*

(the visions of the dead), huge bird faces, faces of mythological dogs, faces of animals of the forest. The peasant forgot the ritual prohibitions, put on one of the masks, and did a few steps of the ritual dance. It was not he who danced, but the face.

With some difficulty I persuaded the peasant to take the masks outside and to put them on, so that I might photograph them. Suddenly I heard somebody shouting from the corner of the square outside the *gön-kang*. It was Lama Ngawang who had come to see what was going on and had "caught" us.

"Put back the masks immediately!" he shouted. "Don't you know they must never see the light? *Oé!* Are you mad? Now evils will descend upon the whole village! If anyone is ill, the fault will be yours! If the harvest fails, the fault will be yours! If animals die, the fault will be yours! . . ."

I tried to calm him.

"Lama Ngawang, I assure you nothing will happen," I said. "If anything happens, it will be my fault. I'll take all the evils upon myself!"

Lama Ngawang approached me, looked at me very seriously, and said nothing. He had understood. He had understood from the light-heartedness with which I spoke that I did not believe. I felt at once that I had hurt him.

41 *Kirimtse: Lama Ngawang holding the keys to the* gön-kang, *shrine of the guardian spirits*

I was very sorry for it, but I had no chance to remedy it. The peasants who had gathered interrupted our silent colloquy.

"Did you hear, Lama Ngawang? Did you hear? The foreigner takes all the evil upon himself! Don't worry!"

They laughed. They looked at me as if I had the plague, and they were glad.

Lama Ngawang accepted the situation. He forgot the anger that he had perhaps felt for a moment. He let me go to the devil as the expiatory sacrifice. I even managed to photograph him against the inner door of the *gön-kang*, next to the face of the terrifying god.

"*Oé!* Don't forget to send me a copy!" he said when I said goodbye. But he spoke coldly. I had disappointed him.

Expiation

The other evening, when I got back to Yatung, I found waiting for me a letter from Pemà Chöki, from Gangtok. She described at length the celebrations that had taken place, at court and in the temple, in connection with the dedication of a new *chorten*. I answered describing my visit to the Lama Ngawang, and I told her how I had finally managed to photograph the masks.

At ten o'clock this morning the post came again. There was another letter from Pemà Chöki, sent by express post from the palace at Gangtok. She told me she was greatly worried at my having dared to take photographs of the *gön-kang*, and at my having carried the masks out into the daylight. "At times the gods can be a bad medicine," she wrote. "I implore you to go back to Kirimtse and have a *kar-sö*, a purification ceremony, conducted by the lama. If you don't believe in these things, please do it all the same for my sake. I'm worried." I was touched by the princess's letter. Apart from her evident concern for me, it was like being asked by a child: "How is it that Father Christmas doesn't get dirty when he comes down the chimney?" or: "Is it true that little Jesus has the loveliest toys in the whole world?"

This morning I woke up shivering, and with a bad pain in my back. It must have been a touch of lumbago. Piero produced a most plausible explanation, reminding me that yesterday it was very cold and damp. But I immediately remembered my light-hearted promise, a few days ago, to take upon myself all the evils that might ensue from the removal of the masks from the *gön-kang*. Then I laughed. Then I felt frightened. It was very stupid. But we are all surrounded by the unknown. Could my promise really have had some occult significance? My reason said "Nonsense". But what is reason worth, after all?

So I climbed up to Kirimtse under the midday sun (which chased the pain away and made me feel better immediately). I found Lama Ngawang sitting in his usual place beside the window, reading. Drolmá, his wife, was boiling *chu-kar* plants in a big saucepan, to dye some woollen cloth red. I drank a cup of tea and waited.

"So you've come back?" was the lama's eventual, cool greeting. "How are you? *Oé!* Have you heard that a mule has died at Pemogang? Luckily they are Bon-po at Pemogang. Otherwise they'd say it was because of the masks. And you? Why aren't you ill?"

"As a matter of fact, Lama Ngawang, I've got pains in my back."

"Just as I said! Just as I said! That's all right! If you're ill after your act of stupidity, we can rest assured that we shan't have to suffer the consequences!"

The lama's manner towards me had changed greatly for the worse. During my first visits I had felt in him the gladness of a man speaking to a distant brother, to whom he is linked by the same faith, and I had not had the courage to undeceive him, because I had felt how much this meant to him, and I did not want to spoil his pleasure. But now we had become strangers. The only link between us was a link in a game of magic. I had performed certain acts, said certain words, set in motion a concatenation of inevitable cause and effect. He was an onlooker. His only surviving interest in me was as a participant in the unhappy incident with the masks; I was a pawn in his game of chess with the invisible.

"Lama Ngawang," I said to him after some time, as I ate one of the fried biscuits which Drolmá offered me, "I've come up here because of that business the other day, when we took the masks outside. Now I want you to say a *kar-sö*, to pacify the gods of the *gön-kang*, in case they're offended. I've brought you five silver rupees."

Lama Ngawang spun round towards me, bent his head forward so that his glasses dropped to the tip of his nose, looked at me, smiled and opened his arms.

"We'll do it straight away," he said. "*Oé!* Drolmá! Bring me my cloak, we're going downstairs!"

Then he looked at me again, as if to say: So I made a mistake after all.

"*Oé!*" he said. "You've done well to come so soon. Bravo! Bravo!"

Our former friendship was re-established as firmly as ever. I knew it was based on a misunderstanding, but I was glad.

A dragonfly memory

In Buddhist countries every kind of life is sacred. In Tibet, where there are no dangerous wild animals, this simply means that the animals on the mountains live fearlessly side by side with man. On my way up to Kirimtse yesterday I came upon a flock of wild sheep (*argali*). They allowed me to approach to within a few paces of them and then calmly moved away; they did not run away. I must say that, however idyllic I found this state of affairs, my instinct would have been to "take" one of them. I do not shoot, but I can see that hunting has deep and natural roots in the mind of man. Fundamentally it offers the satisfaction of getting something of value – food, skins, a trophy – quickly, and perhaps easily, without the labour and patience required to produce it (and in that sense hunting may have similarities with games of chance); an important element is the satisfaction to be obtained from the contest between man and animal (and here the sporting element enters, the assertion of skill and strength); and finally there cannot be altogether absent a sadistic element – pleasure in bloodshed and the infliction of pain and death; and in that hunting often resembles love and always resembles war.

Travelling in Buddhist countries reminds one of problems which have never excessively preoccupied our own civilization; one of them is whether it is or is not legitimate to kill animals, and another, closely though not necessarily connected with it, is whether one should restrict oneself to a vegetarian diet. It must be admitted that there is something inherently repugnant about depriving any creature of life. Even the fly which is now buzzing about my head and annoying me (I shall certainly kill it soon if I can catch it) will suffer, will not want to die, will struggle for its unknown little satisfactions, its own tiny world, and there will be something reprehensible about my almost unthinking act.

On the other hand it is sufficient to look about one to see that life is organized on the principle of struggle, aggression and death, that equilibrium between the species is maintained by mutual destruction; and we, not being the authors of life, cannot hold ourselves responsible for the horror implied in this. If all animals were herbivorous and man alone was a killer, our line of conduct would be clear. But such is not the case. It is sufficient to think of the many animals of entirely different species whose bodies are constructed as elegant *machines à tuer*, who cannot live if they do not kill, whose senses are specialized organs for seeking out prey, whose teeth are built to tear flesh, and whose intestines are constructed to digest it. All we can do, then, is to accept.

In this connection I shall always remember an incident that happened to me a few years ago, in Japan. One of my little daughters was sitting beside me on the grass, near a field of rice. The country before our eyes was basking happily in the sun, and not far away there was a group of peasants' thatched houses, surrounded by a thicket of bamboo. The landscape was as peaceful as it possibly could be: humanity, flora, light, serenity.

I noticed among the blades of grass a praying mantis, a big, green insect with a deceptively pious and innocent appearance. A few seconds later a dragonfly alighted near it. The praying mantis pounced on it, and started eating it. The dragonfly struggled, tried desperately to escape, but the big, green insect immobilized it with a slow, mechanical movement; the poor dragonfly's wings lay open, like human arms in an attitude of hopeless anguish. The mantis's jaws then systematically and with the most complete indifference set about the destruction of one of its victim's huge eyes. It gradually emptied one socket and then the other. It was a horrible sight. It filled the valley in which we were sitting, just as if the poor dragonfly had been able to scream. I thought of setting it free, but what would have been the use? Thousands of other praying mantises were devouring thousands of other dragonflies in just the same way in thousands of other places. It wasn't that particular case that was important. It was the law.

My little girl, who was playing, did not notice what was happening just beside her. Suddenly she looked up and said: "Papa, how good God must be! What He's done is all so beautiful, isn't it? He made the sun for us, and the rice and the flowers, even the straw for the roofs. He's so good, isn't He, papa?"

She turned to me, wanting confirmation. I got up and took the little girl by the hand. I wanted to go away, and we went. I didn't want her to see the last remnants of the dragonfly between the praying mantis's legs, though I'm sure it would not have disturbed her innocent and still completely anthropomorphic faith.

"Yes, darling," I said to her. "God is so good."

Besides, it is sufficient to examine, even for a very few moments, what happens beneath the surface of the sea to be struck by the ferocity of every form of life there. The eel, lying in wait among the rocks for an unsuspecting sargo or gilthead, is an unforgettable sight. Who has not felt fear at the sight of an octopus, gliding among the rocks, ready to seize its prey in its tentacles? Who has not seen a wounded fish being pounced on by its healthy companions? In appearance the world under the sea is a dreamy blue colour, with fairy-tale illuminations and tremulous, delicately-shaded reflections. In reality it is a pit in which struggle never ceases, where silence reigns only because pain is not accompanied by cries or groans.

It may be objected that man is an exception in nature, that he must create new orders of events, more noble and elevated realities. Yes, but first we must put our own house in order, eliminate war and improve social conditions in such a way that there need be no more outbursts of base and violent instincts; after that it will be time to think of the animals. In our present state of civilization what we can do for our humblest companions is to spare them needless suffering. I must note with sadness that, in spite of the lofty ideals professed in Buddhist countries, their animals do not suffer less than ours. In one way they suffer more. While on the one hand innumerable excuses are found to justify a carnivorous diet, on the other no-one will risk the "sin" of removing an old or sick animal. The result is that you see animals about that are living skeletons, a pitiable sight. They won't kill them, but they neglect them. This applies not only to Tibet, but (to a lesser extent) to Japan also.

Flying in the clouds and plunging into entrails

I was sitting at midday in a field at the foot of some huge fir-trees, near Kirimtse, eating buttered *chapati* (Indian-style biscuits). High up towards the sun some crows were flying. They stood out black against the white clouds or vanished into the blue of the sky. Slowly they approached. They flew lower, circling, following one another, grazing the tree tops; the raucousness of their continual cry could not conceal that it was an expression of happiness. How enviable was their freedom from the restrictions of weight, their freedom of the air!

An eagle appeared out of the blue and started circling over my head. It must have seen something among the trees. It used the wind to keep itself aloft, only rarely beating its wings, circling in solemn, slow spirals. Then it dived nearly down to earth, grazed the tree tops, suddenly changed direction, checked its flight, and then started off again. I saw its head and hooked beak turning this way and that with continuous, decisive, proud movements, and I heard the rush of wind between its wings. The crows went on flying, seeming to have no fear of it. But how different was their flight – while they were alone in the sky they had seemed the quintessence of grace and lightness, but now, in comparison with the eagle, they looked heavy and clumsy. The crow has a big body and small wings; the eagle's wings, in comparison with the size of its body, are enormous. The crow has to beat its wings hard to gain height, and it propels itself through the air in a laborious, monotonous and pedestrian manner. The flight of the eagle is all intelligence, grace, agility and power. It uses the wind to gain height without moving its wings at all, and in descending it displays a superb mastery of space.

It grew late, and I had to return to Yatung. Soon after I set out I had a strange encounter. Peasants had thrown a dead mule, perhaps the animal that Lama Ngawang had told me about, among the rocks. About a dozen big, whitish vultures, so intent on their meal that they took no notice of me, were swarming on, around and actually inside the carcass. They were fighting and pushing one another, squawking all the time. Their movements and their voices were horrifyingly human. The most skilful or most fortunate bird managed to get right inside the dead beast's stomach and hacked savagely with its beak to detach the last remnants of the abdominal cavity and the intestines. The whole carcass shook and rocked, seeming to have a ghoulish life of its own. Eventually the vultures left outside managed to dislodge the "inside" bird, which emerged all spattered with blood, with a big piece of entrails hanging from its beak. A horrid battle followed, because the others tried to snatch it from him. They struck one another with their beaks, squawking savagely, and there was a furious beating of wings. The stink of the carcass reached to where I stood. Two birds next managed to get inside the dead mule's stomach, where another battle took place. The carcass, which was balanced unsteadily on a slope, shook so much that eventually it overturned and fell. The two vultures inside it came out, terrified, shrieking, all covered in blood and scraps of putrefying flesh. The others moved away a little, and then they all fell on the carcass again.

Some time passed. One of the birds must have assuaged its appetite. It looked satisfied, and detached itself from the fray. So heavy was it that its departure reminded me of that of an airliner loaded with passengers. It took a long run downhill to gain speed before opening its wings. When it was air-borne it flew off in a slow curve, slowly gaining height, and disappeared like an archangel into an empyrean of clouds and sunshine.

Last day at Yatung: Lama Ngawang's gift

The time came for us to leave Yatung, and today we left. The porters arrived and selected their loads. Many acquaintances came to say goodbye. The *ku-tsab* sent us a big loaf and some bottles of arak from Chumbi, and Mingyur was there with a white silk sash.

A man came hurrying from Kirimtse. "Lama Ngawang sends you this gift," he said to me, handing me a parcel. I opened it. It was the portrait of the lama that I had so often admired in the hall of the Kirimtse monastery, and had tried in vain to buy. Tears were in my eyes when I packed it among my things. I shall keep it always in memory of old Lama Ngawang, a straight, upright, generous and just man. What does the faith in which one was born matter? Civilizations present us with pictures of the universe just as they teach us how to eat certain foods, to dress in a certain way, to have certain ideals in connection with women when we make love to them. But in the last resort all that matters supremely is heart and character.

II

The Giddiness of Discovery

Phari: the wind blows heedless of prayers

Phari is a town of wretched cottages built round the first big Tibetan fortress that one meets coming from the south.[1] It is about 13,000 feet above sea-level, in the middle of a yellowish valley at the foot of Chomolhari (23,930ft). An idea of the scale of these tremendous empty spaces can be had from watching the winding trail that climbs towards Lhasa, along which tiny little black lines can be seen in the distance. They are not ants, but whole caravans of yaks and mules on the way down to India or up to the deserts of Central Asia.

Sometimes the traveller comes across a place where he says to himself: Here a city should be built. The Gulf of Naples would be such a place if Naples were not there. A place where a city should be built is the plain of Phari. Obviously there could be no economic justification for a big city here, at a height of 12,000 feet, but aesthetically it would be incomparable. One's imagination cannot help filling the immense plain with avenues, squares, arches, towers and gardens, and against the background of the isolated and miraculously lovely pyramid of Chomolhari; a whole, living city at the foot of the red rocks and greeny-blue ice of Chomolhari glittering in the sun.

Instead of a big city, however, the first thing we came across when we reached the plain yesterday was a nomad's tent. It made the space around us look even barer, the cathedral of ice still more remote, immense and sacrosanct. Moreover, the experience was so unexpected. After hours of weary climbing up a winding valley enclosed between dark mountains we turned a corner and found ourselves suddenly, and before we were expecting it, in an entirely new world. There were no limits about us but the sky; no more roaring of torrents, but complete silence. Then, after some hours of walking across the open plateau, Phari ("Pig Mountain"), with its square fortress, appeared in the distance. But it was rather like seeing a distant island or cape when out at sea. You see it, and go on seeing it, but you never seem to reach it.

We rested at Phari today. I must again insist on the sense of space. After days in the depths of the Himalayan valleys it is a marvellous experience to find oneself on the Roof of the World. The expression "Roof of the World" is so apt. It is so very like climbing the innumerable stairs of an ancient *palazzo* in an Italian town and finally coming out on the terrace, and being suddenly surrounded by the sky, with a sea of roofs at one's feet. In the neighbourhood of Phari the valley gradually slopes towards a number of big, orange-coloured, dome-shaped hills. The simplicity of their shape, with nothing to break their surface or outline, makes it extremely difficult to form any real idea of their dimensions.

Chomolhari, like every high mountain, is alive all the time. It changes in character and appearance from hour to hour; often from minute to minute. When I went out at dawn this morning it was a huge black mass standing out against the eastern light; the cold magnificence of its icy peaks stabbed into my mind like a sword. A little star was still shining in the sky, right over the summit. It was the only touch of colour in a spectral, sidereal spectacle of frozen purity and space. Later in the day the mountain seems to be changing its dress all the time. It is just like a beautiful, temperamental woman, now playing with subtle wisps of cloud, now putting on bright cloaks or veils, now sulking and hiding itself, now coming out and smiling again. It can be splendid, sublime, mysterious, cold and forbidding, melancholy, spiteful, generous, sinister; or, as at sunset yesterday, it can become a palace of pink biscuit, decorated with wisps of blue silk.

The grey stone fortress is in perfect harmony with the valley. Its walls slope slightly inwards, standing like a barbarian solidly planted with his legs apart. The portico and the windows are painted in vivid colours, red, orange and green. On top a golden pavilion glitters in the sun. But the village is horrible. It must certainly be one of the filthiest places in the world. The hovels of which it consists are built (but "built" is altogether too grand a word – it implies thought) of earth, and an incredible amount of dirt is left lying about in its winding alleys – bones, excrement, rags, kitchen refuse, old tin cans, all among endless expanses of black mud. It is cold and windy all the year round, and the water is generally frozen, so the people never wash. The public lavatories consist of wooden frameworks, open to the four winds. As the air is so dry, so cold and so sterile, solid, pointed hillocks of faeces accumulate underneath.

The wretched, squalid houses of Phari are adorned with innumerable poles and sticks, supporting thousands of little flags with prayers and pious phrases written on them. The wind "utters" and "sings" them. There are prayers in white, red, blue and yellow, old, ragged and neglected prayers, prayers for things long since dead and forgotten, and brand-new prayers, full of anxiety and trepidation, for things that may yet be altered and put right. The wind plays indifferently upon them all, tears them, wears them out. It blows and blows –

42 *Phari: the* Dzong, *or citadel, as it was in 1937*

who knows where? Who knows why? – towards the huge, hungry horizon.

Some houses, built of masonry and bigger than the others, are of recent construction. On the roof of one of them, which is not yet finished, many women are working. They beat the mud-cement rhythmically with their hands to harden it, keeping time by singing in chorus. It is always the same tune, a beautiful one, full of strange half-tones. The wind now brings it near, now blows it away and makes it almost inaudible, now brings it near again. It seems to give a physical sense of the infinite-song, caravans, desert, sky.

Tuna, Dochen: some of the most beautiful places in the world

Let us be clear what we mean by the word "beautiful". If we include under it only gardens, hills and villas, fountains and flower-beds, sea coasts and green, gentle country, if, like Lorenzo the Magnificent, what we want is "A green meadow full of fine flowers / A stream that bathes the grass all about . . ."

un verde praticel pien di bè' fiori
un rivo che l'erbetta intorno bagni . . .

43 *"Tibetan Post Office Pharijong"*

if that is what we want, the Tang pass, the immense Plain of the Three Brothers, the surroundings of Tuna, the lakes of Dochen, the ice-walls of the Himalayas are ugly. The beauty of Tibet is strong, elementary, sublime. It concedes nothing; it is unrelenting.

We crossed the Tang pass (15,000ft) yesterday in storm and mist. Then, as we descended on its northern side, the sky cleared, and all day long we crossed a deserted plain. There was nothing but stones, stones, stones, and a few blades of grass; and the horizon. On one side Chomolhari stood supreme, with its red precipices covered with ice and snow. Ahead of us in the distance there arose other mountains of contorted shape. The colours were crazy: the red, yellow, ochre, orange of the stones, the sand and the rocks; the delicate green of the grass, where the glaciers descended; the blue of the distance and the sky; the brilliant whiteness of the snow. Then there was the everlasting wind, perpetually caressing your face, hands and body and tirelessly murmuring and singing in your ears.

Tuna was the name of a group of six or seven houses standing at the edge of the sky. One was almost afraid to speak; the clip-clop of the mules' hooves on the stones, men's voices, disappeared without echo in the midst of this immensity. The crests of the Himalayas were an unforgettable sight this morning. Everyone knows how a beautiful thing is improved by isolation. Any work of

44 *Mt Chomolhari from the plain of Tuna. The plain lies at 13,000ft, the peak 11,000ft higher*

art is seen to lesser advantage when surrounded and overwhelmed by twenty others. In the Alps the mountains are crowded; no mountain, unless you are quite close to it, can be seen in isolation. But here Chomolhari rises at the edge of an immense plain, imperial, magnificent, alone. Between Tuna and the first hills there are miles and miles of orange desert. Then suddenly the earth curves and rises; there are some yellow hills; then fields of ice; and then the red rocks rise supreme, in a sparkling framework of snow. The giants of the Himalayas are surrounded by an infinity of space and air. Two of the most tremendous sights in nature – deserts and ice – are here combined. The desert, all fire and colour, climbs and fades into the ice. The sparkling ice descends to adorn the stones. A ring of green shows where they meet. Water makes the wilderness flourish.

Dochen – a day's march farther north – is a village with very few houses, some of which look like fortresses. It is cold there, and the wind blows. The solitude penetrates into the rooms, creeps under your blankets at night. It is not a negative thing, a mere lack, but a positive entity, almost with a voice and a face. The village lies on the bank of the lake of Rham. Tibet, apart from huge mountains and enormous deserts, is a country of many great lakes. The Rham-tso is liquid sky that has fallen among the dry stones. When I walked along its banks today the wind died down (a rare event in these parts), and the mountains were reflected in the water with extraordinary clarity. I seemed to be walking along the edge of an abyss of light.

Monastery of Kyangphu: Mara tempts the Buddha one last time

Two days' march beyond Dochen we reached Samada. The plateau is no longer flat. Grim, savage, uncanny mountains, a fit background for shrieks, martyrdoms and visions, are broken by valleys – still at a height of 12,000 feet and more above sea-level – which drop down till they finally reach the great River Tsang-po, as the ultra-Himalayan reaches of the Brahmaputra are called. Here and there we saw houses, and we came to the first meagre fields of barley; we were approaching a domain of men; a domain sacred for more than a thousand years to thought and art. In this area there are some monasteries of exceptional antiquity: they have a name and location but little else is known about them. Tucci is anxious to explore them and make a profound study of the works of art they are bound to contain. He has in his hands a copy of a seventeenth-century guidebook for Tibetan Buddhist pilgrims and wayfarers, the *Nyang-chung*, and he turns to it every step of the way, discussing its contents and descriptions with his Lama-secretary, Sonam.

First thing in the morning we make for the monastery of Kyangphu, about a mile off the caravan trail, a half hour's easy walk up a slight incline through pastures and meadows. Seen from below, Kyangphu looks truly impressive, more a fortress than a monastery. Pressing on, one soon discovers that the numerous buildings – abbot's and monks' quarters, storehouses, refectories, libraries, pilgrims' hostels, cowsheds and so on – are in a painful state of neglect, indeed in most cases they are nothing but ruins. The only thing to have survived intact is the temple itself, a building of some size. The sturdy ring-wall built of sun-baked mud and stones, a good six to eight metres high, which once will have surrounded and protected the entire complex, is now severed here and there by entry points rammed through at will. Tucci's theory is that these represent one or more of the disastrous barbarian raids by the Hor on their way south (Tartars, Mongols, Northern tribes generally speaking) who every now and then put southern Tibet to fire and the sword in past centuries.

It was already hot when we penetrated into the sanctuary; the coolness and silence were a most welcome restorative. The entrance door was tiny (it is notable that nearly every architectural feature was designed with defence in mind); once inside, we were in a courtyard closed for the most part by a colonnade in wood, supporting architraves decorated with stylized animals, an unusually delicate work. The pillars were made quite simply of tree trunks which had been stripped of their bark, leaving intact all their sculptural, muscular beauty. Yet they would have aged to the point of decrepitude, a good thousand years one would say.

"Kyangphu", Tucci observed, "is one of the oldest and most distinguished religious centres in Tibet . . . Well, the *Nyang-chung* maintains it was founded in the time of King Tisong-detsen (755–797), or even in that of Songtsen-gampo (569–649)," he added with a chuckle, "but that is nothing but a engaging fantasy. It's like in Afghanistan, or in the Swat, or in Kashmir, where anything of any importance is attributed to Alexander the Great. Perhaps Kyangphu dates back to the brilliant Tibetan Buddhist renaissance of around 1000. We'll see, we'll work it out. Meanwhile . . . Oh look! . . . "

The master, with his eagle eye for anything philological, epigraphic, historical, had spotted a revealing inscription on one of the stones set into the dried mud, on the inner side of the ring-wall.

"Look," he pursued, babbling blithely, "it's an invocation to Virupa, the esoteric master of the Sakya abbots. Vajradhara, Nairatmya, Virupa . . . typical Sakya triad. I'd suspected it, now we have the proof. So we are in territory that once belonged to the Sakya even if today the *Gelug-pa* lay claim to it, those from the Yellow Sect. So it must be the thirteenth or fourteenth century, when those abbot-princes were at the height of their power."

The master is in good form today. He's thrilled to make discoveries, to plant his banner of learning, never mind how small, in virgin soil. And this makes him fascinating himself, a veritable guru. On such occasions Tucci is galvanized. He's a hound off the leash. He runs hither and yon, he wants to see, to unlock secrets, grab millennia by the throat. There is something of the shaman about him. He comes out with few, excited phrases now and then, dense with meaning, pregnant with suggestion, a language all bone and sinew, like a mathematician's formulae. Then long silences. Then unexpected comparisons, recollections, fancies. Intelligence as a blue flame, thin and highly mobile. His hair stands up like antennae ready to capture the unknowable. Which then does become knowable for the simple reason that it is processed and digested by a brain in which entire libraries lie in ambush, in a babel of different tongues. Poor old problem, it doesn't stand a chance! That extraordinary mind collars it, grinds it up, smashes it to bits, pulverizes it and extracts from it a synthesis, a bloom.

Today it is lucky that the master is thoroughly voluble. He has tales to tell, things to say.

As I listen I find myself closing my eyes to imagine the splendid scenes of times past, when the high dignitaries of the Sakya church (they were the real sovereigns of Tibet in the days of Kublai Khan and Marco Polo) would have been received here with a pomp that partook more of the royal court than of the monastery, dressed in their splendid costumes, at the centre of lavish rituals (photo 75 gives a pale example). Today, alas, there are no more lamas, ascetics, doctors, abbots. A family of uncouth if worthy peasants has charge of the ruin and has transformed it into a sort of convenient farmhouse. Everywhere are to be seen spades, ploughs, saddles, sieves, old rifles, butter-churns, ropes, pouches, sacks, pelts. An old monk appears from somewhere; he is dirty and listless. His costume gives him away as a member of the Yellow Sect. Exactly, it is they who now dominate a large tract of Tibet. These shrines, which they have inherited, as it were, from churches that have come under their orders, now tend to be regarded as step-children, kept alive out of pure charity, or maybe out of sheer inertia. Where once upon a time masters and pupils assembled to discuss philosophy, now crows flap about cawing, or else high-spirited children with little on play tag and shout amid the grass and wild flowers sprouting in the courtyard.

In the entrance, by the ancient wooden pillars, we notice several sacks of grain piled up. A closer look reveals that these are concealing the foot of a wall on which it is possible to make out (but only just) a mural of extraordinary, exquisite, forgotten beauty. Tucci is thrilled. "Stupendous!" he repeats several times. "They are the Five Supreme Buddhas with their retinue of *Bodhisattva*s. Look at the elegance and majesty of the composition, how finely drawn it is in every tiniest detail. The colours are faded, but how they still sing! There's nothing Sakya about this, it goes back a long way earlier. Perhaps to the year 1000 or not long after. It's an exquisitely Indian style. We are looking at a masterpiece from one of the most prosperous periods in the whole of Tibetan art, when exchanges with India were at their most dynamic and stirred up a quite extraordinary spiritual insemination. Could the old, dog-eared *Nyang-chung* be right? According to it, the temple was founded by Chökyi Lodrö, one of Rinchen-tsangpo's disciples. We'd be exactly between 1000 and 1100, and it would all add up!"

The temple proper is a massive building, exquisitely Tibetan, its walls slightly inclined inwards and coloured in a pale wine-red, crowned with white and brown fasciae, which provide a rim to the flat roof. It is on two floors and has numerous chapels adorned with statues and pictures in varying styles and from different periods.

Guided by the listless monk, Tucci and I go on an initial reconnaissance. We look at the doors, visit one room after another. Our footsteps resound in the empty passages, the deserted corridors; the old doors squeak on their hinges, releasing a cloud of fine dust the moment the custodian opens them. Every now and then monstrous faces, bodies contorted in frantic gestures, terrifying gods, local guardians appeared, lit by a ray of sunlight. In the excitement of exploration Professor Tucci and I separated. While I was climbing a staircase, leading I don't know where, he called out:

"Come here, come and see!"

I went down, and found Professor Tucci in a chapel that was smaller than the rest.

"Did you ever imagine that anything like that was conceivable?"

Just for once I found him thunderstruck. At first I found it bewildering and unintelligible. We were in a cramped little chapel that was unbelievably crowded with sculptures. It was an infernal dance of wooden monsters, painted in vivid colours.

"It's the Temptation of the Buddha, or better, the Distraction of the Buddha," Tucci explained. "It's Mara tempting the Buddha for the last time before his final enlightenment."

45 *Kyangphu monastery: the last temptation of Buddha: detail*

Sure enough, at the bottom of the chapel there was a fine statue of the sage, serene and victorious, having attained the plane of the Absolute and freed himself for ever from the illusions of substantiality and becoming, while Mara (love, attachment, death) wove fantastic spells about him, conjuring from the most turgid depths of the imagination a whole population of monsters, half animals and half men, some grotesque, some lustful, some cruel, some stark, raving mad; every one of them quivering with some passion or excitement, in dramatic contrast to the serenity expressed in the features of the Buddha.

The subject is a common one in Buddhist art, but so disconcerting a "temptation" can rarely have been carried out in sculpture. One was reminded of Hieronymus Bosch and the monsters of Palagonia in Sicily. The dissociative technique was admirable. Many modern artists have believed themselves to be making an extraordinary discovery in taking the human form and treating its elements – eyes, nose, mouth, limbs – as independent entities, which by adding, subtracting, amputating, getting inside them, could be welded into new harmonies and constellations. But here, carved in all innocence centuries ago, were torsos turned into faces, eyes grafted on to trunks, whole festoons of eyes; there were also pig-breasts, dog-shoulders, beings with three bodies or four heads, Polyphemuses and hydra-headed monsters, a whole fairground of triumphant monstrosity; forms which would be but toys if each one of them had not been endowed with a soul. Their expressions were often incomprehensible to us. What was moving them? What was disturbing them? Were they crying, laughing, screaming, lowing like cattle, grinning? Were they terrified or raving mad, passionate or vengeful?

Kyangphu Monastery: "We are fantastically privileged, you know? . . . "

Shaken, almost reduced to gibbering, by the mad saraband of shapes in the Temptations of Buddha, by those "horrendous faces" (to quote a sixteenth-century inscription in the famous garden of Bomarzo, north of Rome), we move on to the peace of the South Chapel (Tsang-kang Lho). The walls are crammed with books (Tibetan-style, of course, see Fig 95). Luckily I am beginning to get my bearings; I know now that the large volumes contain the *Kangyur* (the 108 books of the scriptures), while the small ones contain the *Tangyur* (the 225 books of commentaries); it is almost like unearthing in some ancient, neglected, cobweb-cluttered European convent Migne's *Patrologia Graeca et Latina*. But here, more than the chaos and the dust, there are clear signs of violence and past vandalism that leave one thoroughly dismayed. Statues are to be seen that have been patched up any old how (I mean patched up, not repaired), and pedestals

46 *Kyangphu monastery: the last temptation of Buddha: another detail*

for statues that are no longer there – they have been stolen, smashed, destroyed. The scene is all the more depressing on account of the scraps of old *kata* (tributary scarves in cotton or silk), which hang all dusty and falling to pieces and covered in cobwebs, just like cadavers, from arms, necks, heads of saints and gods. Finally there are the broken, wobbly cups for rancid butter, all mildewed and mummified. Offerings someone made that were then forgotten. Who made the offering? When? What for?

But there's something to distract us amid so much squalor. A large part of the chapel is taken up by a remarkable *chorten* in gilt bronze, some three metres high; nobody can explain it or account for it. Tucci studied it with great attention and admiration, like an important physician confronting a rare clinical case.

"Perhaps it holds the ashes, even the mummified remains, of some venerable lama," he remarked, more or less to himself. "It's certainly a fine piece of work. It would look impressive in any museum! The pictures . . . ? Ah, but it's obvious. It's the Vairocana cycle, with the thirty-six Buddhas and attendant *Bodhisattva*s.

It's the Vajradhātu mandala, the one known to the Japanese as the Kongā-kai. Gilded scrap bronze. Could it be Indian? It is quite reminiscent of Bengali art of the late Pala period. Heaven knows how it fetched up here! Via Nepal? Anything can happen in this bizarre world. Besides, the distance from cities, the solitude, the climate, the isolation preserve such things for centuries. Eventually we turn up and are bowled over. We are hugely privileged, you know? What will happen tomorrow? Greedy antiquarians? A fresh Hor incursion?"

At the sides of the entrance to the north chapel (Tsang-kang Chang) we come across two statues not often met with in Tibetan art: one represents the fire-god (Me-lha) and the other one the water-goddess (Chu-lha). Me-lha is the colour of red molten lava, with an aura of fierce flames, and he looks as dramatically terrifying as one would expect. He is also, be it said, fairly rigid and tough. Chu-lha, however, is unforgettable, not so much for the highly original hair-style she has been given, in the guise of snakelike veins of water, as for her horribly expressive grin. "Come on, folks," she seems to be saying, "I am Water. I love

47 *Kyangphu monastery: detail from the mandala of Vairocana. Gilded wood, 14th century*

48 *Kyangphu monastery: the Supreme Buddha Amoghasiddhi (now destroyed)*

you, did you know? I quench your thirst, you'd all die without me. Even so, if I take it into my head, I grind you up, I crush you! Have you seen those Himalayan rivers in flood? So you know what I mean! I inundate you, I drown you, I bury you, I dissolve you. Man, woman, pay me your respects, pray to me, I am Water!"

For some reason Tucci suddenly scowled. He seemed to be looking for something but could not find it. He peered, made notes, turned back on his steps, but no longer spoke. The marvellous thread of illuminations conceded to the commoners had snapped. I asked no questions, of course. I knew by now that in such circumstances the thing was to say nothing, to make oneself scarce if possible. My companion was a man of high intellect but by no means a simple soul, he was a complex of traps and pitfalls. What's more he himself kept saying: "I can't stand men, it's animals I love! I like those who have been punished by their *karma*, not those who have reaped their reward. Perhaps one should except the Buddhas . . . But we see them only in works of art." There are days, hours when all is sunshine and celebration, then whoops! something's

49 *Kyangphu monastery: Chu-lha, goddess of water. Painted stucco*

come adrift and we land in a desert. There is something of the night in Tucci, something feline, Tantric, not to say sinister. And he guards his inner keep most jealously!

It sometimes makes me laugh. Imagine two Italians on their own, who have disappeared up on to the roof of the world, maybe sitting over supper in a shepherds' hut. The attentive Khalil hands us each a half chicken off the griddle; their tendons seem to be wire, and one practically tears out one's teeth eating the flesh. "Would Your Excellency favour the breast or the thigh?" I ask. I tell no lie: "Excellency" as was prescribed by the Reale Accademia d'Italia in those formal days. The master never did absolve me from this verbal homage, this high-flown language which, in Japanese or Tibetan, would be the equivalent of a high degree of ceremonious usage. What can I do but comply, albeit with an occasional secret smile.

One evening the master had drunk a little liquor to get over a headache. He was far more cheerful and expansive than usual. "Those Indian women," he confided to me, "when they turn up it's a catastrophe! Sighs, whinneys, yells and screams. They dig their nails into your back. And the yoni is a Ganges of delight!" Then we talked of further journeys. I think that at one point he was all ready to say, "Oh come on, cut out the Excellencies, just call me Professor or Master, if you want." But instead he came out with the stunning assertion: "You have absolutely no idea of the sort of power I wield in Rome."

Kyangphu Monastery: as though truffle-hunting in the field of science

"Hey, where've you got to? Get your camera and hurry!"

I scramble together my cameras, pouch of magnesium and other bits of attendant magic and make a dash for the north chapel. Here I find Tucci on his knees at an angle on the dirty, dusty floor with a small magnifying glass precariously grasped between his fingers busy deciphering an inscription carved on the pedestal of one of the statues that had vanished heaven knows when.

"Ah, well done, at last! Look, take a picture of this inscription. Then I'll explain. It's a miracle! Precisely as I thought. Look at it closely, take note: what is the name on it? It's the monk Cho-blos, or Cho Lo-dros, or Chökyi-Lodrö. In other words the disciple of Rinchen-tsangpo we talked about earlier! You see, once you take a close look at a thing it all stands out, takes shape. The old legends eventually turn out to be true. The founding of Kyangphu in the days of the great kings, Tisong-detsen etc. is undoubtedly a myth; but the story of its being founded in 1000 or 1100, under Rinchen-tsangpo and his disciples, including Chökyi-Lodrö – now we have the proof! It is authentic. Perhaps these pedestals for lost statues are all that survive from those distant days. And the marvellous frescoes that are now so faded, beneath the veranda in the courtyard. The rest dates back to the Sakya. Thirteenth, fourteenth century. Well, Kyangphu is a miracle! Every era, every witness, from pure Indian influences to equally pure Chinese influences. Incidentally, have you taken a look at those vigorous *dvarapala* (guardians) by the door? How they remind one of Japanese plastic arts from the time of Kamakura, when the samurai were in charge and even the artists had warrior blood coursing through their veins."

While I photograph the inscription on the empty pedestal Tucci has got up; he is chuckling mischievously and rubbing his hands several times in a characteristic gesture. To have come upon evidence of the ancient lama Chökyi-Lodrö, of whom he had written on a previous occasion in connection with western Tibet, gives him keen and quite unexpected pleasure and satisfaction. He has succeeded in devouring centuries and continents, entire languages and literatures, religions and philosophies, in throwing out fine meshes connecting data far apart in time and distance, making them rebound from the unknown to the known by virtue of spot-on exercises in comparison and matching. So the storm was over, it would seem. And with the return of fair weather and with it a lavish flow of knowledge, a royal bounty. And I rejoin the dance. I know perfectly well how Tucci loathes teaching. Getting onto his audience's wavelength is something he finds quite tedious. When he's in a sunny mood what he enjoys is tossing out ideas, which is quite another matter. That is simply the guru thinking out loud, and it is a privilege to be in his company.

Tucci casts an eye over each corner of the north chapel, a clutter of sculptures, paintings, flags. He sniffs the place like a bloodhound of knowledge, a truffle-hunter of science. Three large, noble images of seated Buddhas, in gilt stucco, occupy part of the room; they are accompanied by elegant, svelte carved figures of standing *Bodhisattva*s. Who are they? What do they represent? "Everything, or nearly everything in Buddhist *Mahayana* art of the Great Vehicle is symbolic," the master often says. I dare not ask for an explanation. To watch and wait, that is the best thing to do. But fair weather has set in, thanks to the ghost of Chökyi Lodrö.

"What stupendous thinkers they were, those Indians," the guru exclaims. "And the Buddhists in their wake. Their minds function on a grand scale, they flourish in the gigantic, the boundless. Take an example: each universe has its own Buddha. When poor old Giordano Bruno spoke of multiple worlds, they sent him to the stake. In India he would have been a great pundit at the very least. Right, these three lovely statues represent the eternity of revelation: in the present, past and future universes. As for the statue in the middle, that's Dipamkara, whom the Tibetans know as Marmedze. He carried the message of salvation to heaven knows which humanities of an unfathomable past, humanities evaporated in unknown *nirvana*s. To the right we have (so to speak) us . . . the Sakya-Muni Buddha, the historical one. And to the left you find the highly popular Maitreya, the Buddha of the future.

"*Champa! Champa*!" says the custodian monk, pointing at the statue.

Tucci laughs. "Just look at the unblushing ignorance among these last degenerate offshoots of the faith. The only name he has for it is the Tibetan one: *Champa*. What is needed is a new *kalpa*, a new Buddha, a new everything, and soon!"

Surrounding the Buddhas of the three universes stand eight elaborately adorned *Bodhisattva*s (mediators between the Absolute and the Contingent), standing in, as it were, for the thousand or 996 great saints of our era. There is nothing exceptional about them as works of art, but there is something pleasing about their meditative serenity. Tucci scorns them, however. "Those well-fed faces are late," he concludes after a brief scrutiny. In his book "late" for a style in art is the equivalent of "late" in relation to the Roman Empire.

"What about the statue with the legs cruelly broken, then bound up any old how?" I venture to ask, seeing that we are in *kalpa* of genial availability.

"Here, old son, we've dropped in the social scale, at least iconographically!"

I am quick to grasp the truth of Tucci's remark from the fact that our monk who has been so listless and distrait, comes to life and shows every sign of devotion before the statue of the *Bodhisattva* Avalokitesvara/Chen-re-zi, whose living incarnation is the Dalai Lama, so it is thought. Our monk clasps his hands, bows his head, murmurs prayers in an unexpectedly melodious and deep voice. Norbhu the cook, too, has materialized and joins in the little improvised ritual.

"The empty bases supported statues of Vajrapani and Manjusri," Tucci explained. "That is plain from the inscriptions. So what we had here was the most popular triad in Tibet – Chen-re-zi, the Supreme Compassion, Chanadorje, Adamantine Power, and Jampeyan, Gnostic Wisdom – to give them their Tibetan rather than their Sanskrit names. We'll find them all over Tibet, you'll see; in the temples (painted and carved), on mountain rockfaces, depicted on the *tangka*, in domestic shrines, even formed out of butter and coloured at country fairs. We shall find them looking peaceful and serene but also – Chanadorje most of all – looking terrifying, with flaming auras, girdled with serpents, skulls for necklaces, member erect and bejewelled, etc.

We left the chapel. Norbhu remained kneeling in front of the statue of Chen-re-zi of the broken legs, contemplating the face with a rapt expression.

Kyangphu Monastery: the universe has the secret structure of a crystal

The Tibetan jungle of Buddhas and *Bodhisattva*s, in their peaceful and terrifying manifestations, whether isolated from or united with their gnostic feminine energies (*Shakti*), in mystical coition, with the entire undergrowth of keepers and henchmen, local divinities and guardians of the cardinal points, of saints and teachers, seems to be quite without boundaries, without scale or compass. At first one is perplexed, then dazed, eventually overwhelmed, quite knocked out. No rule is valid in all places and times, exceptions and special cases keep cropping up. "As a rule the symbols held in the hands of the two principal arms are of diagnostic value . . . " the master once let slip, without further comment, as though he'd blurted out a trick of the trade. But even this principle is valid up to a point. Then sometimes one wonders: in the monstrous confusion of talons, torsos, members, jewels, flowers, skulls, serpents, animal skins, axes, entrails, rosaries, banners, goblets, which are the "principal arms"?

Some glimmer of order, some record or census for forcing a passage through the endless horde of lamaist iconographic personages can be achieved by starting with a single well-known group, the Five Top Buddhas, variously referred to as the Supreme Pentad (Tucci), the Five Tathagata, the Five Jina, the Five Heavenly Buddhas, the Five Cosmic Buddhas, and so on. Brian Hodgson, an Englishman who was among the first to study Nepalese and Tibetan Buddhism a hundred years ago, spoke of Five *Dhyani* Buddhas (Buddhas of Meditation): the term is nowadays considered unsuitable, but for a while was all the rage and still remains in use. The Tibetans speak of *Gyalrig-nga* (the Five Sovereigns), while the Japanese speak of *Gochi Nyorai* (the Five Gnostic Buddhas).[2]

The truth is that not even here are we on solid ground. The names of the five can change in certain circumstances; there are occasions when the Five are joined by a Sixth, sometimes even by a Seventh. But as a rule the Pentad makes a useful point of reference. It seems that originally the Pentad grew out of four Buddhas who presided over the four directions of space, with a fifth one acting as centre point, axis and sovereign.

"Just take a look at this!" cried Tucci, from a chapel window on the upper floor of the temple. "Come on up, we've got things of quite some importance to fix on film."

Allured by the monsters of the Temptation (or Distraction) of Buddha, I had gone back during an interval of calm to make further pictures, secure further details.

"Interesting, delectable, no doubt about it," the master observed when I joined him upstairs, "but at the end of the day it's a sort of Buddhist *grand guignol*, a crowd-pleaser, even if it conveys a deep message. What we have here is a wholly new, different chapter in the story of Tibetan art. There is no end to the surprises here at Kyangphu: it's some sort of Noah's Ark containing the beauty of Asia, gone aground on these endless Ararats! If only we could pick it up and carry it to Paris or Berlin, I'd love to see the faces and hear the oohs and ahs of all those top pundits. Take a look at those rich garments, these substantial draperies, these heavy, ornate sashes that adorn the frames of the Buddhas and *Bodhisattva*s. So different to those flimsy Indian veils. Obviously we're looking at stylistic influences from Central Asia, probably from Khotan. Sakya, Mongolia, Kublai Khan, Phags-pa, Central Asia . . . *Tout se tient!* It's all converged on Kyangphu from every point of the compass: from Southern India, from the West and the kingdom of Guge, from Ladakh, from China in the East, Khotan in the North, and the oases of Central Asia."

The two first-floor chapels are spacious and light. And beautifully dry. None of that slightly macabre and rather repulsive stench emanating from the windowless basement chapels. In the first, where Tucci stands observing the scene, his arms folded on his chest, I'm quick to recognize the Five Supreme Buddhas, represented by statues of unusual splendour, in gilded stucco, full-size, accompanied by some thirty lesser figures.

"It makes you gape!" exclaimed Tucci. "Go on, snap every single one."

I'm left on my own. As I try to get the statues in the frame I admire the exquisite, assured modelling of the gilded stucco. The proportions between heads, limbs, bodies, auras, ornaments seem to be gauged with classical sobriety and elegance. In the minor figures, especially the female ones, the harmony between mystic inspiration and sweetly sensual seductiveness expresses the tastes of a civilization so refined and sophisticated as to seem suspended on the brow of a voluptuous decadence. There is no telling whether these statues are intended for a shrine or for the salon of some exigent, elegant, mystical Louis XV of the Buddhist uplands. They are almost perfectly preserved; only the hands, which are fragile as pistils, show the ravages of time. The few figures in agitated poses display a symbolical rage, at once theatrical and genteel; they are not charged with the grim and ponderous symbolism of other places and times.

I stop and admire the august, severe, knowing statue of the Supreme Buddha Amoghasiddhi (photo 48) for I find it particularly moving. If the Absolute is the ineffable mystery at the root of all wonder and horror in the world, could this not be its face? Like some unexpected gap in the series the tone of this image is different from that of almost all the rest. It is as if one wandered through a park amid flowers and tropical palms suffused with little clouds, then all of a sudden, upon a gust of wind, to espy through the vapours and cloying sweetness the pure outline of a Himalayan peak, astonishing, terrifying, unattainable. The regal and impassive countenance of Amoghasiddhi is set in bold contrasting relief, by a vast and stupendous curtain-aura in pierced and gilded wood, sumptuously Baroque. The effervescent tails of the *makara* dragons are changed into repeated rhythmic volutes which maybe symbolize the Dantesque vortices of the *samsara*, the illusory world in which life-deaths unwind in the measureless aeons of time. Other volutes arise from the tails of the humanoid *nagas*, gods of the waters, the horses, the peacocks. The elephant gives weight and dynamism to the earth beneath, the mythical *garuda* bird suggests the heavens, air, space above.

I pause to contemplate. To think. Strange, awkward reflections like shafts of lightning assail my mind. In its fascination with the human drama of Jesus and Mary, the West has almost completely neglected any representation of the Absolute. True, the Christ *pantocrator* of the Normans and Byzantines comes close, but that is a lucky stroke that had missed its aim. Christ is too much like us in His suffering. He partakes of human kind. In the matter of pain He belongs with the workers, not with the bosses. The Absolute is mysterious, sublime, terrible. It has to answer for filthy, atrocious things; and also for the most heart-wrenching beauties, the most enticing perfections. Christianity has swept the problem aside, immersing itself (largely through St Augustine) in Manicheism. Everything bad, ugly and terrible has been charged to Lucifer, to Satan and his companions. Thus the Absolute has grown limp. It has become sugary, analgesic.

If I am not mistaken it should be God the Father who holds title to the Absolute. But in the vast panorama of Christian iconography it is hard to imagine any figure that is more vapid, flabby, gelatinous than He. An old-age pensioner. A worthy retired alderman. A reverend abbot with no further responsibilities or influence. Not even Michelangelo succeeded in lifting Him out of this wretched condition. Blake aims high but then is dragged down by the irresistible weight of tradition. Only the Indians, with Siva, Brahma, occasionally with Vishnu, and the Buddhists with Tathagata have confronted the challenge head on, and they too often fail and only occasionally get close to the goal.

A hand slaps my shoulder. It is the listless lama. "The *kushog-sahib* is waiting for you over there." In the opposite chapel I find Tucci taking notes.

"What a strange medley of people here," he exclaims. "But the level of artistry does not falter."

In the centre of the chapel, an imposing pedestal supports a large statue of mediocre execution: the sacred scripture *Prajnāpāramitā* (the Treatise of the Perfect Gnosis) is represented in the guise of a female seated figure, with four arms. Ten large Buddhas, five a side, stand next to her, vigorously modelled. They stand for the Ten Directions of Space, and thus a different tabulation to the usual one. Some of the profiles show a sober, almost Hellenic, linear grace . I suggest a distant echo of the Hellenic art of Gandhara, but the master laughs.

"Indeed, there is a touch of Ghandara in nearly all Buddhist art, after a certain point, but here the dominant influences are Central Asian. Look at those long, heavy robes, their bell-like shape. Note the auras with their flaming Gothic points."

Samada: potatoes and mandalas

We are happily ensconced for a short visit to Samada, a stopping place on the way to or from Lhasa. We are staying in a cottage. There is shelter for horses and yaks and basic supplies are on sale. "What a relief it will be when there's a road," sighed Tucci's lama-secretary. "They'll build it some day, I'll bet. See how level it is here. But of course everyone knows Lhasa is always a hundred years behind the times!" Lama Sonam is forty, of medium build; his face is hairless, he is a swarthy Tibetan but comes from Darjeeling in India, and he makes a point of letting the hill folk know that his ideas are modern and progressive, he's not like those bumpkins who live back of beyond. He wears a vaguely Alpine woollen beret that never leaves his head, not even indoors: it is the symbol of his belonging to a more advanced, richer civilization, accustomed to such objects as motor cars, motorcycles, trains and aeroplanes, things regarded here as partaking of science-fiction. Lama Sonam is reserved, silent, on occasions I'd call him rather haughty; he generally has a slight smile on his face, as much as to say, "All right, carry on, you simpletons, it takes all sorts to make a world!". He clearly likes to stand on his dignity. From the start he refused, for instance, to go on foot as Tucci and I and the others are doing; he insisted on a mount. In the picture of Lake Rham some figures can be seen in the foreground; the little man walking on ahead on his own wearing a big hat is Tucci; the figure seen from behind on horseback is Lama Sonam (with his woollen beret); the long-haired youth is Thondup.

I confess that I'm at one here with my master in relishing the mediaeval situation in which we are living, not least in the matter of transport and communications. Accustomed as we are to dashing about madly in conveyances of every kind, how delightful it is to resume an idle, leisurely contact with the landscape, a sweet communion. Covering twenty or thirty kilometres a day, instead of two or three hundred (or thousand) means enjoying each one, savouring it, engaging with the landscape in a serene amorous clinch. Set out at dawn, for instance, and you see a mountain with a highly recognizable profile (never mind whether or not you find it appealing) in the pale-blue distance. We know that this evening we shall have reached the foot of it. That mountain remains our goal all day. Little by little it draws nearer, changes shape, colour, comes into sharper focus. Meanwhile hills and valleys, torrents and crags may be studied at leisure, they become friends, kinsmen. Meetings with people too, are so much more human. We see each other from afar, slowly we close the distance, then if the situation allows we exchange greetings and stop for a

50 *Iwang, near Samada: Lama Sonam at the entrance to the shrine*

51 *On the caravan route, by L. Rham. Professor Tucci strides on ahead, Lama Sonam is mounted, Thondup walks beside him*

chat, maybe even sitting down on the grass for a bite and something to drink.

"Your Excellency, tonight all we have are potatoes," I tell the master. "Norbhu didn't manage to find so much as a chicken in the village; some gentlemen from Shigatse came that way yesterday and made a clean sweep."

"Splendid," replied Tucci in Tibetan, so that the lama would understand, "we shall celebrate this day of discoveries in the field like good vegetarian Buddhists! Tell Norbhu that rice and curried potatoes will do fine."

Tucci and Lama Sonam are absorbed in an archaic text that is hard to interpret. The pair remind me of the Dalai Lama and his theology tutor I've read about so often. Tucci is the Dalai of learning, of course; all those tomes that float on the horizon – *Zeitschrift fur . . . Annales de . . . Transactions of . . .* – would crush poor old Sonam like a flea. If Tucci started spouting Obermiller, Bacot, Grunwedel, Evans-Wentz, Thomas, Sarat Chandra Das, Stcherbatsky, he would reduce him to a pulp. Conversely, when it comes to local gossip, oral tradition, dialect deformities in vocabulary and syntax, Lama Sonam would seem a veritable lion – Tucci listens to him carefully and takes notes. Tucci is indefatigable; most evenings he stays up till late studying by the light of a kerosene lamp, surrounded by papers and scribbles.

I have quite an appetite, indeed I'm ravenous. I go into the kitchen to see how supper is coming on. The kitchen is, of course, the realm of Norbhu, a tall gangling fellow of about fifty. He too is Tibetan (the name means "Jewel", with several religious connotations), and he too is from Darjeeling, but his attitude to Tibet is quite different from the erudite Sonam's. Norbhu is ugly, hideous – Nature endowed him with an excessively Mongoloid face, with four white hairs bristling on his angular chin – but he is meek, gentle, silent, hard-working and almost excessively devout. While Lama Sonam looks down his nose at his fellow countrymen up in the hills, taking them for poor half-asleep hicks stuck in the Middle Ages, and dirty to boot, Norbhu feels he's in the Holy Land ever since he crossed the border. He is enormously moved by everything, he's like a mediaeval pilgrim arriving in trepidation at Santiago de Compostella, Rome, Jerusalem. Whenever we visit a temple, if he has a moment to spare, he will sneak in after us and make the ritual circuit with numerous genuflections, muttering endless prayers and invocations in an undertone. His odds and ends include a prayer-wheel, and when there is the odd moment of leisure he spins it with nonchalant gentleness. He was once in Lhasa and says that he made the tour of Potala in a series of prostrations flat on the ground; a painful ascetic trial of great faith. The devout Norbhu is willing to cook the flesh of slaughtered animals but refuses, with smiles and bows of embarrassed but remarkable determination, to take life. When a hen has to have its neck wrung he blushes, then shouts for Khalil. "Khalil! . . . Ah Khalil . . . Chuza!" (chicken in Hindustani, the lingua franca in the kitchen). Thus we have two views of the world, normally in conflict but here to be found in a happy and useful symbiosis!

Khalil is from Kashmir and is thirty-five; he is tall, slender, good-looking and always dressed with simple, commendable elegance, even in the worst occasions. Being a Muslim he can send chickens and other creatures to the creator without incurring the wrath of Allah. Of course he slaughters according to Muslim rites, which are not as rigorous as those of the Jews' kosher prescriptions, but he still adheres to them devoutly. Khalil (Friend of God) has known Professor Tucci and accompanied him on his journeys for many years now, and serves him as his attendant, his majordomo, his factotum, his Jeeves. At first glance he reminds one of a South Italian *carabiniere* who has taken early retirement. One guesses that he won't depart from his orders by one jot or tittle, ready to die for the least article of the Regulations, perhaps somewhat

52 *Tucci's Kashmiri servant Khalil*

rigid, but of constant and absolute loyalty. Unlike our South Italian *carabinieri*, who tend instinctively to be grumpy, Khalil's face is constantly lit by a cheery smile, almost as in an advertisement. One never knows quite what it betokens: conciliation, secret mockery or a simple mask?

Whenever Tucci is feeling light-hearted and not overborne with logistical problems or questions relating to *Mahayana* Buddhist logic or Tantric art-historical problems to resolve, he enjoys telling "Khalil stories". Of which there are a great many! Like this: "I was only just back in Italy when a letter came from Srinagar. It must be Khalil, I told myself. Quite so. Greetings. News of the family and mutual friends and so forth. Then: 'Master-sahib, there's been a little accident. I was in a boat on the lake. My friend Ahmed fell in. He's dead. He had my watch on his wrist. Would you please send me another? Best wishes, Khalil.'"

We also have a deputy-Khalil in Thondup, a patient young man of few words who generally carries my photographic equipment and helps with taking the pictures. Unlike the others, Thondup is a "local recruit", so to speak. We hired him at Yatung. Which makes him pure Tibetan, not only by race and language but also in customs and habits. He wears his hair in a pigtail bound with red thread, halfway down his back. A strange historical fossil! The Manchurians of the Ch'ing dynasty (1644–1912) imposed the custom on the Chinese as a sign of humility and submission; the Tibetans have copied the Chinese, without perhaps grasping the symbolism involved; now the pigtail is quite defunct in China but survives here and there in the remoter fields and meadows of Tibet. Thondup speaks only Tibetan. I find this all to the good for it gives me practice in the difficult language of Tsongkhapa.

When we are en route the caravan is quite showy; it comprises six regulars plus four or five mule- (or yak-, depending) drivers, with a dozen beasts burdened with various loads. Additionally, of course, there is the lama's white pony. When, as at present, we are not under way the personnel is trimmed to the bare essential. Tucci likes to feel surrounded by this little court. But everyone is to know his place! "Anyone who doesn't fall in with me one hundred per cent may as well go," he keeps saying. "Otherwise I'll crush him like an insect . . . !" And again that mischievous laugh and the characteristic rubbing of the hands. Not that I see any doubts anywhere about. On one occasion the lama sat down to eat with us, but fortunately he felt out of place. At any rate, Khalil follows the form to the letter, and knows exactly what he is about. "The lama, Norbhu and Thondup over there; the sahib over here; me, I'm the bridge, it's the same whether I'm in the kitchen or the living room." Once he whispered to me with a knowing wink, defining his Buddhist friends in the kitchen as "those heathens".

"Not you," he added, as though to dissipate any misconception, "you are men of the Book, the *khitab*!" You might say that spirits and demiurges of half the human race waft and spiral invisibly over the cottage in Samada.

Once at table I exclaim: "Your Excellency, that's one delicious curry our Norbhu has managed to make with his potatoes!"

"It's not the curry, my friend, it's the appetite!" remarked the master with a grin. "We've had a day of battle. But also of victory. How splendid! I feel as if I'm back for a moment in the days of Western Tibet . . . Now those were voyages, expeditions, enterprises! Passes five and six thousand metres high, snow, ice, yaks rolling down into the precipices, whole buried cities to unearth, hermits, brigands, sorcerers, deserts, hunger and thirst often enough, but glimpses of paradise. Lake Manasarovar, Mount Kailasa! This is nothing but a short hop outside the gate. A day-trip from Rome to Frascati! So cool down.

53 *On the caravan route: a Tibetan mule-driver*

54 *On the caravan route: grazing yaks*

A cook, lama, majordomo, who could ever have afforded them in those days? Anyway, today has been a positive pleasure. Just think, we've found the traces of a disciple of my great Rinchen-tsangpo, from the year 1000 or thereabouts – I wrote a book about him."[3]

"I see you're pleased, Your Excellency. But why have I seen you lately so preoccupied, as though you were grappling with a problem?"

"A problem? A dozen problems! I'll have months of work with the material collected at Kyangphu. You'll see. One thing in particular: you remember the upstairs chapel with the statues of the Five Supreme Buddhas?"

"Of course. They made a deep impression on me."

"Good. I can tell you they make a mandala, a huge, rich, extravagant three-dimensional mandala. You thought that mandalas were simply those geometric pictures we've seen in various temples and books, like the Getty we have with us and you keep looking through.[4] That is the commoner aspect of mandalas. But let's look at things more generally."

"Master-sahib, *anda, anda*! (eggs, eggs)." Khalil, standing respectfully to his master's left, offers him a large white plate containing a small yellow omelette, with the irreproachable gestures of a head waiter in a luxury hotel in a fashionable spa. He explains that Norbhu has finally succeeded in finding this modest

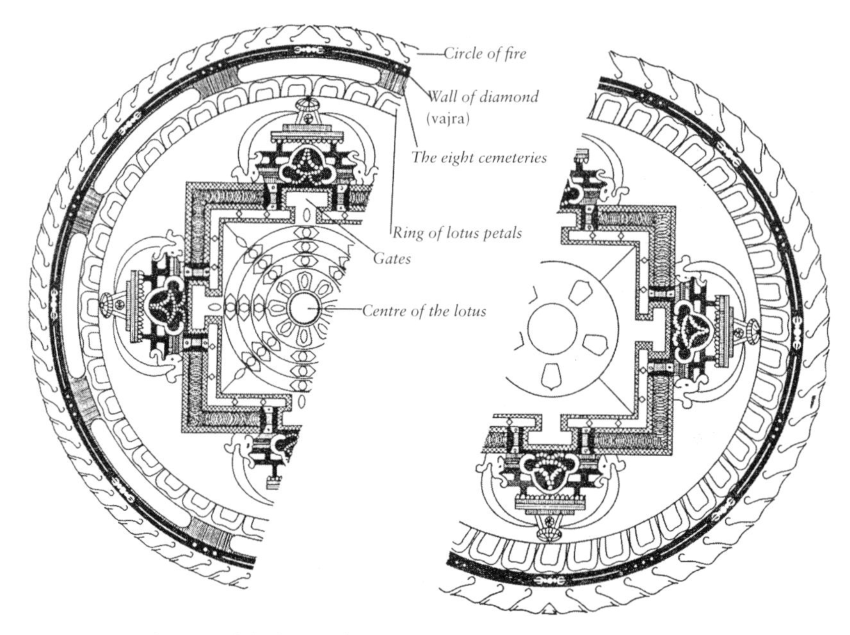

55 *Left: a mandala for terrifying gods. Right: a mandala for peaceful gods. The former is told apart from the latter chiefly by the additional ring, "the circle of the eight cemeteries". (A. and P. Keilhauer:* Ladakh, *p. 94, Dumont, 1982)*

addition to the meal. His Excellency Professor Giuseppe Tucci of the Accademia Italiana helps himself to his share of the omelette and pursues:

"We have to ask: basically, just what is a mandala? Simple: a spatial compendium of mystical truths! You follow? Bear this in mind. A broadly generalized principle therefore. A mandala may be drawn or painted and this is the commonest case. But it can also be a simple graffito in the sand. Just as it may be an important, elaborate complex of statues. Or a building. Borobodur in Java is basically a colossal mandala. Many of the temples in Angkor in Cambodia are mandalas. Now the thing about the Kyangphu statues is they pose me quite a problem: what the devil kind of mandala does it represent? As a rule those mandalas that feature Vairocana (or Namparnangdse as the Tibetans call him) as the central Buddha are ancient. The further you go back in time, the more popular they seem to have been with the faithful. I've seen plenty. At Spiti and at Kunuvar, in Indian Tibet, at Tsaparang, at Toling, in the territory of the ancient kingdom of Guge, where the Jesuit d'Andrade lived all those years, in the seventeenth century; then at Tabo. But each one was slightly different from the last. Why? Maybe some help is to be derived from a study of the Japanese ones, which are well known. Tajima has written brilliantly about them in French. It is strange that the Japanese too went for mandalas centred on Vairocana. But there's a reason. The great Kobo Daishi, ninth-century, acted as a bridge; lamaism and the Shingon sect have much in common. The Japanese have polarized between two mandalas in particular: the *kongo-kai* (the adamantine universe), and the *taizō-kai* (the uterine universe)."

"What superb symbolism, Professor! On the one hand the purity and indestructability of the stars, on the other the creating fire of love."

Tucci turned round and fixed me for a moment with that ruthless, icy, needle-sharp stare of his that suddenly glints in his eye when he is contradicted. Like the Tibetan gods, he can move in a flash from *shiwo* (peace, serenity) to *trowo* (disturbance, ferocity, terror). Somehow my observation stepped too far into the discussion, threatening to subvert the secret hierarchy of the expedition and its universe. The photographer is permitted to understand a fraction of what he sees, if he insists, but he has no business butting into the scientific *prajna*. Some doors are simply closed to him. And that's that.

Little by little I am beginning to grasp the odd, vague element of Tucci-ology; it is an arduous and subtle doctrine, highly inter-disciplinary, involving both intellect and emotions, body and psyche, *tatemae* (the façade) and *honne* (the substance) – as the Japanese put it – and it disposes of prestigious sums, overt and covert, tied up with sibylline mafias in the realms of government and the universities and spreads an invisible net over embassies and foreign governments. Like the rain forests of Sikkim, the levels, the extensions, the flatlands are almost infinite. At the bottom you have the dripping, dark, mossy caves or the dark, suffocating Kremlins, where snakes and throbbing monsters move about, betraying no definable profile or consistency; halfway up you admire the robust, prodigious pillars that support immense vaults of lush foliage and flowers; higher up still you catch sight of the peaks, almost miraculous in their unsullied brightness.

The following is, for instance, an important principle of Tucci-ology: a sharp distinction is to be maintained between travelling companions and pupils. The former ought ideally to be military men, strong, willing characters who see just so far and no further, or else technicians who concentrate on their own little patch; the latter are chosen among the finest brains at university, but let them be, how shall I put it? pedantic, hide-bound, little attracted by, indeed scared stiff of, vast spaces, by dirt and sweat, by solitude and cold, by a hard slog up on the high mountain passes. And woe betide if the two sectors start contaminating each other! The entire Tucci-ology would risk cracking up.

This evening, however, there is a happy conjunction. After a second the opposition melts away. The master smiles a genial smile. Maybe he realized he'd overdone it.

"Excuse me, Professor," I say then, plucking up courage, "Why are the mandalas in such profusion? Differing fantasies of masters? Schools at sixes and sevens? Regional types?"

"Good question. However the reasons you adduce are marginal. The truly fundamental one is quite another. Buddhism, you see, is a religion entirely different to ours, I mean the Judaeo-Christian and Islamic. It is not exclusive but inclusive. It does not obliterate, it absorbs. It does not destroy, it digests. Almost anywhere that it has flourished it has adapted to pre-existing cults. Here you have Bon, in China Taoism, in Japan Shinto, the Thais have their Nat, and so on. And yet all these countries are wholly or largely Buddhist or used to be. So much for the peoples as a whole; when it comes to individuals, Buddhism tries to adapt to the variety of single dispositions, to the moral personalities, to the level of intellect and culture, to the colour and warmth of character, to the karmic heredity, to past religious experience; you have to consider each case from a number of intersecting angles. A mandala, you remember, is a visible compendium of mystical truths, an instrument for capturing the light with immediate experience, not for knowing it merely in an abstract, intellectual way. So a master who knows his business needs to have at hand a great number of mandalas, and adapt one each time to the particular situation of his pupil, possibly in a number of attempts. There are mandalas for intuitive people and mandalas for people whose approach is analytic, mandalas for those who approach things visually and mandalas for ears that absorb truth through words, mandalas for those who have no time for forms and mandalas for those who are moved by sacred rites. There are occasions when passion is used to subdue passion, anger to subdue anger. I can't for the moment go further into the full complexity of the matter, but I've given you the nub of it. Bear in mind that the great Buton-Rimpoche [1290–1364] (we were looking at some of his writings just now with our lama) lists a good 343 mandalas, I believe, and that is only counting those with some bearing on the Supreme Buddha Vairocana, or his manifestations. Mandalas are a forest, an ocean, a galaxy!"[5]

As Tucci is talking I notice Khalil standing in the shadow, as though waiting to convey a message. Finally he steps forward.

"Master-sahib," he says as he advances and bows, "some lama come with old thing. Very good fellow; very good old thing."

We get up. Supper is over, as also the brief chromatic fantasy for mandala and potatoes. I retire into a closet to develop the photos I took of Kyangphu. It is an important task that I impose on myself on a daily basis, sometimes under pretty trying conditions. And yet it would be dreadful to discover, perhaps six months later, that some of the photographs had not come out properly. By developing them at once I can check; any that have not worked may always be retaken.

While I'm busy with the methyl, water, hyposulphite etc., I vaguely hear the voices of Tucci and the monk in the room next door. The word I keep hearing them repeat is *gormo,* rupees. That is another side to the infinite facets of my polyhedral guru: here he is in action as the no-nonsense dealer in Tibetan antiques. By now I know the score. It is evening. With the twilight, furtive monks with monstrous profiles come sidling in. Are they suffering from a multiplicity of arms, oversized scrotums, dropsical backs? Not in the least. They have large, fragile, rare, stupendous treasures beneath their grubby, greasy habits. They go into the secrecy of the guru's bedroom. After endless negotiations (the master is not readily taken for a ride) the works of art remain behind and the monks return to their impoverished monasteries with handfuls of (for them quite fabulous) *gormo.*

How I should like to be present at these secret nocturnal transactions! Not out of mischief or for the pleasure of scandal, but simply to have a better understanding, in the round, of this extraordinary person of whom it has been my singular good fortune to be able to say that I was his companion across the deserts of Tibet. A scientist bordering on genius; a tireless hiker; a past master at manipulating millionaires, governments, institutions, colleagues; in love with art, women, literature, food and wine; a voluptuous antiquary who gets high on caressing his latest acquisition; a bibliophile with an unerring nose; a bloodhound for following religious trails; as gentle as could be when he is so minded, but savage, ruthless, obnoxious when it suits him to be.

Tucci has been accused on various occasions by the irresponsible of exporting a large, a too large number of artistic treasures from Tibet (by purchase, of course). I have to speak out most robustly here in the professor's defence. If only he had exported more, a great many more, he would have rescued them from the iconoclastic onslaught of the Chinese! Under this heading I must also speak up for Sir Aurel Stein, von Le Coq, Paul Pelliot, Jacques Bacot, Edoardo Chiossone, Ernesto Fenollosa, Guimet, and all those other Europeans and Americans who have saved for mankind entire treasure-houses of artefacts which their possessors did not appreciate and which were liable to be lost or destroyed in the course of popular political or religious upheavals of one kind and another. I take the view that even in regard to Italy's own artistic heritage it is all to the good to allow them some measure of dispersion throughout the world: there is no knowing what disasters (earthquakes, fires, ideological insanity) may strike. The *Mona Lisa*'s residence in Paris and the Parthenon marbles' in London are both to be accounted a blessing rather than a misfortune.

Samada: an unknown lama turns up in the developer

Last night as I was developing the photographs and today as I was printing them by the primitive method of direct sunlight, I had a surprise. Next to the statue of poor Avalokitesvara from Kyangphu monastery, with his broken legs patched up any old how by means of rags and *kata* scarves, I find a most unusual portrait-bust of a lama. I had not noticed it when I took the picture. I noticed it only now as I looked at the proof sheets.

What makes it so unusual? Why, its features, expression, its face, the cold, clear eyes: imagine meeting someone like that seated on a small gilded throne in some palace-monastery, amid the whispers of deacons and clergy! Tucci gave the bust a moment's attention but found it of little interest. Perhaps he is right: it could be that in real life the man was merely some petty monastic bureaucrat.

And yet, why carve his image, and why put it on the altar next to the most venerable *Bodhisattvas*? It is clear that in his day, whenever that was, this man will have been quite magnetic. Indeed, the more one looks at him the more one is intrigued. His expression is at once fascinating and repellent: those cold, glaucous eyes reminiscent of a Prussian baron stare at you, watch you, bore into you relentlessly. Meanwhile the great mouth with its puffy lips – those of a late Medici grand duke – wears an ironic, knowing, not entirely mean smile, a true hedonist's smile, in complete contrast to the eyes. It's as if you amuse him with your presence, but he could be on the point of coming out with something grisly, of inviting his minions to throw you into the grimmest of dungeons. There is also a certain connivance with the onlooker, but that could suddenly change to disdain. He holds a rosary in his hands, but that double chin, that plump, self-indulgent body, remind one of habits maybe picked up in the seminary.

Then doubts arise. Have I read his psychology aright? Am I not conditioned by acquired cultural reflexes, which so easily send us off the track? Perhaps in the psychological terms of Tibet the entire facial landscape is open to a quite different interpretation. Perhaps. Not to mention the possibility that the artist misconstrued the reality of the sitter. Might it be the revenge of a sculptor who had been humiliated, frustrated? At all events, the more I observe and study my lama, the more sibylline I find him, the more he escapes definition and resists normal readings. Yet another of the many mysteries in this mysterious country.

56 The unknown lama who turned up in the developer

Dregun monastery: the cave of terrors

The weather is still beautiful. Just to think what it was like a few days ago, on the southern slopes of the Himalayas, bearing the full force of the mists and rains of the summer monsoons! We are living in two contrasting worlds: back there, damp, clammy heat, air heavy with steam, excessive vegetation, greenery in full sway; this side, dry, fresh light air, blue sky, steppes, desert, yellow and orange hold sway, whiteness of the ice – and the continuous festival of sunlight. At this height, the light falls like hail on a stupendous, savage, landscape, it isolates each detail, it sculpts the surfaces of stone and rock, it models the mountains near and far. One might think that Van Gogh had brought his brushes from Provence to these Tibetan mountainsides!

We are starting to see huts surrounded by little walls enclosing areas for the domestic animals. It is immediately clear from the roofs that we have penetrated into a region with a dry climate. South of the Himalayan watershed the roofs were made of wood, with a steep pitch to them, while here they are flat and made of baked mud. Brick made from sun-baked mud is often and readily used hereabouts as well as stone. One sees piles of these bricks here and there, laid out neatly in the air to dry. Along the valley floors there is a stream in which children bathe noisily, cheerfully as Tibetans will, except for the youngest who fall silent at the sight of strangers.

A half hour's walk from Samada brings us to a small monastery, Dregun *gompá*. We draw near. A low building, some thirty metres long. The walls are in rough stone sloppily whitewashed. All in all it looks more like a fort than a monastery. The effect stems from the fact that Tibetan architects nearly always choose lines that converge gently upwards in preference to rigid verticals; the stylistic motif, which moderately influences the eaves and walls, is repeated in a more marked manner in the design of the windows. The end result is nearly always happily unsophisticated: it gives the impression that the entire building has been born from the rock, from the mountainside, from the valley slope, a spontaneous offering of nature. The labour of man is wedded to the local geology, it completes and perfects it. Obviously the final impression is generally somewhat more warlike than priestly. The supreme example of this architectural style is the Potala in Lhasa, which we shall consider by and by.

The Dregun *gompá* belongs today to the Yellow Sect, the *Gelug-pa*, but Tucci already knows, from reading the *Nyang-chung* (his dog-eared guide for the seventeenth-century traveller), that it was built in ancient times by the Sakya abbots. The main building gives directly onto the caravan route, which is perhaps why it was badly damaged by the Anglo-Indian troops during the skirmishes of 1904. Thus the building is new for the most part, having been rebuilt a few decades back. In we go. The usual courtyard. Silence, sunlight, flowers, spades, baskets, all very picturesque. We are welcomed by a youngish monk; he is kind, quiet, extremely shy. Three steps up and we are in the temple itself. The master looks around much as an expert philatelist would who has been brought a packet of letters discovered in grandfather's chest.

"No point taking pictures, I should say. It's all small stuff that's been made over lately. Still, a good school! It maintains the tradition. Reminds one of that master at the Dung-kar *gompá* – what a sure touch, what masterly brush strokes! Tibet is a bit like Mount Athos: there they still paint Byzantine icons, here they keep on with seventeenth- and eighteenth-century frescoes. On the whole what's missing is the breath, the spirit. That Buddha with the sixteen *arhat*, the sixteen saints, in their niches, repeats a motif that is universal in Asiatic art, from Nepal to Japan. [Other instances of Buddha with the sixteen *arhat* can be found at Gyantse, and in the monastery of Sera at Lhasa.] Maitreya/Champa, the human Buddha of the future seated in European fashion is immensely popular everywhere, though not as much as the Supreme Buddha. He is Akshobhya/Mikyö-pa, you can see that at once, partly from the distinguishing blue colour, a bit from the *mudra* (ritual position of the hands). Around him stand his 108 emanations."

Tucci steps forward for a closer look at the painting. "Not at all bad! Perhaps it forms part of the original fresco that survived destruction in 1904. In that case it could date back to the sixteenth century. What a lot of discoveries to make along this well trodden caravan route, and yet so little investigated! What a lot of discoveries!"

The temple is larger than one would have thought; part of the walls are covered with murals depicting terrifying gods, haloed with flames, caught in furious ritual couplings.

"Professor, do these depict guardians or am I wrong?"

However the master is not forthcoming this morning. "Those? They're the thirteen forms of Vajrabhairava," he answers curtly on his way to the door. "I've written a whole lot about it in connection with the temples at Tsaparang in western Tibet. If you feel like it, read *Indo-Tibetica*, Volume Three, Part Two, etc. There must be a copy knocking around. Ask Khalil."

(Left thus empty-handed I did that evening take a look in *Indo-Tibetica*, Volume Three, Part Two. Khalil brought me two or three volumes but let me choose only one, for he cannot read the titles; then he handed it to me as though it were an ancient and venerable copy of the Koran. Soon I am

57 *Dregung monastery: mural in the* gön-kang *chapel depicting avenging Furies*

an expert on the Vajrabhairava and its metamorphoses.)

A while later Tucci called me; he could not be far, but from the sound of the voice, from the echoes, he seemed to be in a confined space. I turned and followed the sound. Ah, I've got it! He had fetched up in the *gön-kang*, the dark, subterranean shrine of the violent tutelary deities. Tucci is beaming again, as he does in "moments of discovery".

"Go and fetch your gear! This is a quite fascinating chapel. Splendid paintings. Notable Chinese influence. Era? Heaven knows, but old at any rate. Sakya inspiration, you follow? Which makes it thirteenth- or fourteenth-century."

While he is speaking, the master hands some more rupees to the gentle, shy lama, who pockets them but with little enthusiasm: fear is more potent than any reward. The honest fellow stands hanging his head, and when he looks up a little I notice that he is staring wide-eyed, like someone standing next to an object on the point of exploding. The terror of the local tutelary deities is so instinctive that there is no surmounting it. The lama wants to do as we wish, but those demons, those furious devils on the walls, those unchained Furies, what are they going to say? What if they took offence, if they felt they had been disturbed? To look at the grimace of anguish clawing at the lama's features, one would think that pernicious gamma rays are emanating from the wall.

The little chapel seems to be dedicated to Gur-gon, Protector of the Tent (though the name could also refer to other more esoteric meanings), patron of the lamas of the *Sakya-pa* school.[6] One wall, not all that big but not easy to photograph owing to the narrowness of the shrine, is occupied by a superbly wrought fresco, in colours matured and softened by time, depicting Gur-gon's court in a frantic, grim cavalcade. The field seems to be crossed by tongues of flame (restless will o' the wisps, as it were, born out of nothing), that are dragged diagonally, towards the right and upwards, by a violent wind. The ground is strewn with mutilated corpses in various stages of putrefaction, from the newly dead to the skeletal. Shrieking Furies, semi-naked or entirely so, ride foals, boars, yaks, dragons, giant hounds, camel-like creatures, bears, imaginary beasts, and brandish daggers, scythes, axes, ripped-out hearts, entrails, serpents, flayed skins. Some of them are exposing their vaginas, gaping voraciously; all of them have great big pendulous dugs that dance like bells; on their heads they all wear a crown of skulls. Giant crows wheel above, black as ink; one of them is about to plummet in an almost feline posture on to the field of macabre delights. A pensive wizard in one of the large black hats of his confraternity, and modestly mantled like a Confucian sage, looks out of place, but he is conscientiously pummelling a corpse.

This scene of rabid fury has a certain grandeur about it, and was born heaven knows when, from the brush of some anonymous painter, but the imagination, the bravura and power is extraordinary. He seems effortlessly to have imbued his human and animal characters with the erotic and violent passions with which he found them possessed, dashing them off effortlessly, all in one go; and he knew how to make them move, gallop, almost fly over the grisly fire-licked plain. In other words, he creates: he does not repeat what has been seen time and time again, but digs down into the depths of his own fantasy to uncover if not the characters, at least their aspect at that moment, and groups them according to his own assured taste.

Another mural nearby is interesting for its complex symbolism, though it is much more static: it boils down essentially to a fairly random catalogue of objects. There is a conspicuous Chinese influence in both panels: the horses (remarkably like those in terracotta in the T'ang tombs), the scaly dragon, the offertory tables and so on are sufficient evidence. Note also the eyes in the grinning skulls that make an ornamental framework at the base of the wall: look at them quickly from left to right, or vice versa, and they will seem to turn. Here the rampantly, uncompromisingly macabre style of the large panels above is collated with the grotesque mockery of one who has a total grip on subject and emotions.

Iwang monastery: at the origins of Tibetan art

What a dream, what an unforgettable experience, the remote and tiny sanctuary of Iwang!

A few kilometres downstream from Samada, beyond Selu (with the monastery of Gyani, belonging to the Yellow Sect – alas it is heavily restored and almost bereft of anything of interest), we leave the caravan trail to the right and take a lonely, dusty track. Some neighbourhood boys are our guides. What shall we see today? Will Iwang prove to be a big monastery? Or small? Recent or ancient? Interesting or so-so? Tucci holds his peace and ponders. I know by now from experience that to bother him with questions is a wholly pointless exercise. I can almost understand that drawbridge which is "Your Excellency". If he is in outgoing mood he lowers the drawbridge and chats, prattles, lets himself go, spreads the pollen of his learning; otherwise he raises the mediaeval contraption and remains alone in his castle protected by a moat of formality.

The tiny caravan keeps climbing. Tucci goes on ahead with the broad hat he wears on treks; then comes the lama-secretary Sonam on his little white pony followed by Norbhu leading the other horse laden on one side with baskets for lunch and on the other with baskets full of books, dictionaries, the seventeenth-century "touring guide" and so on. Then comes Thondup humping the bag of photographic equipment. I bring up the rear of this odd procession (see photo 51). I enjoy the landscape as I walk. A few steps off the caravan trail and it is as if we were not on the high seas but in the "high deserts". No longer a trace of human kind. Certain arid, powerful mountains the colour of burnt sienna rear up ever closer. They dominate the horizon exclusively. But do not, dear reader, imagine that they are fixed, empty, dead, oppressive! Meanwhile, to cheer them here and there, like drops of living turquoise, we have the loveliest, most precious blue poppies of Tibet: it seems impossible but these delicate gentian-hued flowers actually thrive in these dry, lonely places. Then up in the sky we have loose, scurrying clouds galloping like mad in the wind up there; their shadows race along the hillsides, caressing them, momentarily altering their tone and temper – from bright yellow to ochre, to purple, to violet, and from the stern or ugly and lowering to brightness and gaiety. It is a continuous dance of shadow and light: the mountains begin to flow like a sea with giant waves.

Suddenly, after a bend, here is Iwang. I don't know what I was really expecting, but what I found is certainly far beyond what I would have imagined. In the absolute human emptiness of a sort of irregular valley we come upon a small rectangle of straw-coloured walls with traces of red paint; it lies crouched up the hillside amid stones, scree, and a bit of ash-coloured scrub. Strange tapered battlements that have little respect for any rules give the complex the feel of a castle that somehow stirs the imagination.

Nowadays the little monastery belongs to the Yellow Sect, the *Gelug-pa*, but it is virtually deserted. The situation is worse than the one we met with at Kyangphu: there a family of peasants was ensconced, and if a beam or floor timber were suddenly to give, at least there was an able-bodied man to carry out repairs. Here at Iwang, who should come to open the door to us and show us round but a wretched old crone sloppily dressed and filthy beyond words. It seems that some shepherds live there too but they're not around. Inside, in the little courtyard and along the walls, weeds and a tangle of brambles are growing. Every object of ritual use has completely disappeared: stepping into the chapels, which evidently stay open whatever the weather, all we find is statues and frescoes. It is one of those places where, the moment you step inside, you are possessed by an instinctive sense of wonder and awe.

58 *The remote monastery of Iwang*

The present state of the monastery, abandoned, miles from anywhere, brings back in an almost physical sensation, the presence of the sages who lived here once upon a time, in meditation and asceticism, and that of the artists who so nobly embodied their ideals. The words of the Japanese poet Bashō spring to mind: "Ah the grass and the wind / And here amid these stones / The shadow of a dream."

What suggested this haiku to the seventeenth-century poet was a visit to the ruins of a fort in distant Tohoku; but it perfectly fits Iwang monastery. "The shadow of a dream!" : the sense so dear to Pascal of man as something fragile, perishable, transitory, "wretched" in the extreme, and yet great; great even in the shadows of his dreams.

Tucci looks around him, dashes off some notes. The old woman obviously doesn't know anything about anything, the lama Sonam is in a black mood. The master, with his seventeenth-century guidebook under his arm, is the best informed of all. And today, as luck would have it, he feels like thinking out loud.

"How predictable," he exclaims as she shuffles through some pages of the *Nyang-chung*, "that this Iwang should be an authentic gem! It's small but chock-a-block with riches. And of no little antiquity. Eleventh-century, maybe twelfth, certainly no later than early thirteenth. Which takes us back to "the second foundation of Buddhism in Tibet", after the horrors of the tenth century. The days of Rinchen-tsangpo or Atisha. Or soon after. One legend speaks of the monastery being founded by Lhaje-chöjung, who seems to have lived in the twelfth century. In those days the monastery was called Yemar. What a lot one can glean from this splendid manual for pilgrims!"

Some details turn out to be quite novel and unexpected, and the seventeenth-century guidebook makes no mention of them. For instance the unusual lay-out of the temple with three parallel chapels, each one longer than it is broad. Tucci makes a rough sketch.

"If only we had Ghersi with us!" he mutters as he sketches. "That was the man to take measurements and make sketches."[7] I suggest that maybe I can stand in and do the measuring, but for some reason the guru does not like the idea. "You take care of the photography, that's more important."

The main chapel is more reminiscent of a granary than of a shrine; the wooden pillars are hewed with axes, as are the roof-beams. Even so there is a subtle charm about the place. Its very simplicity and innocence are a delight. Certainly the big statues in gilt stucco that fill the room lack the technical skill, the stylistic refinement of those we admired at Kyangphu, yet there is something moving about their hieratic fixity, the way certain Byzantine mosaics are moving. The heavy draperies (possibly an echo of Hellenic incursions as far as Gandhara) would once have been gilded. The years have given them a precious patina that veers oddly towards purple, and results in a whole exquisite landscape of equivocal lights, of disillusioned reflections. The imposing central figure represents an unusual Buddha, Amoghadarshin; the image is half covered in old *katas* offered in homage by pilgrims; they look like giant cobwebs or forest lichen. On the halo there reappears the motif of the ten Buddhas of the "celestial regions" so popular hereabouts. On either side of Amoghadarshin is a tribunal of six immensely solemn and regal Buddhas, seated in European fashion, their hands in the *dharma-chakra-mudra* position, "gesture of one setting in motion the Wheel of the Law".

In the chapel next door we come once more upon "the family of Buddhas of the Directions of Space", represented by life-sized statues. At Kyangphu there were ten, here there are sixteen. There seem to be two sides to the concept underlying this iconographic motif: on the one hand there is the idea of presiding (one might call it), of ruling, of having charge of every sector of the horizon (not omitting the top and the bottom, the zenith and the nadir); on the other hand there is the idea of mission, the notion of Buddha being present in every quarter of the globe. The statues are very much like those at Kyangphu, except they are more rigid, drowsier, somewhat stereotyped.

"Here too, just as at Kyangphu," Tucci exclaims, stroking the draperies of one of the sixteen Buddhas, "see what a vigorous influence derives from Central Asia! Put it simply: in India it was hot and the saints went about with almost nothing on; in Central Asia it was cold, in fact freezing for a great part of the year, and the artists out there gave their venerated gods a generous layer of clothing. Sometimes styles have these homely origins, they derive from the elementary conditions of living. Later on the eminent professors draw all manner of conclusions. Now look at those pointed auras."

"Might one call them 'Gothic auras'"?

"If it amuses you. At all events they are typical of Central Asian styles. And of the northern Chinese. The Wei, for example. The Wei artists create proper flames on the shoulders of their saints, never mind auras! But look at the differences between these Buddhas painted on the walls. Purest Indian air, wouldn't you say? At Kyangphu you also found this proximity of India-Central Asia, India-China, but you had to reconstruct it in your mind as you moved from one chapel to the next. Here they're right under your nose! Between one statue and the next under Central Asian influence you come upon an exquisitely Indian fresco. Here we are at the origins, at the roots of Tibetan art. The Indian stream and the Nordic and Chinese are still independent of each other, quite distinct, barely juxtaposed. So the fusion, the birth of Tibetan art properly speaking comes much later. Perhaps in the fifteenth century. We shall see. Let's hope we find something at Gyantse. For the present the harvest is indeed great."

While the master moves on to copy some inscriptions – or rather to have his lama-secretary Sonam copy them – I get ready to photograph the murals. To photograph is also to observe. It is, moreover, a special way to immerse oneself in the object whose image one wants to lay hold of. It is true: the painted Buddhas are radically different from the carved ones right beside them. Apart from the semi-nakedness from India in contrast with the heavy Central-Asiatic draperies, it is clear that the spirit that imbued the one school of artists was in sharp contrast to the one animating the other. The brush of the "Indian" master looked towards synthesis, to capturing the essential with the minimum of

59 *Iwang monastery: ancient mural in purest Indian style of Buddha*

60 Iwang monastery: ancient mural in purest Indian style of Bodhisattva

technical outlay, boldly throwing onto the walls lines of almost calligraphic elegance, and making use of only a few basic colours (wine-red, dark brown, pink) distributed in great splotches; his colleague the sculptor, however, was absorbed in a pedantic analysis of the drapery, in the liturgical precision of each gesture, and meanwhile he loses sight of the whole, which is submerged under the typical rigidity of the symbolic, of the ideogram.

Some of the painted figures have a seraphic look on their face, vaguely didactic, others are more feeble, even while remaining pleasingly decorative. One figure is striking for its vigorous presence as an "athletic Buddha", for all the world like an Olympian Illuminato, champion not merely in contests of holiness, of logic and metaphysics but also in sporting contests. Slim waist, massive, powerful shoulders, bull neck, full face, an assured, determined look on his face, all this leaves one oddly perplexed to begin with; then one has to ask why. After all, the artist wanted to represent the Buddha as a champion and an Illuminato, a perfect man. Has he not succeeded?

Now the remarkable standing Buddha, his hands making a symbolical gesture commands an immediate assent, sympathy, perhaps even devotion, so it seems to me. His face expresses serene concentration with a touch of enigmatic spirituality. The brutally gawky feet, far from diminishing the nobility of the whole, move one by their rustic humanity. Maybe we wish to think in a typical Buddhist image of the lotus flower that grows in splendour from the mud.

I come to the end of my photographic tour. Among other things I have discovered that here too, as at Kyangphu, there is a chapel with the hundreds of "ghastly faces" of the Temptation of Buddha. The two collections are assuredly from the same school and perhaps, from their similarities, the work of the same artists.

Out in the courtyard I hear footsteps; the sound of decisive steps, of feet shod in great big stout leather sandals, the kind used to walking the mountain frontiers. It may sound silly but I would swear that Buddhist footsteps sound subtly different to Islamic footsteps. Maybe Buddhists tread more delicately, more furtively. Over the millennia the notion will have seeped into their blood that all is illusion, that we are on our way from one life to the next along vales of tears towards the Great Extinction. The Muslims set out a whole millennium later, but their message was more reassuring, and they hurled themselves with massive energy into the conquest of the world. Their basic doctrine gives them a huge confidence. And what of the rest of the world? Well, they're either pagans or they're People of the Book. The People of the Book deserve some measure of consideration but, when you get down to it, Jews and Christians have to admit that they are reactionary oafs, blind to the message of the last and supreme prophet, of the "Seal of the Prophets". Those with Islam in their hearts possess an inner citadel that is well-nigh impregnable, from which they may enjoy the Earth as their final and assured possession by divine right. Which inevitably shows in their footsteps, in the sound their steps make, the echoes they awaken beneath loggias and in gateways. As here.

I turn round and there is Khalil. He wears one of his broadest and most potent smiles. "Master, here post," he says, panting a little from having run, and hands a bundle of letters to Tucci, who has just sat down on a low wall. Much of the post is for "Sua Eccellenza" or "His Excellency", etc., but there are also letters for Sonam, Norbhu and me. What a strange feeling, this little arrow that arrives from across oceans, plains, mountains to fetch up here, amid blue poppies and Buddhas swathed in holy scarves that look like lichen! Obviously those lines of love, written out on flimsy paper that the wind tries to snatch from one's fingers, they offer happiness and inner warmth. And yet it is strange, all of a sudden it is Iwang that absorbs the world, not the other way round. As luck would have it the news was cheerful; had it been bad, maybe it would be different. As it is, after a few moments Iwang presses forward to assert itself. It enchants us and wrests us away. The letters are consigned to a bag.

Noticing the interruption, Norbhu steps in with table napkin, bowls, chapati, rice in one pot, curry in another. We eat with a hearty appetite. The bedraggled old woman crouches in a corner of the loggia looking at us. Khalil would drive her out but Tucci insists on her getting a bowl of rice and curry. The master today is in an effervescent, ebullient mood. Good news in the mail? Perhaps. But the chief reason for his high spirits, I think, is Iwang.

"Did you see? I told you so!" he cried as he drank a toast with a cup of that jet-black Indian tea, to which we have grown accustomed, as though it were

61 *Professor Giuseppe Tucci, on a visit to the Abbot of Kar-gyu, July 1937. He drinks tea with butter and salt from a jade cup*

wine. "It all adds up, it really does. That inscription beneath the portraits of the chapel donors tells us a great deal; now I have the painter's name, for instance. One Gyantsen-de. He declares, mark this, he declares in writing, for the benefit of posterity – that's us – that he painted his scenes on the walls 'in the Indian fashion' (*Gyagar-lu*). All doubts dispelled, then, all signed and sealed as though in the presence of a notary back there in the abysm of time. And back there in the third chapel too. You took their pictures, didn't you, those other Buddhas of the Cardinal Points, dressed like true Khotanese plutocrats? There again the artist has made his bold declaration. Not easy to make out. The name is obscured. Even so he states that he has worked in the Khotanese manner (*Li-lu*). It's as if two different schools, a southern and a northern, had been working in competition, and left a note for posterity stating which one each belonged to! A style competition. More curry? It's not at all bad. This spot of breeze whets the appetite."

When we leave Iwang there is a touch of evening in the air. The blue of the sky is more delicate, mature, piquant, the clouds have slowed down their frantic race and are taking on a vaguely pink hue. What a bounteous day of discoveries, tasty morsels for the spirit! In these last hours – thanks to the master, of course – the art of a thousand years has taken on meaning and depth before my eyes. In my imagination I followed pilgrims of yore making the journey up from India, laden with the odd bag of grain and a whole load of books on their shoulders; strange men driven by their dream, making for the crystalline solitude of the mountains. Others, driven to flee from the plains, put to fire and the sword by the Islamic conquerors, came up here for sanctuary. I have accompanied merchants' caravans on the silk routes, the gold routes, the routes for wool and salt. I have "seen" the Hor barbarians arrive on their horses from the north to sack and destroy, to kill and plunder, only to vanish on a sudden back into the desert from which they had come. I have known nomads wandering for millennia from horizon to horizon.

And each one of these groups carried in its hearts and minds a world, and an artistic language in which to express it. Thus India has climbed up to the Himalayan plateau from the south, the civilization of Central Asia has reached it from the north, bringing with it residual echoes of Gandhara, of Greece; and China infiltrated later on from the eastern valleys. Little by little Tibetan art as such was to take shape from these encounters. Today Tibet is like a living museum. Situated at the centre of Asia, remote but not peripheral, it has somehow captured and reflected every spiritual movement of the continent, each one has had its Tibetan moment. Congeries of facts that have vanished elsewhere but remain intact up here – living fossils.

Reconsideration, 1998

What ghastly news, it brings shame on the human race!

One day (the exact date is unknown) in one of those years of fire and shit between 1966 and 1977, the paranoid Mao determined in his insanity to unleash the whirlwind of the so-called Cultural Revolution in China and its colonies; and along the newly-built road from Gyantse to Phari lorries were to be seen crammed with young thugs shrieking and brandishing red flags, machine guns, rifles, picks and shovels. Who were they? One is almost ashamed to admit it but there is now little doubt that they were mostly young Tibetans, aged between twelve and twenty, led, urged on, set loose by a handful of adult Chinese fanatics. And where were they headed for? Kyangphu among other places. Luckily there was nobody there: the monks had left years ago, the peasants had fled, so this time nobody was killed (or so it would seem). But the ancient temple with all its chapels and its splendid statues, its paintings, its books, its precious furnishings, was mined, destroyed, torn apart, reduced to dust and shards.

In 1986 a young man from Turin, Roberto Vitali, a brilliant expert on Tibet, succeeded in obtaining permission to visit the temples along the caravan route (today a metalled road) connecting Gyantse and Phari. Where Kyangphu once stood all he found was "a stretch of shards", as he was later to write in his seminal study *The Temples of Southern Tibet* (London: Serindia, 1989).

I tell you this with tears in my eyes, dear reader: of all the marvellous and age-old works of art preserved at Kyangphu, which reflected the human spirit at a time of the sublimest faith and interior civilization, nothing remains with us here on earth save for the pale shadow – the photographs here reproduced. It is tragic, heart-breaking, but that is the simple truth.

At the monastery of Iwang (or Yemar) things fared a little better. Perhaps it was considered of smaller importance than the others because it was smaller, or perhaps the brutes were in a hurry; the fact is they contented themselves with taking the roof off the chapels. The vagaries of the weather – rain, snow, frost, sun, wind – did the rest. Some of the photographs taken by Roberto Vitali give an idea of the disaster. At Iwang the worst loss was not of statues, which were considerably inferior in terms of art to those at Kyangphu, it was the frescos (see photos 59, 60), which Tucci dated back to the twelfth century and which displayed the vigour of Indian influence at the beginnings of Tibetan art.

62 *Iwang monastery: heads of two Buddhas damaged in the Cultural Revolution (photograph by R. Vitali, 1986)*

1 This chapter refers to a journey made before 1948.

2 On Pentads, see Buddhas, Five Supreme, in Glossary.

3 G. Tucci: *Indo-Tibetica*, II: *Rin c'en bzang po e la rinascita del Buddhismo nel Tibet intorno al mille*

4 A. Getty: *The Gods of Northern Buddhism*, Oxford University Press, 1928

5 The question of the variety of mandalas is fully discussed by Tucci in *Indo-Tibetica*, IV/1, pp. 106–19.

6 Statues and paintings of the *gön-kang* in Dregun are analysed in depth with the usual scholarship by G. Tucci in *Indo-Tibetica*, IV/1, pp. 122–32.

7 Tucci is alluding to Captain Ghersi, who accompanied him on the previous expeditions to Tibet.

12

Gyantse, "The Royal Summit"

Gyantse: golden roofs gleaming in the distance

Yesterday afternoon we reached Gyantse after many days' travel.

It was not yet midday when the valley, which we had been following for several days' marches, slowly widened out and transformed itself into an open plain. At first there were only a few isolated human dwellings, but gradually they became more frequent, and eventually they became a normal feature of the landscape, and we were surrounded by fields of barley and other crops. At the foot of the grim, rocky, yellow mountains that rose in the distance in every direction the green of the valley broke off sharply, as if it were a lake. After so much travelling in the wilderness the soil, which at home would have seemed wretched and meagre, struck us as a marvel of fertility; in talking of the low poplars, the humble willows, that were to be seen every now and then, one was almost tempted to use the word "luxuriant". The white gentians and edelweiss growing between the cultivated plots seemed equally extraordinary.

The route – it was still an extremely irregular mule-track – grew populous. We had a distinct feeling of "arriving", of having left a now remote world, traversed great solitudes and of now entering another, different, world, a world entirely *sui generis*, a shut-off, isolated, archaic world. Though the route grew populous, there were no vehicles. Peasants passed, little local caravans of yaks and mules, and occasionally a lama on horseback, wrapped in his brownish robe and accompanied by junior clerics or servants; then we would pass a group of wandering players, or a local lord with his escort, or pilgrims, or a shepherdess, or merchants.

The houses became still more frequent, and handsomer. Some were country villas or the residences of nobles. In the distance there came into sight some low hills, among which there gleamed some golden roofs. "Gyantse!" the men exclaimed. We went on walking for a long time. We were tired; it was hot, and I was thirsty. The golden roofs gleamed more brightly. Now we could see the white walls of the monasteries, and soon we made out the city walls, which climb over the hills like the Great Wall of China. Finally the wind brought us the deep voice of the long trumpets being sounded in the monasteries. We crossed a stream. Thousands of little white "prayers" sang in the wind. The golden roofs gleamed like drops of sunshine fallen among the hills. It was like coming out of the wilderness into a land of fable, approaching a fairy-tale city. The yaks' bells tinkled, and round us men and women were working in the fields.

In our machine age rapid means of transport have deprived arrivals of any significance. Apart from certain places approached from the sea – Naples, New York, Rio – a city wraps its railway lines, its wires, pipes and tubes about us before we ever get a chance of seeing it. True, the aeroplane has restored a certain dignity to the all-important experience of arrival, but it is a momentary experience only; a few panoramic glimpses, a brief vision of giddily revolving houses and squares, the population reduced to tiny dots creeping about. But no-one who has not experienced it knows what it means to arrive in a famous and beautiful city after days and days of travel by means of the most primitive means of locomotion, on foot or on horseback; to catch a first glimpse of a city on the distant horizon; to approach nearer and start being able to pick out

63 *Gyantse: the ancient walls*

its most famous monuments; and then, instead of penetrating rapidly into it, to allow it gradually and slowly to enclose and absorb you, with all the fascination of an almost human personality. Who can tell what arrival at Florence must have been like for our grandfathers, coming down by carriage from the hills of Bivigliano into its enchanted valley? Gyantse today revived for us those exquisite, lost sensations. It should be added that it lies in a remote situation, difficult to reach, in a valley of great beauty, and that we came to it on a glorious July afternoon; and it will be understood that the experience will remain one of our most vivid and precious memories.

Philosophical duel between Tucci and the Khampo

The first thing we did today was to pay a visit to the Khampo, the head of the big group of monasteries that constitutes the sacred city of Gyantse.

It was a magnificent morning; the colour of the sky was indescribable. I don't know whether it was the height (12,000 feet), our closeness to the tropics, or the dryness of the air (the reasons the physicists give to explain the blueness of the sky are incidentally extremely complicated and abstruse); the fact remains that this morning it was of unsurpassed splendour and vividness. The day's colour-scheme could be divided into three levels; the cobalt and turquoise of the sky above, the ochre and orange of the rocks, the walls, the mountains around us, and the green grass below. Those are the colours of Tibet, blue, orange and green.

We lodged in the little bungalow, a little way outside the city, which is used by passing officials, the Political Officer from Gangtok, and the few other foreigners who occasionally pass this way. It seems very comfortable. The professor has a room and a study to himself, and there is also a room I can use as a dark room, an invaluable thing for a travelling photographer, because film can be developed the same evening, and unsuccessful "shots" can be retaken next day.

When you emerge from the bungalow you see facing you, about half-a-mile away, the *dzong*, the fortress, of Gyantse. It rises from a great yellow rock, surrounded by steep cliffs; "rises from" is the right word, because it looks less like a man-made building than a special kind of rock, a fantastic example of natural geometry, a new kind of hilltop. Its colour, surface, and "feel" are all rock.

Architecture is perhaps the form of art in which the spirit of this country has found its most original outlet. It is certainly the aspect of Tibetan culture which is most in harmony with its surroundings. Its distinguishing marks are

64 *Gyantse: the* Dzong

65 *Gyantse: a street, with the* Dzong *in the background*

the simplicity of its vast surfaces, its elementary, Babylonic lines, its grandiose and solemn proportions, its buttresses, and the tendency to build walls sloping inwards, suggesting a man standing with his legs apart, firmly planted on rock or on the ground. It is a courageous and noble architecture, simultaneously suggesting both a fortress and a monastery. It is not just an expression of brute strength; there is mind behind it, a desire for religious isolation, a sublime sense of beauty, with no trace whatever of frivolity or the baroque. It has the same beauty as the horizons and colours of these high plateaux. Those who have seen the Potala at Lhasa, the Buddhist Vatican, say that it combines in the happiest and most consummate manner all the best characteristics of the Tibetan architectural style.

When we walked round the bottom of the rock on which the fortress rises, we came suddenly upon the city of Gyantse. The shops and the houses of the lay population are on the plain, and standing in a semi-circle among the hills are

66 *Gyantse: view from the* Dzong

the temples, the monasteries, the libraries, the retreats, and the big *chorten* called the Kum-Bum ("the hundred thousand" – the word "images" is understood). The second, the sacred city, is separated from the lay city by a huge, thick wall of mud and stones. Both are protected by big walls that climb over the hills towards the north.

When we reached the first houses, we were greeted again, as we were yesterday, by the sound of trumpets being blown by the monks in the monasteries. In Tibet trumpets and bugles more or less correspond with our church bells. Like church bells, they can fill a whole countryside with something which is more than just sound, a physical vibration in the air, but has powerful emotional overtones. On a more physical plane we were greeted and assaulted by the usual horde of Tibetan children. Thus we penetrated into the city preceded, accompanied and followed by a whole army of grinning, leaping, laughing and shouting urchins. People crowded to the doors of their houses, because a white man is still an unusual spectacle in these parts. Nearly every woman wore on her head a big *patruk* of wood and coral; the men all wore a round earring, making them look like pirates. Here and there we saw a Nepalese or an Indian, and occasionally a girl of rather suspicious appearance, painted like a doll, and there were many beggars with prayer-wheels, which they whirled giddily.

To enter the sacred city we had to pass through a huge wooden door in the wall. Monks immediately came forward to meet us, for they had already heard of our arrival. First we were shown the Great Temple and the Kum-Bum, and then we were taken to the Khampo, the abbot-administrator of the sacred city. Three different sects – the Sakya, the Sha-lu and the Yellow Sect (*Gelug-pa*) – live peacefully side by side in the sacred city of Gyantse, each with its own temples, monasteries and retreats, but the Khampo, who is sent direct from Lhasa, is the undisputed head of them all.

We were led through narrow alleys, across courtyards, down passages, up steep steps, until we finally reached the Khampo's apartments. We were shown into a room where we sat on cushions and awaited that dignitary's arrival. The room was small and self-contained. The ceiling rested on wooden pillars, the capitals of which were decorated with the usual vivid but harmonizing colours. There were many pictures on the walls. On one side of the room was an altar, books, a statue, and in the middle some furniture. A shaft of blinding light, reflected from a white wall opposite, came through the window and lit the room with all the cheerfulness of the summer morning.

When the Khampo entered with rustling robes and took his seat on his own little throne this shaft of light illuminated his face from below. He was a man of about forty, fat and short; his features suggested a strong will, few scruples and

67 *Gyantse: girl in what used to be the traditional festive attire of the Tsang region. Her hair is adorned with a* patruk

great self-control. Perhaps nothing so clearly reveals a lama's character as the way in which he sits down. There are the ceremonious lamas, who take their seats slowly and delicately, carefully arranging the folds of their garments about them with broad, decorative gestures; and there are the ascetics, whose robes, by some secret virtue of their own, seem to fall into folds exactly as they are depicted in the statues of the Buddha. Finally there are the strong men, the born leaders, like the Khampo, who enter hurriedly, sit down anyhow and then quickly adjust their robes to leave their hands free, as if to seize invisible battalions of demons by their horns or direct the building of an enormous palace on a mountain-top. It should be added that the character of the Khampo's round and sometimes almost jovial face was sensibly modified by a noticeable admixture of fat, and that there was a calmness about him which led one to suspect Asian habits of dissimulation and observant watching and waiting.

After the exchange of the usual courtesies, Tucci and the Khampo embarked

68 *Gyantse: Abbot Ngawang Lodrö, the Sakya Lama of Ngor*

on a conversation that swiftly left the earth and mounted to exalted philosophical altitudes. Every now and then I managed to catch a phrase which I could understand, but I was like a man who has lost his way in a forest at night and is able only occasionally to glean some idea of his whereabouts from an occasional light. It struck me that in metaphysics, as in other things, the Khampo was a colonel rather than a philosopher. I could see from his face and gestures that he was marshalling his arguments like rooks and knights in an invisible game of chess. They seemed to be not so much thoughts and ideas as well-learned rules of logic and dialectics. He reminded me of some Dominican who knew his *darii* and *ferio* inside out and was deploying his scholastic syllogisms with skill. Apart from that, there was also the difficulty of the language, which at that level was no joke even for Giuseppe Tucci.

The arrival of tea and biscuits interrupted the learned disputation, and the Khampo and the professor started talking of simpler things; our journey, our programme at Gyantse, Tibetan gastronomical habits. Finally we left, with the Khampo's permission to photograph anything we liked in the sacred city and a flavour of stale fried biscuits in our mouths.

The sinfulness of meat

We have recently struck up a friendship with the Tibetan doctor of Gyantse. I don't know what his name is, but everyone here calls him the *am-chi*, the doctor, and we do the same. He is a man of about forty, tall, thin and bony, who always bends forward when he walks, as if he were just about to fall or were miraculously leaning on the air. His normal expression suggests that he is ready to accept imminent disaster with resignation, but he often smiles, and then his appearance changes completely. His face lights up as instantaneously as a room when the light is switched on, and he seems to be able to switch on his smile at will.

69 *Gyantse: the local physician* (am-chi). *The broad-brimmed hat was formerly used by men of science*

Today he came to fetch us, and we went "to town" together. It was market day. Stalls were lined up along the principal street, near the entrance to the monasteries, and there was a big crowd. I noticed that butcher's meat was openly, almost ostentatiously, on sale. The adaptation of the Buddhist conscience to this must be so long-standing as to have become ingrained. Or is the theory that the sin of meat-eating would only be encouraged by repression? If it were rigorously forbidden, would a plate of meat have all the attraction of forbidden fruit? It is interesting in this connection to note that Europe, with its obsession with chastity and sex, has for ages produced works of art which Asians find completely shocking; to a Chinese or Japanese who has not yet adapted himself to our conventions, not only Rubens, but even Giorgione or Botticelli are pure pornography.

Hwuy-ung, a Mandarin of the Fourth Button, wrote from a Western city on September 8th, 1900, to a friend in China:

> "The pictures in the palace set apart for them not please cultured mind of my venerable brother. The female form is represented, nude or half nude. This would obtain fault from our propriety. One fraction of this indecency would in the streets gather a crowd of watch-street men, and occasion a scene of disorder; in the palace anything may be depicted, and girls and children contemplate it . . . Morality with these strange people is not a fixed thing, but question of time and place. They have statues of plaster, and some of marble, in the public gardens and in this palace, most of them naked. In the winter's ice it makes me want to cover them. The artists not know the attraction of rich flowing drapery." [1]

But to return to the market. It had little to offer, except cheap and shoddy goods from India and gimcrack products of Chinese factories. Occasionally, however, you saw pleasing examples of Tibetan craftsmanship – Derge tea-pots or jars, Lhasa silver, and a few antiques. Every stall-holder also had a heap of rough turquoises, often big, but rarely of a really beautiful blue. Many women were selling at the stalls – not attractive girls employed to attract a little extra custom, but matrons with faces disfigured with layers of butter, who displayed their prosperity by wearing rings with stones of exaggerated size and heavy and ostentatious amulet boxes. I watched them bargaining with their customers. Their frank and confident manner again demonstrated, if there were any need of such demonstration, the equality of the sexes which is so characteristic of Tibet.

Indian rupees circulate in the market as freely as Tibetan *tanka*. Rupees are actually much sought after. The Tibetan coinage is brass and silver; there used to be gold coins, too, but these have now vanished from circulation. The silver coins have an attractive, archaic look. There is also paper money-notes of ten, fifty, a hundred and five hundred *srang*; they are huge notes, covered with fantastic patterns in bright colours, showing the Tibetan lion, the mountains, the Eight Glorious Emblems, as well as impressive stamps and seals.

The doctor's house is near the market; it is, indeed, right that such an important personage should live in the centre of the town. From our point of view he is an amateur, working on purely empirical principles, but at Gyantse he is *the* doctor. He is an intelligent and cultivated man. He knows all about the local plants, with which he makes dozens of different decoctions, and from the roots of which he extracts various active principles as remedies for many ills. He has a great respect for Western medicine, and, like most Tibetans, a blind faith in injections.

He has been a widower for several years, and lives with an old servant, a daughter of twelve and an assistant. He moves with great dignity among his thousands of possessions; the *am-chi* is one of those men who solemnize everything they touch. As soon as you look at him his smile lights up. At heart he must be a very sad man. It is immediately obvious how devoted he is to his little daughter. She appeared for a moment when we arrived, but her father packed her upstairs to change and make herself beautiful. The *am-chi* has many books, some of which interested Professor Tucci. The two talked for a long time, looking through book after book. The *am-chi* wore his big scientist's hat all the time, and did not remove it in the house. In the East a hat is a symbol rather than a head covering. Then he sat down opposite the little family altar, on which there were offerings, little cups for holy water, a prayer-wheel, some religious books wrapped in pieces of cloth, artificial flowers, ceremonial silk sashes and two big pictures on poles. The cracks in the wooden partitions between one room and the next were plastered over with old English newspapers.

Nima-üser, the little mistress of the house, came down again. She had changed, and put on her dead mother's jewellery, and she came and sat with us. She was an adorable child. She was shy, but not so shy as to hide completely the pleasure of feeling herself so important. When the servant brought tea she rose, arranged the cups and offered us biscuits. Then she sat down again, like a little statue, admiring her father, of whom she was obviously extremely fond.

Protective horrors

Photography is a double-edged weapon, a dangerous thing to practise in these parts. At first no-one would agree to be photographed, and a few days ago a

70 *Gyantse: the doctor's daughter, wearing her late mother's jewellery*

man made as if to pick up a stone and throw it at me because I persisted in trying to photograph him. But, now that I have given away some prints, badly printed in the bungalow, I notice a complete change. Not only do people allow me to take all the photographs I want, but many seek me out and insist on my photographing them. I foresee that very soon I shall have no more peace. One of the most persistent of those who besiege me is a young monk, who calls on us several times a day. Fortunately he is a likeable, friendly and always good-humoured young man, and we have started using him as a guide. His name is Kumphel, and he is, I think, twenty-four or twenty-five years old.

Today Tucci and I went to see and photograph the *gön-kang* belonging to the great temple of the sacred city. As usual, it was a dark cellar, full of horrors. The black statues of the terrifying deities were covered with dusty rags, the straw-filled carcasses hanging on the wall were falling to pieces. Masks and ancient swords and halberds were standing about, mingled with offerings of rancid butter. Terrifying, bloodthirsty shapes were painted on the walls. After only a very short time in a *gön-kang* you feel oppressed as if by an incubus, and you long for daylight and the sun like a drowning man longing for air. But

I have often noticed that lamas seem actually to like being in such places. Today I asked Kumphel whether he did not feel frightened in such surroundings.

"On the contrary," he answered. "One always feels fine in a *gön-kang*, one is more protected here than anywhere else. The terrifying gods are our guardians!"

It is always fascinating to see things through other people's eyes, particularly if they are very different from one's own. Kumphel's answer showed how much more important in life are the things you believe in than the things you see. What you see or feel you simultaneously incorporate into your inner landscape. Western thought, twenty centuries behind Eastern thought, has now become thoroughly convinced of this. But too little attention is still paid to the fact that it is the cultural constant rather than the individual variable which is the decisive factor in the transformation which the cosmos undergoes in the psyche. In other words, if we had been born and bred in a lamaist environment we too, no doubt, would find a *gön-kang* the most comforting of places. To give an opposite example, what we consider to be the agreeable strain and exertion of games and sport appear to most orientals to be either simply crazy or to be a form of punishment.

All our activities are "cultural"; there is no such thing as "natural" man. I am incapable of blowing my nose or admiring a sunset without revealing a whole tradition, an attitude towards society and the world. But it is by leaving the greenhouse of one's civilization that one becomes aware of this – the greenhouse

71 *Gyantse: wild beasts and flames in a graveyard strewn with corpses, from a mural in the* gön-kang

72 *Gyantse: the goddess Dö-kam lha-mo in the* gön-kang, *instilling terror*

of one's own civilization in which the most random little plants end by taking on resemblances to the oaks of the Absolute.

Son of the Rock

The great rock is markedly stratified, bare, a luminous shade of yellow, and rises suddenly out of the plain; it will undoubtedly have been fortified from the earliest, indeed from prehistoric, times. It is one of those places like San Marino, which are asking for a castle, yearn for one, require, insist upon one! It is not for nothing that the place has taken its name from this characteristic. What we have is Gyantse, that is, the *tsé* (the peak, summit or apex) of the Gyal(po) (the sovereign, lord, kind); in other words the Royal peak, or Regal summit. The fortifications we see today would seem to go back at least to the fourteenth century in their essential nucleus, when Nangchen Phags-pa founded a local dynasty of some importance. Of course much was added later, bringing the agglomeration to that symphony of ascending lines that crowns the walls with such bold power. I never tire of admiring the *dzong*, in every light, from the great variety of angles that the surrounding plain vouchsafes to the eye. The term *dzong* itself could not be more pertinent: at once peremptory, incisive and sonorous!

I went up early this morning on the *tsé* to visit the fort. I have to confess that I was disappointed, save for the view. It was here in 1904 that the Tibetans put up a massive resistance to the advancing British military expedition led by Colonel Francis Younghusband, and the damage then suffered was only partially repaired by the Tibetans, as best they could. Nobody lives there now except for a pair of wretched keepers. In those days it must have been seething with life. Once upon a time the *dzong* would not have been simply a fortress, it would have been the Prefect's headquarters, the centre of the provincial administration, temple, school, granary, prison and heaven knows what else besides; in a word it was the lay centre of the city, as distinct from the ecclesiastical centre in the monastery.

I wander here and there among the deserted alleys, the battlements, the towers and walkways of the bold fortress, much as we would do at Narni, Lerici, Caccamo, Mussomeli. Crows which perhaps nest up here wheel above us, cawing noisily. I recollect the description made by Waddell of the place many a decade before, when he climbed up here shortly after the Tibetans had abandoned their positions. There is a photograph of the entrance in his book, with four conspicuous wild yak carcasses stuffed with straw and dangling from the ceiling, to scare off enemies whether visible or not: bear in mind that wild yak is an extremely savage beast, a great deal larger and more powerful than the domestic variety, with which it has little commerce. And there is no forgetting the discovery made by Waddell and his companions when they visited the fortress. "While we were looking for grain stores, we stumbled on a roomful of horrors, crammed with the decapitated heads of men, women and children. One of the male heads could have passed for European. The gory hills of heads betrayed the fact that the decapitations had all been inflicted on living people."[2]

A modicum of horror (even if it is attenuated with time) is part and parcel of life in Tibet. I look out from the parapet of the furthest tower and my thoughts are cleansed in the incomparable splendour of the view over the city, the monasteries, the bare mountains, ochreous and boundless. The monastery of Gyantse is truly a holy city on a large scale. One already has some sense of this as one walks, as we did, through its streets and alleys, its squares large and small, its flights of steps climbing up and tumbling downhill (reminiscent of Amalfi and Volterra) – but one gets a clearer impression of it looking at the whole place from above.

The holy city, called Palkhor-choide (Eminent circular enclosure of the Faith), is precisely that. There is no doubting that it is eminent; it takes up a good half of the inhabited city. And it is eminent not only by virtue of its extent but thanks to the harmony and grace of its urban development (for lack of a better word). It nests perfectly in the lap of the barren, orange-yellow hillsides baked by the sun, a true Thebaid of hermits, crowned by garlands of walls that dance from one hilltop to the next, from tower to tower. The complete isolation is stupendous in itself, emphasized as it is by the desert background bare of any sign of human life.

It is equally obvious that it is an enclosure: imposing mediaeval walls protect it on every side, giving it the perfect compactness of a Carcassone or San Gimignano. And the adjective circular fits it too just as well. To anyone looking carefully at the whole, it constitutes a subtle geometrical harmony of rectangles and circles that follow each other in a fugue of lines, inscribed in the wide oval that encloses the whole. Finally, that the Palkhor-choide is all to do with Faith can be gleaned, even up here, from the importance accorded to the principal temple, Tsugla-kang, and the colossal *chorten* with its golden dome that glints in the sun.

It is said that the complex embraces more than twenty be it monasteries or temples housing some eight hundred religious of various categories, *trapa* (monks), lama (masters), and *geshe* (theologians); and often they receive visits from *trul-ku* (living embodiments of some celebrated saint). Unusually, the monasteries, as we have said, for complicated reasons of history, are divided among various sects: the *Sakya-pa*, the actual founders of the sanctuary in the fourteenth century, the followers of Buton-Rimpoche, and most of all the ever-present *Gelug-pa*, who hold sway in Lhasa and effectively in the whole of Tibet.

A great temple: a Babel of treasures

Our destination today is the Tsugla-kang, the Great Temple.

Yesterday, no sooner had we set foot in the *gön-kang*, the dark shrine of the guardian divinities, Tucci – with his unerring nose, a veritable Berenson of the snows and deserts – exclaimed: "Ah yes, here we are in ancient Sakya territory! My good old *Gelug-pa* never give a thought to these subtleties: they occupy, adopt, rake in, but quite neglect every trace of the founders, the erstwhile masters. It is enough to observe the image of the guardian spirit Gur-gon (Gur mgon) standing by the door for the true story to emerge. It is a typical Sakya name. Indeed it is, that's the pluralist policy set in hand by Tsongkhapa and pursued also by the Fifth Dalai Lama."

I am discovering that the master nurtures an admiration approaching idolization, a reverence close to passion, for the Sakya abbots; meanwhile he is cool

73 *Gyantse: the living incarnation of Buton-Rimpoche, the Great Precious One who lived 1290–1364*

if not downright frosty towards the *Gelug-pa*, the Yellow Sect, who have been the true masters of Tibet from the Fifth Dalai Lama (mid-seventeenth century) onwards. Maybe it is one further manifestation of his curious love for those whom the English playfully define as "the underdog". At all events, the master speaks of the Sakya with the greatest deference, ("now there you had enlightened spenders! Look at how they always opted for the right masters, the most inspired artists. While the *Gelug-pa* . . . strutting generals in a Falangist church! A lamaist Salvation Army . . . "). He also has a high regard for the Gyantse princes, a local dynasty of no little importance, great benefactors ("you might almost call them the Medicis of Tsang") who reigned for several generations over Gyantse and the surrounding district. They were more or less vassals, where not kinsmen, of the Sakya abbots, through family ties with the overlords of Shalu, a small territory between here and Shigatse, the place where the great theologian Buton-Rimpoche lived, wrote and taught.

As we approached the temple Tucci discovered in the ring-wall a stone slab with a rudimentary bas relief eroded by time: it must have been the portrait of Chogyal Rabten (or Rapten, or Rabtan), the fourth prince of the Gyantse dynasty, and founder of the splendid pagoda-*chorten* known as Kum-Bum, which stands close by and will be studied in a moment.

It seems extremely difficult to establish a chronology. Tucci discusses this at length, with various lamas who keep coming to call on him. On two or three occasions the master has sat down to supper (the usual chicken in tinfoil with stainless steel tendons, the usual undercooked potatoes on account of the altitude) with a look on his face that I secretly set down as "a victory-grin", vigorously rubbing his hands together in his own inimitable fashion, while announcing to me: "Now we have it: Rabten was born in . . . " only to come out with a glum correction a few days later. And now we must really be there: the date of birth has to be 1389; as to the date of death, that is wrapped in silence.

Some monks are awaiting us. Authority is represented by a young one with

74 *Gyantse: large prayer wheel*

slender philosopher's hands but an expression that suggests that he's very pleased with himself. Greetings. Exchange of *kata* scarves. We climb a few steps to the temple atrium and are welcomed by the vast, colourful, cheerful murals depicting the Four Kings of the Cardinal Points. I notice also a big Wheel of Life. Once past the massive wooden door, as heavy as could be, lacquered in red, and past a narrow little room, here we are in the impressive principal aisle of the temple, where the many rites of feastdays and feria take place. There are long, low stuffed cushions for a hundred monks and more to sit on (but they are rock-hard and greasy). There is not much light, and the air is steeped in that *foetor thibeticus* compounded of butter, various kinds of incense, human odours, a metaphysical-pastoral combination which one has to smell only once to recall forever.

It has to be said that Tibetan architects have always been absolute magicians in designing and building the exterior of their civil, religious and military buildings; but when they come to the interiors they prove to be timid, pusillanimous,

75 *Gyantse: monks reading the* Kangyur *scriptures*

faint-hearted. When it's a question of covering no more than a few square metres, they will not move until they have planted a veritable thicket of wooden pillars for support; they are like those circumspect climbers who need a solid piton at the foot of every passage that presents the smallest difficulty or exposure. So the principal room of the temple is more than a nave (which might conjure up an image of an inverted ship's hull) but rather might be called a forest. Masses of wooden pillars, finely carved and painted in cheerful colours, hold up the ceiling, precluding by their density any overall view of the place.

In the sanctuary at the end of the room there is a tall statue of the Crowned Buddha (Jowo Rimpoche), which is evidently a reproduction of the famous statue of the same name at Lhasa. According to Tucci it is modern and hideous ("the usual *Gelug-pa* stuff"), and not worth the bother of photographing. He is right of course, if one thinks of the sublime works of art that we have had the good fortune to see and admire along the road from India. It has to be said, though, that the image has been installed with enormous skill, and expresses quite dazzlingly that strange parallel between Catholicism and lamaism which so struck the French abbés Huc and Gabet a hundred years ago. A small window let into the wall above and in front of the statue throws light on it with all the effectiveness of a Caravaggio painting. To complete the mystical atmosphere there are numerous lamps fed on butter, the rich and heavy white silk scarves, the coloured silk drapes hanging from the ceiling, the haloes carved in

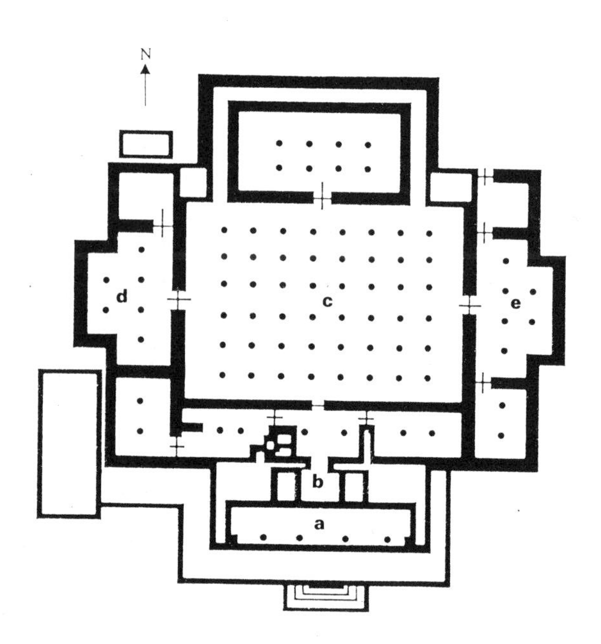

76 *Plan of the Great Temple* (Tsugla-kang) *at Gyantse: ground floor (M. Henss:* Tibet, *p. 154, Atlantis, 1981)*

a. Painting of the Four Guardians of Space (Gyalchen-de-shi). *b. Entrance. c. Great chapel for meetings. d. Chapel of the Vajradhatumandala of Vairocana. e. Chapel of Maitreya/Champa, formerly of Avalokitesvara.*

wood and gilded, the silver holy water stoups, the peacock feathers, in a word all those signs of popular devotion that give a statue a human dimension to the point of bringing it to life, endowing it with a personality.

Everyone who entered the chapel with us, dozens of people, whether monks or layfolk, fell prostrate in front of the Crowned Buddha in an act of total devotion, reciting ejaculations and sacret ritual formulae in a deep-voiced, cavernous singsong. Norbhu, who sidled in with us, seemed to be beside himself with ecstasy. Kumphel approached and said something in my ear: "You know,

77 *Gyantse: large statue in gilded copper of the Crowned Buddha, Jowo Rimpoche*

to make this marvellous statue they used so much copper and so much gold." I gather from his gestures and his bashful miming that the quantities involved are beyond counting. When we were back at the house we made the calculation: it worked out at some eleven tons of copper and five kilos of gold – not bad! "In Ripin (Japan)," I tell Kumphel, "twelve hundred years ago, at Nara, they made a Buddha in which they cast 130 kilos of gold!" I don't know whether Kumphel believed me, but he gave every sign of being thoroughly impressed.

From the central nave we made for the chapel of Vairocana; it was smaller and contained any number of holy images. I recognized the Five Supreme Buddhas (but was confirmed in this by the master in a brief aside). It took the form of a three-dimensional mandala, like the one we saw in the monastery at Kyangphu. Ancient though they are (early fifteenth-century), I must admit that these sculptures impress me a good deal less than those we admired at Kyangphu. There's something rigid and pedantic in the faces and bodies that leave one cold. The noble Cosmic Buddhas have put on weight, grown flabby, turned bourgeois; for all the world like somewhat listless imperial eunuchs. What has become of that vibrant presence, the absolute vehicle for the spirit, above and beyond any imaginable religion, which is the true sign of inspiration, of authentic grandeur. The 999 images painted on the walls, however, that represent various aspects of the Supreme Buddha Dorje-sempa in an obsessive repetition – how delicate, how sensitive and exquisite they are!

We crossed the great nave once again – at this point some fifty monks have assembled for some function of maybe a restricted nature – and entered the Chapel of Maitreya. It seems it used to be dedicated to Avalokitesvara, before adding a statue to the Buddha of the future, Maitreya/Champa, and the name changed.

"Now these really are first-rate!" said the master, stopping before three statues in stucco, to which time has lent a remarkable patina. "I am quite at a loss, for I've never seen anything like them." But Tucci is swept up on a wave of enthusiasm and recovers his saving habit of thinking out loud.

"Yes, of course, they are the Three Holy Kings. It is a rare theme in iconography, and what is more it is handled here with absolute mastery."

I stop to take their photographs. The retinue of notables move off, the masters at their head. At last I am alone with my kings. It is not at all easy to admire, to feel, to read the sculptures and paintings properly while being deafened by the crowd. Now in the silence and recollection of the empty chapel I am free to savour to the full the harmonious proportions, the subtlety of the details, the softness of those hands in the dances of the various *mudra*, the faces of these statues, at once so human and so inspired. The influence of Chinese masters is beyond doubt, while there is a strong Indian residue in the faces, in the adornment of their dress; truly Tibetan art is being born, in the deep assimilation of inspiration wafted in by the winds from every point of the compass, almost in secret.

The temple is vast and complex, with its two storeys, its passages, its stairs, its chapels great and small, its courtyards and terraces. We continue our visit. Here it is not as in the monastery of Kyangphu, way out in the desert, where Tucci and I wandered about blissfully, discovering age-old, forgotten masterpieces; now we are moving in a procession led by the elegant and authoritarian young lama who is short of patience; to judge by the respect with which everyone treats him, he must be uncommonly important.

We go upstairs.

"Just as well, just as well!" Tucci keeps remarking as he looks at paintings and sculptures. "Just as well that the great patrimony of the Sakya abbots has remained almost intact. Look! Just what I expected. Here is the true, authentic exclusive forum of the mystical masters of all doctrine, according to the

78 *Gyantse: the 8th-century King Tison-detsen, the greatest ruler of Tibet*

Sakya-pa: in the middle, Vajradhara/Dorje-chang, the primordial ancestor, the Supreme Buddha . . . The Buddha-in-chief, you might say. Then Nairatmya/ Damema on one side, Virupa on the other . . . In a word the historical dignitaries of the Sakya church."

Apart from Vajradhara, who repeats the usual iconographic canons, with no great inspiration, so it seems to me, the rest of the statues are of a kind entirely different from those we have seen hitherto. There is something strangely torrid and impetuous in the saucy way in which the various characters are represented, in their crazed, aggressive smiles brazenly trumpeting their hidden meanings – they defy classification. Once again, as with the mysterious lama of Kyangphu, perhaps we are faced with an entire psychology that needs reinterpreting. Can our response be quite outside the bandwidth? Here the divine breathes through unusual pores, as it does in the Orpheus of Douanier Rousseau – "douanier" for want of a better word: he was the shrewdest of innocents!

Still more disturbing (but at least in this case it is to be expected) are the paintings all around us on the chapel walls; they feature those mad, sublime, bizarre characters, somewhere between heroic and erotic, great philosophers and great savages, the 84 *maha-siddha*, the 84 "holy miracle-workers" or better, the 84 incredible magicians.

This strange family was born in India in the dim and distant past; some of them are mythological, some legendary, others possibly carry echoes of authentic living beings of yore, and they are venerated saints, eminent magicians, irresistible yogis, supreme miracle-workers. Several lists of *maha-siddha* are known. The popularity of the cohort was extraordinary, both with the Hindus and the Buddhists. At the root of it all lies the belief, common to Hindus and Buddhists, that hard ascetic penances and long meditations bring one to acquire special psychic and physical powers, unusual energies that go vastly further than any normal man's equipment in these fields. Such capabilities might include levitation, ubiquity, clairvoyance, insensitivity to pain, telepathy, the generation of body heat in the cold, and so on. In a word, by putting his body and his mental faculties through a special regimen, the *siddha* has successfully achieved his goal (*siddhi*) and acquired extraordinary powers. Each one of the 84 *maha-siddha*s became famous for some spectacular undertaking. The *siddhas* belong to every social class, often their birth makes them outcasts, but they end by excelling with unbending willpower. Under the influence of Tantrism and its technique of sexual yoga, the *maha-siddha* acquired female companions, the *shakti*s.

Buddhism accepted this popular cult of magicians and witches, investing it with a symbolic value. True success (*siddhi*) was no longer considered to be the conquest of prodigious powers over nature but the attainment of supreme illumination. This explains their acceptance in the temples.

As for the chapel in Gyantse, what is most interesting is the extraordinary artistic interpretation given to the various motifs connected with the lives and deeds of the *maha-siddha*s. The holy magicians are projected onto the walls in acrobatic, tightrope-walking attitudes, balanced between the fantastic and the impossible, masters of a yoga that partakes at once of coition and the dance. Their reptilian bodies are contorted in positions redolent of ecstatic harlequins, wonderfully interlaced with those of the intense, lascivious, malleable, naked and bejewelled little *shakti*s. Is it liturgy, dance, or erotic acrobatics? The artist is alert to every possible offshoot of his bold theme with a naughty, free-wheeling sensitivity, ready to stress, underline, highlight the ballet of his scandalous saints.

79 *Gyantse: chapel of Dorje-sempa in the great temple. Detail of 15th-century mural showing a* maha-siddha *engaged in Tantric yoga with his* shakti

80 *Gyantse: chapel of Dorje-sempa in the great temple. Another detail of 15th-century mural showing a* maha-siddha *engaged in Tantric yoga with his* shakti

And around the *siddha*s, around their loose-jointed, fiery contortions there is a hint of Nature at its most lavish and succulent, of tropics dreamt about rather than experienced. Trees, with roots like tentacles, imitate the humans in a dance of branches. Flowers, clouds, flames, tigers, jewels add a supplement of cream to the gluttonous feast of colours and shapes. Perhaps what we are looking at is one of the most ingenious and astonishing creations in Asiatic art.

The special morning, which had begun very early, ends late, after a marathon of Buddhas and saints, statues, paintings, inscriptions. We also visit various book collections. One of them includes the immensely heavy and sumptuous volumes of the *Prajnāpāramitā* in eight thousand lines, a work of the most special value which is not simply read but is carried in procession, so it seems, at moments of crisis or disaster. To open a volume is not only a ritual that requires the singing of certain ritual words but also a long, precise, difficult technical operation. The outside ribbons have to be undone, the "cover" – a highly precious slab of heavy, carved and gilded wood – removed; then comes the inner "clothing", a series of pieces of silk folded on the pages with extreme care; finally we come to the great sheaf of pages; each one has its central part dyed with a band of indigo ink applied with assured precision; on it is inscribed the text, in diligent, precise, exquisite calligraphy; the characters are in gold.

When we eventually leave it is past noon. Everyone has gone off for lunch. Here and there in the great courtyard in front of the temple, bathed by sunshine that seems to us ferocious after so much shadow, there wander only a few barefoot, somewhat mysterious men in hoods.

The Kum-Bum; the hundred thousand images

The Kum-Bum ("The Hundred Thousand Images") is one of the most famous temples and one of the most interesting monuments in Tibet. If the Potala is the Vatican of Upper Asian Buddhism, the Kum-Bum is its Assisi; it is as much a sanctuary for the faithful, for those for whom the myth is alive, as for the whole of humanity, for the men of all times and all countries who believe in beauty and bow before the mystery of inspiration.

Even from a distance the Kum-Bum is very striking. The whole of the upper part is gilded and glitters in the sun, and the rest of the building is white or painted in vivid colours. When you go nearer you see that two big, enigmatic eyes are painted on the dome; these give it personality and presence. The Kum-Bum is essentially a *chorten*, a pagoda. As a piece of architecture it certainly lacks the slender, lyrical quality of Japanese pagodas, which are delicate timber traceries, rhythmical poems of roofs and spirals. The Kum-Bum is Tibetan; that is to say, it is static and massive, like a mountain or the pyramids. It is Egyptian or Aztec; solid rock, carved and painted by the hand of man. Like the Potala, it marvellously expresses the final, immutable, hierarchical feeling of Tibetan civilization.

But the architecture of the walls and dome is only one aspect of the Kum-Bum. What really counts is its invisible architecture. As we have said, it is primarily a *chorten*; in other words, it is a reasoned and systematic synthesis of the Buddhist universe; the physics of the metaphysical; an exotic Divine Comedy in stone, proportions and colour. The pictures which adorn practically every wall of the seventy-three chapels which open on to the four levels of the Kum-Bum take up, develop and put the finishing touches to the fundamental themes expressed by the architectural structure. Thus the Kum-Bum as a whole conceals the complexity of a living organism. Leibnitz said that the difference between man-made mechanisms and natural ones lay in the fact that the former were mechanisms only on the surface, while the latter, however much they might be dismantled, always remained mechanisms. The Kum-Bum, like a natural

81 *Gyantse: the Kum-Bum pagoda, early 15th-century*

mechanism, is, even in its remote recesses and most fugitive aspects, a cosmography, a guide to the Buddhist heavens and ultra-heavens. It is therefore also called the *Chö-ku*, "the embodiment of the Faith".

The structure rests on a massive foundation measuring 108 cubits. (108 is a sacred number; there are 108 volumes of the *Kangyur*, 108 signs of Buddhahood, 108 votive lamps, etc., etc.) This foundation is called the Lunar Lotus, because on it, in the last analysis, there rests Dorje-chang, the Absolute, which is represented in the form of a statue concealed in the highest chapel of the Kum-Bum and is "serene, beatific, lunar". The basement "symbolizes the fusion of the two elements from which there arise the thought of enlightenment, that is to say praxis (*upaya*) and gnosis (*prajna*), or the two aspects of being, beatitude and unsubstantiality (*mahasukha* and *sunyata*)."[3] The next section of the building, resting on this, symbolizes "the four imperturbabilities of the Buddha"; succeeding storeys are built concentrically on this one. Each has five faces, each bearing the symbol of one of the five *Dhyani* Buddhas; the lion of Vairocana (Imperturbability), the elephant of Akshobya (the Ten Mystic Forces), the horse of Ratna Sambhava (the Thaumaturgic Powers), the peacock of Amitābha (the Ten Dominant Capacities), the eagle of Amoghasiddhi (the Force of Non-Attachment).

This symbolical counterpoint (the broad nature of which I have only hinted at) is continued, extended and echoed from the bottom of the structure to the top. It develops like a dance, or a fugue. The paintings, which are often of great beauty, respond to the symbols, the measurements, the proportions, like groups of instruments responding to other groups of instruments in an orchestra, and thus the symbolic structure rises to its summit, where Dorje-chang is enthroned, the Absolute, the beginning and the end, the All. Thus the whole universe is reproduced in the Kum-Bum for the edification of the faithful; it is at once Bible, planetarium, encyclopedia, museum and temple; the sum of Tibetan knowledge. The pious visitor, ascending from one level to the next, enjoys the advantages of progressive illumination at every stage.

The first storey symbolizes the "four coefficients of consciousness", the second

82 *Gyantse: mural in the Kum-Bum, showing a minor goddess, Thrang-wa-ma, with rosary*

83 *Gyantse: mural in the Kum-Bum, a personification of song*

that of the "four renunciations', and the third that of the "four elements of mystic power". On the fourth storey the Tantric doctrines are expressed in sacred diagrams called *mandala*, which have as much meaning to an initiate as the complex symbols of an equation have for a mathematician. Finally, the pictures in the shrines immediately under the dome "are intended to express by symbols those Tantric experiences which lead to the realization of the absolute and undifferentiated unity of the coefficients of supreme illumination, that is to say of practice and mystical gnosis"; a union which, as we know, is represented by the hieratic embrace.

> "At the extreme summit of the structure, in a shadowy cell the walls of which were also covered with paintings, which, however, are no longer discernible today, the statue of Dorje-chang, the symbol of the Absolute in its essential immutability, smiles its mysterious smile. Having thus completed the ascent of the monument and arrived in the presence of the supreme principle of all things, the visitor has passed through the

84 *Gyantse: mural in the Kum-Bum, Vajrabhairava/Dorje instilling terror. The god's terrifying expression is a menace not to the good but to evil-doers*

> various stages of phenomenal life and, by means of mystical knowledge, he has in the process reunited himself with that cosmic, colourless and undifferentiated awareness of which Dorje-chang is the symbol. The mystic, having completed in reverse the evolutionary process which leads to the birth of all things, has therefore annihilated it by becoming aware of it, himself merging into the light which gives existence to everything." (Tucci).

We have for several days been tirelessly studying and measuring the Kum-Bum. The temple has been known for many years, and many travellers have briefly described and even photographed it, but no-one has ever taken the trouble to examine it thoroughly and in detail. Tucci faced this task with his incisive character and his formidable learned equipment (Sanskrit, Tibetan, Chinese; knowledge of Asian history and symbological and artistic technique). We rise early, go to the Kum-Bum, work indefatigably through one chapel after another. Tucci copies inscriptions, makes copious notes, and from time to time seeks a lama's help in a piece of artistic, symbological or palaeographic interpretation; meanwhile I photograph all that is photographable, and make notes too. In the afternoon work goes on in the same way. In the evening the professor transcribes and arranges his notes, while I develop the pictures taken during the day. At an altitude of 12,000 feet it is an exhausting routine. But the continual sense of discovery, of intellectual adventure, and the pleasure of contributing knowledge of this masterpiece of Eastern civilization to the civilization of the West, is a continual spur.

"Stay in this cell," Professor Tucci said to me this morning, "and choose some detail from the frescoes for a photograph that will show the spirit of the whole, while I go in there to go on copying inscriptions. Do you know that they are of exceptional interest? They reveal the names of the artists who painted these walls. It's the first abandonment of anonymity in classical Tibetan art. We shall be able to study influences and derivations. We may be able to discover some personality more alive than the rest."

I was left alone with my camera, tripod, flashlight, and other equipment of a twentieth-century craftsman, in front of some wall-paintings of the most penetrating beauty. I was in the chapel of the Maitreya, the future Buddha, the embodiment of charity. In front of me was a whole population of divine and human figures. They represented the heaven which the god would renounce, to descend again among mankind and resume his apostolate. The artist had taken a humanist's delight in giving life to his theme. He had shaken himself free from the schematic, hieratic formalism so often associated with it, and made the figures move and breathe. He set them in a real world, under a real sky, in a real spring. How much Chinese influence there was in all this! In the neighbouring chapels the Indian style predominated – flesh and cerebrality, sensuality and symbolism, nudity, contortions, monstrosities; a metaphysical filigree of jewels, couplings, caresses and blood for esoteric connoisseurs. But here China made a glorious entry. Here was not just space, but earth and sky. Here were portraiture, proportion and serenity, humanity and ceremony instead of cryptograms and syllogisms. Here were men as individuals, not as phases or states or categories; and the universe was a home, a place in which one lived.

While I was working in the chapel, into which a warm, bright ray of sunshine entered, I heard footsteps. A bent old man entered, carrying a shabby bag. He greeted me with a smile, and did not seem at all surprised at seeing me there with all my equipment. He was completely absorbed in his visit to the Kum-Bum, and looked at the gods with mystic emotion. For him they were not walls or frescoes, but a window. I asked him where he came from. He told me the name of the place, and added: "*Taring po*" ("Far away"). Then he said goodbye and left.

Solitude as poison: solitude as flame

This morning we went up to the retreat of the monks, a group of little houses on the mountainside above Gyantse, at a height of nearly 15,000 feet. We walked for hours, surrounded by nothing but rocks and stones, and occasionally we saw blue poppies. On the way we stopped at one of the little mortuary hills on which the bodies of the dead are hacked to pieces and then left to be devoured by birds of prey. A body had been left there only the day before yesterday, but this morning nothing remained; the birds had quickly finished their macabre feast. Nothing was to be seen but some greasy stains on the smooth stones, warm in the sun; and there was a certain slaughterhouse smell hanging about. Death here is like the end of a wave that has broken on the shore.

After visiting the chapels of a *ri-trö* (hermitage) and a short rest, we continued on our way. We climbed a desolate, windy slope of rock until we reached the hermits' cells. Imagine a bare, remote mountainside, with nothing in sight but rock and sky, and no sound but that of the wind. Such were the surroundings in which we found some tiny houses, situated a short distance from each other, each with its little cell for meditation. Nowadays there are not so many hermits as there used to be. Today, indeed, we found only one, Lama Tsampa Tendar, who had not left his narrow prison for eight years.

His little house was like a box. It had a courtyard two square yards in extent, on to which the door and window of the cell opened; the hermit must see nothing of the world outside, nothing of that which is mere illusion, a transitory state of non-being. I sat down for a moment near Lama Tendar. Apart from the surrounding walls, all I could see was a little triangle of sky, with some bright clouds, among which a big bird was flying in slow curves. Who knows if the Lama Tendar ever looked longingly or with regret through that little triangle? To me it seemed the most delightful sight imaginable in that tomb-like cell. Perhaps it was to resist the last glimmer of temptation that, when the lama meditated, he drew over his eyes the little visor that he now had perched on his brow.

Solitude is such a powerful experience that it leaves indelible marks on those who have been through it. It acts on some like a stimulus, refining the flame of their spirit; but in ordinary mortals the flame grows dim or is extinguished. It is like some kinds of poison, which in certain proportions on certain organisms have a marvellous tonic effect, while on others the same dose is fatal. Who has not heard of people who have "died" of loneliness – Europeans isolated in remote places, or persons of sensibility and culture exiled in spiritual deserts of provincialism and ignorance? For such people human contacts become

85 *Gyantse: the hermit Tsampa Tendar in his cell in the mountain above the city*

abnormal, tormenting experiences, and disorder and idleness eat like gangrene into their lives.

But Lama Tendar is a great and supreme lord of the white oceans of silence. You felt instinctively, without need of argument or proof, that solitude and ascetic discipline had had an exquisitely purifying effect on him; that he had emerged victorious from the experience. In any case our call upon him was exceedingly brief. We spoke little, and made no reference to the greater things. It is a fact that our relations with people are to a large extent conducted at the level of the sub-conscious. Vague hints and intuitions reinforce the feelings of like or dislike that we have for people, the often instinctive feeling we have about people that they are either good or bad. Lama Tendar emanates peace and benevolence almost as if they were physical realities; he radiates an inner light.

He is undoubtedly the strongest personality whom we have met on our travels. It is not for nothing that he enjoys a reputation for sanctity, and that on certain religious festivals people make the long climb up the rocky mountain in the hope of receiving his blessing. We too were blessed when we left, and it left us with a feeling of deep peace. The ultra-terrestrial forces are no respecters of emblems or hierarchies. Any religion can be a vehicle between God and man, just as any religion can deteriorate into magical or commercial practices, or be turned into an instrument for tormenting one's fellow-men.

How much I should have liked to have been able to talk to Lama Tendar without the obstacle of language! There were so many things that I should have liked to ask him – about life, and all the things that agitate us, about death and love, about the powers of the earth and of the invisible. In an obscure way I felt that his answers would have been memorable and profound. As it was, I brought away only a mental picture and some feelings, and the memory of a smile which was different from all other smiles.

Today, according to our way of looking at things, a hermit's way of life seems an incredible thing, almost an enormity. But hermits once played an important part in the West, in the history of Christianity. The theoretical justification for the hermit's life is sound enough. If God is everything and the world is vanity, why not renounce vanity and illusion and live entirely for the eternal? For centuries religion reached its loftiest heights among hermits scattered from the Thebaid to Cappadocia, from Sinai to Palestine. St. Paul of Thebes, St. Anthony and St. Hilary had innumerable followers and disciples in the West. The social trends inherent in the West caused the hermits almost completely to disappear. Today their practices strike us as monstrous, and their attitude to life seems indefensible. But would it be surprising if after the fifth or sixth world war, there occurred a revival of dwelling in the desert? Perhaps the only way of escape from the madness of society might then be to take refuge from it.

Milarepa, wizard, hermit and poet

The subject of hermits inevitably reminds one of Milarepa ("cotton-clad Mila"), one of the most extraordinary personalities that Asia has produced. Tibet has contributed to history at least two names of world significance – the Sixth Dalai Lama, living god and poet, an outburst of joyful paganism in a gilded cell, and Milarepa, wizard, hermit, poet, philosopher, sinner, a tumultuous soul ever in anguish or frenzy, with an unlimited capacity for both good and evil, and unbounded spiritual energy amid the Himalayan ice.

For nearly a thousand years Tibetans have been deeply moved by Milarepa's life-story, written by his pupil Rechung.[4] It is a kind of thriller at a mystical level, full of crimes and visions, fisticuffs and metaphysics, written in a strain now of esoteric poetry, now of a piece of crime reporting, now of hagiography, but always with a human warmth and vividness which is compelling even to a sophisticated modern reader. Milarepa's early childhood was a happy one. He was born in about the year 1030 in a prosperous or actually wealthy family in Himalayan Tibet. But his father died when he was seven, and his troubles began. His mother was the dominating figure in his early life. She was devoted to her family, but was extreme in everything, given to cursing, weeping, hating, threatening suicide, and her appetite for revenge was not exhausted even when her son had killed by magic no fewer than thirty-five of her personal enemies in the village.

What drove her to these excesses was this. When her husband died he left his property in the care of his brother and sister-in-law, to look after until Milarepa should grow to manhood. Instead he treated it as if it were his own and forced Milarepa, his younger sister and his mother to work for him. "In summer, when the fields were cultivated, we were my uncle's servants," Milarepa said. "In winter, when the wool was carded, we were my aunt's servants. They fed us like dogs and worked us like donkeys."

One day, when Milarepa had reached the age of fifteen, his mother sold a small piece of land and invited all their relatives to a feast. When it was over she read out her husband's will and invited her brother-in-law and his wife to restore Milarepa's rights. But her unscrupulous brother-in-law declared that he had only lent the property concerned to her husband many years before, and that he therefore owed nothing, either to Milarepa or to his mother. Lacking any way of obtaining redress, the widow and her two children had no choice but to go away and live in extreme poverty, derided rather than pitied by the rest of the village.

One day Milarepa came home drunk after a feast. His mother fell into a rage, flung a handful of ashes in her son's face, struck him with a stick, called on the spirit of her dead husband, so that he too might be disgusted at the spectacle of his son's drunkenness, and collapsed fainting on the floor. Her daughter hurried to her assistance and Milarepa recovered from his drunkenness. "Then I too wept many tears. Weeping, we rubbed our mother's hands and called her. After a moment she opened her eyes and rose." It was only a moment's weakness on his mother's part. Her strength promptly returned. She devised a plan. Her son must become a sorcerer, and destroy his accursed relatives by spells.

So Milarepa departed in search of a master to teach him the magic arts. His mother sold another plot of land, and gave him a turquoise and a horse. "You must have an implacable will," she told him when she bade him farewell. "If you return without having shown your magic power in the village, I, your old mother, will kill myself before your eyes." After much travelling Milarepa found a wizard, who was, however, unable to satisfy him, so he went in search of another. Eventually, after long months of devoted and exhausting study, he was initiated into the black arts. The great day arrived. In Milarepa's village his uncle invited a crowd of people to attend the celebration of his son's marriage. Milarepa's magic worked from afar, and the house collapsed. The letter that Milarepa's mother thereupon wrote him was rather like a war *communiqué*: "Thirty-five people were killed in the collapse of the house. The people here therefore hate me and your sister. Therefore make hail fall . . . then your old mother's last wishes will have been fulfilled."

Milarepa grew to manhood surrounded by implacable hate and excessive love; he knew poverty and riches, death, black magic and revenge. Then he underwent the remarkable experience that has left an indelible mark upon so many exceptional characters, both in the East and in the West – the phenomenon of conversion, a total upheaval of the personality as a result of which the forces in the mind that were previously devoted to evil, or to success or glory on the earthly plane, are suddenly directed towards good, to glory on the eternal plane. "I felt my mind full of remorse for the evil I had done with magic and the hail," said Milarepa. "I was haunted by the doctrine (of the Buddha), and I even forgot to eat. If I moved I wanted to be still, if I were still I yearned to move. At night I could not sleep."

Milarepa turned his back on his previous life and set out to find a master, a *guru*, to guide him to mystic wisdom. After various vicissitudes, he met Marpa, the translator of Sanskrit texts. Just as the first part of his life had been dominated by his passionate and vengeful mother, so was the second part dominated by the far more memorable figure of Marpa, a doctor learned in esoteric knowledge, a pugilist, a violent, quarrelsome, proud, temperamental man, eternally dissatisfied because of the unattainability of perfection, given at times to drunkenness, unfairness or cruelty, a kind of natural genius with the spirit of lightning and the splendour of a storm. Every now and then Marpa's wife appears in the narrative, a good, kind, maternal woman, who tried to protect poor Milarepa from her apocalyptic husband's lightning and thunder, for Milarepa was subjected to the most pitiful ordeals in the course of his preparation for initiation. In one way Marpa's wife became a kind of mother to Milarepa, at any rate in the more sweet and consolatory implications of the word, because he never wavered in his frantic attachment to his real mother, his almost sexual love for her.

Marpa and Milarepa were bound by the relationship, so dear to the East, of master and pupil. Marpa was the *guru*, the guide, and Milarepa submitted to him body and soul, in thought and deed. Marpa, who had discerned the great possibilities in Milarepa, tested his constancy of purpose by subjecting him to

86 *Marpa (above) and Milarepa (below), idealized portraits in a Tibetan print.*

the most searching ordeals. He made him build houses, then ordered him to pull them down, erect towers and then destroy them while they were still incomplete. He deceived him, struck him, cursed him, sent him away, brought him back again, derided him, but sometimes changed his tone and praised him; though this too seemed to have been but mockery when he started persecuting him again. Finally, after many vicissitudes, after Milarepa had twice run away from his hard master and twice returned, the time came for his initiation. Marpa gave his pupil a maxim to be kept always brightly burning in his heart: "Be ardent; fly the banner of perfection."

In the long run the continued association of two such strong and decisive characters as Marpa and Milarepa was bound to be impossible. After Milarepa's initiation into the Tantric mysteries he therefore left his master. Their farewell, as was natural in the case of a friendship in which there had been so much love, hate and violence, was moving. At the moment of parting the two men felt all the strength of the bond that had kept them together. The pupil's veneration for his master was coloured with a new affection, the master's confidence in his pupil was warmed by new friendship.

The only thing that still bound Milarepa to the world was his desire to see his mother again. So he returned to his native place, but he found his house destroyed, and all that was left of his mother was her bones. His sister had gone away. Dzese, the fiancée of his distant childhood, had waited for him, but the result of his conversion was that their lives had drifted so far apart that there could no longer be any question of marriage, so Milarepa left the village again, "with his mother's bones between his clothing and his breast", and composed a poem about the vanity of life.

> Country, home, the paternal fields
> Are things belonging to an unreal world.
> Who wants them may have them . . .
> I, a hermit, go in search of liberation.

Milarepa sought refuge in a cave in the mountains, and devoted himself to the life of the ascetic with all the fire that had inspired his passionate and revengeful youth. Every day he took less food, until in the end he lived on nettles only. Months and years passed; his clothing wore out and was not replaced, so that he was partially naked, his unshorn hair grew wild and unkempt, his untended nails grew long, and his body was reduced to a bag of skin enclosing a skeleton; he was ugly, filthy, and looked like a ghost, "with green hair and skin". He had abstracted himself from the world and lived in the realm of the Absolute, but knew unspeakable intoxications of the mind.

After many years his sister succeeded in tracking him down. She climbed to his cave, and was horrified at the state in which she found him. She tried to dissuade him from persisting in such an insane way of life and to persuade him to return among men. She offered him food, and tried to clothe his body to protect him from the cold. Milarepa was moved, but his way of life was marked out. The words of Marpa, his *guru*, sounded perpetually in his ears. He answered his sister with a poem:

> Oh sister, creature still so bound to the world . . .
> This place really is a den fit for wild beasts;
> Anyone seeing it would be filled with indignation.
> My food is that of dogs and pigs;
> Anyone would be nauseated at the sight of it.
> My body is like a skeleton;
> The sight of it would make even a mortal enemy weep.

> My conduct seems that of a madman;
> And it makes my sister blush with shame.
> But my spirit has attained illumination . . .

Many more years of solitude and mortification of the flesh passed by, and Milarepa attained such a degree of domination of the bundle of nerves which his organism had become that he was able to produce warmth at will and could perform the miracle of levitation. "During the nights of my visions I was able freely and without any obstacle to explore the whole universe, from the abysses of the infernal regions to the most giddy heights . . . My body was as if incandescent."

One day, when Milarepa emerged from his cave to repair to another and more remote retreat, he broke the vessel in which he cooked his nettles. "I consoled myself with the thought that everything made is by its very nature as ephemeral as that. Understanding that this too constituted an exhortation to meditate . . . I sang:

> "A moment ago I had a jug, and now I have it no longer!
> This negligible fact throws light
> On the whole law of impermanence,
> And shows us
> What is the condition of man.
> The jug, which was my only wealth,
> At the moment when it broke
> Became a lama
> Preaching a marvellous sermon
> On the necessary impermanence of things."

While Milarepa was composing this poem some hunters arrived at his cave, and were astonished at finding a human being in such a state.

"Whence comes the thinness of thy body, oh hermit, and this green colour?" they asked. They were full of pity for him, but Milarepa replied:

"In your eyes I may appear excessively wretched. You are unaware that no-one in the world is happier than I." He thereupon composed for the hunters "The Song of the Horse".

> The horse that is my spirit flies like the wind . . .

Milarepa, always composing and singing and moving from cave to cave, eventually reached old age. Every word and action of his remained dramatic, even to the end. A famous scholar, who gave him hospitality during a journey, was offended at the slight worldly respect that the crazy old hermit paid him, and gave him poison to drink. The dialogue between the scholar, who had read all the learned treatises and counted for something in the world, and the naked hermit, who owned no books, illustrates Milarepa's supreme contempt of all worldly forms and conventions:

> I have the superiority of indifference,
> My audacity knows no obstacles.
> Diseases, evil spirits, sins, wretchedness
> Adorn the hermit who I am.

At last, surrounded by disciples, he abandoned "the cycle of transmigrations" murmuring his last thoughts:

> Do if you like that which may seem sinful
> But helps living beings,
> Because that is truly pious work.[5]

The fortress captain's horrible possessions

It sometimes happens that during the night one wakes up so late that it is already morning. In such cases, if one is not too tired, it is best to get up. That is what happened to me this morning. It must have been about five o'clock. I thought that everyone was asleep, but as soon as I was out of the house I heard a monotonous sing-song of human voices. Not a living soul was to be seen, but in one room Khalil, Tucci's Kashmiri servant, was saying his Muslim prayers, and in the other Norbhu, the cook, was saying his Buddhist prayers. I, a so-called Christian, felt ashamed at being silent in the middle. Is there perhaps a collective way of talking to God in different tongues and languages? I do not know . . . In the first red of sunrise the mountains were really divine.

At about ten o'clock the *am-chi*, the doctor, came and fetched me. He had promised to take me to a mountain where "there are many strange herbs". First we called at his house, because he wanted to show me his stock of "medicines". These were in about 180 little boxes, containing a most incongruous variety of objects; stones of various colours, crystals, hollow stones lined with crystals, seeds of unusual shape, dried roots, hair, bits of bone, small fossils. Medicinal qualities were attributed to anything out of the ordinary. The rarest exhibit was, if I understood correctly, an incrustation of dragon's blood, but to my disrespectful eyes it seemed to be an ordinary piece of sealing wax.

The mountain where there are "so many strange herbs" is Tse-shen, a hill shaped like a ship, which arises nearly in isolation in the middle of the plain on which Gyantse stands. A big monastery "grows out of" one side of the hill. The "strange plants" grow on the north side, where there are nearly vertical red rocks and it is shady and damp. When we reached the red rocks and the *am-chi* showed me the "strange plants", I saw that they were timid little ferns. I picked them carefully for the botanical collection of the University of Florence.

Our respective searches caused us to separate. After a while I saw the *am-chi* in the distance, wandering alone on the slope against the sky; a passing cloud was just about to obscure him. I don't know why, but I was reminded of a Chinese poem:

> The master has gone alone
> To search for plants on the mountain
> Hidden among the clouds.
> Where? I do not know.

I climbed up to the top to find the *am-chi*. The cloud disappeared as suddenly as it came; it was just a freak of the changeable summer weather. The *am-chi* was lying on his back, enjoying the warmth of the sun. From the top of the hill there is a superb view of the whole of the Gyantse valley. So vast was the landscape that you had to make comparisons and calculations before being able to appreciate the immensity of its scale. The hugeness of the space before us was shown by the number of different "weathers" that were to be seen between us and the horizon. Where we were it was fine, but over there it was cloudy, and in the distance there were about a dozen storms to choose from; there was one over there in the valley, another among those mountains, a third on the plateau in the direction of Lhasa; and each one of them was accompanied by a downpour of rain and a stupendous play of light and shade. Meanwhile the *am-chi* had discovered some more "strange herbs" which he was carefully gathering.

On the way back to Gyantse we saw several groups of tents pitched along the canal banks and little water-courses of the plain. It was summer, the time of holidays, excursions, singing, drinking and feasting. The Tibetans enjoy summer just like children. Everywhere there were people undressing and plunging into the water; for a few days their brown bodies would actually be clean. Breasts, legs, shoulders shone in the sun; there was shouting, jokes and laughter; then they would drink, eat, sleep, and above all pass the time in an absolutely carefree manner. Hurry? What an idea! The secret of liberty is to live like a flower or a stone; sheltering from the rain in bad weather, enjoying the sun if it is fine, breathing in the fullness of the afternoon, the sweetness of evening, the mysteriousness of night with equal joy and wisdom. Perhaps that is why you heard singing everywhere, fine music that faded away into space as if it were spontaneously generated; a tremulous variation of semi-tones ending in long-drawn-out notes, shouted into the wind, entrusted to the wind, dissolved by the wind.

Everyone knew the *am-chi*; they greeted him; they greeted us. We stopped for a while at a tent in which relatives of his were staying. They offered us *chang* and wanted us to stay with them for the rest of the day. It would have been delightful to have done so; nothing is more delightful than basking in the midst of nature, watching the fall of evening reflected in the slow changing of the light, breathing in the smell of the earth and the grass, listening to the wind singing in the branches. But we had to return to Gyantse. The *dzong-pön* was expecting me, and I could not fail him. Goodbye! Goodbye!

The house of the *dzong-pön* (literally "fortress captain", in reality "governor") was a little way outside Gyantse, at the foot of the rock on which the *dzong*, the fortress, stands. It is a solid structure of grey stone, the façade of which is covered with a multitude of gaily-coloured blinds and awnings of bright material to protect the door and the windows from the excessive light of an altitude of 12,000 feet. Inside the door I saw the classic wall-painting of good augury, the "Mongol with a tiger on the leash", and I walked through a cheerful courtyard, among flowers growing in terracotta vases.

87 *Gyantse: children at their lessons*

88 *Gyantse: children playing in the river*

The *dzong-pön* was aged about thirty, and his wife twenty-five or twenty-six. Both were tall, slim, silent and smiling. The *dzong-pön* looked more like a gentleman of the palace than a fortress captain, so fine were his manners and so elegant his appearance in his long, light blue *chuba*, with his plaited, jet black hair gathered at the top of his head in a shining, complicated knot, and the gold and turquoise earring hanging from his left car. His wife might have walked straight out of one of the ancient diaries kept by ladies of the Japanese court:

> "Lady Koshosho, all noble and charming. She is like a weeping-willow at budding-time. Her style is very elegant, and we all envy her her manners. She is so shy and retiring that she seems to hide her heart even from herself. She is of childlike purity even to a painful degree – should there be a low-minded person who would treat her ill or slander her, her spirit would be overwhelmed and she would die. Such delicacy and helplessness make us anxious about her."[6]

The hospitality of this Tibetan couple was cordial and exquisite. As I sipped my tea I could not resist looking about me at my surroundings. The drawing-room-chapel in which we were sitting contained the most heterogeneous collection of objects. Apart from a number of Tibetan things (cups, tea-pots, pictures), which had been chosen with the most civilized taste, there were a number of the most revolting European or quasi-European objects; among other things there were a cheap vase with angels and Cupids, for instance, a clock with a marble base and a bronze lion, and a china view of London. Immediately in front of me the striking beauty of a big Tibetan wall-painting was hidden by some modern Chinese oleographs advertising I don't know what brand of cigarettes; one of them was a picture of a smiling, semi-nude blonde of unsurpassed vulgarity. The furniture, in so far as it was not Tibetan, was also a stab in the eye; the lacquered rush chairs, for instance, and a little table with a silk centre on which a sailing ship was embroidered in criminal colours.

The Tibetan things, however, showed a unity and refinement of taste. It was easy to see that each one of them had been carefully chosen from among many others as the best, the finest, the most elegant, the most likely to please the requirements of the most cultivated and civilized eye. But in the face of the things of European origin the most complete and unexpected blindness,

89 *Gyantse: one of the two fortress-captains* (dzong-pön) *and his wife. Behind him, scenes from the life of Milarepa*

a kind of mental paralysis, prevailed. The value which the *dzong-pön* and his wife attributed to this tasteless bric-à-brac was pathetic. They showed me each object as if it were a trophy or a treasure. For them these things were exotic, the products of the fascinating and mysterious West, which came, not from realms of pearl and ivory, jade and spices, but from the equally fabulous world of microscopes, aluminium, aeroplanes and fountain-pens. I detected a fleeting look of disappointment in the *dzong-pön*'s eyes because I did not make so much fuss of these things as I should have done, because they did not make me feel "at home". (As a matter of fact there was an under-current of that kind of feeling too, but my dominant emotion was shame that Europe always shows its most trivial and rubbishy face to Asia.)

I have noticed the same phenomenon in India, Japan, and China, in fact everywhere. With us it exhibits itself the other way round, in our attitude to oriental objects. The phenomenon is so constant and so widespread that it leads to broader conclusions, suggesting that absolute standards of beauty do not exist, and that aesthetic standards are valid only in the civilization within which they are established. Paul Valéry has said that beauty is the supreme degree of appearance. One might paraphrase the thought and say that beauty is the supreme degree of the ways in which a civilization manifests itself, the culmination and fruit of centuries, the quintessence into which myriads of individual joys and griefs are distilled, the spring at which saps and juices come to the surface after thousands of years of underground wanderings.

The beautiful is that which is declared to be such by the most competent judges in every epoch and every civilization. Who are the most competent judges? The most civilized, those who take the fullest part in the invisible life of the great spiritual organism which nourishes them. But even these, if they venture outside the borders of their own civilization, are at first no better than fumblers, groping in the dark. Time, patience, humility and good will are needed before the beautiful can be distinguished from the ugly in new surroundings which have not yet become familiar. It is only thus that one can explain the fact that persons of alert and educated taste in their own civilization turn out to be barbarians in another.

We often discussed these things in the evening with Tucci.

Leopardi in the heart of Asia

We did have moments of homesickness. We remembered excursions into the Abruzzi mountains or little villages in Tuscany, persons dear to us, or our favourite Italian poets. One evening I came across a little volume of Leopardi

90 *Gyantse: painter at work on a "wheel of life"*

which had gone astray and found its way to the bottom of a trunk. Tucci snatched it from me, as a man dying of thirst might snatch a bottle, and started reading aloud the *Canto Notturno*, the song of the wandering shepherd under the night sky of Asia, with the worn little volume resting among the pages of an ancient Buddhist treatise. When he had finished reading we both had tears in our eyes. We went outside, "to look up at the moon". Each of us was ashamed in front of the other.

Reconsideration, 1998

We have precise and recent news from Gyantse, as also an abundance of photographs taken in recent years. Friends who visited the city and the sanctuary just a few months ago have returned to Italy to report: "Quite beautiful, but an empty shell!" That is precisely the feeling one gets if one compares the photographs of "before" and "after". The vast ring-wall of the sanctuary, which used to appear crammed with buildings, like one of those cities carried

91 *Gyantse: a scribe*

in their hands by our thirteenth- and fourteenth-century saints, is now seen to be empty, abandoned, oppressed by a solitude that speaks of squalor and dereliction. In place of the twenty and more buildings there used to be all that remains standing is the big pagoda (Kum-Bum), the great temple (Tsugla-kang), and the Labrang. As for the rest, it is as if everything was carried off, right down to the ruins, so bare is the rock bed now. One is reminded of a valley scoured by the fury of a tremendous flash flood.

The Labrang (the Abbot's lodging, so to speak) seems to be empty, derelict, open to wind and weather. The Tsugla-kang on the other hand seems to be in a reasonable state of repair, both outside and in. The noble statues of the Three Holy Kings are in place as are those of the Supreme Buddhas and of the *Sakya-pa* patriarchs. Even the murals appear not to have suffered damage or disfigurement.

In the case of the Kum-Bum, conditions were found to be much better than previously feared, by Professors Lo Bue and Ricca, during their very thorough survey of the famous building in 1990: "It has to be said," Lo Bue observes, "that the general picture offered by the paintings . . . remains on the whole fairly good, and that the majority of the wall paintings lend themselves to aesthetic appreciation and critical analysis."[7]

This last of the "Reconsiderations, 1998" will have to be linked to the memory of Giuseppe Tucci, who devoted so much labour and enthusiasm to throwing light on the iconography of the Gyantse temples, and in particular the murals of the Kum-Bum.

It was in April 1984 that the master passed away. Many years before, he had retired to a small house at San Polo de' Cavalieri, where Lazio merges with the Abruzzi, in a circle of huge mountains of elemental shape that get lost in a vast horizon. Up there everything is reminiscent of Tibet. If one manages to evade the sight of the nearest houses and some ribbon of road that interrupts the profile of the hills, it would be easy enough to imagine oneself on a plateau of the Roof of the World.

That April day the Tibetan aspect of the landscape was particularly suggestive. Light and dark clouds, smiling here, frowning there, raced across the sky dragging their shadows, along with glints of sunlight, across mountains still brown from winter. I thought of Iwang so many years before, of the days during which I had experienced with the master the frenzy of continual and unrepeatable discoveries.

What I was expecting as I climbed up to San Polo for this final leavetaking I really do not know. Vaguely, but only vaguely, I envisaged a presence of those wine-coloured togas worn by the lamas. Perhaps I was envisaging the shadow of Lama Ngawang: "I'll read you the *Bardo Tö-döl* myself out loud; it'll do you good." So I was quite shaken when, at a certain point, a long and substantial procession (public authorities, top professors, pupils, relatives, friends) formed and moved with the coffin towards the parish church, where a solemn Requiem Mass was said. The flowers sent by President Pertini, those from Indira Gandhi, looked right; more ambiguous was the sermon roundly applauding "our brother Giuseppe who finally, after much wandering, has returned to his own".

What to say? What to think? I was unable to find within myself "the ten directions of space", so much did this unexpectedly conventional end contrast with the character as I had known him in real life. I was embarrassed. I felt utterly demoralized. It was sad to think of anyone taking advantage of the extreme physical and mental incapacity of a dying man to secure his assent to a world from which he had quite clearly distanced himself during all those years of physical and intellectual vigour. A man of Giuseppe Tucci's stamp does not wait for the last moment, the final breath, to give a public definition of his own position in matters of such importance. Or perhaps, with his mocking relativism, he simply brushed it all aside – this is not wholly implausible.

At some point in this book I stated that "to study and love the East does not mean being converted and renouncing one's own civilization." I have wanted to keep this passage intact, even if today I would adhere to it with a number of reservations. In any event it does not imply at all a subjection to Christianity. The West has two sovereign and parallel traditions: the secular spirit and the spirit of Faith. From some angles the West is less than Christianity, a religion of universal character, while from other angles it is much more: there were millennia of a spectacular non-Christian West, and we are on our way towards a not entirely despicable post-Christian West.

I have always seen, heard and admired Tucci as a sovereign master of the great secular tradition of the West. He brought to his work all the independence of the lay spirit, ready to accord the greatest respect to the data of experience, wherever it might lead him, along with a humanistic warmth that enabled him to approach the great the world over as brothers. He did indeed possess a strong sense of mysticism, but neither does that necessarily correspond with Christianity. What was the point of pulling the old man by the hair, in his last hour, into a boat he had always regarded with suspicion? Simply to crow over a "victory"? As if souls were mountain goats and life a hunt!

Not to mention that extracting a yes from a master, in the failing light of his final shipwreck, means exposing the less edifying sides of his character. So we are left in some doubt as to whether we may not be in the presence of a stupendous brain, a living computer in which whole libraries and scores of languages have been splendidly classified, a brain in which at the smallest prompting the most complicated relationships between data and theories, between data and dates, between Names and names, between chronologies, scripts, quotations, recollections are lucidly projected onto a screen – and yet whether the whole thing is not grafted onto a petty, shifty personality, capable of shabby, spiteful behaviour, inordinately clever at trimming his sails to every tiny puff of wind. The final act of metaphysical and cosmic opportunism, if it is true, would be a reminder of a whole lot of others: praise for the Duce in some of his Prefaces, verbal and written declarations of fidelity to Buddhism in order to be able to set foot in Lhasa, the door shut in the Dalai Lama's face once dispossessed, on his visit to Rome (presumably so as not to offend the Chinese).

At this point there comes to mind, too, a brief campaign in favour of the Flat Earth, useful for making a favourable impression on those in power at the moment, the great Lamas of the Potala. "In 1948", writes Heinrich Harrer,[8] the famous Tibetologist Professor Tucci came to Lhasa from Rome. He was regarded as the most eminent expert on the history and civilization of Tibet. He left Chinese, Nepalese, Indians and Tibetans open-mouthed by his knowledge of their countries' history. I often met him at receptions; then on one occasion, with a large crowd present, he put me in a very false position by taking the Tibetans' side in a discussion about the shape of the earth. Tibetan tradition holds that the earth is a flat disc. And this is precisely what was being discussed at the reception, and I maintained the obvious theory whereby the earth is a sphere. My impression was that my arguments were making headway with the Tibetans, and I appealed to Professor Tucci for his support. Much to my surprise he took an agnostic position and stated that, in his opinion, scientists should continue to review their own theories and that, one fine day, the Tibetan doctrine might well turn out to be the right one! Everybody chortled, knowing me as they did for a geography teacher."

It only remains for me to return here to the conversation on board ship in the Red Sea, all those years ago: "You believe in science. You are under an illusion: science postulates an I and a non-I fixed in an immutable relationship to each other. Fiddlesticks!" All things change, revolve, evaporate; all mutates, flows, is transmuted, flows into its opposite.

In fact, then and forever after, one found oneself confronted with secret, invisible lines of defence with which a highly sensitive, mistrustful ego defended its inner citadel. The truth, the final, exquisite barycentre, the one that supported the interpretation and understanding of these and other acrobatic somersaults – sometimes they were spectacularly, indeed enchantingly, scandalous – was represented by a fanatical dedication to one's own work. All that seconded it was legitimate, all that obstructed it was to be swept aside.

Was the success of this or that expedition really dependent on the Duce's blessing? Well then, let us invoke it. Stalin's would have been equally welcome had it been of any use. In order to overcome certain walls is one to declare oneself a Buddhist? Gentlemen, at your service! To stay in the swim is the earth to be defined as a flat disc? Of course, my friends – every theory was true once upon a time, or is true today, or will be true tomorrow. This supreme pliability would eventually have been second nature to him and betrayed him at the end, in his weakness and the befuddlement of his illness.

No harm done. What remains is precisely that which he would have wanted to remain: his work.

1 *A Chinaman's Opinion of Us and His Own Country*, written by Hwuy-ung, Mandarin of the Fourth Button, translated by J.A. Makepeace, Chatto & Windus, 1927. (By permission of A.G. Tourrier)
2 A. Waddell: *Lhasa and its Mysteries*, London, Murray, 1905, p. 203
3 These and the following quotations are from G. Tucci, *Indo-Tibetica*, IV, 1.
4 For the translation, see Evans-Wentz in Bibliography V.
5 For a complete English translation of the songs see Chang, G.C.C. in Bibliography V.
6 From the diary of Murasaki Shikibu, in *Diaries of Court Ladies of Old Japan*. Translated by Annie Sheplay Omori and Kochi Doi, Constable and Houghton Mifflin, 1920
7 F. Ricca & E. Lo Bue: *The Great Stupa of Gyantse*, London, Serindia, 1933, p. 52
8 *Seven Years in Tibet*, London, Rupert Hart-Davis, 1954

13

Lhasa, "The Land of the Gods" (1998)

What a lovely dream, to admire the Potala amid its mountains! As a young man it was impossible, for one reason or another, for me to set foot in the valley of Lhasa. Later the whole country was closed to foreigners for years. Now that it would be possible, indeed easy to travel there I am prevented by the cruel wasting away that attends old age: the place is at too great an altitude, too close to the sky. How good it would be to be able to say of a certainty: it will be for another life. Well, we leave things under their rightful veil of mystery.

At any rate, I have read so much about Lhasa, pored so long over books, that I really feel as though I have been there. What pleasure it is, for instance, to follow Desideri in his adventures, particularly for his Italian which is so much our own and yet not without its delicious curlicues. He speaks of Lhasa as being "greatly populated by persons who are natives of those lands and by a very great number of foreigners from divers nations, Tartars, Chinese, Muscovites, Armenians, Kashmiri, Hindustani, and Nepalese who pursue their merchants' calling. The houses are on the whole made of stone, on three storeys, the rooms nicely fashioned. The Potala is a mountain made all of stone. One climbs conveniently up the cliff by broad staircases with balustrades, of excellent architecture, and at the top is a most magnificent palace."

Perceval Landon, special correspondent for *The Times* on the Younghusband expedition of 1904, was more carried away. Not surprisingly. He had been on the march for months. And it was no mere stroll. Finally, one August day they were past the small valley connecting the Chagpo-ri (Hill of the College of Medicine) with the hill of Potala, and on a sudden "there the great palace of the god-king was . . . Even if we had found Lhasa to be a handful of hovels scattered on a dusty plain, one side of our fierce curiosity would, no doubt, have been slaked sufficiently, but here was a different thing indeed. Here, in these uttermost parts of the earth, uplifted high above humanity, guarded by impenetrable passes of rock and ice, by cliffs of sheer granite, by the hostility of man and by the want of food and fuel, here was no poor Oriental town arrogating to itself the dignity which mystery can in itself confer.

From the first moment, the splendour of the Potala cannot be hidden."

Giuseppe Tucci was strangely cool, or so he comes across in his book. Perhaps he reached Lhasa during one of those moments of sudden withdrawal inside the interior fortress of his feelings, reluctant to concede himself. Possibly. "Towards noon", he writes, "I pass beneath the Potala." He adds that the palace "has grown out of its rock like a diamond secured to its setting." And he speaks of a central body that is red, "and above it a sparkle of golden domes and pinnacles".[1] Beautiful, competent brushstrokes, but oddly unfeeling.

In the few lines written by Alexandra David-Neel[2] there is certainly a sense of emotion. After a prodigious journey from Yunnan disguised as a beggar, in 1924, accompanied by the faithful Lama Yongden, she was finally able to see the Potala in the distance. Then she felt she wanted to "*entonner un chant triomphal*", but this had by force of circumstance to be "*réduit à un murmure*", otherwise at the last step of the great adventure somebody might have unmasked the clandestine lady-traveller. The Japanese monk Ekai Kawaguchi was no less revealing in the shiver his heart felt when in 1903 he was finally able to look across the plain of Lhasa. "The Potala is so splendid that even the illustrations made of it look beautiful," he exclaims in the innocence of his *majime* soul, candid and pure as it was.

It was great good fortune that the Potala was garrisoned by the Chinese army during the worst period of the depredations carried out in Lhasa by the Red Guards in 1966 and the years following. Had they been given a free hand, those vandals would have wrecked everything. Of course the troops were not motivated by any desire to protect works of art so much as by the wish to ensure that the great quantities of gold and jewels lavished on the paintings and decorations were not stolen. In any event, for whatever reason, the Potala today is largely saved; indeed, times have moved on to such a point that the parts that had suffered over the years from neglect are now being actively restored. A panoramic view of the whole, taken some years ago, betrayed even in photographs the signs of some degree of neglect. Today the palace looks pristine once more, like a high mountain that has overnight been covered in a fresh fall of snow, with the red central crag crowned by the pontifical apartments. Like Greek churches, the houses of Capri, Positano, Panarea, the Potala is not the least bit damaged by a fresh coat of whitewash, indeed it demands one.

What is altogether more depressing is the other principal pole of Tibetan Buddhism, the Jokhang (Cathedral of Lhasa), hemmed in among houses and lanes. A long time ago I had the good fortune to draft the spoken commentary for a documentary on Lhasa made for Italian-Swiss television by Gianluigi

Quarti. Viewing the filmed sequences time and time again on the Moviola was just like actually experiencing a visit to the temple. I cannot say why, but the impression I was left with was not all that inviting. The place seemed to me gloomy and claustrophobic and much too crowded with devout folk and rich in pious baubles. Oh, I thought, for our deserted and abandoned temples, amid the yellow shale of the mountains, where abandoned and forgotten splendours were to be discovered!

What moved me a great deal more than the place were the people. As I watched the faces of those peasants and shepherds, those eyes fixed upon an authentic mystical experience, I felt myself in the presence of an unusual dimension of the human spirit. What was borne in on me particularly was the way religion, Buddhism – whether that of Padma Sambhava or of Tsongkhapa makes no odds – now stood for the life, the sea-anchor to keep a hold on an identity so cruelly and subtly threatened.

1 *Lhasa and Beyond*, Rome, 1950
2 *Voyage d'une Parisienne à Lhasa*

14

Across the Himalayas: Return to the West

The Tang-kar valley: "Noble Faith's" disapproval

The vicissitudes of the expedition have resulted in my being left alone. Nothing remains for me but to go home.

I set out from Yatung early this morning with a few porters. We left the big valley which the caravan route climbs in the direction of Lhasa and made for places in which few white men have ever set foot. The path was narrow; it mounted, descended again, and crossed patches of marsh-land in the forest; we had to surmount huge tree-trunks struck down by storms. The path followed a stream and clambered up the side of the valley to avoid overhanging rocks. It was typical of all the paths in this part of the Himalayas. There were good, recently-constructed bridges made of big deal beams squared with the adze. The timber still had a perfume.

The weather, which was fine this morning, deteriorated. The valley grew dark. The mountain-tops were hidden in mist, which crept down among the fir-trees growing tall and steep over the mountainsides. Soon it began to rain. We stopped at an abandoned hut. The men lit a fire to dry themselves and boil some water, and the torment of smoke in one's eyes began. Outside it grew darker and darker. Night gradually closed in round us, quietly and sadly, with mist and drizzle.

I have five porters with me. The oldest is Tam-chö ("Noble Faith"). He is fifty-three years old, small, but still strong. He is much more civilized than the others. He greets me with respect, bows and smiles. The others all call him *apha*, "dad", and I do the same. He wears his hair long, in plaits wound round his head. He dresses completely in the Tibetan style. He wears rag slippers with leather soles (*lham*), a woollen robe (*chuba*) and a white cotton shirt; on his left ear he wears a big, round earring (*along*); and at his waist he carries a dagger (*tri*). Signs of his religion are not wanting. On his wrist he has a rosary (*threng-wa*), a cloth amulet hangs from his neck, and at his waist he carries a box for amulets (*kau*), containing a sacred statue.

The next in order of age is Si-thar, who is about thirty. He is tall, strong, with rather good features, wears his hair long, and can read and write, having spent some time in a monastery. His clothes are almost completely Tibetan, but foreign infiltration has left its mark; he wears a pair of American army boots. The others are Ten-zin, aged twenty-seven, Tsi-rin, aged twenty-four, and Dorje (Tam-chö's son), who is eighteen. Ten-zin still has long hair, but the others wear their hair short, in conformity with modern usage. It is interesting to note that the traditional clothing (which in Tam-chö's case is still complete) suffers its first contamination in Si-thar (American boots), and a considerably bigger one in Ten-zin (American boots, "G. I." sweater and badges). In the younger ones it is displaced entirely; they wear a horrible collection of Indian-Gurkha-American left-overs. But all of them wear amulets; a sign that it is easier to change fashions than faith, and that styles of clothing are more fluid than cosmologies.

After dinner Si-thar, who is the minstrel of the company, produced a bottle of arak, and we drank. We also sang. Then we started gossiping about the people of Yatung. The time passed slowly. There were great guffaws when the names of certain girls were mentioned. Mema? She was easy, but ugly. Drolmá? Pretty, but affected; she seemed to think she was the only pebble on the beach. I discovered that the Tibetan ideal of female beauty was still "a face as round as the moon". The models of their ancient literature were unconsciously respected by beings who were outwardly as hybrid, as lost to any sense of civilization, as Tsi-rin and Dorje.

Tam-chö sat in a corner repeating *Om mani padme hum*. He scorned our irreverent chatter.

In the nomads' tent: the beautiful slinger

This morning I left the hut early. The sky was still white, and mist hung motionless over the bottom of the valley, but overhead you could see that the weather was going to be fine. Soon the sun's first rays shone on the rocks on the other side of the stream. The forest was bejewelled; glittering pearls of dew clung to the lichens and the spiders' webs. I went on ahead by myself. Tam-chö shouted after me to beware of the bears.

The bottom of the valley suddenly became completely flat. I crossed some marsh-like country among enormous trees. I had to take off my boots to wade through pools of freezing water. It is strange that forests on the flat seem much more mysterious than those on a slope.

When the sun began to shine I stopped near the stream and waited for the others. Running water reminds one strangely of human life. It first emerges so thin and small and devoid of strength. In its infancy it runs sparkling through meadows, among flowers and shining stones. Then the waters gain in weight and vigour and rush downhill; their youth is bold and happy, a time of singing and dancing in the sun, celebrating noisy marriages with tributaries, forming crazy little waterfalls and exultant little lakes. All is joy and high spirits. But gradually the slope diminishes, and the stream grows and becomes a river; youth turns into manhood. Its course is now more regular; it no longer runs crazily, but has become sensible and strong. It is less beautiful, but has become useful to agriculture and industry. What makes it attractive now is its calm, serene maturity. Enthusiasm, love, passion, beauty, have given way to quiet, useful purposefulness. At last it imperceptibly approaches the estuary; the lagoon-like expanses, the sadness and sweetness of old age. Then it once more mixes with the original waters.

A forest also reminds one of so many things; a nation, for example. But not just for the simple reason that it is a crowd of plants; there is something deeper and more significant about it. The trees that shine in the sun or whisper in the wind or seem absorbed and thoughtful in the sadness of the mist are the image of that part of a nation that lives visibly in the daylight. But every forest is double. There is the forest that we see, and the invisible forest, that of the roots; a forest of crowded trunks and branches that no wind ever moves, on which no sun ever shines, that never knows the splendour of the snow, the singing of birds, the cries of woodmen or the voices of children; a buried, motionless, slow-growing, mysterious forest, winding its way between the stones like myriads of snakes. It is this which is the primary forest; the other draws its sap, its life, from the roots. It is the same with a nation. Underneath it, concealed from sight, there is a powerful, obscure, terrible, inverted forest of primordial impulses, traditions stronger than reason, fixed tendencies which never rise up to consciousness, but condition acts, unleash wars, lead to atrocities, or alternatively lead to self-sacrifice and heroism.

"*Kushog-sahib*! This way! This way!" Tam-chö and the others called out. I rose and followed. We continued our way among huge fir-trees. Two hours later the trees had grown smaller, and after three hours we emerged into the open. We were at about 12,000 feet. Before us now was only the bare, high mountain. We stopped to eat and boil water for tea, without which Tibetans do not seem able to live. "But, *kushog-sahib*, here there's no wood to boil water," is a remark sufficient to disqualify as a camping site any place whatever, no matter what other advantages it may have to offer. Tea, incidentally, is also a primary necessity in Japan. During the war, when the civil population was subjected to almost insuperable privations, we often heard the statement: "*Cha-mo nai!*" ("There's not even any more tea!"), which was practically equivalent to announcing the end of the world.

The weather grew bad, as it always seems to after a certain hour in the afternoon. Clouds closed over the mountains, and it started to drizzle. At about four o'clock we saw in the distance the tents of the nomads of Tang-kar-shimo. As soon as we approached, a number of ferocious watch-dogs started baying and barking. A woman appeared at the entrance of the camp, and then came to meet us. She was Si-thar's sister, the wife of one Dondruk-dorje, part-owner of the herd, so we were welcomed in the tent like relatives.

The porters put down their loads, we took off our wet coats, and squatted on the wild sheep-skins which were spread around the fire burning in a hollow squared out in the centre of the tent. Outside it was raining, and inside the crowded tent it was extremely pleasant. An agreeable, hospitable, more than merely physical warmth seemed to prevail. Our host, Dondruk-dorje, certainly understood hospitality rather in his own way. He had two intelligent eyes, but an impudent face. He was one of those people who find it amusing to tease strangers with jokes and awkward questions which they cannot understand, making everybody laugh with embarrassment. However, we were cheerful, though it was at my expense. The Tibetans are, after all, a people of fairly wild mountaineers, capable of great generosity and of great ferocity at five minutes' interval, always ready for a joke, open and frank but rather given to leg-pulling, sometimes quick with their fists, rarely cruel; emotional, hospitable, superstitious, fond of drink, women, travelling and splendour.

Fortunately Kandron, Si-thar's sister and our hostess, protected me. She was a huge mare of a woman, handsome in a rather barbarous way. Whenever her husband made everybody laugh by a particularly outrageous remark, she apologized, or made a grimace, or bent her head to one side, as if to say: "Don't take any notice," and offered me milk. It was wonderful *dri* milk (the *dri* is the female of the yak), creamy, smelling of alpine flowers, seemingly the distilled essence of sun, snow and petals; and then there was delicious yoghourt, whey and cheese.

Si-thar and the others handed round stinking cigarettes and talked. Dondruk-dorje started making butter, a long and wearisome process. First Kandron poured about fifty pints of milk from a number of earthenware pots into a big cow-skin bag, and her husband started the long and hard work of shaking it. Dondruk-dorje, sitting on the ground, beat the skin, rolled it, dragged it this way and that. He went on doing this for about an hour-and-a-half. Then he opened the bag and took out a huge lump of butter. Meanwhile Kandron boiled the skimmed milk with yoghourt to make cheese. This was a long and wearisome process too. She went on lifting huge saucepans, carrying sacks, moving shapes, filling pails for hour after hour.

The weather improved, and milking time came. Dondruk-dorje and Kandron both left the tent. The man went up the mountainside to collect the yaks and *dris*, I watched his tiny figure in the distance and heard his shouts in the great silence. Above him rose huge towers of rock, and pinnacles of ice, pink in the sunset, outlined the sky. Silence and flowers; larks and flowers; bells and flowers. When the yaks were near enough Kandron guided them towards the tent by throwing stones with a sling. She picked up a stone, placed it between the strings, bent backwards and, with her strong legs planted on the ground, swivelled her chest and shoulders from the waist and sent her projectile whistling through the air to land exactly where she wanted it, quite near the yak, on the side where she wanted to frighten it, to persuade it to come home.

When it got dark and the milking was finished, we had supper. The meal was a long and glorious succession of milk dishes: yoghourt, whey, rivers of milk, fresh cheese, dry cheese, milk so wonderful that one could almost get drunk on it. Sitting round the fire in the middle of the tent, a kind of beatific torpor eventually came over us, and we could have sworn that bliss had quietly descended upon earth. Dondruk-dorje and the others went on talking. I gathered scraps of the conversation. The life of the valley passed before my eyes – why Ishe's son wouldn't work, why Ten-zin had sold his calves so early, why the price of butter had not gone up as it should have. It is delightful when you start feeling you're beginning to know everyone in a remote place, and you start feeling almost at home.

There were too many people in Dondruk-dorje's tent, and it was impossible to sleep. Besides, who knows how late they would go on talking? Another nomad, who had a tent not far away, and shared it with a youth who worked for him, offered me hospitality. I accepted, and went with him. Outside it was raining and cold. The darkness seemed solid. In the new tent we lit a big fire and drank tea, and Ri-tar, my new host, talked to me about his yaks. The link between a Tibetan and his yaks is as strong as that between an Arab and his camels. The yak and the *dri* are the alpha and omega of a nomad's life in Central Asia. The hair is spun and woven into the coarse cloth of which tents are made, and the milk and cheese products not only serve for daily nourishment, but produce wealth.

"I send the boy down to Yatung once a week with about 40 lb. of butter," Ri-tar told me. "This year the price is low."

When a yak dies, the meat is eaten. What is left is either dried in the sun or salted. The horns are used to make utensils, and gum is made from the hooves. The yak and the *dri* are also used for transport. Every now and then I heard the ringing of bells; this was the yaks and *dris* moving about; they were tied to a long rope stretched along the ground. Every time the bells rang Ri-tar raised his head and listened. He could tell from the sound whether the animals' movements were normal, or whether something was wrong.

The fire died down and the silences grew longer. The great silence of the world outside penetrated into our tent, and descended into the mind with a feeling of unspeakable peace and serenity. Only the wind occasionally murmured something.

The Tang-kar pass; Anthony Trollope in the Himalayas

This morning we rose early.

How the world changes as soon as the first light of dawn strikes the eyes! The night seems like a memory of a distant and different country; it is like a transition, not from little light to much light, but from one world to another world, with different laws and a different soul. Who knows the night who has not really slept with it? That involves sleeping out, where the night holds undisputed sway. In a house, even with the windows open, the night enters shyly, is humanized, and tends to become a uniform texture of darkness. Really to know the night you have to sleep in a tent, or bivouac. Then you really hear its breath and know its secrets, its changes of mood, its humours and its loves.

When I went outside the tent this morning I stepped into a new world; a world so new and pure that it might have been created only half-an-hour before. The sharpness of the outlines was almost painful. Up above the sun had already started firing the ice with splendour – a colour between pink and blue – but the walls of rock in the shadow were still plunged in night. I felt like singing a paean of victory for all that is great and noble and pure and worthy of dedication and sacrifice in human life. Instead I solemnly drank the milk that Ri-tar offered me, removed with my finger the cream that remained on the edge of the cup, and swallowed it.

I should have liked to have gone on looking at the mountains, and to have watched the yellow tongues of sunlight creeping down and setting the channels of ice alight, but Ri-tar would not permit it. He took me by the arm and insisted on my joining him to inspect his yaks and his *dris* one by one. This one was strong, the strongest of them all; that one produced enough milk to flood a valley; this one was small, but would become very powerful; that one was born in the year when they crowned the Great Protector (the Dalai Lama). The nomad's love of his beasts, the pride he felt for all their qualities, the care he lavished on them, were touching.

After another meal of milk and cheese, we went back to Dondruk-dorje's tent, where the porters were, and soon afterwards we left. Goodbye, Ri-tar! Goodbye, Kandron and Dondruk-dorje! Goodbye, happy nomads, companions of a day in the remote fastnesses of the Himalayas! How beautiful and serene is your life remote from the toils of the world! You will always remain alive in the mind and heart of the traveller who spent such a short time with you; Ri-tar, who showed me your finest yaks with such pride, Sönam, who lit the fire at dawn, Kandron, who slung stones to guide the *dri,* and you, Dondruk-dorje, who made a final crack at my expense as we departed. Everybody laughed. What was it he said? Something indecent . . .

From the plain where the nomads were living we slowly climbed an interminable valley with ancient moraines here and there. We started feeling the height, and had to rest every now and then. The sky was a solid blue. It seemed to be resting on the mountain-tops like a solid, metallic roof. Then clouds suddenly appeared from nowhere. First they were young, light clouds, then they became heavier, darker, and full of menace. I reached the top of the pass ahead of the porters, just in time to see the opposite side. Soon afterwards the mists closed down and it started to rain. The men arrived two hours later (they had stopped for one of their dozen daily teas). We put up the tent and prepared for the night.

We had a meal and slept for a while. A storm, with fine snow and a gale of wind, howled round us for two hours. When we finally awoke it had died down. I went outside. The sun was setting and the sky had cleared; not completely, because angry clouds still hung ominously above, but sufficiently to allow us to catch glimpses of the crests of the mountains about us. It was a grim, wild place, with jagged rocks, thin green sheets of ice, towering peaks that seemed to be poised precariously; a whole geology in a state of becoming; the bare bones of the world exposed to the fury of the elements; ruins and abysses filled with slag; and overhead the moon.

Eventually I went back into the tent while Si-thar made tea. Later on I read for a time. Dante? Milarepa? The *Bhagavad-gita*? No, that would have been practically impossible. When you are living, breathing, touching, treading, digesting the sublime, it is sweet and consoling to take refuge from the sublime. You need to return to normality as a rest from it. On this occasion my defence against the sublime was a novel of Anthony Trollope's. I had picked it up at Yatung, where it had been left by some passing traveller; a solid English novel, as innocent and well disposed as a maiden aunt – two hundred pages to the first shy kiss and another hundred to the marriage and the end. There is also much talk of parishes, benefices, violets and country walks. How delightful such things are at a height of 15,000 feet in the Himalayas!

Outside was the boundless silence of Asia and gigantic pinnacles of ice and rock towering up to hide the stars, and inside the tent there was this precious corner of provincial Europe.

Lachung: Jampel Thrashi's witches

The descent from the top of the Tang-kar pass seemed interminable. Down and down we went, as if descending into the entrails of the earth. First there was ice, then snow and moraines, which were ever more ancient and corroded by the elements. Then we came to huge torrents, meadows, the first thickets of rhododendrons, the first trees. Then down we went through fir woods, and came to the first signs of tropical vegetation, among mist and rain the whole time, and with leeches that attacked our ankles. We descended from 16,500 to 7,500 feet, and at last reached Lachung. We were exhausted, and slept like logs.

Lachung is the only important village in this part of Sikkim. Its most notable possessions are undoubtedly some of the wall-paintings in the little local monastery. They are recent, the work of a painter whose name, as I found out after a good deal of inquiry, was Jampel Thrashi, who died about 1940. The dancing witches of the Great Vision of the Dead (*shi-trö*) have not only phenomenal physical exuberance, all the wild and pulsating motion of the dance, but will, personality, distinct attitudes towards the onlooker. Each is endowed with a soul of her own, accursed or mocking, ferocious or sensual, cruel or comic.

As I looked at them I seemed to hear Lama Ngawang of Kirimtse by my side, saying: "*Oé!* Look at them well! You'll see them one day too! But remember they are only apparitions, illusions, nothing, and you will be saved!"

Gangtok: reception by Scarlatti

From Lachung we went down to Tsung-tang, half-a-day's march down a grandiose valley, with enormous waterfalls on either side and forests clinging to the vertical walls of rock. We saw lilies and the first butterflies, and heard the first crickets. We went through the last Bhutia (Tibetan) villages, with apple orchards and thatched cottages. The girls here are beautiful, tall, slim, healthy, as succulent as ripe peaches. Then we gradually dropped down into territory inhabited by Lepchas, shy, furtive people who practically never appear on the mule-track. They hide among the trees or in the undergrowth, and then cross it cautiously, like suspicious, fugitive animals.

From Tsung-tang to Sing-hik was another day's march, through forest that was now becoming tropical. We left Sing-hik this morning, and this evening reached Gangtok – a march along nearly twenty-five miles of mule-track, starting with a drop of 3,000 feet and followed by a climb of nearly 5,000 feet. It was a killing day in the rain and the accursed, damp heat of the forest. Darkness came down on us while we were still on the way, but when we got to Gangtok how light it was! Of course, electric light, I had nearly forgotten!

It was thus in a way a real return to the West, a resumption of contact with "normal" life, a re-emergence from the Middle Ages into the age of matches, petrol cans, coal and steel wire. Fortunately the civilization to which I belong did not, as it generally does at its periphery, present itself only under its petty, material aspects. When I reached the bungalow I found a letter from Pemà Chöki waiting for me, with a basket of fruit; and a gramophone, with several records of good music. What a delight! Who else would have thought of such a charming welcome? While I rested I listened to Brahms, Mozart, Scarlatti. It was like bathing in a fresh, clear river after a long period of sweat and fatigue. Nothing could have been more restful and enchanting. Never have I had such a lively sense of "homecoming", not just to what is by chance my native country of Italy, but to my true, my greater home, Europe.

Perhaps in the future there will be learned and heated disputes about whether the arts of the East are superior to those of the West or not. Viewing them as a whole, one must acknowledge that in the sculpture and painting of the East there is a spiritual quality far more subtle and exalted than there is in the corresponding arts of the West, preoccupied as we have always been with the myth of "truth". But there is one art which is a supreme exception, and that is music. In music the vicissitudes and struggles of the human spirit are entrusted to an abstract, almost mathematical, language, which is nevertheless capable of expressing them as nothing else can. About music there is no doubt; it is the European art *par excellence*, and in it the spirit of a whole civilization reaches its loftiest heights. The whole torment, passion, heart of Europe, is contained in it, as well as its heroic intellect, its proud spirit of analysis, on which it erects invisible palaces to the sky.

Chartres, Cologne, the Parthenon, Pisa can be countered with Horiuji, Agra, Beijing, Angkor Vat. The Ludovisi Throne, the Ara Pacis, Jacopo della Quercia can be answered with the Buddha of Sarnath, the Maitreya of Koryu-ji or the bas-reliefs of Borobodur. Pompeii, the Sistine Chapel and Botticelli can be answered with Ajanta, the works of Kukaichi or Sesshu. But music towers alone, a splendid and unequalled flower of the civilization to which we belong; an invisible flower, entrusted for its perception to the most analytical, the most solitary and most noble of man's faculties. Nothing in any other part of the world has ever been created corresponding with the invisible cathedrals of Mozart, Vivaldi, Beethoven.

When I read Dante or Blake, when I am moved by Piero della Francesca or Masaccio, I am certainly proud to be a European. But, when I listen to Palestrina or Bach, there is added to my pride a sense of wonder; the knowledge that no other civilization has ever reached such heights or bestowed such a gift for all future ages and men; and that, even if Europe went down in some frightful cataclysm, music would still remain to proclaim its greatness.

Tashi-babu: antiquities and revolutions

I spent today paying calls and seeing people. After weeks of solitude company is pleasurable. This morning I went to see the British Political Officer, who was just about to leave for a brief business visit to Calcutta. I went to see him, not because he is the Political Officer, but because I like him.

"My dear fellow," he said, as we walked down to the village. "These are difficult times for us all. Now they are dismantling the British Empire, and I shall have to look for a job. What can one do when one is nearly half-a-century old and has spent the best years of one's life among official documents? I know several Indian languages, and I know Tibetan, but is that any use? Do you think you could find me a job teaching English in Italy, for instance? Just look at what we are reduced to, after being lords of half the earth! Apart from that, I feel old already. You see, India is a great lady, but she sucks the life out of you; you're finished before you notice it. However, that's how it is. You come into the world, you have to dance according to the music, and then the time comes for you to go. That applies to empires and to individuals."

Nearly thirty years in the East had given the Political Officer a vast, calm and humble vision of things, the kind of vision that a Chinese sage might have. He laughed, stopped and relit his cigar, replied to the greeting of some passing peasants, and went on:

"Work? I've no more desire to work, and that's the truth. Not because it's troublesome – actually I like it – but because now it all seems so relative and useless. My real inclination would be to retire, in the Eastern sense of the word. Do you know what I mean?"

"I think so."

"The West, among other things, is obsessed with youth. Even Christ died young, at the age of thirty-three; but the sages of Asia – the Buddha, Confucius, Lao Tse – all reached a ripe old age before abandoning the scene. In the West the old are barely tolerated. They try to imitate the young – 'life begins at forty', and so on. Only orientals understand the art of living. Every age has its own ideals, myths and ceremonies. I'm not old in years, but India has aged me in spirit. Do you know what the infallible sign of old age is?"

"No . . . Or is it the feeling that after all nothing really matters?"

"That's it! When you start being convinced that there are very few things that really matter, you are ready to join the sages. But with us retreating to meditate under a tree doesn't make sense. People would just say it was madness or cowardice. With us the only recluses are comic figures – misanthropists or people who regard the world with contempt. But in Asia to retire from life and spend one's last years writing poems or composing religious hymns or visiting sanctuaries or the tombs of ancient courtesans is a recognized custom. Yes, I should like to spend the rest of my days away from the tumult of life, but not away from the perfume of life. Do you understand?"

Talking thus, we reached the village. The mail for Siliguri was not due to leave for another half-an-hour, so we called at the shop where Tashi-babu sold "Antiquities and Objects from Tibet". Tashi-babu is a Tibetan. He is a man of about fifty, sturdy and strong, and looks a man of action. His hair is cropped, though he is not a lama. On the contrary, he is the only Communist in this part of the world. He heads parades and demonstrations against the Maharajah, and reads the left-wing Calcutta newspapers. He is a revolutionary more by character than out of any material interest, because he is rich enough.

He appeared out of the backshop while we were examining and talking about a Tibetan picture. After the usual greetings, he gave us a long and clever little sales talk in the hope of persuading one of us to buy.

"It's all stuff that I'd willingly see destroyed," he said. "It's pure rubbish, the lot of it! I don't even know what it all means. You seem to understand more about it than I do. But I'd be glad to sell it to you, because you'd use it as an ornament. But I wouldn't sell it for anything in the world to these idiots in Gangtok, who believe in it and would take it home to light cups of butter underneath it . . . Huh! Priests, capitalists, and you English! But now you're going away, aren't you?"

"Yes," said the Political Officer, with a sigh, evidently thinking about his own affairs. "Are you glad?"

"Heaven forbid! It's not you personally I dislike! Have we ever quarrelled in all these years?"

"I suppose not . . . Or perhaps we have every now and then, because of the millionaire's prices you ask for your antiquities . . . Tashi, old man, you may seem innocent, but you're as cunning an old rogue as . . ."

"Well, I've got to live . . . Besides, you always have money. It's the system I hate. The English support the rich, and the rich support the lamas, they're all in league with one another . . . The lamas ought to go and work in the fields instead of chanting litanies from morning to night. Can you tell me what the lamas have done in the last thousand years? But this Lu . . . Le . . . Wait a minute!" He vanished into the backshop and came back with a magazine. "This Lysenko," he went on, "this Lysenko makes wheat grow I don't know how many times in a season . . . I believe in science, not in all the nonsense in that picture!"

At this point one of Tashi's wives called him, and he vanished into the backshop again. I don't know how, but we started talking about hermits again; perhaps it was because we were looking at the Tibetan picture, in which some ascetics were to be seen, meditating on high in some caves among imaginary rocks, drawn with the most delightful ingenuousness.

"It's a great shame that our world has lost all tradition of solitude," the Political Officer said. "A hermit incarnates the ideal of individual perfection; he is a champion, but on the plane of the spirit; he is a man on intimate terms with God. He's the antidote we need so much in an age obsessed with the masses . . . Just look at that exquisite touch in the gold that illuminates the landscape! What a sense of magic and vision! . . . But what was I saying? . . . Oh, yes, the masses. Man in the mass tends to become zero as an individual. The end-result is the man-formula, Huxley's alpha-plus or beta-minus. He identifies himself with his position. Frankly, hardly a desirable state of affairs . . ."

"I should say it was better to die."

"Don't exaggerate, be sensible. The obstacles are more inside than out."

The driver of the mail-van appeared at the shop-door. "Just going, sir," he said. So I said goodbye to the Political Officer and wished him a good journey.

"Try to take a photograph of the tree-ferns in the Residence garden," he said. "I should very much like to have one."

Climbing up to the village again on my way back to the bungalow, I met a young Indian whose acquaintance I had just made. He is the son of an Indian professional man who has recently established himself here, and he is studying medicine in one of the big universities near Delhi. He has all the terrifying narrowness of vision of the barbarians of the future. He dismisses all tradition with one word: "Rubbish!" From this zero level (which is not the zero level of Descartes, which is so sensitive and alive and so ready to pounce on the least ideal suggestion) he reconstructs the world, using nineteenth-century mechanics as his raw material. As is usual with those who have recently adopted a new faith, he divides everything into black and white. Anything connected with the magic word "industrialization" is white, and anything connected with "feudalism" is black. The young man speaks English well enough, and he can certainly express himself, but he keeps bringing the conversation back to the same thing. How is industrialization progressing in Italy? The Muslims do not understand industrialization. Tibet is feudal, and is therefore not civilized. As for Europe, he says it's completely finished.

The princess reads the hermit's poems

Finding a note from Pemà Chöki waiting for me on my return to the bungalow was therefore a very great consolation. She asked whether I was going to be in later on in the day, because she intended to drop in for a moment to bring me some books. The thought of her – so civilized, so refined, so ready to be moved by any form of beauty – seemed almost sacred in this world of hatreds, racial struggles, religious intolerance, political ferocity and endless new barbarisms, the glittering barbarisms of our atomic age shining with gamma rays, an age whose precious stones are uranium and plutonium, an age getting ready for interplanetary flight and the scientific destruction of whole peoples.

I sent the bearer out at once to fetch flowers, while I tidied the room. At four o'clock precisely a long, shining limousine stopped outside the bungalow. Tse-ten, the Maharajah's private secretary, opened the door, Pemà bent forward to get out, advanced a tiny, sandalled foot – good gracious! her toe-nails were painted red – and jumped out, small, light and neat. She was also escorted by the Enche Kasi, a thin, bespectacled man of about thirty-five, with an intelligent face and an ironic, observer's look; he is reputed to be the best-educated person in Gangtok.

We went in and sat in a circle at the open window facing the valley. Pemà, in her Tibetan clothes and jewels, looked extremely pretty. A slight excitement shining in her eyes made her irresistible. She wore a dark blue *chuba* (coat), a red vest, and a *pang-den* (apron), all in colours which might have clashed horribly if they had not been chosen with an imaginative and fastidious taste. Her black hair was gathered in the usual thick plait, as sinuous as a snake, and fell over one shoulder. She wore big, round, flat earrings and had a ring with brilliants on one finger; her fingers were like fleshy little stalks supporting the bright red fruit of her finger-nails.

The conversation was at first very formal, but not in a derogatory sense. Formality is abominable when it is an empty shell, but, where there is real feeling behind it, that feeling can be made more significant by being enclosed in a formal pattern; just as movement can be made more significant when turned into dance, or sound when turned into music. It must be recalled that we are at Gangtok, where Pemà Chöki is "the princess", and that only a few days ago she became engaged to the son of a Tibetan high official. Followed by her little court, but defying many prejudices, she came to pay a visit to a foreigner, including him in the category of passing scholars, whom it was possible for her to visit for the sake of improving her mind.

She brought me a number of books as gifts. I accepted them, raising them to my brow, as is the custom.

"This volume contains the collected poems of Milarepa, as well as his life," she said, carefully adjusting the folds of her *pang-den*. I thanked her. Then she continued, talking now with the complete naturalness with which she had talked about magic and poisons a few months before, at Changu:

"The whole of Tibet is in the books I'm giving you. We are so different from what people imagine us to be, you know . . . Often, when I read books written about us by foreigners, I think that they don't understand us at all. A country of saints and ascetics who care nothing for the world, indeed! Ah! you must read the life of Milarepa if you want to understand us. Greed, magic spells, passion, revenge, crimes, love, envy, torture . . . Besides, what need would there be to preach the law to us so much if we were always good and full of virtue?"

"But that is just why Tibet is so fascinating," I replied. "Would the Tibetans be at all interesting if they were merely figures in a tapestry or in literary miniatures? The fascinating thing about Tibet is its delightful, disastrous, irrepressible humanity. Perhaps one day I shall write a book and call it Secret Tibet. The secret will be, not the strange things that it will reveal, but the normal things in it – real people, flesh and blood, love, desire, repentance, pride and cowardice. You know what I mean?"

"Yes, but you mustn't forget that religion and the gods have extreme importance in our country."

"Gods never impoverish a people, but always enrich it. The invisible gives meaning and depth to the visible. Man only really lives when he lives in a cosmic drama."

"To sum it all up then, considering that there are so few of us, and that we have created so many beautiful things, might one also perhaps say that the Tibetans are the greatest little people in the world?"

Pemà raised her head and laughed proudly; she was delighted at this idea of hers. Then she grew serious again. She untied the book, took off its lacquered and gilded "covers", unwrapped the cloth that protected it and finally opened the pages. Her nervous and well-cared-for hands touched with religious respect the crude and archaic paper, printed by woodcut in some remote Tibetan monastery. I asked her to read me a poem. She started turning the pages. I saw that she was searching. I heard her murmuring some phrases, but then she started turning the pages again. She was undecided, and knitted her little brows. Finally she found what she wanted, and she started reading, in liquid and modulated tones. She sounded the tones so emphatically and with such sinuous continuity that she made Tibetan sound something very like Chinese. Then we translated together the verse beginning:

I, an old man, am like a box of poems . . .

Here and there the Enche Kasi helped us out with a word, not without preliminary whispered consultation with Tse-ten. Milarepa's imagery, describing his sensations as a hermit during his nights in the frozen wilderness, gradually became alive.

"Marvellous, isn't it?" Pemà exclaimed. Then she went on: "Do you have poets like Mila? At school they made me read Tennyson, but I couldn't stand him. How boring! Full of complicated words, without any madness . . . I've always heard it said that Europeans and Americans are excellent with machines and medicines, but are not much good for anything else. Now tell me in confidence, is it true?"

She smiled, bent her head to one side and half-closed her eyes. She knew perfectly well that that was being unfair, and that she was repeating a commonplace in which she did not believe, just as she often knew perfectly well that she was being frivolous, or vain, or malicious, as indeed she was; she was delightful in being it, and in knowing it.

To answer her I thought of Villon, Rimbaud, Blake, Lorca, but ended by reciting to her, and translating into English, one of the few things I know by heart: *Votre âme est un paysage choisi . . .*

"It must be my English governess's fault," Pemà went on. "For years she made me believe that Westerners were all chaste, well-bred, unselfish, religious people, dedicated solely to their duty and to the task of illuminating the darkness of us poor, irreligious and uncivilized barbarians. You know, it was a real blow to me when I saw my first film at Darjeeling! I discovered in an hour that you are almost worse than we Tibetans! Tell me, is it amusing in Italy? Most of all I should like to see Egypt, I don't know why. And then Greece. I adore Greek temples. I've never seen one, but they must be very beautiful. Is it true that they are as white as sugar? Then I should like to see Italy too. Why don't you ever sing? When my brother heard your expedition was coming, he said: 'Ah! they're Italians, you'll see how they'll sing! We shall have such a lot of music!' Instead . . . You know, you were a serious disappointment!"

A low whistle made me look outside. I saw Sönam, the bearer, signalling to me. I signalled back at him, using the code that we had agreed on to indicate that it was time to bring in tea, sweets and food. We had arranged everything very carefully, but I was trembling with anxiety that Sönam might forget something, or upset the tea, or not know how to serve the biscuits. However, he brought in the tray in the most self-possessed manner, and did everything quickly, skilfully and silently. He was barefooted, but had actually managed to find a pair of white cotton gloves – an unheard-of thing! Well done, Sönam!

While we drank tea Pemà Chöki looked at some of the things that I had brought from Tibet.

"That is a beautiful reliquary. Where did you find it?" she said. "Do you know that there are some very special *kau*s, blessed by a lama who died many years ago, which give protection against knife wounds and even against pistol shots?"

"With us too," I could not help interrupting, "there are certain images of certain saints that are considered to provide infallible protection against certain dangers; against the lava of volcanoes, for instance."

"Really? Afterwards you must tell me all about volcanoes. What terrible mountains they must be! But they must be very beautiful! Perhaps the more terrible a thing is, the more beautiful it is, or am I wrong? Let me tell you the story of the miraculous *kau*. A few years ago there was a bandit whom nobody could catch. He killed, robbed and looted on the road from Lhasa to China entirely at his convenience. Eventually his secret was discovered. He had a *kau* of the really safe kind – bullets simply bounced off him as if he were made of iron. He grew so self-confident that one day he actually went to Lhasa, got off his horse, and went to the market, among all the people. He was recognized, but nobody dared to touch him. In the end someone tried to lay hands on him, but he defended himself and started shooting. Others started shooting too, but without doing him any harm; the bullets simply slid off him like ice. In the end a lama recited a miraculous formula. The bandit suddenly repented and saw the folly of his ways. He took off his *kau*, kissed it and fell at once, perforated by I don't know how many bullets!"

"And what happened to the *kau*?"

"There was a terrible struggle for it. Many were wounded or crushed in the fray . . . That is Tibet too! Do you still like us? Ah! we are a strange people!"

The sun was rapidly descending towards the wooded mountains facing Gangtok. I noticed the Enche Kasi and Tse-ten consulting their watches. Pemà rose, and it was time to say goodbye.

"Don't forget the dance of the lamas next week. We shall expect you," she said, getting into the car, which was as black and solemn as a mausoleum.

I returned to my room and put the chairs back in their places. A little red handkerchief was lying on the ground. I picked it up. In the corner I saw written the word: *jeudi.* It was simple forgetfulness, not a message. But in its way it was charming all the same.

"Why should I sign my work?"

Gangtok is a little village isolated in the mountains, but, when you get to know it, it turns out to be much more interesting than it might seem at first sight. Its situation in a borderland between India and Tibet means that you meet people of all sorts. On the mornings of festival days the bazaar is a living anthropological museum. Cheerful big Tibetans, built for the spaciousness of their huge deserted plateaux, pass like horses through the throng of tiny Nepalese and rub shoulders with silent Hindus, and with Muslims from the north-west, who are tall and virile too; but the Muslims' proud bearing seems always ready to take offence.

Regions where two or more civilizations meet always provide plenty of material for observation. Here the West (the Latin alphabet, mechanical inventions, Christianity, trousers and soutanes, monogamy, hygiene, artistic realism, and so on) comes into contact with a number of other complexes: with the Tibetan (Buddhism, economic and social feudalism, long hair worn both by men and women, butter); with the Nepalese, the Hindu, and others besides. How do these civilizations act and react on one another? It is obvious at first sight that material loans are the easiest and quickest to be made, while moral and spiritual influences become effective much more slowly, or not at all. The West is indisputably dominant on people's head and feet. Felt hats and leather shoes have been adopted by everybody. Badges (British-Indian military influence), cigarette smoking, the bicycle and the fountain-pen are very common. Also marriage based on romantic love is, I am told, beginning to be a widespread practice.

The general tendency of the Asian peoples, in view of their great cultural traditions, is to accept from the West only its technical advantages. Their attitude towards our spiritual message remains decidedly critical. During the nineteenth century the West inspired respect because of its strength and its success. Only a pathetic shadow of all that remains, and the message has now to stand by itself. The Eastern answer is that, if two thousand years of Christianity have not made us any better than they, have not been able to bring us peace even in our own home, what are the special virtues of that doctrine which make it in any way superior to their own? The mental attitude of many orientals towards us is admirably expressed in Lin Yu-tang's book, *My Country and my People*:

"The fact that Westerners, too, have a well-organized social life, and that a London policeman would help an old woman across the street without any knowledge of the Confucian doctrine of respect for old age, comes to the Chinese always as more or less of a shock."

The play of influences is always particularly revealing in the field of art. It was, therefore, with great curiosity that today I went to see Rig-zin, who is the best Tibetan painter south of Shigatse, at any rate in the opinion of the Enche Kasi and several other people in Gangtok. Rig-zin lives in a Lepcha-type house on the hill behind the bazaar. It is really more of a hut than a house; it stands on piles and is built of stone and timber. When I arrived I found two of his children making mud-pies outside the door and his wife sitting at the window with a suckling in her arms. She greeted me, and showed me into her husband's studio – a tiny room, full of frames, boxes, sacred pictures and rolls of cloth for painting on. He was working on a big "Wheel of Life" that Piero Mele had commissioned in April and that he was to hand over to me in a few days' time. He had been working on it for a month, and all that remained to be done was some slight retouching. It was a big picture in the traditional Tibetan style; Rig-zin's only personal innovations were three figures he had inserted into the "Life of Men" section, representing an Indian, a European and a Chinese. Incidentally these three figures, both in line and in composition, were the only ones that were out of harmony with the rest of the picture, which was otherwise really perfect in its way. (See photo 90, p. 277)

Rig-zin is a little man of thirty-seven, not very likeable, though one felt he had character and an unusual wealth of personality. He is a passionate worker; he did not put down his brushes, but went on painting while we talked.

"Who was your teacher?" I asked.

"I studied for several years with the *che-mo* (head painter) Wang-dü, of Shigatse," he replied, not turning his head, but actually leaning forward till it nearly touched the cloth, as if straining to give the lightest possible strokes of the brush from as close as possible. "Wang-dü now lives at Kalimpong, he's sixty-three. He's a great master. Have you heard of him? But he's old now, he paints very little."

"And how many pictures do you paint in a year?"

"What does it matter? I don't know. Perhaps twenty or thirty. I have a great deal of work. I can't complain. They send for me from all over Sikkim, from Darjeeling, and also from Gyantse and Shigatse. Next month I'm going to paint some frescoes in a new temple at Darjeeling. If only my eyes didn't trouble me! You know, they get tired and water, and they ache. Could you perhaps recommend me a medicine?"

"Perhaps, yes. I'll send it up to you tomorrow. But tell me, when you paint a big, difficult and complicated picture like this 'Wheel', do you do it all from memory?"

"I've painted so many 'Wheels of Life' now that I do them from memory. But first I studied under a master. Also there's a book, you know, which gives all the details; the divisions, the characters, the animals, the saints, the devils, even the colours. Every colour has a meaning."

"So you can't change anything?"

"Some things, yes. The backgrounds, the landscapes, the positions of the lesser characters, some of the details, some of the colours."

"But there are very fine 'Wheels' and also very poor ones."

"Certainly. You can tell the good painter by the life he puts into his figures. They must fly, leap, run! That is the important thing."

Eventually Rig-zin turned, removed his spectacles and looked at me for a moment. He is a man completely absorbed in his work; a quiet, calm, obstinate devotee. When he had looked me over sufficiently to weigh me up and classify me, he put his spectacles back on his nose and resumed his painful and minute labour.

"And does the work take long? How do you start?"

"It's very simple. First you take the cloth, cut it and spread it in the frame. Then you carefully spread the gum and white lead. When you've finished preparing the background you draw the design with charcoal. Then you spread the colours dissolved in gum. Finally you put in the lighting with gold, and the picture's done. That's all!"

"Then what happens? You hand it over to the customer?"

"Yes, if he pays. Every now and then someone doesn't pay, but all the same I manage to place what I paint."

"Tell me something. Have you ever thought of signing your pictures?"

"Writing my name on them? What an idea! Why should I sign my work? Is that the custom with you?"

Rig-zin stopped his gold work for a moment, and looked at me over his spectacles. I think he was silently re-classifying me. Then he went on painting.

He changed his brush, took a very fine one, retouched the background landscapes and became completely absorbed in his microscopic work. Other paintings of his were in the room. There was always a peculiar felicity, a spontaneous and convincing life about his drawing, but the colours were sometimes abominable. At one time painters used to make their own paints by mixing certain earths. Today all they have to do is go to a shop and buy chemicals. This saves trouble and is cheaper, but the result is criminal. I told Rig-zin so.

"You are right," he said. "But what is one to do? You must remember the time and the expense. I've got a family to keep, you know."

So the painter of the "Wheel of Life" was himself caught up in the wheel of present-day life. He depended on industry for his cloth, his colours, his brushes, for everything. But his style was still intact. In his paintings there was not the slightest trace of the influence of the covers of the Indian illustrated newspapers that I saw lying about the house and in the hands of his children. For how much longer, though?

Love and polyandry: at the dance of the lamas

My manoeuvres to sit next to Pemà Chöki were long and complicated, but were eventually successful. First of all the way was blocked by Wangchuk, who insisted on talking to me about cameras. ("I have a Zeiss with a magnificent lens, but I don't know how to use the shutter.") Then there was Jigme, who wanted to tell me all about his plan to provide skis for the postmen who cross the Himalayas. ("We should have express services all the year round.") Finally a big lama was just going to tell me something, but I noticed a free place next to the princess and pounced on it. I reached it just ahead of the Abbot of Tumlong.

Big white tents, with the usual imaginative blue flourishes, had been erected the evening before opposite the big temple of Gangtok. The central tent was for the guests, and there were many of us. There were benches at the back, armchairs in the middle and divans in the front row. The dances were about to begin. An orchestra of five or six lamas had been placed in a pavilion in front of the temple. Two young coenobites with strong lungs were going to blow the *tung-chens*, the six-yard-long trumpets which give out notes as deep as distant thunder, while two others were going to blow the *gyaling*, little silver trumpets, which squeak. Then there were drums and cymbals to provide the rhythm.

For a few moments the heavy clouds that hang over the mountains at this season lifted, and Kanchenjunga, the third highest mountain in the world, appeared shining in the sun. Everyone considered this a most favourable omen. The dances were in fact being held in honour of the god Kuvera, who resides on Kanchenjunga.

Kuvera, according to the legend, practised extreme asceticism for a thousand years, whereupon Brahma decided to reward him by conferring immortality upon him and making him guardian of the treasures of the earth, with authority to distribute them to men according to his pleasure. Kuvera was adopted by the Buddhists, and later emigrated in the direction of Tibet, undergoing various

92 *July, and the first warnings of the monsoons; the clouds drive in from the south*

metamorphoses and being fused with other divinities on the way. He became god of war and of martial strength, as well as the guardian of the north. It was in this composite form that he was honoured as the godhead of the great Himalayan mountain, together with a companion, Maha-Kala ("The Great Black One"), the commander-in-chief of the Champions of the Faith. So at least I was informed by the Enche Kasi, who came and sat beside us. The guests' tent was crowded. All the local notabilities were there, as well as a number of Indians and white men who had motored up from Kalimpong or Darjeeling. I also noticed some wives, or sisters, or daughters, of British or American tourists or residents. In comparison with Pemà Chöki they looked like cart horses next to a highly-strung thoroughbred. On such occasions Pemà Chöki, having taken in the situation at a glance, instantly assumes a pose of frightened humility, as if she were a humble flower of the field that had by chance found its way into an orchid house. Everyone, women included, searched her out, called her, surrounded her, feeling that they had made a rare discovery, wanting to show her to others and have the pleasure of protecting her. Every now and then, after circulating among the guests, she returned to her seat, and we went on talking. She laughed. She knew that I had seen through her little game.

"Have you ever tried wearing European clothes?" I asked her.

"Papa would never permit it, he's very firm on that point . . . I tried wearing European clothes just once, secretly, at Darjeeling, but I didn't like them. Papa's too intelligent to tell me outright that the clothes I wear have been modelled for centuries to go with the shape of our Mongolian bodies, to hide our legs, which are too short, and our breasts, which are too small, and emphasize the neck and face, which are often very beautiful . . ."

The dancing began. Pemà's duties as hostess called her away again. The Maharajah set great store on his reception's being a success, and he counted greatly on his daughter's help.

Meanwhile about thirty monks were dancing in the space in front of us. They were dressed as soldiers – soldiers of Kublai Khan, soldiers who might have served in Marco Polo's escort. They wheeled rhythmically about themselves in a measured and solemn step called *dorje-dro*, "the thunderbolt step". It was less a dance than a ritual, a grandiose, slightly grotesque and subtly melancholy performance of a mediaeval mystery play. The monks disguised as warriors cleft the air with their swords, cutting evil spirits in two, three, a hundred pieces. The orchestra gave the rhythm with music which Montaigne would have described as *poisante, sévère et spondaïque*.

At one point a herald came forward and slowly sang the invocation to Kuvera: "Oh destroyer of the enemies guilty of the ten kinds of sin! Oh prince of the guardians of this noble country of rice! Oh lord of all the spirits, known by the name of the Summit of Junga! Oh warlike divinity of martial youth . . . ."

The Maharajah, wrapped in his brocade robe decorated with golden flowers and wearing a doge's hat on his head, was sitting rather rigidly on a long blue divan and following every phase of the sacred mystery from behind his dark glasses. He was heraldic and precise, something between a lily and a scientific instrument. Beside him was the wife of the Political Officer, looking dignified and a little cold, but full of character, a last farewell of Victorian England to the Asia of dream and fable.

In another burst of sunshine Kuvera appeared in person at the temple door, all covered with gold, brocade and silk, and wearing a red mask that flashed in the bright light; it was beautiful, fantastic, metaphysical. It was a moment of intense excitement for all the Sikkimese. The children shrieked, the girls clapped, the old people who had come down from the mountains held their breath and watched in amazement. Kuvera, impersonated by a great, strong lama who was an excellent dancer, descended the steps and started a long series of evolutions and sudden leaps, with numerous pauses and complicated balancing movements which required months of training. The six-yard-long trumpets broke the silence with a triumphant boom.

Pemà Chöki had quietly returned and was sitting between the Enche Kasi and me. "Look at that mask! Isn't it wonderful?" she said. "It was remade last year. The red lacquer is superb . . . By the way, what was that lipstick called that I asked you to send me? You've forgotten, have you?"

"Riv . . . rev . . . I can't recall it for the moment."

"It was Revlon, Bachelor's Carnation . . . Don't you dare forget it again! I'm relying on you to send it to me from Calcutta. Don't forget, will you?"

Now it was the turn of Maha-Kala, the Great Black One. Another herald advanced and sang another invocation to the Principal of the Guardians of the Faith. A servant wearing a red-patterned uniform passed with a tray.

93 *Gangtok: the dances of the lamas – Kuvera appears at the temple gate*

94 *Gangtok: the dance of the lamas – two masked actors*

"Won't you have some tea?" Pemà Chöki asked me. "It's not Tibetan tea, it's ordinary tea; I ordered it for you."

The servant poured us out some tea. The music ended in a glorious outburst of dissonance between the temple and the sky. The comic, horrible, stupendous mask glittered in the sun.

"I like Tibetan tea," I remarked.

"Nonsense, that's your way of paying compliments; or you do it to give yourself airs as a great traveller! You swallow it like a medicine, and say: 'Good! *yagpo*!' but you don't take me in!"

Pemà laughed, her white teeth flashing in the sunlight. A few moments later she told me about her fiancé.

"Perhaps I'm not in love with him, but we shall get on well all the same, I think . . . First the family wanted me to marry someone else, belonging to an older family and very rich, but he had several brothers."

"What then?"

"We are in Tibet, where polyandry is practised. A younger brother's wife is also the wife of his elder brother, or brothers."

"And you didn't like the elder brother?"

"No."

"And if you had liked him?"

"Oh! what a lot of questions! You know, you're far too inquisitive! . . .

Look at Maha-Kala standing ready at the temple door! Wait for the invocation to finish. Be quiet! If you behave yourself, I'll translate what he says for you. 'The fierce, proud, unconquered Maha-Kala, victorious over all, today arises to fulfil his duty . . . Arrows, lances, swords and every sort of weapon are directed towards the enemy, and glitter and shine. Mountains of corpses are consumed like food, oceans of blood are poured like drink . . . Let him who sets store by his life keep away from me. Let him who wants to die approach. I shall cut off the red source of life and offer it in sacrifice. I am the destroyer who assuages his thirst with blood. Glory to Maha-Kala, Kiki-huhu, Kiki-huhu!' Do you like it? You see what a nice place your Tibet is? You know, we are like the Spaniards, only our bulls are devils; the terrifying gods are our *toreros*. I'm an *aficionada* of Kuvera, the one who danced first. He's handsomer, he's braver, he's more everything!"

The servant passed again, this time with pineapples and melons.

"Won't you have a piece of pineapple?" Pemà asked. "They came straight from Rangpo this morning. Two loads for the Dalai Lama are leaving today. Ah! Lhasa! What beauty! What life! All those festivals! You've no idea how much you can enjoy yourself there!"

"And I thought it was a city of meditation and silence, inhabited exclusively by monks, abbots and theologians."

"Oh, yes! They have those there too, of course, but there are so many other people who have nothing to do with the monasteries, and want life to be beautiful . . . Besides, don't the ascetics practise purity and make sacrifices for us? it's like a bank. They pay in the money, and all of us draw the benefit. That's how they acquire eternal merit."

The dances drew to an end. It started drizzling. Pemà took a small piece of pineapple and carefully raised it towards her lips. But a small drop of juice fell on her brand-new *pang-den*, made of special Bhutan cloth. She threw the fruit away, called her maid, who was standing at the bottom of the tent, and made some whispered complaint to her in Tibetan. Then she laughed and repeated, like a small child going into ecstasies about a remarkable cake:

"Ah! Lhasa!"

Lunar rainbow

It is my last evening at Gangtok. It rained all day, but now the weather seems to be clearing up. The moon is painfully opening herself a path, still a very shadowy one, between heavy, almost motionless, clouds. The play of light on the showers across the valley has taken the form of that rare and unspeakably beautiful phenomenon, a lunar rainbow.

A faint, ethereal – I should like to call it silent – curve of light emerges imperceptibly from the dark abysses of the forest and stretches across the sky to fade equally imperceptibly into the patches of light reflected from the roofs, above the temple and the palace, where Pemà Chöki lies asleep with her black hair on a white pillow. It is only the ghost, the memory of a rainbow, the faintest suggestion of pink and blue tones, to be guessed at rather than seen, suspended between one nothing and another in the darkness of the night.

Mechanical wind-man: Asia disappearing down below

We had left; we were in the sky. Climbing out of the suffocating monsoon heat of Calcutta into the clear sunlight of 9,000 feet was magnificent. We travelled through a forest of clouds shaped like pillars, towers, enormous mushrooms reminiscent of the Hiroshima mushroom. Every now and then we passed close to one of those superb white monuments, those huge, carnal bulges, or plunged into its midst, to emerge suddenly with a sensation of entering a void. I strained to see whether I could make out the Himalayas in the distance, but who could be sure that those distant white undulations were mountains? Down below, between one cloud mass and the next, was a region of many lakes and hundreds of villages, surrounded by yellowish expanses of water. Millions of people down there would not be able to move from their homes for weeks; moving only a few miles would mean dragging oneself through mud; lighting a fire was a problem, sleeping in the dry very difficult, burning the dead absolutely impossible. Perhaps someone looking up noticed a tiny aeroplane in the sky, a tiny aeroplane that by next evening would be in Rome.

We reached Karachi very late. During the night we left again for Iraq. Every now and then, half-asleep and half-awake, I said to myself: “Down there is Persia; mountains, deserts, estuaries, rivers, cities, mausoleums, rock sculpture, caravans, brigands.” Overhead in the luggage rack were Tibetan books and pictures. Milarepa, used to travelling by levitation, would certainly not be surprised at this new experience. If he were now suddenly to arise after a thousand years of trance in a cave of the Himalayas and find himself here, perhaps he would compose a poem about a mechanical wind-man. What thoughts might not be suggested to him by the life of these ingenious Western barbarians, dominators of *samsara*, the world of illusion?

With the first light we reached Basra, a trail of palm-groves along the united Tigris and Euphrates, between two wastes of boundless, orange sand. Then deserts and deserts all the way to Cairo. No more clouds were to be seen; the clearness of the sky was absolute in every direction. At Cairo we stopped an hour for a meal. During the afternoon we passed over Crete, and at sunset reached the heel of Italy. The passengers started moving about, getting ready; we had the feeling that Rome was only a few yards away. Indeed, so it was. After what seemed a moment we saw Capri and, almost before we realized it, there were the lights of Ciampino airport.

"Yesterday we were in Calcutta."

15

Notes on Tibetan Buddhism

The metaphysical adventure of Prince Gautama

Lamaism represents an important philosophic and religious complex within the far vaster orbit of Buddhism. From one point of view, because of its rites, and its institutions culminating in a pope, the Dalai Lama, it could be said to correspond with Roman Catholicism in the Christian world. But in other respects it has greater affinities with the Protestant Churches. Lamaism, unlike Catholicism, is a relatively recent development among the various Buddhist sects, dating from the seventh and subsequent centuries of our era; also it is to a great extent a "reformed" variety of Buddhism. However, all such comparisons, however external and superficial, are inexact, and no real parallel can be drawn.

Buddhism, as a historical phenomenon, represents one of the most grandiose edifices of the human spirit. It is sufficient to point to the influence that it has exercised in the course of 2,500 years in countries as diverse as India, Ceylon, the Indo-Greek kingdoms of the generals of Alexander the Great, Central Asia, China, Japan, Tibet, Mongolia, Indo-China, Siam, the East Indies and parts of Siberia. It has inspired whole literatures, and an art to which we owe some of the most noble and inspired works of man. Consider what a vast and complicated task it would be to write a general and all-embracing history of Christianity, tracing its influence on every form of human activity, following all its mystical and philosophical developments, the growth and development of its religious communities and organizations, its influence on the art, the political and social history, the ordinary life, of the people of a whole continent. The material offered by a study of Buddhism is no less vast, either quantitatively or in its universal implications.

If, therefore, we wish to understand lamaism, we must start with him who initiated the great movement of which lamaism is only a part; that is to say, with Gautama Buddha, the "Enlightened One". He was born in north India in the sixth century B.C., and lived, preached and died at the foot of the Himalayas, in what is now border territory between Nepal and Bihar. The most ancient documents, written in Pali, enable his life story to be reconstructed in reasonably detailed fashion. This is not the place to discuss the controversies between orientalists on which episodes in his life are historical, which are imaginary and which are merely probable. In certain cases legend has special rights which no-one will wish to deny. I shall therefore follow the story of his life as preserved by Tibetan tradition, adding some information established by modern research.

"The Twelve Episodes of the Life" (of the Buddha) – in Tibetan *tse-pa chu-ni* – provide one of the themes which have most frequently inspired Tibetan artists. They deal with it in twelve scenes, often divided into two big frescoes, or grouped into one big one in which the following incidents can be observed:

(1) The future Buddha resolves temporarily to abandon his celestial abode to be incarnated on earth.

We are thus at the outset plunged into myth. We shall see later that as Buddhism developed it was unable to resist the temptation to deify its founder. Here he is presented as a supernatural being from the start.

(2) Queen Maya sees in a dream a white elephant descending from heaven.

A little white elephant is the emblem of gentleness, and for many centuries the child Buddha was represented exclusively by this charming symbol. According to the biographies Queen Maya (the name means "Admirable Virtue"), who was then aged forty-five and had previously had no children, conceived miraculously. Her vision of the little white elephant was a kind of Annunciation. Gautama was now about to begin his terrestrial life. Where, how, in what stratum of society was he to be born? His father, according to legend, was a great king. But it seems much more probable that he was a small rajah (the word is the same as *rex*) belonging to the Sakya clan ("Sakya" means "the powerful"), who occupied a limited area of land at the foot of the Nepalese Himalayas. His name was Suddhodhana, and he lived at Kapilavastu. Maya, the Buddha's future mother, and one of her sisters, became Suddhodhana's wives. They were the daughters of a feudal lord whose home was not far distant from Kapilavastu. When Queen Maya felt that her time was approaching she left for her parents' house, but when she reached the park of Lumbini her son was born.

(3) Sakya-Muni (in Tibetan, *Sakya-Thupa*, "the ascetic of the Sakyas") is born while his mother is in the act of picking an olive-branch.

The new-born child, according to the legend, immediately rose to his feet and walked seven paces towards each point of the compass, exclaiming: "This is my last reincarnation!" He was given the name of Siddhartha ("He who has Attained the Goal"). Queen Maya died barely seven days after giving him birth, so he was suckled with his little cousins by his aunt foster-mother, Prajapati. Legend describes how it was prophesied to his father that the little Siddhartha was destined for great things; to be a conqueror of empires, or a Buddha. King Suddhodhana, fearing the latter alternative, had his son brought up isolated from life in the refined, luxurious, gilded cage of the palace.

With the birth of Prince Siddhartha we reach an important point in the story in which tradition, historical documents and archaeological research confirm one another. In 1895 there was discovered at Lumbini (now Rummindei) the commemorative pillar erected by the Emperor Asoka in 249 B.C., *i.e.* little more than two hundred years after the Buddha's death, when the traditions must have been very much alive. An inscription on the column records that the emperor exempted the village of Lumbini from taxation, because "here the Buddha was born".

(4) The young Siddhartha confounds his masters by the exceptional knowledge he displays for his age, and he defeats his contemporaries at wrestling and athletics.

(5) Prince Siddhartha marries Yasodhara.

Gautama was then aged nineteen. Yasodhara was his cousin, the daughter of a maternal uncle. After several years a child was born, Rahula. The biographers all speak of the secluded and luxurious life lived by the young prince, who, free from every care, passed his days in the tranquillity of shady gardens or in the pleasures of love. But a profound dissatisfaction with the uselessness of such an existence, and the feeling that reality must be very different from what it might appear from inside the palace walls, seem gradually to have made headway in Siddhartha's mind. Tradition has synthesized what must have been a long, inner struggle into three episodes, which constitute the sixth picture.

(6) Prince Siddhartha, during his walks in the park, sees a wretched old man on the point of death, a corpse, a sick man and a mendicant ascetic.

These experiences bore fruit in a mind of exquisite sensibility, inclined by nature to observe the world as a philosopher. Life, he discovered, was not as it seemed to be in the gilded cage of the palace, in the shade of the trees, among the perfume of the flowers in the big garden, or in Yasodhara's jewelled arms. Beyond the precincts was a world of tears and pain, of ugliness and decay, of suffering and death. The nature of the man who was both sage and saint, who was Bhagava, "the Eminent One", was here revealed. He did not try to retreat into the unreal world into which he was born, to make of it an oasis in the wilderness of suffering. He saw that reality lay, not in shady retreats, silken clothing, luxury, the pleasures of security, youth and love, but in wounds and sores, painful, livid flesh, poverty and care, old age, disease and death. He decided to withdraw into solitude and meditate, to cut himself off from the world, and put himself into contact with ultimate truth and find a way for mankind to liberation from pain.

(7) Prince Siddhartha leaves his father's palace and enters the forest as a beggar.

This was the great renunciation, the first of the fundamental acts with which Gautama affirmed his personality as the future Enlightened One. Tradition has taken charge of this moving episode, and made of it one of the supreme masterpieces of human poetry. Siddhartha takes his departure in the middle of the night. He goes on tiptoe to embrace his son, but the child is clinging to his mother, and he cannot touch one without waking the other. After gazing long at these two creatures, who are still infinitely dear to him, he leaves in silence. Channa, his faithful groom, and Kanthaka, his white palfrey, are waiting for him outside. Siddhartha leaps on his horse, and the gods make a carpet for its hoofs with their hands, enabling him to leave the town without being seen or heard. At dawn, in the open country, the prince hands to Channa his perfumed clothing, all the precious things that he has with him, puts on a beggar's cloak, and with a few strokes of his sabre cuts off his hair. The great renunciation is complete. Siddhartha no longer exists. His place has been taken by Gautama, the ascetic of the Sakyas.

(8) Sakya-Muni seeks truth by way of asceticism.

After the great renunciation Gautama sought for a teacher. He became the pupil first of one famous ascetic, then of another, but their teaching did not seem to him to lead in the direction of the goal which he had set himself. He therefore shut himself up with five faithful companions in a forest to the south of Patna, where he lived for six long years, mortifying his body with the cruellest privations – one grain of rice a day – until he was reduced to a skeleton. One day he collapsed, and remained unconscious for many hours. When he came to himself he realized that this was not the path that led to true wisdom, and he went to a neighbouring village in search of nourishment. His companions called him a coward, a weakling who abandoned the struggle, and left him. This grieved Gautama, but he persisted in his conviction. While sitting under a pipal tree he found germinating within himself supreme and final illumination.

(9) Mara tempts Buddha for the last time.

Gautama remained under the pipal tree for many, many hours. As often happens just before a supreme crisis, he went through a period of intense anguish and dismay. Having tasted once more the simple pleasure of a bowl of rice, he asked himself whether it were really worth while renouncing life for a goal that was perhaps unattainable and was certainly remote. He thought of the family he had left, his past life of ease, the comforts to which he could at any moment return if he abandoned the goal on which he had set his heart. When Mara saw that this simpler form of temptation was vain, because Gautama had attained complete enlightenment and had passed beyond the cycle of rebirth, he tempted him to vanish into *nirvana* and leave mankind in the darkness of ignorance and sin. But Mara was frustrated again, for the Buddha had decided to bring enlightenment to the world. This intense, inner struggle, which makes Gautama an immediate, real figure to us, a man like ourselves in the fullest sense, not a dim, hieratic figure belonging to another continent and another age, has been transformed by tradition, and is represented as the final assault upon Gautama, intended to break his will, of Mara and his demons in their innumerable aspects, some terrifying, some monstrous, and some almost irresistibly voluptuous. The artists represent Gautama in this scene as serene and motionless, while around him there rages the maelstrom of illusory forms.

(10) Gautama finally becomes the Enlightened One.

The sage, having won his last, supreme battle, was aware of an infinite peace; he was now the Enlightened One. The causes of suffering were now known to him with a terrible clarity, and he had seen the way that must be followed to obtain liberation from it.

(11) The first sermon in the Park of the Gazelles at Benares.

After spending further time under the tree, the Buddha decided to announce his doctrine to his former masters. But these were dead. So he made for Benares, to search for the five companions who had forsaken him. He found them there, in the Park of the Gazelles, proclaimed his doctrine to them, and converted them. Henceforward the life of the Buddha was a continual apostolate. For forty-five years, except during the annual rainy season, which was reserved for meditation and communal study, he was continually travelling about, followed by an ever-increasing band of disciples, converts, worshippers and admirers.

(12) The Buddha's death.

When he is nearly eighty years old the Buddha feels the end approaching. He gathers his disciples and spends his last hours with them, and then passes finally into *nirvana*.

There are two possible attitudes to life, and every individual can be said to base his life on a compromise between them. On the one hand there is what we may call the pagan attitude, according to which the world is this world, to which the good, the true, the beautiful belong (or will one day if they do not now): the sun, harvest time, the traffic in the market-place and the ship's prow cutting through the water, the girl at the window and the artisan in his shop, the plough, the hammer and the sword. In contrast to this is the spiritual attitude, according to which the real centre of the universe, the true reason for living, enjoying, suffering, loving and hating, is invisible and lies elsewhere; this world is a place of transit only, and life is a testing period, an ordeal to be overcome, or an illusion, or a puzzling ideogram, or possibly a cruel farce; we breathe among shadows and for shadows, what seems most real is least real, the real truth is not discernible by the senses, but belongs to the remote, the future, the eternal. The doctrine of the Buddha, like that of Christ, belongs definitely to the second category. Life is pain and tears, this world is but the illusory scene of transient episodes concerning impermanent, changing aggregates, involved in an endless drama.

The Buddha, like Socrates, Christ and many other Great Initiates (to use Schuré's celebrated phrase), left no works written in his own hand, but proclaimed his teaching by word of mouth to his disciples or to the crowd. Buddhism therefore has its own problem of the scriptures. Which among the many books, all of them written centuries later, faithfully reflect the master's words? And, when the choice has been made, how much interpolation is there, how much fantasy, how much poetical embellishment? To reconstruct the Buddha's teaching in its original form one must turn to the canon preserved by the Buddhists of Ceylon. It is written in Pali (which is related to Sanskrit) and is called the *Tri-pitaka*. The title itself takes us back to a rural age, when sages disputed about metaphysics in the shade of the trees or walked barefooted through the fields from village to village. *Tri-pitaka* means "three baskets", because the complete scriptures, bound in volumes of palm-leaf, could be contained in three receptacles.

The first, the *Vinaya*, the "repository of discipline", contains monastic, disciplinary rules and so forth. The second, the *Sutra*, is the "repository of sermons", and probably contains the most ancient material, that most directly inspired by the master; the third and last, the *Abhidhamma*, the "repository of metaphysics", contains philosophical discussions, and is the least ancient of the three.

To understand the Buddha's teaching, which, like all the sublime things which have really influenced the history of the world, is essentially simple – its essence is contained in the Four Noble Truths, the Eightfold Path and the Twelve Causes (the Chain of Causation) – one must bear in mind a most important point. The Buddha did not appear suddenly out of the blue; he did not emerge as a colossal figure of thought in a speculative void. He belonged to the rich Indian philosophical tradition. Just as Christ spoke a language intelligible to His listeners and used Western terms and ideas – soul, creation, paradise – so did the Buddha speak to his disciples of *karma, arhat* and *nirvana*; the term "Buddha" had been used to honour sages and seers before him. The idea of the soul was common to Greco-Roman philosophy and to Christianity; it was part of the common patrimony of a whole civilization. Similarly terms like *samsara* and *karma* were used not only by Buddhists, but by Jains, and the philosophers of the *samkya* school, the dualists of their age.

Samsara means rebirth, but has far deeper implications than that. It indicates the theory of the transmigration of souls and the "vortex of life" (Tucci) in which that transmigration takes place. *Samsara* is thus the complicated, irrational, unstable universe, in a state of continual becoming, the realm of suffering and death; it is the realm of matter and decomposition, of ephemeral pleasures and blinding passions. Man, and indeed, all living things, are bound to *samsara* by the cycle of birth and rebirth, by ignorance (*avydia*) and attachment (*upadana*). All the efforts of the sage must be directed to the liberation of man from *samsara*, from all illusory hopes.

An *arhat* is one who has attained liberation and "loses himself in *nirvana*" (Tucci). There is a subtle distinction between an *arhat* and the Buddha. Both are no longer subject to rebirth, but the Buddha is by far the superior of the two. He is an active force, simultaneously enlightened and enlightening, while the *arhat* is he who takes advantage of his teaching, is liberated, but as a follower walking in the Buddha's footsteps, inasmuch as the Buddha preceded him. He has freed himself from his burden of *karma* and finds rest in *nirvana*, disappearing from the scene of life.

What are *karma* and *nirvana*? They are subtle concepts, riddled like Gothic spires by centuries of disputation. *Karma* originally meant "action", but then assumed the meaning of "the effect of action", including the merit or demerit which everyone acquires in the course of his existences in this or in other worlds. Liberation from *samsara* signifies the final annihilation of one's *karma*; good or bad modifications of one's *karma* decide one's progress or regression in future births.

When *karma* is exhausted, all that remains is *nirvana*. This term now has certain associations for us; it implies a sense of dreamy reverie or a vague, ecstatic plunge into the void. Indian interpretations of the term, however contradictory, are far more precise. Ontologically it is a mere limit. It is that which remains after the annihilation of psychic activity; it is total liberation from *samsara*. Like the infinite, it can only be defined negatively. In the *Tri-pitaka* it is used to indicate entirely different psychological states. Sometimes it implies true annihilation, sometimes it is something indefinable, transcending all experience and thought, and at other times it is described, more materialistically, as a state of ineffable peace and serenity. The Buddha, wisely concerned with the far more human and immediate problems of suffering and of the way to liberate mankind from attachment to life, did not trouble about this, or about many other eschatological and metaphysical problems, and left no opinions about them. Did Jesus concern Himself with establishing grades and hierarchies of angels? Let us ignore the laborious hair-splittings of Dionysius the Pseudo-Areopagite's *Concerning the Celestial Hierarchy*, and the logical subtleties of a Dharmakirti.

It should, however, be borne in mind that this summary gives an idea of only some aspects of each principle. Nothing is more foreign to the Eastern spirit than codification and intransigence in philosophical and religious matters. There are a thousand paths to truth, just as there are many paths to the top of a mountain. True, there is a tremendous diversity of schools and a wealth of differing and conflicting interpretations. One should, incidentally, consider the baffling wealth of material with which, say, a Chinese student would find himself confronted if he set out to write about the concept of the soul in the West. What a distance from the atomists to Plato, from St. Paul to Descartes, from Dante to Freud! But fundamentally every thinker in the West, whether he denies the soul, idealizes it, or reduces it to atoms, whether he turns it into an afflatus or an essence or a chemical formula, has to come to terms with it. The various philosophies and schools of thought bear the same relation to the cultural foundations of the civilization from which they derive as the laws of a people bear to that people's customs.

At this point let the Buddha himself announce the true foundations of his doctrine, the Four Noble Truths about pain, as he did in his sermon at Benares. The first truth declares that existence involves pain; the second declares the origin of pain; the third the possibility of the extinction of pain; and the fourth the way that leads to the extinction of pain.

"(1) Now this, monks, is the noble truth of pain: birth is painful, old age is painful, sickness is painful, death is painful, sorrow, lamentation, dejection and despair are painful. Contact with unpleasant things is painful, not getting what one wishes is painful . . .

"(2) Now this, monks, is the noble truth of the cause of pain: the craving which tends to rebirth, combined with pleasure and lust, finding pleasure here and there, namely the craving for passion, the craving for existence, the craving for non-existence.

"(3) Now this, monks, is the noble truth of the cessation of pain, the cessation without a remainder of craving, the abandonment, forsaking, release, non-attachment.

"(4) Now this, monks, is the noble truth of the way that leads to the cessation of pain: this is the noble Eightfold Way, namely right views, right intention, right speech, right action, right livelihood, right effort, right mindfulness, right concentration.

"This is the noble truth of pain: Thus, monks, among doctrines unheard before, in me sight and knowledge arose, wisdom arose, knowledge arose, light arose." [1]

The last of the Four Truths foreshadows the Eightfold Path, which is the basis of and guide to the Buddhist good life. *Right views* means not falling into heresy. Heresy could take three main forms: one might doubt the reality of suffering, or conceive it to be a negative aspect of pleasure or enjoyment; one might mistake the impermanent for the abiding, the changing for the immutable, the transient for the eternal; or one might succumb to illusions about the existence of the soul as something individual, that survives and is transmissible. This last is one of the most thorny and difficult points in the whole Buddhist doctrine. But there is no doubt about it; it is clearly and repeatedly stated that the so-called soul is only an unstable compound of the five elements of which the universe is made, and that at death these are dispersed and return whence they came. Only the *karma* survives and remains active, providing the nucleus round which the elements of a new being – in the course of centuries the elements of innumerable new beings – will congregate. But this *karma* is not consciousness, is not a self; that is pure illusion. In the age-long journey through *samsara* towards liberation *karma* provides the only thread of personal identity.

Right intention must include the desire not to harm other living beings, to emancipate oneself from slavery to the senses and to love one's neighbour. *Right speech, right action, right livelihood, right effort* more immediately concern conduct. Here one may recall the Buddhist decalogue, consisting of five commandments for laymen (thou shalt not kill, thou shalt not rob, thou shalt not commit adultery, thou shalt not lie, thou shalt not drink alcoholic liquor), with five additional precepts for monks, who are forbidden to accept food outside the prescribed hours, to attend spectacles of music, songs or dancing, to use garlands, perfumes, pomades or scent, to sleep in high or wide beds, and to accept gold or silver. For monks sexual abstention is also assumed.

Right mindfulness indicates the awareness of the fundamental truths that every man must always carry with him. Finally *right concentration* concerns the higher activities of the spirit; meditation must culminate by way of various states of ecstasy in the abolition of sensibility and consciousness. These final stages of perfection can, of course, only be achieved in the ascetic life of the sage.

The final important theory of primitive Buddhism may be considered as a completion and an explanation of the second truth about suffering. This is the Twelve Causal Connections (*pratitya samutphada*), which explain in complicated and somewhat obscure fashion the fundamental reasons why desire, attachment to life and consequently suffering perpetuate themselves.

It will be seen from a consideration of the broad outlines of this primitive Buddhism that it is essentially a pessimistic philosophy rather than a religion. Life and the universe are nothing but evil, pain and ugliness. The gods are mentioned, true, but as poetical, decorative figures possessing the majestic, frigid and crystalline impersonality of principles that govern the universe. Primitive Buddhism provides a scientific, dispassionate analysis of the causes of suffering and a dispassionate, scientific search for the remedy.

The thing that marks it off so sharply from the Brahmanism of its time is its insistence that liberation is not attainable by way of propitiatory rites, liturgies, sacraments, which are not the path to virtue and sanctity; liberation is attainable only by the deliberate, inner development of the self. It is useless to pray, weep, make sacrifices, mortify oneself or attempt magical practices, for none of these things is effective; the only thing that is effective is right thought and right action. Moral abasement and evil do not offend any god, but harm only those who succumb to them. It is a metaphysics based on morality, with the human personality, and its will for virtue and purification, elevated to a supreme place and put in the very centre of the All.

On the practical level primitive Buddhism is also more of a philosophy than a religion. It sanctions, indeed encourages, the monastic life, but admits no priesthood. No mage, no professional intermediary, must intervene between man and the truth. The life of the coenobite, remote from the temptations of the world and free from family ties, is the best-adapted for meditation and the gaining of understanding, but the monk is a selected soldier, not an exorcist or a possessor of secrets.

In conclusion, if we wish to understand the main lines of Buddhism as Gautama probably understood them, we must bear in mind the fundamental points: the Four Noble Truths, the Noble Eightfold Path, and the concepts of *samsara*, *karma*, *arhat*, *buddha* and *nirvana*.

The great propulsive force of Buddhism was not due to its novelty or originality, because nearly all its constituent elements were to be found in contemporary Indian thought. Its strength derived rather from its lofty moral sense, the universality of its message, its serene philosophical tone, its scorn for the miracle-mongering, the theatrical excesses, of asceticism, and above all the personality, so strong, so human and so fascinating, of the prince-ascetic Gautama Sakya-Muni.

As we know, he was opposed to the establishment of a church or priesthood, with the result that after his death the large number of disciples who had gathered about him in his long life of preaching very soon divided along the lines of different interpretations of the master's sayings. As happens when a spiritual movement is alive and deeply touches the hearts of men, Buddhism became diversified and complicated, and many variations arose. True, for several centuries there was a succession of patriarchs, twenty-seven in all, down to Bodhidharma, who visited China in A.D. 526, but their authority seems to have been recognized in only a very general sense. Every three or four generations the more responsible elements tried in vain to arrange a council to discuss and settle controversial points: at Rajagriha soon after the Buddha's death, at Vaisali about 370 B.C., at Pataliputra in 246 B.C. Meanwhile a slow but inexorable trend began, transforming the original philosophy into a religion, the original order into a church, the master into a god, *nirvana* into paradise and the psyche into a soul. There also developed a notable tendency to believe that *karma* must be modifiable by prayer.

With the conversion to Buddhism of the Emperor Asoka (269–232 B.C.) the philosophy of Gautama entered upon its triumphant career as a religion of the masses. In the year 261 Asoka proclaimed it to be the state religion, set up monuments and inscriptions and established monasteries and temples throughout India, caused learned men to assemble the first canon (it is from this that the Pali *Tri-pitaka* derives), and himself became a monk. The Buddhism of Asoka's time was already notably different from primitive Buddhism. The emphasis was very definitely on ethical and moral virtue, on the good life; there was much less pessimism and hatred of life, and much less was heard about the ideal of *nirvana*. Buddhism had undergone a humanizing process, and regarded life and living creatures with greater benevolence. Processions and ceremonies had crept in, a priesthood existed in embryo, exorcism was practised, benedictions were given, dreams were interpreted and horoscopes read.

After the collapse of Asoka's empire Buddhism frankly headed away from Gautama's agnosticism or atheism towards a metaphysical polytheism. In the popular imagination, always receptive to the supernatural, the Buddha was irresistibly transformed from master into Lord, and solar myths, fire cults, ancient autochthonous fantasies and immemorial legends contributed to his idealized figure. From the Enlightened he came the Enlightening One, the spreader of light; in other words, God. A parallel development took place in the speculations of the philosophers. They ended by taking less interest in the Buddha than in the state of Buddhahood. From an individual he was transformed into a category, and Gautama became one Buddha among many. The story of Gautama gave way to a science of Buddhahood. The individual Gautama disappeared, to be replaced by a symbol, a manifestation of the Absolute.

The fundamental division of Buddhism into two great branches, the *Hinayana*, or Little Vehicle, and the *Mahayana*, or Great Vehicle, dates from this time. The *Hinayana* stood for faithfulness to the Buddha's original doctrines, was opposed to theistic developments, and adhered loyally to the *arhat* ideal; it was the right hand of Buddhism. Its fortune in the course of centuries was far inferior to that of the *Mahayana*, and it survives to the present day, though in a much-modified form, in Ceylon, Burma and Siam. The *Mahayana* accepted theistic, magic, mystagogic developments with alacrity, almost with enthusiasm, did not oppose the incipient sacerdotalism, and proclaimed that salvation was available not only to a few chosen ascetics, but to all (hence its name, the "Great" Vehicle). The *Mahayana* substituted for Gautama's agnosticism the adoration of a vast empyrean of gods. It adopted symbolism again, and tended to attach greater importance to the recitation of sacred formulae than to the performance of meritorious actions.

Simultaneously it abandoned the philosophical rigour of primitive Buddhism for religiousness of a more popular type. But in doing so it became more human, more well-disposed and helpful to humanity; it no longer misanthropically, though for the most sublime motives, turned its back on life. Thus the ideal of the *arhat* ("the worthy"), preoccupied with his own individual liberation, his own escape from the world of *samsara* into *nirvana*, gave way to the active, compassionate, warm-hearted principle of the *Bodhisattva* ("he whose essence is enlightenment"). A *Bodhisattva* is a being who has reached the stage of perfection and is on the point of escaping for ever from *samsara,* but deliberately renounces *nirvana* to remain among his fellow-men, who are still the slaves of ignorance, desire and attachment to sensuality and illusion, to help them to attain the final goal.

As for the scriptures, Mahayanic Buddhism always maintained the doctrine of multiple revelation. Men are diverse, and times are diverse. What may be suitable for one individual in one social environment at one level of education may be of no use to another individual a hundred years later or a thousand miles away. The traditional scriptures (those accepted by the *Hinayana*) are undoubtedly genuine, but the Buddha preserved more profound or difficult doctrines for other times, and gnosis, or direct knowledge of spiritual mysteries (*prajna*), for the elect. It was thus that it was possible for the works of a Nagarjuna or a Vasubhandu (two of the greatest thinkers of Asia) to exercise so much influence and obtain so much agreement across the centuries. The acceptance of this progressive principle, opening the way to every conceivable development of thought, unquestionably gave the *Mahayana* a metaphysical vitality, a lasting power of seeing new visions, creating new myths and making fresh imaginative excursions, fresh plunges into the realm of psychological introspection, while the *Hinayana* remained secluded, conservative, traditionalist in a time without duration.

By the first centuries of the Christian era Mahayanic Buddhism can be said to have become completely unrecognizable. Innumerable celestial Buddhas, together with demons, giants, heroes and saints, competed for the favour of the religious. The category of *Bodhisattva*s had been enormously enriched, both "from below" (human beings who had become divine) and "from above" (terrestrial manifestations of celestial Buddhas). Thus the transition from agnosticism to theism had been completed by a further transition to polytheism, idolatry and demonology. Every Buddhist doctrine had been radically transformed including the doctrine of *karma*, for example. The universe was now peopled with gods, who had all the characteristics of human beings. They had wills and feelings, could be moved or offended, could change their minds, punish or forgive. That being the case, they could be propitiated, and prayer and sacrifice had acquired a value. *Karma* was no longer the impassive, immutable, practically physical law that it was in primitive Buddhism. Doctrines of grace and forgiveness arose. *Karma* actually ended by becoming transferable, and there arose the conception of a collective *karma*, in which the merits of a *Bodhisattva* served to wipe out the deeds of sinners.

In short, while the *Hinayana* takes as its starting point the immediate world of suffering and change (*samsara*) and then considers an absolute (*nirvana*), the *Mahayana* takes its departure from the Absolute, the empyrean of eternal Buddhas and archetypal ideas, and descends to *samsara*, a world that is pale, dim and unreal in the light of ultra-terrestrial perfection. The *Mahayana* therefore imagines a whole series of states intermediary between the Absolute and the immediate world of everyday experience. Every one of the celestial Buddhas in whom the unity and immutability of the Absolute is reflected has three primary manifestations. He has his own ideal form as the Logos (*dharma-kaya*); he has a form of perceptible perfection (*sambhoga-kaya*); and finally he has a terrestrial, phenomenal body (*nirmana-kaya*).

At this point there took place the third and final stage of Buddhist evolution, under the influence of the philosophy set out in the Tantras, the sacred books of the cult of Siva, dating from the sixth and seventh centuries A.D. The *Mahayana* had grown gradually out of the *Hinayana*, and the *Vajrayana* (Adamantine Vehicle) now developed out of the *Mahayana* in the same way. The Tantras are the final fruit of Sanskrit literature; fruit so over-ripe, so heavy with scent and sweetness, that it is on the point of turning into poison and putrefaction. They can be said to be the final triumph of autochthonous India, the dark, mysterious India of jungles and snakes, female deities and orgies, phallic cults and magical practices, over the serene Aryan India, the Himalayan India of pastures, cattle, epic poems and patriarchs.

In form the Tantras consist of dialogues between Siva and his Female Energy, who has many names, one of which is Durga ("the Inaccessible"). Nominally they deal with the Five Great Themes (the creation of worlds, the destruction of worlds, religion, the acquisition of supernatural powers, and union with the Absolute). Actually they are mainly concerned with ritual matters, mystical and magic ways of acquiring occult powers, the use and meaning of formulae and enchantments, the uses of letters of the alphabet, esoteric diagrams and talismans, and the symbolism of gestures (*mudra*).

The philosophy of the Tantras is fundamentally a pantheistic monism. Its essential postulate is the identity of the self and the Absolute. To state it as simply as possible, the universe is pervaded and permeated by a single spirit, a single secret and profound power. It is therefore the ascetic's task to turn it to his advantage. Here there arises the connection between philosophy and yoga. There is not only identity between the spiritual self and the universe, but between the body as microcosm and the universe as macrocosm. Truth is not a thing to be learned, but a thing to be lived; it must become an inner physical experience, a trance. The ascetic therefore aims, not just at evoking and dominating the secret forces that govern the universe, but at making himself one with them. Long and complicated rituals, lifting him from one mystical level to the next, enable him finally to identify himself for a short time with the divinity invoked.

An idea typical of the Tantras is that of the Energy which a god emanates; it becomes something external and objective, and ends by incarnating itself in a female body (*shakti*). Metaphysically a *shakti* is the line of force according to which the One, the Absolute, differentiates itself and acts. A *shakti* is generally represented as engaged in a carnal embrace with the god who generated her and has become her mate. This orgiastic symbolism became enormously popular, and initiates read innumerable meanings into it. Perhaps the most widespread and best-known interpretation is that the male divinity represents *karuna*, compassion, while the female stands for *prajna*, gnosis, or perfect knowledge. Gnosis means a lightning intuition of the truth which leads to liberation, but that is nothing if it is not intimately united with the active, altruistic force of compassion, which causes him who knows and sees to immolate and sacrifice himself for him who does not know and does not see. Such unity can only adequately be represented by the symbolism of a lovers' union. That is what the eye of the initiate reads into the amorous embrace which confronts him on the altar.

Another thing emphasized in the Tantras is the terrifying aspect assumed by benevolent deities in order to combat and overcome the powers of evil. Many lamaist divinities are as frequently represented in their terrifying aspect (*tro-wo*) as in their pacific aspect (*shi-wo*).

Our path is now complete. It was this Buddhism of the Adamantine Vehicle which penetrated into Tibet, and still reigns undisputed there today. This makes less unintelligible the profound contrast between the interior world of the Tibetans and the crystalline splendour of their natural surroundings. Tibet is like a living museum. In the darkness of the Tibetan temples there still survives the India which was transplanted there more than a thousand years ago. It is an invisible jungle of the spirit, invisibly fossilized among the ice.

I have thus tried very briefly to summarize the life of the Buddha and what can reasonably be supposed to have been his teaching, as well as the transformations which it underwent before it was introduced into Tibet. (Its introduction was chiefly due to the efforts of Padma Sambhava, in the eighth century A.D.) I shall now try to give a picture of the universe as it might appear to the mind of a Tibetan, restricting myself to the figures of primary importance in the lamaist empyrean. The picture I shall give is a simplification, and the beliefs I shall describe should not be taken to be dogma. There is a Tibetan proverb which says:

Lung-pa re re, ke-lu re,	Every village its own dialect,
Lama re re, chö-lu re.	Every lama his own doctrine.

Every teacher, every school of thought, has a private point of view on all these problems.

The internal impulse of Buddhism towards more and more distinctly theistic forms had been working itself out through the centuries along two substantially different lines. On the one hand there was the popular trend continually to accept and incorporate new protective deities, new demons and new furies into their mythology. On the other there was the philosophical trend, which one way or another had necessarily to culminate in an absolute, uncreated primary essence. It seems to me to be a matter of surprise that the complete fulfilment of this process was delayed until the tenth century of our era, when it was finally achieved by various Nepalese schools. Perhaps it shows how profoundly rooted agnosticism was in Buddhism – the belief that the ultimate reality of the universe lay in the physics of *karma*.

The Nepalese schools finally gave a name to the One, the External, the Uncreated, the *svayambhu* ("the Existing-for-Himself"). They called him the Adi Buddha, or first Buddha. An Adi Buddha is commonly accepted in present-day Tibet; but a different personality, at any rate a different superficial personality, is attributed to him by each of the three most important sects.

The *Gelug-pa* ("the Virtuous"), those of the Yellow Sect, so-called because of the colour of their hats, identify the Adi Buddha as Vajradhara, ("He who holds the lightning", in Tibetan *Dorje-chang*), "the indestructible lord of all mysteries, the master of all secrets". Vajradhara, is represented in a sitting position, wearing a jewelled crown and the clothing of a young Indian prince. As symbols he holds a thunderbolt and a mystical bell in the attitude known as *vajra-hum-kara*. He is often shown united with his *shakti*, Prajnāpāramitā ("Perfect Gnosis").

According to the Kar-gyu-pa lamas ("Those of the oral tradition"), the Adi Buddha is Vajrasattva ("Whose essence is light" – the Tibetan equivalent is *Dorje-sempa*), a metaphysical personality very similar to Vajradhara, represented in art in very much the same way. However, the *Nima-pa* sects ("the Ancient Ones") consider a very different figure to be the Adi Buddha, namely Samantabhadra ("Universal Kindness"), who is pictured as completely naked and coloured dark blue, embracing his *shakti*, who is also naked, but white.

It is truly an impressive experience to penetrate into the stuffy and venerable darkness of a temple, where the silence seems to be a positive thing, having a solidity and a consistency of its own, and there, in its innermost depths, on a golden altar, among dragons, lotus flowers, brocades, peacock feathers, the flickering of butter burning in tiny cups, and butter worked into elaborate shapes and patterns for offerings, to find oneself face to face with the Absolute, the Ultimate, the First, the Eternal, the Everlasting and the All-pervading, in the form of a bejewelled prince voluptuously embracing his own *shakti*. What fantastic imagination, what metaphysical daring, to represent the most abstract possible concept, a concept only definable by negatives, like mathematical infinity, by the most concrete, the most carnal picture that it is possible to imagine; to symbolize that which is without beginning and without end by that which is par excellence ephemeral and fugitive; to identify extreme serenity with extreme passion, the crystal light of the stars with the fire of love, the invisible and the intangible with the intoxication of all the senses; and to recall the oneness of the universe – to awareness of which the mind only rarely attains, as a result of a supreme effort, in a flash of illumination – by a representation of the moment in which thought is completely annihilated.

On the one hand, then, we have the adamantine purity of the Adi Buddha, on the other *samsara*, the transient, uncertain, painful, irrational world. But between these two extremes there are intermediary, transitional phases. The first step between the One and the multiple, between being and becoming, is the differentiation of the Adi Buddha into his five manifestations or reflections, the Five *Dhyani* Buddhas ("Buddhas of meditation"). These exist motionless, meditating, almost like Platonic ideas, archetypes of the real, in their "body of the law" (*dharma-kaya*), in entirely immaterial form.[2]

Each *Dhyani* Buddha presides over one of the five epochs of the world (*kalpa*). Each of these epochs lasts for thousands of years; the number varies from school to school. Three *kalpa*s have now passed, and we are now in the fourth. From each of the five *Dhyani* Buddhas there emanate one of the five colours, one of the five elements, one of the five senses and one of the five vowels. Each presides over a point of space, is seated on his own mystic animal, has his own mystic symbol and his own mystic flower, and has his hands arranged in a mystic gesture. All the elements which, according to Indian thought, constitute the universe, all the immutable germs of the mutable and of becoming, originate from one of the *Dhyani* Buddhas. The colours and the physical elements are as important as the senses and the syllables; macrocosm and microcosm turn out to be interchangeable, to be projections of one another, phases, moments of the identical All.

The *Dhyani* Buddhas are represented as ascetics, monks, unadorned, without tiaras or jewels; they are seated in the adamantine position, the position of most profound meditation. Very rarely they are represented as united with their own Energies (*shakti*). When this occurs, they are represented as richly adorned, with all the attributes of royalty.

The *Dhyani* Buddhas represent the first stage in the cosmic process of differentiation; they are static, and stand for the thought and order behind the multiple universe. The next stage is the stage of dynamic creation, represented by the *Dhyani Bodhisattva*s. Each *Dhyani* Buddha generates a *Dhyani Bodhisattva*, and each *Dhyani Bodhisattva* creates a universe, a samsaric universe, over which he presides. The *Dhyani Bodhisattva*s exist in "bodies of absolute completeness" (*sambhoga-kaya*), and are therefore represented in adorned form, with all the attributes, ornaments and sumptuous clothes of princes. Each has his own Energy (*shakti*), but is rarely pictured with her. The *Dhyani Bodhisattva*s often assume their terrifying form, which is perfectly consonant with their nature. A *Dhyani Bodhisattva* is Buddahood in action; his terrifying form indicates his full participation in *samsara* as a militant hero engaged in the conquest of evil. In his pacific form he is *karuna* itself, benevolent compassion and compassionate benevolence; the hand stretched out to help all living things to guide them to liberation.

The last stage, a most important one, is that in which the Absolute puts on flesh and blood and comes down to live and suffer among men. Once in every *kalpa*, or epoch, each *Dhyani* Buddha generates a *Manushi* Buddha, a terrestrial Buddha, who appears among mankind as a gentle, yet glorious, prince of the faith and with his inspired words and the fascinating example of his life provides enlightenment for those who do not yet see, converts heretics and liberates the slaves of desire and attachment from the tyranny of their own selves. A *Manushi* Buddha, according to one ancient doctrine, is nothing but appearance, as his body is a *nirmana-kaya*, a "phenomenal body" only, an illusion; his real essence is truth, law, the adamantine nature of the Adi Buddha. This doctrine is distinctly reminiscent of that of the Docetae, who maintained more or less the same proposition with respect to the body of Christ in the early centuries of Christianity.

Thus each of the five great ages (*kalpa*) into which the history of the universe is thought of as being divided is conceived in the mind of a *Dhyani* Buddha, is created by a *Dhyani Bodhisattva*, and is blessed by the apostolate of a

95 *Tibetan book, closed (above) and open (below)*

Manushi Buddha. Pictures of the *Dhyani* Buddha, the *Dhyani Bodhisattva* and the *Manushi* Buddha of our own fourth epoch may be inspected on the next page. It is worth while impressing them on one's mind, because we shall meet them over and over again wherever we go in Tibet – in art, literature, religion, everyday life, past history and present-day politics.

The most striking thing about all this is the strange destiny of Gautama, the Buddha. All the historical evidence points to the fact that throughout his terrestrial life he preached a courageous, rigorous, agnostic philosophy based on a grim diagnosis of the innermost nature of man, denying the soul and binding all that he feels to be most human and most sacred, all the good and all the evil of which he is capable, to the mysterious thread of *karma*. Throughout his life he sought to disillusion men, to liberate them from their false faith in gods, and to lead them back to looking into themselves and to feeling themselves to be the masters of their fate. Yet here we see him transformed into the emanation of an emanation of an emanation – a god in a fantastically elaborate and complicated system of other gods, a celestial actor in a stupendous, cosmic drama, preceded by others and followed by others.

Category	*Sanskrit name*	*Tibetan name*	*Usual Aspect*	*Notes*
Dhyani Buddha	Amitābha	Ö-pa-me		Incarnated in the Panchen Lama
Dhyani Bodhisattva	Avalokitesvara	Chen-re-zi		Incarnated in the Dalai Lama
Manushi Buddha	Sakya-Muni	Sakya-Thupa		The Prince Siddhartha of history, who became the ascetic Gautama

96 *The Buddhas of the Fourth Epoch, the present*

1 Edward J. Thomas's translation in *Early Buddhist Scriptures*, London, Routledge, 1935

2 The term *Dhyani* Buddha is nowadays no longer in use. Alternatives are *Tathagata* or Supreme Buddha. It is a question of terminology, not of substance.

16

Notes on Tibetan History

From the kings who descend from the heavens
to the commissars who come up from the plain

The last forty years of the history of the Tibetan people have been tragic, a continuous chain of sorrows. The uninstructed visitor who travels the country will wonder: what is the reason for these persecutions? Why this unleashing of such visceral hatreds? To clarify the matter it is necessary to give a quick glance at Tibetan history.

Let us leave aside prehistoric and the earliest history of Tibet; it could be of great interest but we know very little about it.[1] We shall establish one point of importance, however: the earliest Tibetans were called Ch'iang/Qiang by the Chinese, and belonged to a race that was basically not all that different from the Chinese. In their physical appearance (both belonging to the Mongol race), and in particular in their language (Chinese and Tibetan spring from the same family even though they are mutually incomprehensible), the Ch'iang/Qiang and their descendants the Tibetans embark on their career in history from a position very little removed from that of the Chinese. The two peoples' prehistoric roots undoubtedly have something in common.

In the pages that follow we shall see the development of a process of progressive separation, the increasingly conspicuous distancing of the one tribe from the other. The fifteen centuries or so of Tibetan history we know about constitute, save for certain particular moments, a continual and ever more notable alienation from the Chinese, not so much in political as in cultural and religious terms. This brings us to the present situation in which the two peoples, however similar in physiognomy and speech, are radically different in the way they think, in their vision of life and the world, in their most intimate scales of values, in a word in all that constitutes the most jealously preserved spiritual heredity of a people, a race, a nation.

One might arrive at not dissimilar conclusions in considering two great European nations, the French and the Germans. Originally the Franks appeared in the West as a conglomerate of Germanic tribes akin to the Alemanni, the Teutons, the Longobards, the Angles and so on. Once they had migrated into

Gaul, conquered it and settled there, they ended up not only adopting a neo-Latin tongue but underwent a cultural leavening nourished by both Roman and Celtic elements which was so deep that fifteen centuries later, on the occasion of certain disastrous crises in Europe, they were able to confront the Germans, who were now so glaringly different from them, as foursquare, inflexible opponents. And it was not just a question of armies doing battle: it was civilization vs Kultur, two visions of the world locked in battle. That is precisely what is happening today on the roof of the world.

The kingdom (c.600–850)[2]

Tibet appears almost unexpectedly in the history of Asia as a small state vigorously expanding under the royal dynasty of Yarlung (the name comes from the place of origin of the tribe, in a valley some two hundred kilometres south-east of Lhasa). The Yarlung dynasty, like the Japanese one of the same era, claimed descent from Heaven: both dynasties offered the world a gaudy genealogical tree taking them back in remote times to their divine ancestors. For the Japanese, the descent to earth took place in 660 B.C., for the Tibetans, about a hundred years later. Needless to say, in Tibet as in Japan we are talking of myths and legends; the historical events evoked in these narratives, the establishment of a kingdom and a state, may perhaps be situated in both cases around the first centuries of the Common Era.

In Tibet at the start of the seventh century we come upon a person who is authentically historical, King Namri-songtsen, who extended his rule over most of the high plateau and south to the Himalayas. His son Songtsen-gampo (569–649) is considered the true founder of Tibet as a power. The date of birth has been widely debated; our greatest living Tibetologist, Luciano Petech, inclines towards 569 and we support him. A more recent date of 629 is considered by many to be his date of birth but is more likely to be the opening year of his reign. Songtsen-gampo was extremely active and took decisions which have remained relevant to our own day. Not only did he extend and consolidate the kingdom inherited from his father, not only did he reorganize and centralize the administration, but he transferred the capital from Yarlung to Lhasa. In 635 he married a Nepalese princess (Bhrikuti Devi) and in 641, after long and difficult negotiations with the Imperial court, a Chinese princess (Wen Ch'eng). Apparently the two princely brides brought with them to Tibet the first rudiments of Buddhist worship, the sacred scriptures, religious images; one of them possessed, according to popular tradition, the deeply venerated image still to be found in the Jokhang temple (Lhasa's "cathedral").[3]

In those days the religion practised in Tibet and recognized by the state consisted of a very elaborate form of shamanism, usually identified as Bon (or Pon, or Pön). Within the context of this religion the king occupied a highly sacred position, of sovereign charisma. From this angle the Tibetan Bon of the time could have had notable points of similarity with the corresponding Japanese cult later known as Shinto.

Regrettably we know all too little about the cultural, and in particular the religious, conditions at this period which was so influential in the development of Tibet. The histories of the country were often so lavish in detail but had not yet been written; they came a great deal later, after the almost total victory of Buddhism, and were written by learned, well-meaning monks who obviously saw in the past no matter for scientific enquiry but perfect occasions to indulge in sentimental hagiography or religious propaganda. In particular, King Songtsen-gampo and his two wives were picked out and raised to the altars as holy apostles of Tibetan Buddhism. In Lhasa the Potala and Jokhang are adorned in a number of places with famous groups of gilded sculptures representing the king and his devout wives. Songtsen-gampo is considered to be the incarnation of the *Bodhisattva* Avalokitesvara; he is represented with a tiny head of the supreme Buddha Amitābha (whose manifestation in contact with the world is considered to be Avalokitesvara/Chen-re-zi) crowning his royal turban. In other words Songtsen-gampo is considered to prefigure the Dalai Lama.

Well, this is all most poetic, and undoubtedly served to bind the masses to the pontifical throne, but it still leaves us in the land of legend, not of history. Both Tucci and other eminent scholars have often expressed their doubts as to the degree to which Buddhism had penetrated Tibet during the reign of Songtsen-gampo. It is possible that it was practised in some limited form at court, but otherwise the chances are that the indigenous religion, which may not yet have been known by the name of Bon, held unopposed sway in matters of faith and liturgical practice. Important Tibetan documents from the eighth century, found at Tun-Huang/Dunhuang, the eastern starting point of the Silk Road, have been recently translated[4] and give a picture of the kingdom that looks quite different from the traditional one depicted by the Buddhists. We find Bon priests, shamans and soothsayers, animal sacrifices, and evidently human as well in exceptional circumstances such as a king's funeral – a picture of religion and culture that would horrify the pacific vegetarian Buddhists of later eras. The world in which Songtsen-gampo ("the Constantine of Buddhism") lived was thus purified of such iniquities and its history was rewritten with conspicuous distortions due to a sort of instinctive censorship.

Among Songtsen-gampo's many initiatives there was one no doubt deemed at the time to be of little importance but which turned out to have remarkable consequences for the future. We have arrived at the first of four crucial moments in the loosening of ties with China: it involved sending to India, at the king's command, a delegation of young scholars led by the famous minister Thonmi Sambhota, with the task of adapting to Tibetan use one of the many writing systems employed by Indian scholars. All the peoples with whom Tibet entertained relations, Indians, Iranians, Chinese, inhabitants of the city-states of Central Asia, had long ago developed their own scripts. Songtsen-gampo clearly understood that if he wanted his state, which was now extensive and powerful, to be properly governed, he needed to teach his subjects to record sounds by means of signs, to invest thought with a material basis that was incon-trovertible, permanent, easy to transmit in time and space. A few years later Thonmi Sambhota returned to Tibet – on his own, it would seem, having lost his companions in the course of the venturesome expedition – carrying with him an ingenious and elegant lexicon that he had elaborated on the model of Brahmi and Gupta script; these were current in the foothills of the Himalayas, and were not too far removed from the script used in Sanskrit and Indian classic texts.

In theory Songtsen-gampo's minister might have spared himself the journey to India by studying Chinese ideograms and adapting them to his own tongue. As we have seen, Tibetan is not far removed from Chinese; the basic monosyllabic structure is clearly evident while declensions and inflections are scarce. The choice was evidently determined by quite different considerations. Perhaps Songtsen-gampo wanted to maintain a respectful distance from China, an altogether too vast, rich, crowded, armed and aggressive country, to make a shrewd approach to India, which was just as civilized but not so formidable, and anyway less concerned with what went on up on the high plateau behind them. Certainly neither the king nor his ministers could imagine what colossal importance this choice of theirs would have down the centuries, restricted as it appeared to be to a limited field of cultural endeavour.

The fact remains that the adoption of one writing system in preference to another does not boil down purely to a question of semiotic technique. We are confronting a fundamental decision in the life of a people; it is a case of a true marriage attended by a cultural convergence, indeed conversions and bondings as unforeseen as inevitable. What is more, the writing system eventually adopted ends by exercising an aesthetic domination over the entire cultural landscape, attaching itself emotionally to the most living and sensitive nucleus of the ethnic, national and religious heredity. One has only to think of how Gothic followed and fertilized the spirit of Germany, in many cases the spirit of Protestantism, or to think of the notable and irreplaceable situation of the ideogram in Chinese and Japanese civilization – not to mention the close relationship between Arabic script and the Koran, Hebraic script and the Torah. One has only to think of the way in which Catholicism is attended by the Latin alphabet and Orthodoxy by the Cyrillic one. The most extensive language of the Indian sub-continent is substantially a single one and is called Urdu and written with Arabic characters when employed by the Pakistanis or other Muslim groups, while it is called Hindi and follows the Devanagari lexicon when employed by the Hindus. Not for nothing did Kemal Ataturk, meaning to break with the past and bring his country into closer contract with Europe, replace Arabic with Latin characters in 1924. And not for nothing is the nationalistic interest within Turkey now reasserting itself and pressing for a return to the characters formerly in use. Lastly, while pursuing this line of thought: much as Cyrillic was a tool in the hands of the Soviet government to Russify the various populations of its vast empire, so do the alternative alphabets function as a banner of resistance for those who resent such a process – for instance the Latin alphabet for the Baltic nations, the Georgian and Armenian for the peoples of the Caucasus.[5]

It is interesting here to note a parallel (and a contrast) that bring Tibet and Japan into contact once again. While the Japanese, starting from a language fundamentally different from Chinese, being Altaic in the matter of grammar and syntax, Malay-Polynesian in terms of phonetics and certain aspects of its vocabulary, have chosen the use of ideograms, thus entering into a close cultural correlation with China, the Tibetans, starting from a linguistic structure in common with the Chinese, have opted for a phonetic, syllabic script of Indian origin, thus turning their backs on the Far East and immersing themselves in the spiritual world of the south. In both cases nature has had its hand forced, the chromosomatic dowry of the language was betrayed.

To enter the syllabic orbit, to reject the ideogram signified for the Tibetans redirecting the new-born culture of their nation towards the sources of metaphysics, faiths, wisdom, literature and arts of India and shut their door in the face of the Chinese tradition. The weight of this change of direction has been felt down the centuries to the present day; indeed it is today that the consequences are singularly dramatic. At Lhasa and elsewhere in Tibet, beneath our very eyes, the ideogram and the Tibetan lexicon often confront each other like two banners, graphical and symbolic quintessences of two worlds in collision.

Add two factors that are of considerably greater moment than they might seem. Ideographic characters have for centuries followed a vertical alignment and a development that starts on the right and moves towards the left; Tibetan writing, on the other hand, has always developed along horizontal lines, starting from the left and moving towards the right. The influence of the Chinese vertical alignment has been profound on the bordering states; Mongol and Manchurian, although written phonetically, are both laid out on the page in vertical lines. Such graphical magnetism has never been felt at all in Tibetan writing.

Lastly, Chinese literary works are inscribed either on rolls or in books whose pages are turned from right to left; Tibetan literary works follow the Indian model, originally set down on palm-leaves like packets of pages clamped together between stiff covers made of wood or other material. In a word, the entire basis of Tibetan culture is radically different from the Chinese one in terms of the materials employed.

The immediate successors of Songtsen-gampo continued the work of territorial expansion started by the first kings, and greatly extended the boundaries of Tibetan suzerainty with rapid military campaigns which quite disoriented the enemy; one could now speak not so much of a kingdom as of a true empire whose frontiers extended from present-day Afghanistan to the western provinces of China, and from Bengal to the foot of the Altai ranges in Central Asia. The Tibetan empire reached its apogee under the great Tisong-detsen (755–797). At a certain point, in 763, his army was for a short while in occupation of the Chinese capital at the time, Ch'ang-an/Chang'an.

But Tisong-detsen was not only pre-eminent as a military leader of the Tibetans; he was a virtually tireless promoter of Buddhism, in which he saw not simply a great universal religion capable of uniting men of differing races, languages and traditions, but an extraordinary cultural vehicle. At a certain moment, maybe in 779, he proclaimed it the official state religion. Of course this missionary campaign was not without its political motivations: in making himself the champion of the new faith the king armed himself with a strong spiritual lever in his ongoing struggles with the leading aristocratic families, who backed the Bon shamans.

With the intention of spreading the new religion throughout the country Tisong-detsen sent to India first for the master Shantirakshita, who encountered some difficulties in converting the rustic mountain folk to the king, then for the master and miracle-worker Padma Sambhava, who for his part met with instant and spectacular success. Padma Sambhava represented perhaps the ideal apostle of Buddhism among an extremely primitive and violent people as the Tibetans then still were. More than a master of spirituality and asceticism, he was a mindboggling miracle-worker with a clever knack for slaking the thirst for prodigies, miraculous cures, shamanic oracles, impressive prophecies, so prevalent among the shepherds, peasants and merchants of the high plateau. Padma Sambhava's Buddhism was, furthermore, subtly linked to practices of mystic sexuality that many could interpret as boldly symbolic, while others could take them literally, and to which in any event the Tibetans were drawn, convivial, pleasure-loving, impetuous as they were, not to say insatiable.

Padma Sambhava is represented even today not as a monk or a penitential ascetic but as a prince in an orgiastic ecstasy, dressed in golden apparel, much bejewelled, with a halo of prodigious rainbows, accompanied by his many

97 *Padma Sambhava*

faithful ladies, and two in particular, Mandarava and Yeshe Tsogyal. Padma Sambhava brought with him a Buddhism conceived of a magical power, domination of the elements, irresistible knowledge of spells. Popular tradition asserts that Padma Sambhava converted the myriad demons that were infesting Tibet, turning them into champions of the faith. Padma Sambhava's religion was later to be overtaken by that of reformers like Atisha, Sakya Pandita, Buton-Rimpoche and especially Tsonghkapa (1357–1419), but his influence remains visible in the Tibetan arts of every confession, style and era, arts wherein is expressed an age-old irrepressible love for the grisly, the cruel, the terrifying, often combined with clearly erotic motifs.[6]

For Padma Sambhava Tisong-detsen built the great shrine of Samye, south of Lhasa – shamefully destroyed by the fanatics of the Cultural Revolution, and recently rebuilt. This brings us to the second determining moment for Tibet. It seems that the ritualistic, miracle-working Buddhism based on texts known as Tantra, which Padma Sambhava was presenting to the Tibetans, was strongly opposed by many masters particularly those of Chinese origin, who championed a style of religion not greatly different, it might be said, from that being developed in China under the name of Chan, and which was to become very popular in Japan under the name of Zen. At this point the king summoned a council, the Council of Lhasa, which assembled partly at Samye, partly at Lhasa, in the years 792–794. The Indian masters, led by that eloquent barrack-room lawyer Kamalasila, swept the board: their Chinese opponents had to leave Tibet and return home discomfited. Evidently there were scenes of violence among the onlookers, just as occur in our present-day football matches! Here too we are confronted with a fact which may appear trivial but was, in the long term, absolutely crucial. "Tibet thus entered once and for all into the Indian sphere of cultural influence."[7]

After the death of Tisong-detsen (797) there was a rapid decay which became a disaster when King Lang-darma (838–842) – a Julian the Apostate of Tibet – tried to return to the ancestral faith, Bon, and set in train a very harsh persecution of the Buddhists, religious and lay. Lang-darma was eventually assassinated by a monk in disguise (842), and the Yarlung dynasty died out a few years later amid civil strife. Heirs of the royal house did, however, found two important kingdoms in western Tibet: the kingdom of Guge (that lasted until 1630), and that of Ladakh (that retained its independence until 1842) and which to this day survives as a cultural Little-Tibet on the extreme edge of Indian Kashmir.

Crisis and rebirth (850–1200)

From the end of the Kingdom, for the whole of the tenth and into the eleventh centuries Tibet lapsed into a dark age. Bon reacquired to some degree its erstwhile hold, but lacked a central authority, a state to support it. Much of the country was in the hands of local chiefs who ruled their patches in a framework of total anarchy. As for Buddhism, it managed to cling on somehow in eastern Tibet. Around 1000 and during the eleventh century there were the first signs of a religious and civil revival. Tibetan Buddhists look back on this period as the one in which "a second spread of the faith took place". Celebrated Tibetan masters, like Rinchen-tsangpo (958–1054), settled for a long period in India and came back with many sacred texts already translated or to be translated; and Indian holy men, like Atisha (982–1054) for example, travelled up into Tibet bringing the light of their own teachings and new, much stricter monastic rules. In these exchanges the benefactors were largely the Guge kings.

The rebirth of Tibetan Buddhism largely coincided with the tragic, irremediable collapse of Buddhism in India. Soon after 1000, under the leadership of Mahmud of Ghazni (998–1030), there was the start of incursions by Muslim bands who swooped down from the Afghan mountains, where Islam was already well established; with time this led to the definitive conquest by Islam of a great part of northern India. The Muslims, a people who in those days were short on piety and long on savagery, were prepared to spare the People of the Book (Jews and Christians), but considered everyone else to be pagans only fit for slaughter, for eradication. Obviously it was not possible to purge the world of the boundless multitudes of Indians, so in time they arrived at various forms of co-habitation. In this unstable peace the Hindus secured their position well enough thanks to the many links their religion maintained with the Brahmin caste and the family in general. Buddhism, on the other hand, was fundamentally linked to the prosperity of the monasteries, to the community of religious. When the savage invaders put the renowned monastic universities – Nalanda, Vikramasila, Odantapuri, etc. – to fire and the sword Buddhism was mortally wounded. Indeed during these centuries of continuing violence Buddhism, targeted by the Muslims, driven to the wall by renascent Hinduism, was to vanish almost completely from India.

Which brings us to the third defining moment in the process of alienating Tibet from China. Most of the Indian Buddhists, including many great masters, preferred to forsake their country, which was now dominated by intolerant fanatics, and seek refuge in the Himalayan mountains, or in Tibet itself. The migratory push went hand in hand with the vigorous rebirth of Buddhism in Tibet. This was a time when a great many masters of outstanding intellect were flourishing – Marpa (1012–1096), Milarepa (1040–1123), Gampo-pa (1079–1153), Bronton (1005–1064), and not long after Phamodru (1118–1170) and later still Buton-Rimpoche (1290–1364). In this period the links between Tibet and India became even closer and more intimate, warmer and more fruitful. With the gradual disappearance of Buddhism from India, the Tibetans came to feel the true, legitimate heirs of every authentic Buddhist tradition. The religion of Gautama was dying in India but surviving in Tibet. Just as Byzantium was the second Rome, Lhasa could call itself the second Bhodgaya.

The abbots of Sakya (1200–1350)

In this period of intense intellectual activity and disastrous political disarray, Tibetan Buddhism began to acquire many of its singular characteristics. Various schools, various sects, for instance, began to take recognizable shape; they organized themselves, and acquired each one a distinctive form of philosophical doctrine, ascetic discipline, monastic rules, liturgy and customs. As a rule each of the large monasteries depended on a renowned master for the one part and on a powerful family for the other. Such families exercised a sort of patronage over the foundation, protecting it by force of arms and deriving prestige from it at the same time.

Those who remained faithful to the teachings of Padma Sambhava, who were not a few, ended by constituting themselves the church of "the Ancients" (Ni-ma-pa), in contradistinction to the rest. Atisha was the founder of a highly important line of masters, whose followers were called *Kadam-pa*; later on this school, once reformed by Tsongkhapa, emerged into the powerful church of the *Gelug-pa* ("the Virtuous"), and into the dynasty of the Dalai Lama. Prince Kongchog-gyalpo founded a great monastery in 1073, that of the Sakya, which was destined to achieve sovereign importance. Naropa, Marpa, Milarepa, Gampo-pa were some of the famous patriarchs of the *Kargyu-pa* sect which flourishes to this day, and produced several offshoots.

At the beginning of the thirteenth century it looked as if Genghis Khan meant to occupy Tibet, but changed his mind in view of other military campaigns pressing him. In 1239, a few years after his death, the Mongols under Goden, a descendant of Genghis Khan, returned to the charge. Tibetan nobles and monks, cowed by the threat, engaged the abbot of the monastery of Sakya, the celebrated Lama Kunga Gyaltsen (1182–1251) to negotiate with the dangerous invaders. From the beginning of the thirteenth century Sakya had become a great centre of power, political as well as religious, overcoming the influence of the rival organization, the *Karma-pa*. The abbots of Sakya were renowned for being capable and astute men in government rather than learned and ascetic prelates – the more so because they married and maintained a splendid court.

Kunga Gyaltsen (also known as Sakya Pandita) played his hand with consummate mastery. Not only did he succeed in holding the Mongols at bay, but with great self-possession he ceded to the sovereigns of the north a protectorate over the country, then had them appoint him their deputy and representative: in a word he became to all intents and purposes a theocratic viceroy of Tibet under the aegis of the distant rulers of the steppes. A little later (1260) the Mongols conquered China and the position of the *Sakya-pa* became all the more important and assured. The collaboration between Kublai Khan and Phags-pa (1235–1280), descendant of Kunga-gyaltsen, and renowned superior of the Sakya, marked the culmination of these remarkable prelates in their splendour, truly prince-bishops in the land of the snows. Phags-pa contrived to have himself appointed *ti-she* (Imperial Preceptor), thus establishing a precedent for a special relationship between Tibetan pontiffs and Chinese sovereigns; this was to become the cornerstone of every claim made by Beijing to a protectorate over the territories and people of the mountains. The great lama of Sakya offered himself to the emperor as special intercessor for divine favours, and the Chinese emperor repaid him with a guarantee of earthly protection: obviously this compact carried with it certain limitations to the abbots' sovereignty, particularly in regard to relationships with other powers. The doctrine of the coupling between China and Tibet in the framework of a patron-guru relationship has continued to ferment over the centuries, and is often taken out and dusted even today, when assuredly no president, party secretary, or commissar feels the smallest need to go in search of mediators for heavenly intervention in the affairs of this world.

Prelates and Lords (fourteenth to seventeenth centuries)

From the second half of the fourteenth century the Mongol power declined, and as a consequence the Sakya abbots lost their grip over the greater part of Tibet; thenceforth they had to rest content with exercising a regal influence (that continued until 1959) only in part of the region of Tsang, where their principal monasteries were sited. The emperors of the Chinese Ming dynasty (1368–1644) frequently asserted in their edicts their protectorate over Tibet, effectively exercised by their Mongol predecessors; in practice there never were any military operations up in the mountains. For about three hundred years Tibet maintained its independence for all practical purposes, despite its lack of any central authority that was continuous and generally recognized.

This long period, whose limits cannot be readily established in time, and which anyway overlapped with the period that followed, presents a picture of persistent confusion. At one point it is a sect or certain monasteries that succeed in imposing themselves on a given area, at another it is a petty baron who conquers a small provincial fiefdom, passing it to his descendants over a number of generations, creating an obscure, minor dynasty. What we are looking at in fact is a Tibet made up of monastery-fortresses, castles, endless battles, sieges, destruction and reconstruction, in which both monks and layfolk are involved.

In the complicated plot of the chronicles of these centuries, three ascendancies may be noted[8] as signalling some measure of continuity, and embracing territories of conspicuous extent. The first to emerge, chronologically, were the Phamodru-pa abbots, secure in their great fortress-monastery of Densathil, south-east of Lhasa. The Phamodru-pa constituted a real power for almost a century (1350–1436), until internecine quarrels stopped its ascent and brought it low. Their inheritance passed in part to the nobility of the house of Rinpung, who were prominent from the mid-fifteenth to the mid-sixteenth centuries, and thence to the kings of Tsang, the region embracing Gyantse and Shigatse. For some decades it looked as though this ascendancy was destined to re-establish the ancient and illustrious kingdom of Tibet, but events were to take a quite different turn: a battle lost in 1642 spelled the end for them, while at the same time a new and unsuspected power had established itself.

The rise of the Gelug-pa (1400–1720)

In 1357 a not uncommon event occurred: a baby was born. The happy event occurred in the extreme north of Tibet, close to the banks of Lake Koko-nor (or Ch'ing-hai, or Qinghai); the boy was called Lobsang. A few years later Lobsang had become a monk and spent long periods of study in his country's most famous monasteries (Tshal, Sakya, Phamodru, Shalu, Jonang), making himself familiar with the doctrines of the various sects, giving evidence of extraordinary intelligence and remarkable gifts for organization. Coming as he did from a valley famous for its onions, he was given a curious nickname, Tsong-kha-pa, "Him from the land of the onions".

Within a few years Tsongkhapa rose to a position of eminence in the church of *Kadam-pa*, whose patriarchs included the great Atisha, and which he meant to reform radically. Tsongkhapa imposed on his followers the most rigorous celibacy, individual poverty, a vegetarian diet, and abstinence from alcohol; on account of this discipline, which was taken very seriously, the monks of the reformed *Kadam-pa* sect were called *Gelug-pa* (Models of Virtue). In effect a new church was born that was soon to become extremely powerful.

Tsongkhapa, who had already come to prominence for an erudite and inspired work, the *Lamrinchenmo* ("Synthesis of Doctrine"), achieved enormous popularity when in 1408 he instituted lavish festivities at Lhasa to celebrate the new year (Monlam-chenmo) in the cathedral of Jokhang; the tradition was to be continued with every respect for some five hundred years until 1959. Monks and laity venerated Tsongkhapa to the point of setting him on a pedestal and building in his honour the monastery of Galden (or Gaden), "The Happy Mountain", in 1409. This was destined to become a complete religious city, inhabited during certain periods of its long history by close to ten thousand religious, including brothers (*trapa*), masters, priests (*lama*), and theologians (*geshe*).[9] Two of Tsongkhapa's most famous disciples went on to found the monasteries of Drepung (or Depung) in 1416 and Sera in 1419. In 1447 the shrine of Tashilhumpo, near Shigatse, was added to this triad of great monasteries which survived as strongholds of the *Gelug-pa* until 1959.

Tsongkhapa's death led to a savage fight between the *Gelug-pa* (thenceforth known as "the Yellow ones" from the colour of their headgear) and the more ancient sects, generally called "Red", again from the dominant colour in their habits and headgear. "From the middle of the fifteenth century and for almost the next two hundred years the history of Tibet is the history of political and religious strife between the Yellow Sect and the various Red Sects (particularly the *Karma-pa*) for ascendancy in the land of the snows."[10]

There is little point in trying to follow this long and complex struggle as it developed. Rather I shall record one important particular. From very early times, perhaps the twelfth century, the custom had grown up among the monks of certain sects (the *Karma-pa* and the *Drikung-pa*) to provide for the succession of their abbots not by family inheritance or by election but through reincarnation; what they looked for was a boy who had been born shortly after the death of the departed dignitary in the belief that the soul of the venerable person could have returned to earth in the body of the child.[11] The system had a number of disadvantages, such as the long minority of the new chief, and occasions for error, but on the other hand it combined the virtues of election with those of co-optation, at the same time satisfying the exigencies of metempsychosis that subsisted in popular Buddhism. Tsongkhapa was succeeded by an able and energetic man, Gedun Truppa (1391–1475), founder of the monastery of Tashilhumpo. Gedun Truppa was succeeded by the Lama Gedun Gyatso (1475–1542), and it was generally accepted that in him the soul of his predecessor was reincarnated. It was only at this point, in 1475, that succession by reincarnation was adopted by the abbots of the *Gelug-pa* – each one of whom was for the moment styled Gyalwa Rimpoche ("Great Precious Sovereign").

The third abbot in the sequence, Sonam Gyatso (1543–1588) contrived to give the *Gelug-pa* immense prestige. Among other things, on meeting the Mongol prince Altan Khan in 1578 by Lake Koko-nor, he exercised such a fascination on the uncouth horsemen of the steppes as to convert a large number to Tibetan Buddhism. Altan Khan then wanted to give his new spiritual mentor the Mongol title of Dalai ("Ocean" "of Wisdom" being understood). Subsequently the title was accorded retrospectively to Gedun Truppa (who became the First Dalai), and to Gedun Gyatso (considered the Second). Thus Sonam Gyatso was identified in Tibetan history not as the First, as he ought to have been, but the Third Dalai Lama. Tsongkhapa, by now virtually deified as incarnation of Manjusri/Jampeyan, *Bodhisattva* of Mystical Wisdom (his symbols were a book and a sword), remained outside and above all of this.

When Sonam Gyatso died in 1588, his successor was discovered, with metaphysical diplomacy, among the grandsons of Altan Khan himself. Obviously from that point on the Mongol princes considered themselves the lawful protectors of the pontiffs in Lhasa. The happy child, on his twelfth birthday, was enthroned at Lhasa in the Potala as the Fourth Dalai Lama, under the name of Yonten Gyatso (1589–1616). A similar rapid growth in power of the Yellow Sect obviously aroused jealousies, both among the other sects and among the numerous semi-independent princelings of Tibet: their reaction was savage, and for a time it looked as if the *Gelug-pa* were destined to succumb to the intrigues and head-on assaults of their enemies.

Luckily for the sect, on the death of Yonten-Gyatso the choice fell on a child who in a few years was to reveal himself as a statesman of exceptional capabilities. This was Ngawang Lobsang Gyatso (1617–1682), the Fifth Dalai Lama, "the Great Fifth", as he was recorded by the Tibetans. Indeed his regents, during the pontiff's infancy and minority, had shown themselves to be very able men. The times were difficult and particular flair and energy was needed in order to be safe from attacks that were often unexpected. The protection of the Mongol princes offered an excellent shield, but in the boundless northern steppes there was an absence of unity and good order. Other chiefs, jealous of the Altan Khan's prestige and of that of his kin, descended on Lhasa with the excuse of protecting the Holy Father – and their visits looked more like brigand incursions than like devout faithful on pilgrimage.

No sooner turned twenty than the Great Fifth had to confront a new, fearsome "protector", Gushri Khan, head of the tribe known as Qoshot. By dint of clever footwork the young Dalai contrived to exercise his fascination to the full on the tough but barbarian lord of the steppes, both by virtue of his position of spiritual privilege, and by that of his personality, so much so that the meeting concluded in an alliance. Eastern Tibet, the Kham, where the Bon-po seemed still to exert a strong ascendancy, was fiercely ground down; likewise the province of Tsang was pacified. In 1642 Gushri Khan, now the master of most of Tibet, made a gift of his conquests to the Great Fifth. When Gushri Khan died in 1656 the Dalai Lama's dominions extended from Mount Kailasa, far to the west, all the way to the eastern frontier with China, and from the Himalayan chain to Kun-Lun.

Now this brings us to the fourth determining moment in the alienation of Tibet from the Celestial Empire. Tsongkhapa's reforms, which had started within the context of monastic administration, gradually, in the course of decades, developed into a full-blown, powerful theocracy. The donation of Gushri Khan in 1642 ("the foundation of the temporal power of the Dalai Lama" – Petech), succession by reincarnation, with its arcane fascination for the masses, the iron-clad organization conferred on the Church by a succession of able and dynamic pontiffs, the monumental reconstruction, the royal enlargement, the sumptuous embellishment of the Potala at Lhasa by the Fifth Dalai, all these factors created on the Roof of the World a spectacular political, economic, cultural, religious and artistic entity that was totally distinct, and very proudly independent, from China; and yet all this took place in lands and among people that the emperors in Beijing considered to be under their sway, however spectral. Let it be remembered (a principle valid to this day) that the rulers of the Celestial Empire have always considered those lands to be Chinese that at any time in the past formed a part of their dominions. And effectively Kublai Khan had, after all, delegated to the abbots of Sakya a slice of his temporal power in place of an actual invasion.

The death of the Great Fifth took place in 1682, but this was kept a secret for a good thirteen years by the regent (*desì*) Sengye Gyatso (who was said to be his natural son). Under the pretence that the pontiff had withdrawn into a very strict, cloistered regime of meditation, the able minister, a very erudite historian and a wily politician, contrived to hold the reins in Tibet for more than a decade.[12] Sengye Gyatso wasted no time: for one thing he substantially expanded Tibetan territory by sending a military expedition against Ladakh; it failed in its primary object but did succeed in annexing the now declining kingdom of Guge, with its passes open to India, and with its famous shrines of Tsaparang and Toling. He also chose in great secrecy, among the various pretenders, the child who was to become the Sixth Dalai

Lama with the name Tsangyang Gyatso ("Ocean of Pure Melody").

And now occurred one of the most extraordinary episodes in the already extraordinary history of Tibet. Scarcely was the Ocean of Pure Melody out of his childhood and beginning to grow whiskers than he revealed himself for a man of high intelligence, brilliant, undoubtedly, but not in the realm of theological doctrine, nor of historical expertise, in which it was expected that he would shine, but rather in the florid field of unconventional, romantic, occasionally melancholy but always inspired love poems. The winged lyrics were not only the fruit of a heady fantasy but reflected brave nights in the actual life of a worldly pontiff intent on sowing his wild oats. "Many Tibetans", Snellgrove writes, "can still recall the traditional account of his appearance – in the blue silk robe of a lay nobleman, wearing his hair in long black locks, bedecked with rings and jewellery, and carrying a bow and quiver."[13] He would make for the discotheques of the day, where he was made welcome by his young friends and pretty mistresses.

Such was the charisma of the one who incarnated the *Bodhisattva* Avalokitesvara/Chen-re-zi and such was probably the personal magnetism of the Ocean of Pure Melody that the majority of Tibetans, while being occasionally disconcerted, accepted his bizarrely unconventional propensities. Instead of saying "we made a mistake" they would say "it is He wanting to put our faith to the test". For the first time, moreover, love songs and songs of everyday life which at all events existed (and how!) in the patrimony of oral folklore[14] were written down. Thus was born a new literary form that enjoyed an immediate success: the love songs of the Sixth Dalai Lama were on everyone's lips, and so they have remained.[15]

Words written with black ink
Have been effaced by water drops.
Unwritten designs in the mind,
[You] cannot erase them even if [you] want to.

The Lama's face which I try to meditate upon
Does not appear in my mind.
The lover's face which I do not meditate upon
Appears in my mind clear and distinct.

If I reciprocate with the feelings of the girl,
My share in religion during this life will be deprived.
If I wander among the solitary mountain ranges,
It would be contradictory to the wishes of the girl.

The Dalai Lamas and the Manchu presence (1720–1912)

If the Tibetans, lay and monastic, looked the other way, "the case of the poetic Dalai Lama" offered the numerous enemies of the *Gelug-pa*, and of the now well established Tibetan independence, some excellent hand-holds to forge ahead. Sengye Gyatso took the precaution of requiring the young Dalai to renounce his spiritual prerogatives (1701), but the provision made little difference. The arch-enemy of Tibetan independence resided as ever in Beijing. I have already mentioned that the Ming sovereigns (1368–1644) were plainly Chinese, and had taken only a Platonic and desultory interest in Tibet. By the middle of the seventeenth century, however, the Ming dynasty was showing those fatal signs of decline that have ever characterized royal houses after two centuries on the throne. The Celestial Mandate was running out; it was poised to pass into the vigorous and warlike hands of certain Manchurian tribes which, after a number of campaigns, succeeded in wiping out the Ming and their supporters. A key date in this highly important change in China's ruling class is considered to be 1644, when the warlord Nurhaci entered Beijing with his troops.

The sovereigns of the Ch'ing/Qing dynasty (1644–1912), one of the most glorious in the long history of the Middle Kingdom, were not Chinese (for several generations the language spoken at court continued to be Manchurian), but they were fully conscious of the weight of the august mission laid upon them by Fate. Among the most urgent and important tasks they considered was that of re-establishing the dragon emblem in every land which in the past had in any way been subject to the Empire's rule. This involved the reconquest of lands in Central Asia (Sinkiang/Xinjiang, "the New Colony") and assertion of suzerainty, be it never so loose, over Tibet. Moreover it was now becoming very important for Beijing to exert some sort of control over the pontiff in Lhasa, given the enormous spiritual influence that he exercised on those restless peoples of the north, an ever-present danger for the dynasty.

The case of the aberrant Dalai Lama now presented itself as an unexpected blessing. The first occasion for the Chinese to take advantage of it came about quite indirectly. The Emperor K'ang-hsi/Kangxi (1644–1722) astutely lent his backing to Lazhang Khan, the son of the already nominated Gushri Khan, and he fell upon Lhasa in 1705 with a small, well-organized army, ejected Sengye Gyatso and decreed his death, declaring Tsangyang Gyatso a spurious reincarnation, and sent the young lama under escort back to China. As was to be predicted, on the way there, not far from Lake Koko-nor, the hapless pontiff-poet met his end in mysterious circumstances; the official version states that he was struck down by a sudden illness, but the likelihood is that he was poisoned or suffocated.

At this point matters grow complicated; all that remains is to give a simplified overview. Lazhang Khan plotted to obtain the recognition of a young man (possibly his own son) as the authentic reincarnation of the Great Fifth. The Emperor K'ang-hsi backed this device, so long as the Khan declared himself a vassal of Beijing; the proposal was accepted. Thus the year 1710, the year in which the agreement was made, is considered by many to be the inaugural date of Chinese sovereignty over Tibet, at least *de jure*. For the moment everything remained as before in spite of the protocols.

The Tibetans, religious and lay, flatly refused to recognize the substitute Dalai (ostensibly the Sixth) proposed by the Khan, and demonstratively accepted a different incarnation, discovered in 1708 in eastern Tibet, as the authentic one: he was to grow up as the Seventh Dalai Lama, given that the Sixth, for all his peculiarities, was universally recognized. And here a great importance was accorded to what was then taken for a prophecy, discovered in the poetry of the Sixth Dalai Lama:

> Ah you who fly, white heron,
> Lend me wings!
> I shall not go far
> Barely to Lithang – then I shall return.

Now Lithang is indeed in eastern Tibet, the place where the young deposed pontiff had mysteriously – and maybe wretchedly – perished. So it all added up. The Emperor K'ang-hsi had the political flair not to want to cross the Tibetans, and eventually recognized the new Dalai Lama as Seventh in the succession. Added to which, the star of Lazhang Khan was apparently now on the wane.

Lazhang Khan's misfortunes had been noticed not only in Beijing but by a shrewd Mongol rival, the Khan of the so-called Zungar tribe. He assembled a small but well armed corps of mounted troops and suddenly appeared at the gates of Lhasa (1717). Lazhang Khan was killed and the Seventh Dalai Lama, still a child, was enthroned in the Potala. The Zungar stayed in Lhasa and Central Tibet for three years, and showed themselves to be inhuman and ferocious in their depredations, their uninterrupted violence, their senseless destruction. And the Tibetans had no-one to whom to turn for help unless it were to the great and magnanimous K'ang-hsi, ruler of the Celestial Empire.

Which brings us to that fateful September day in 1720 when Chinese troops, for the first time in history, occupied Lhasa, then the rest of Tibet. The Qoshot Mongols of Lhazang Khan first, and the Zungar Mongols subsequently, had made themselves so poisonously hated that the Chinese were welcomed as true liberators – rather different to their welcome in 1951 and 1959.

Now began a long settled period. The Tibetan scene remained fundamentally unchanged between 1720 and 1912, when the Manchu dynasty, in its death throes, was unseated by the fledgling Chinese republic. For twenty years, between 1727 and 1747, the country was governed, under Chinese tutelage, by a dynamic and enlightened prince of the Tsang region, called Polhana. For a while there seemed a real chance that the ancient kingdom might be restored, even under the suzerainty of Beijing, but Polhana's son, on succeeding his father in 1747, was clearly not up to the difficult challenge; he was assassinated, and his death raised a sea of disorders.[16]

The Chinese Emperor of the time, the great Chien-lung/Qianlong (who reigned 1736–1795) determined to change the way in which suzerainty over Tibet was exercised. From 1751 the Dalai Lama, assisted by a council of four ministers, became the official temporal sovereign of Tibet, while still remaining head of the lamaist Church. Two Chinese imperial commissioners (the *amban*) were given broadest powers and charged with watching over China's rights and interests. This new order answered well enough to the numerous political requirements of the situation, and was able to endure for a good century and a half.

During the eighteenth century Tibet was not so rigorously closed to foreigners as it was later to become. Many Italian missionaries were able to visit the country and reside there for long periods. Various Capuchin fathers, mostly from the Italian Marche, were at Lhasa in the years 1707–1711, 1716–1733, and 1741–1745, and their writings afford a great deal of useful information on Tibet at that time. It has to be said, though, that the good Capuchins were but pedestrian observers of a world they were unable to understand.[17] The Jesuit Ippolito Desideri, from Pistoia, visited Tibet from 1716 to 1721 and not only mastered spoken and written Tibetan quite remarkably, to leave us a deeply penetrating and intelligent description of the country as he then found it, but he even succeeded in writing important works of Christian apologetics in the language of his hosts.[18] Thus Desideri's name takes its place beside those of Matteo Ricci (1552–1610), the founder of Chinese studies, and of Umberto De' Nobili (1577–1656) who did so much to promote Indian studies. Here we have three outstanding figures in the interpretation of Asia, whose pioneering work was carried out at a time when little was known of non-European civilizations in even the broadest outline.

During the long, sleepy period running from the mid-eighteenth century to the early twentieth century, six Dalai Lamas took turns occupying the throne of the Potala, most of them of little consequence; they were kept under capable and strict control by all those who had an interest in maintaining the institution but would not countenance its slipping out of their grasp. The first four Dalai Lamas of the nineteenth century died very young. A double-edged glory for those unfortunate boys, to find themselves in that position of maximum eminence in the gilded Buddhist Vatican! Too many persons in Tibet and outside were interested in their prompt demise, and did not wish to see them achieving their majority and assuming power, never mind how limited. Each drama was enacted in the soft intimacy of the historic apartments of the gods, possibly amid the gentle aroma of tea mixed with butter and poison, offered in a jade cup.

The slow evolution of the decades was marked by a few events of varying significance. There were two short but bloody wars with Nepal, in 1792 and 1856. In the first instance the prompt intervention of the Chinese hurled the invaders back to Kathmandu; in the second, the Tibetans succeeded on their own, there were no major changes of territory, but the Nepalese ended up with notable trade concessions. An attempt by the Maharajah of Jammu, in north-western India, to conquer Tibet was foiled firmly by the Tibetans, who ruthlessly annihilated the enemy expeditionary force.

The end of the eighteenth century saw the first contacts with the British, who were by then firmly established in India. The Bogle expedition of 1774–75 and the Turner expedition of 1783 penetrated as far as Shigatse and visited the court of the Panchen Lama [see Glossary]. A traveller who had no official backing or assistance, Thomas Manning, contrived, almost as a sporting bet, to reach Lhasa in 1811–12. Two French Lazarist priests, Evariste Huc and Joseph Gabet, undertook a remarkable feat they arrived at Lhasa in 1846 directly from Beijing, after crossing the north-eastern deserts, at the end of a long, difficult, brave and venturesome journey. The account of the adventure is still one of the most rewarding narratives about bygone Tibet.[19]

In 1876 Thubten Gyatso was born; he was to become the Thirteenth Dalai Lama. Probably there were many who thought, and hoped, that he would end as his predecessors had done, and disappear from the scene with judicious tact before reaching his majority. Owing to some happy conjunction of stars this did not happen, and the Thirteenth Dalai Lama grew in time to become one of the most able pontiffs in the history of Tibet. It could be said that the world was now that much smaller than once upon a time: Tibet no longer figured as some sort of Shangri-la up in the clouds, but was turning into a focus of intrigue that involved Great Britain, Russia and, as usual, China. As early as 1893 Tibet had been obliged to cede Sikkim to the British, and open the Chumbi (Trommò) valley to trade.

Possibly daunted by this turn of affairs, and by signs that the British were taking a very firm political stance, the Dalai Lama began to frequent a Buriat monk called Dorjieff, a Russian. This came very soon to the ears of Lord Curzon, Viceroy of India, who was already ill disposed towards the Tibetans on account of their resistance to any sort of diplomatic communication with the world at large. Fearing that the Russians would get there before him, and despite a lukewarm response from London, he eventually despatched a military expedition to the mountains, under the leadership of Colonel Younghusband, with instructions to make the Tibetans sign a treaty regulating political and commercial relations with British India. The Tibetans refused any form of diplomatic overture, therefore Younghusband advanced, from one skirmish to the next, as far as Lhasa, which he reached in August 1904. The Dalai Lama had fled into Mongolia, but the British negotiated a treaty with some of his representatives which partially opened the country to international trade; whereupon the expedition withdrew.[20]

While the British were quite incapable of exploiting the success of the expedition, the Chinese, with canny diplomatic moves, contrived once again to establish their protectorate over Tibet, so much so that in 1910 General Chao Erhfeng/Zhao Erfeng reoccupied Lhasa with an ostentatious show of force. This time the Dalai Lama fled to his ex-enemies in India, and received a most respectful welcome from the British. Tibet seemed to have moved fatally back into the Chinese sphere of influence when, almost unexpectedly, the Ch'ing/Qing dynasty collapsed in 1911–1912. The new republic had other things on its mind. Tibet thus remained isolated. The Tibetans drove out the Chinese and the Thirteenth Dalai Lama was able to return to Lhasa amid great rejoicing.

Independence (1912–1951)

Between 1912 and 1951 Tibet was able to enjoy four decades of independence which it had not known for a very long time. The Thirteenth Dalai Lama, a complex, thoughtful, centralizing personality, revealed himself with time to be very skilful at dealing with the two powers (Britain and China) who were forever threatening to limit his country's independence – he played them off against each other. To the British he conceded just that much of an opening as was needed to assure mutually advantageous diplomatic and commercial relationships; with the Chinese, who in 1917 tried once again to invade Tibet, he was very firm and defeated them time after time. The boundary between eastern Tibet and China remained ill defined owing to the immense difficulties involved in marking it out in such mountainous terrain, but it came to coincide more or less with the ethnic frontier between lamaists who spoke Tibetan and Confucians who spoke Chinese.

The death of the Thirteenth Dalai Lama on 17 December 1933 was mourned by the whole of Tibet. Not since the days of the Great Fifth (1618–1682) had they felt themselves to be under the guidance of a hand so wise, so firm and balanced.[21] The search for the Fourteenth Dalai Lama was long and laborious, but the candidate was eventually discovered in 1936, some twenty months after the demise of his predecessor (see pp. 127 ff).

At Lhasa and in the chief centres of Tibet the initial impact of the Dalai Lama's death was dire, not least because the pontiff's illness had been extremely short, and some of the circumstances surrounding the decease appeared to be suspect, or at any rate were at once declared ominous by the competent authorities. An atmosphere of dark apprehension, of vague dread, hung over the city along with an expectation of miracles. Indeed word went about that the Dalai Lama had miraculously returned to life for a few hours. Then it was said that the *Dronyer Chempo* (Great Chamberlain), feeling responsible for not having anticipated the pontiff's illness, had taken his own life, swallowing powdered glass.

Meanwhile, as the people closeted themselves in their homes and in the temples, reciting prayers and reading the scriptures, a muffled battle for power began among certain eminent people in the capital. According to tradition it was a question of choosing a Regent (*gyeltsab*) to rule the country for the twenty years or so that were expected between the death of the Thirteenth Dalai Lama and his successor's coming of age.

The first name proposed was that of Lama Kunmphel-la, who had been the close companion of the pontiff for many years and the executor of his orders. Kunmphel-la was twenty-eight and had a big following among the monks of the younger generation; he was known for his openness and candour, as also for his impulsiveness.

The plan was thwarted at once and at all costs by a second group of monks and layfolk under the leadership of a layman, Lungshar by name. Dorje Tsegyal Lungshar had been born in 1860 and sent to England in 1912–13, with four carefully selected Tibetan boys to receive a Western education. The voyage formed part of a broader programme for a gentle modernization of Tibet, supervised by Sir Charles Bell, Britain's diplomatic representative with the Dalai Lama.

Lungshar, who came from a good family of the smaller Tibetan aristocracy, was an intelligent, ambitious man with a broad view. It seems that he had diligently turned his months of residence in England to good account, both to learn English and to determine just what a modern democratic government was and how the administration worked in more developed countries. On returning to Tibet, Lungshar had pursued a brilliant career, holding high positions in the Tibetan government of the time.

First of all Lungshar, who had a large following, tried (perhaps incautiously) to have Kunmphel-la condemned to death on the charge of having poisoned the Thirteenth Dalai Lama. The accusation could not be proved, but Lungshar succeeded in having his adversary driven into exile and in having a number of his supporters gaoled.

For some time Lungshar seemed to succeed in dominating the Tibetan political scene. He had founded an apparently innocuous movement called *Kyicho Kuntün* ("Everyone united in happiness") but tending somehow towards the introduction of democracy into the country and reinforcing the National Assembly (*tsong-du*). Perhaps Lungshar was hoping eventually to institute some sort of parliament, such as he had seen in action in various European countries.

Naturally the conservatives united against him, led by Timon, an elderly and respected *sha-pe*. The conservatives had an easy task presenting Lungshar's bland reforms as motivated purely by personal ambition, or as revolutionary proposals. It was said that Lungshar wanted to introduce Bolshevism into Tibet, or that he wanted to turn the nation into a republic, or worse still, that his aim was to have himself appointed king.

It is not clear exactly what he did want, the more so as in the absence of any kind of press in the country, it is difficult to reconstitute the past.[22] Perhaps his aim was to create an oligarchic government with the aid of the most eminent people in the National Assembly, under his influence. Had he succeeded, he would have put into effect the ancient eastern practice of government offstage, and probably that would have satisfied him. Perhaps Lungshar represented something new on the country's political horizon. Perhaps he considered himself a Tibetan nationalist, as one might infer from some of the positions he adopted against Chiang Kai-shek and China.

For a little while, in the early months of 1934, Lungshar's fortune seemed to be in the ascendant. His constant game was to build up the *tsong-du* at the expense of the *kashag*, more elections, that is, and fewer appointments. But he may have overestimated his influence over the National Assembly, and when, on 10 May 1934, he proposed a series of measures tending to reinforce his side, the Assembly supported him at first, but then rejected him.

That is when Timon *sha-pe* saw his moment and organized a counter-attack, inviting Lungshar to come to the Potala to discuss the issue. Lungshar, suspecting a trap, turned up but escorted by armed men, and this was his undoing. His escort were easily disarmed, and Lungshar was obviously open to the charge of wanting to subvert the state.

And now, from the twentieth century, we must prepare for a leap backwards to the Middle Ages!

In the struggle to disarm Lungshar someone wrenched one of his boots off, and some pieces of paper were seen to fall to the ground. Lungshar, struggling free, neatly contrived to pick one up and swallow it, but the rest were gathered together. On them were written the names of Timon *sha-pe* and various members of the government. Black magic! According to Tibetans, to tread under foot the name of one's enemy is in fact one of the most loathsome – and effective – methods of visiting evil and death upon him. The discovery was fatal to Lungshar. The moment the news was out everyone who had been supporting him forsook him. Then Timon *sha-pe* and the most influential members of the *kashag* passed to the attack. There were many arrests. The death penalty hung over Lungshar. But, in view of his merits, he was condemned "merely" to lose his eyes. The cruel sentence was carried out on 20 May 1934, and Lungshar was shut in a freezing, damp dungeon in the cellars of the Potala. In such desperate conditions all that kept him alive was an enormous strength. He was released in 1938, but died the following year.

The most tragic aspect of Lungshar's story is this: the man who risked his life to modernize Tibet condemned himself by virtue of his reliance on archaic practices of sorcery!

Meanwhile, independently of the political activities of the laity, the highest prelates of the Lamaist church had assembled at the start of 1934 and elected a Regent, the abbot of Reting, a monastery some days' journey to the north of Lhasa. Owing to the fact that various of the prelates were unable to come to an agreement, the choice had been arrived at by means of a particular system of balloting (*senriy*), the result of which was taken for the manifestation of the divine will.

The abbot of Reting was a *trul-ku*, a living *Bodhisattva*, in other words he was the reincarnation of former abbots of the famous and ancient monastery. Faced with a divine election, arrived at by the *senriy* method, the elector prelates needs had to hold their tongues. In private conversations, however, various shadows were to be noted. One, the youth of the abbot, barely twenty-four; two, his impulsiveness and his tendency to take decisions on his own without reference to advisers and committees; three, his notorious weakness for pretty women. (Here Goldstein observes that where the *trul-kus* were concerned, their monastic life was not the outcome of a personal choice but of an exterior "recognition" by others, under the Tibetan system of reincarnation, and in cases of a little bit on the side it was customary to turn a blind eye.)

Reting was solemnly enthroned as Regent on 24 January 1934 and took a dominant role in the search for the new Dalai Lama. The story goes that when he visited the famous lake of prophecies Lhamola-tso, in the south of the country, he had a vision that sent him resolutely to the north-east, towards the region of Amdo; this is where a little while later at a place called Taktser the boy was discovered who answered all, or nearly all, the requirements in this most delicate case. The child, born in 1935, was brought with great ceremony to Lhasa, where he arrived on 8 October 1939. To forestall the unexpected (such as the presentation of other candidates) the child had already been officially declared the reincarnation of the Thirteenth Dalai Lama on 23 August, while the caravan was still on the road.

The notable success in the search for the new Dalai Lama afforded the Regent Reting some years of benevolent gratitude from the monks and laity of a great part of Tibet. At a certain point, however, a serious and wholly unexpected crisis blew up. Come 1940, according to an old tradition, the Regent was supposed to accept the monastic vows from the new pontiff, Tenzin Gyatso, the Fourteenth Dalai Lama. One of these vows concerned chastity, purity, the renunciation of carnal pleasure. Now the "impure" Reting, notorious for the way he frequented various concubines, did not seem the most suitable person to enact such a delicate religious rite. Bowing to the pressure of public opinion, Reting thought fit to resign and transfer his charge of Regent to the abbot of Taktra, an elderly and unambitious man who enjoyed everyone's respect; perhaps a bit crusty and stern, but nevertheless a man of the most complete integrity.

It appears that there was an understanding between the two abbots whereby after a given period, possibly two years, once all the ceremonies affecting the new Dalai Lama had been carried out, Taktra would restore the office of Regent to Reting. In 1944 Reting returned to Lhasa obviously intending to resume his place as Regent, but Taktra quite simply rejected the exchange. As may well be imagined, a mortal enmity resulted between the two abbots. In consequence the whole of Tibet was riven between two factions – Taktra's supporters on the one side, Reting's on the other. As these were prime movers in the nation's religious and political life, the falling out was no laughing matter.

At a certain point Reting had the most unfortunate idea of seeking the help of the Chinese dictator, Chiang Kai-shek. Of course he was at once accused of high treason and thrown into prison; he died shortly afterwards, ostensibly of poison. That was not, however, the end of the matter. Reting's supporters, especially those from the monastery of Sera, at the gates of Lhasa, attempted a rising against the government, which had to respond by force of arms, bombing the shrine and the rebel monks and raking them with machine-gun fire – the bloodshed was deplorable (26–30 April 1947).

The British had withdrawn from India on 15 August 1947, and Tibet was isolated in the face of the tough and persistent demands of the Chinese. India inherited the formal treaties with Tibet, but was suffering from internal problems of its own and had in practice to abandon the country to its own devices. Meanwhile in China the weak and corrupt Kuomintang regime of Chiang Kai-shek had been swept aside in the advance of the Communists under Mao Tse-tung (1949). Chiang Kai-shek and his followers took refuge on the island of Taiwan, while the new Communist government expressed itself quite unequivocally: Tibet was an integral part of China.

A person like Mao Tse-tung is easier to understand if he is compared with an archetypal figure in Chinese history like Shih Huangti/Shi Huangdi (246–210 B.C.), founder of a dynasty. Such an exceptional individual rises above his contemporaries like a mountain, he is to be situated above and beyond any sort of common judgment, and enjoys a charisma that is more divine than human, because he demonstrates, in his person and in his achievements, that he has obtained the indefinable blessing of a Heavenly Mandate. The fact that in this particular case we are talking about a Communist, presumably an atheist, is neither here nor there; archetypes do not rest on rational foundations, they function in the deep, emotional, secretive depths of the irrational, and feed on the hidden lymph of the recent and remote past. The barely inaugurated dynasty might transmit its power by co-optation, election or otherwise instead of by inherited seed, but this is beside the point. What mattered was that the new dynasty should be attended by a deep social regeneration on the one hand, and the reaffirmation of Chinese greatness on the other. The Kuomintang had lost the divine mandate because it was considered to be corrupt, weak, unwilling to hold on to its own, too closely linked to foreigners. What the Communists promised was social renewal and greatness for the country. The Mandate went to them.

As has been already seen, China regards itself as owning any land over which at any point in its millennial history it has exercised any form of sovereignty. It was therefore obvious that the new dynasty should think to restore its banners, this time without dragons but with stars, hammer and sickle as soon as possible throughout all the bordering regions including Sinkiang and Tibet, even if inhabited by peoples as different as could be from the Han.

In those minds the deep, glaring differences between the imperial idea and the Communist idea did not even reach the threshold of consideration. The new dynasty was only incidentally Communist, it was first and foremost Chinese.

Tibet in Chinese hands (1951 to the present)

As early as January 1950, the new Chinese government, in the person of General Chu The/Dzu De, announced its decision to "liberate" Tibet. "Liberate" the Land of Eternal Snows? But what if for the first time in more than two centuries it really *was* free? Liberate it from its freedom, therefore? A moment's thought is enough to establish that this was precisely the aim. Aside from the atavistic considerations of prestige, a free Tibet on China's borders, ultimately open to undesirable alliances, was something to be strenuously avoided; thus it behoved China to free Tibet from its freedom at the first opportunity. To this end the Chinese completed that ironic "liberate" with the words "from imperialistic influences". From which ones? Great Britain was withdrawing to home waters, while India had other problems to cope with. Thus what was involved was the most hypocritical set-up imaginable.

The tenuous British protectorate over Tibet had been exercised for decades without effecting the smallest interference in the country's internal affairs: all that was required in New Delhi (and in London) was for the protectorate to have certain negative effects internationally, that is, to discourage the Russians from moving south and the Chinese from moving west. Indeed, if the truth be told, had the British been somewhat greedier and more aggressive in the colonizing of Tibet, this may have been altogether to the good. Had they for instance opened a motor road between Gangtok and Lhasa (possibly a bus route), had they pressed the Tibetans to a somewhat closer acquaintance with petrol and aspirin, with electric light and cheques payable to bearer, with political parties and trade unions, the faithful of the Dalai Lama would not have approached the middle of the twentieth century with their Merovingian spirit, with their virginal mediaeval minds. As we shall now see, it was precisely this that proved their downfall. To accuse the British and Indians of an "imperialistic" influence on Tibet is like accusing a butterfly of snapping at one.

The Chinese opened hostilities on 7 October 1950. The isolated, disorganized Tibetans, with a scratch assortment of weaponry, and no protection against hunger and cold, made a heroic attempt to mount a resistance around Chamdo, in the Kham, but lost more than four thousand men, some dead, others taken prisoner. A few days later, on 13 October, the fortress of Chamdo fell, betrayed to the invaders. Thenceforth it may be said that the road was open to the Chinese; they advanced in two columns, one from Lake Koko-nor in the north-west, the other from the east, the classic road "of the Four Rivers and the Six Chains" (Chushi Kangdruk). In April 1951 they were at the gates of Lhasa. The Dalai Lama had fled south to the monastery of Dung-kar, but was then forced to return to the capital. Meanwhile the Chinese had on their side a big collaborator, Ngapo Ngawang Jigme. The war could be said to have been won. The Chinese troops made their ceremonial entry into Lhasa on 26 October under the command of General Chang Kuo-hua/Zhang Guohua.

Before we continue it will be as well to stop and consider a point which is seldom emphasized. When speaking of Chinese military action against Tibet, seen by some as an authentic colonialist brutality, an aggression against a harmless and unarmed population, and seen by others as liberation from a reactionary regime that defies present-day understanding, while for others it was simply China's reaffirmation of its historic rights, the comment is often made: "And all this happened before the almost totally indifferent eyes of the world!" A subtle, double-edged notion! It could underline the crude insensitivity to others' sufferings displayed by peoples who are comfortably settled, and it can also serve to demonstrate that nobody made a move because nobody challenged China's right to wage such a campaign.

And here a fact must sadly be acknowledged: that a great part of the responsibility for this wall of indifference worldwide lay with the Tibetans themselves. It is true that the supreme crisis hit them at a most delicate moment in their history, and hence caught them on the wrong foot, with a child Dalai Lama and regents locked in civil strife; had the thirteenth pontiff still been alive, things would in all probability have worked out differently, or at least the Chinese conquest would not have been a walkover. Had the Tibetans been more on the alert, had they been living less like desert hermits on top of their pillars, they would have put out feelers here and there.

But time was scarce; they had barely two or three years, from 1947 to 1950. That was the time when they should have been making themselves heard by the world and in the world by every means available; they should have appealed to the United Nations, sent missions to the principal capitals and to the leading political leaders of the day, organized press campaigns, blown up scandals, entrusted their case to a big advertising agency ("Independence for Shangri-la!" "Freedom: Hope of Himalayan Pope!") and so on. All going well, it would have been useful to say and shout: "Look, here we are, a small independent people who want their independence recognized. We want to have our rights protected." Tiny Bhutan, under a king who knew his way around, moved fast enough to have himself recognized by the United Nations, and thus to secure his country's independence. The Tibetans could have and should have done the same.

Blissfully immersed, however, in their age-old isolation, they made no move. They did nothing. They missed the boat. Or in truth they did take one or two pathetic steps, but at the last minute, and all too quietly. For instance they expelled the Chinese mission which had somewhat illicitly established itself in Lhasa in 1934 at the time of the Thirteenth Dalai Lama's funeral. This was too little and too late. All it contrived to do was to infuriate the Chinese. The community of nations, "in view of the persistent claims of the Chinese that Tibet was an integral part of their territory, and given that Lhasa evidently showed little interest in obtaining formal recognition of its complete sovereignty and independence, rightly concluded that they should not pronounce on the matter."[23] A Tibetan appeal to the UN at the end of 1950, requesting the General Assembly to consider the case of the Chinese aggression, was in fact postponed *sine die*. Later on the Dalai Lama was to declare that the Tibetans were thoroughly dismayed at being thus forsaken. This is understandable, but the fault lay for the most part with them.

Let us return to the fateful May of 1951. The Chinese summoned to Beijing a Tibetan delegation of fifteen, and presented them with an important document for their signature. The Chinese could of course impose whatever demands they wished on their neighbours; moreover the weakness of the Tibetans was emphasized by the fact that the delegates themselves were seriously at odds for some of them represented the Dalai Lama, others the lay nobility, others still collaborators of the Chinese in zones that had long been occupied, and so on.

The document carried one of the usual splendid flowery titles: "Agreement on measures for the peaceful liberation of Tibet". Anyone who has read something of ancient Chinese philosophy knows the importance attached to the "rectification of names". The theory of course applies in both senses: if it is right to call a thing by its correct name, then if you call a thing by its incorrect name, the result is wrong. What happens if we give unsuitable names to unjust things? We go back to Square One! Not by chance therefore those that were in effect "impositions towards the forcible enslavement of Tibet" were called an "Agreement on measures for the peaceful liberation".

Leaving aside these comments, which do not seem to me wholly out of place, for they do answer to inveterate Chinese customs, it has to be acknowledged that the contents of the seventeen articles were notably enlightened and generous. Among other things it was established that the Central Authority "shall not make any alteration to the existing political system in Tibet. The position, functions and powers of the Dalai Lama shall remain unchanged. The officials in the various ranks shall retain their duties (Article 4). Religious liberty shall be respected. The faith, customs and practices of the Tibetan people shall be respected. The monasteries of the Lamas shall be protected (Article 7). The education of the Tibetan nation, the study of Tibetan culture and the study of spoken and written Tibetan shall be promoted (Article 9). In the matter of reforms in Tibet the Central Authorities shall be put under no compulsion (Article 11). The People's Army of Liberation, once on Tibetan soil, shall adhere to the above principles in its conduct, shall buy and sell at fair prices, shall not arbitrarily take so much as a needle or thread from the people (Article 13)".[24] An ill-disposed person might insinuate that such a breadth of vision, so handsome a provision might indeed be accorded with any number of smiles and ceremony in a document that, at the end of the day, was not worth the paper it was written on.

At any rate the early years of this strange cohabitation of lamas and commissars, of red flags and *tangka*s, of *Das Kapital* and *Prajnāpāramitā*, of historical materialism and administrative metempsychosis, of Lenin and Tsongkhapa, evolved in an atmosphere of almost disturbing peace and harmony. The Dalai Lama and his government embarked upon a few reforms, others were undertaken by the Chinese, and everyone moved forward cautiously and with full regard to the very special circumstances of Tibetan culture.

An optimistic observer might have deluded himself that the nuptials were destined for a future which if not rosy was at least one of peaceable domesticity.[25] The Chinese were largely preoccupied with the great labours that from a certain point of view we might define as neutral. Road-building, for example. Until 1951 Tibet had neglected the wheel. Now mountains were being excavated, bridges built, plains crossed, with feats of engineering which, in truth, were breathtaking. Lhasa was soon connected with Chengtu/Chengdu by a motor road of some 2,200 kilometres and more, that had to contend with immensely high hills, rivers, near-vertical rock walls, mountainsides subject to landslides. Other roads connected Lhasa with the north through Nagchuka, and with the west via Shigatse. This trunk road continued on to Gartok, then through the desert of Aksai Chin, and eventually linked up with the network of roads in Sinkiang. The roads connected with the Indian network via Yatung and Natu-la, and with Nepal via Nyalam. One is bound to say that the Tibetans were far more impressed with this aspect of the occupation, which for a while won many points in favour of the new arrivals.

Tibet, however, was a long way from being a unitary state, even in its "mediaeval" context. At least three traditional fault-lines were to be intuited at its social core: one of them ran through the *Gelug-pa* bloc, in the difficult relationship between the Dalai Lama and the Panchen Lama; a second was to be noted in the normally covert but still often deadly rivalry between clergy and laity, between abbots and barons; a third, the most serious of all, affected the relations between Lhasa and a number of outlying tribes, especially those in the Kham area, on the Chinese border, or among the Ngolok, a little further north, who were immensely strong, indestructible, proud, quick on the trigger, quick to pull a knife. These folk were accustomed to respecting the Dalai Lama as a venerable holy father, assuredly, but only for so long as he turned a blind eye to their trafficking and raids. Another fault-line was now to be added to these three traditional ones: that between the majority of Tibetans, who endured more or less in silence the presence of foreigners among them, and a growing number of collaborators (who in their turn were split between authentic converts and fellow-travellers). So while China presented itself in Tibet as a monolithic block embodying troops and party activists, Tibet could only be described as a shapeless, eddying mass of bewildered people who were often divided by conflicting ambitions instead of being united by shared values.

After 1953–54 the sky began to darken. The sparks of a great conflagration in store were first to be noted in Kham, in the eastern part of the country, both because it was there that the Chinese embarked on the most radical reforms and because the mountain folk from that province were traditionally the most refractory. In those years the guerrilla warfare between the Kham-pa, the Ngolok and the Chinese lapsed into mind-boggling savagery, with surprise attacks, vendettas, destruction, torture, brutality of every sort perpetrated by all sides. Reading the depositions made by Tibetan refugees to the representatives of the International Juridical Committee in Geneva[26] is even today, so many years later, a horrifying experience. The conflict was for all practical purposes a war of religion, not unlike those fought ferociously between Catholics and Anabaptists, Muslims and Kaffirs. If a conventional religion, Buddhism, represented the one side, the other was represented by what was self-confessedly a non-religion, but promoted with religious fervour. To be even modestly wealthy meant to sin not against the gods, but against the one god, The People. So the guilty party was stripped of all he owned, and if he put up the least resistance he was destroyed. The lamas sinned in that they consumed without producing, so the same principles applied to them. The shrines and monasteries were desecrated, relieved of every useless bauble, made over to be stables, barracks, granaries, workshops. Children were taken away from their parents, if the latter showed the smallest sign of heresy, and would be sent to China to be re-educated in a "healthier" atmosphere.

Fugitives from areas of worst persecution arrived at Lhasa with news that caused the greatest alarm. Little by little a gulf of hatred was being dug between the Tibetans and the Chinese. Many of the Kham-pa had banded together to set up a highly mobile "Volunteers for National Defence"; at times these controlled vast areas of southern and western Tibet. By March 1959 the temperature was at boiling point everywhere. The Dalai Lama was in a most difficult position. The Chinese insisted that he sent his household troops, a force of some five thousand men, to fight alongside the occupying army against the Kham rebels. Of course the Dalai Lama refused to co-operate; it would have meant sending Tibetans to open fire on other Tibetans, to engage in a civil war.

At this juncture General Chang Ching-wu invited the Dalai Lama to attend a performance at the Chinese military camp on 10 March; he was to come on his own, absolutely without any armed escort. The moment the news was known in the city, a crowd estimated at thirty thousand people surrounded the Norbhu-Lingka, the Summer Palace, where the Dalai Lama was then residing, and prevented his leaving. The incident continued for several days. The crowd, largely made up of Kham-pa guerrillas, grew more restless by the hour, more difficult to rein in. General Chang sent new and repeated messages, each one ruder and more imperious, addressed simply to "Dalai". He played for time, explaining that the crowds of faithful were preventing him from moving.[27]

The situation was at once grotesque and explosive. On March 17 the Tibetan government finally took a decision that was now inevitable: the Dalai Lama would escape. That same evening, disguised as a labourer-monk, under cover of darkness, the twenty-four-year-old pontiff escaped from Lhasa with a handful of devotees and one or two members of his household. At Nethang he was joined by a great many more followers. From there they crossed the impervious Che pass and descended to the River Tsang-po. After crossing it the caravan was in territory under the control of the Kham-pa, and it was possible to breathe more easily. The only danger now was from aircraft and paratroops, but luckily the weather remained propitious to escape, for it was cloudy and misty. All preparations had been made in the greatest secrecy, but even so, heaven knows how, local shepherds, peasants, nomads all seemed to be in the know and crowded along the roadside, in the villages, to obtain the Dalai Lama's blessing. Soon the giant mountains on the frontier with Bhutan, the Kula Kangri and its court of ice-bound peaks shut off the horizon to the south. The pass which crosses the Himalayan range was reached on May 31. Pandit Nehru, given advance notice of what was happening, had opened the way to India. A few days later the Dalai Lama and his suite were safe in the great

Buddhist monastery of Tawang, sixty kilometres within the Indian border. They had made it!

The Chinese learnt of the escape two days later. Naturally they expressed anger, very great anger, and undoubtedly the feeling was genuine enough among the troops at Lhasa; but in the secret, subterranean meanders of high politics, in the gleaming, silent corridors of Beijing, it could be that this defection was not entirely deplored. It is hard seriously to imagine that the Chinese, with all the military might at their command, were incapable of stopping a large caravan comprising people travelling slowly across open terrain on foot and on horseback. True, the three principal guardian divinities of Tibet, Chen-re-zi, Jampeyan, and Chanadorje provided wisps of low cloud over the valleys to conceal the flight of the living *Bodhisattva* and his followers, but there will certainly have been some breaks in the cloud cover in the course of two weeks! The fact is that the escape of the Dalai Lama served to resolve a situation that everybody had been finding impossible. This action had put the Tibetans in the wrong – from their new masters' point of view – and thus every engagement undertaken could be rescinded whereby they had been supposed to engage in a number of bold joint-ventures, a number of delicate compromises between the requirements of socialism and those of theocracy. Now they could make a clean sweep and rewrite the rules of engagement. The most brutal among the far-sighted will probably have heaved a blatant satisfied sigh of relief.

In terms of tactics the first step was to put down the rebellion in Lhasa. This was accomplished in a few days by means of cannon- and machine-gun fire. Lhasa was an inferno, fortunately for only a few days. It is said that twelve thousand people were killed,[28] and an equal number were deported. The Tibetan government was immediately relieved of its authority, to be replaced by "Committees of Military Control".[29] The disorganized, listless Tibetans had been unable to form a united front, to go through with their rebellions, which in any event affected only Lhasa and its immediate environs.

The famous reforms that were supposed to be taking place gradually in the light of the particular social and religious conditions of the Tibetan world, in accordance with Article 17 of the Treaty, were now instead put into immediate effect in the most radical way, in June 1959. Rights to real estate, housing, cattle were everywhere reassessed, with straightforward confiscations for anyone who in any way had been connected with the revolt; for the rest there were various forms of compensation, (more theoretical than practical). Tibetan society was subjected to a complete upheaval. Refugees in their tens of thousands started to cross the Himalayas and seek refuge in India, Bhutan, Nepal, often in the direst conditions. It was not only the rich who were targeted, so were the very small landowners; and of course so were the monasteries, even more harshly. At Sakya, for example, at the beginning of 1959 there were five hundred monks; by the end of the year (we read in B. R. Burman) the number had dropped to thirty-six, all elderly. This was a typical case of what had befallen eastern Tibet now for a long time, and of what was happening in the centre and south.

This is not the place to follow the story step by step. As in all these socio-cultural cyclones, especially when they blow in from outside, there were countless individual tragedies (which by the same token become a collective phenomenon); some echo of them may be captured in the accounts of the refugees, which are almost always touching, often desperately heart-rending.[30] The forces who occasioned such tragedies would seek justification in arguments familiar from earlier colonial eras, arguments I used to hear as a child when Italy was involved in Libya, in Eritrea, Ethiopia and Somaliland: "I mean, after all, we are bringing them peace, security, wellbeing, we're building roads, railways, airstrips, teaching them the use of electricity and the telephone, building hospitals, schools, factories, bringing the natives up to date in agricultural methods that are modern, scientific and mechanized." Such is the capricious complexity of human activity that there is a grain of truth in all this. And it is thus correct to say that the Chinese brought in (and imposed) many benefits on the Tibetans. But colonialism it still remained, of that there can be no doubt.

And the truth is that the final balance worked in the favour of the Chinese. The Chinese improved one thing and another, but they also left a whole lot of other things in ruins. First and foremost the country, which was poor and scrawny, had to support a population of two hundred or three hundred thousand troops and as many civilians all from China: shortages built up and prices rose. Secondly there was the exploitation of primary resources. For the present this largely means the despoliation of Tibet's primaeval forests in the south-east, on the foothills of the Himalayas and the Burmese border. Further depredations are to follow: mineral exploration in the high plateaux has just begun – it has been known since the time of Herodotus that there are gold deposits, but apparently there are even more precious and useful minerals to exploit.

Lastly, a single fundamental fact needs to be faced: that a people's freedom is an asset that is of transcendent value, an asset that nobody is entitled to confiscate. It is one of the great paradoxes of our time that the "capitalist, reactionary, imperialist" world has fully recognized this fact for close on fifty years and acted upon it. All its colonial empires have been dismantled, dismembered, dissolved. The only colonial empire still extant is that of the Chinese "socialist and progressive" world, which, with its fine speeches and lovely doves of peace is in practice acting like the reviled colonial powers of the nineteenth century.

It is also necessary to bear in mind that the Chinese colonial yoke is particularly burdensome for reasons that date back thousands of years. If the original China of Shi Huang-ti/Shi Huangdi had expanded entirely by demographic growth, today we should have a populous nation, though certainly not to be compared with the one actually in existence in the Far East. The Han nucleus of two thousand years ago continued to expand over the centuries by continuously incorporating further ethnic groups. After two, three, ten generations the erstwhile barbarians had eventually been transformed into civilized human beings that could gradually consort with Han Chinese. Time counts for little in this sort of operation. The Chinese have a gift for stability. Time is measured by geological eras. China is built like sedimentary deposits, layer upon layer.

The work of Chinese assimilation is of course based upon the concept of an intrinsic, absolute superiority of Chinese civilization over all other such fruits of human evolution. The Ch'ing dynasty, for instance, which lasted until 1912, not all that long ago, never completely accepted the idea that relations with other countries could be pursued on a basis of equality. By no means. At the centre there was China ("The Centre-Flower"), the depository of every civilized value, and around China there were the barbarians, not excluding those from the "Western Oceans", who were admitted, if the need arose, to bring tribute and receive a benediction, but in no sense to be treated as equals. The European colonialists had of course many and mean defects, but as a rule they did not stick their noses in the affairs of the natives. The case of the missionaries, with their light and shadow, was peripheral(except in Central and South America). The Chinese as colonialists, however, by deep instinct and ethnic tradition, tend to impose themselves: therefore they exercise a subtle, continuous, involuntary pressure to make the "barbarians" abandon their rough, uncouth ways of eating, dressing, entertaining themselves, sleeping, singing, writing, thinking, and adapt to methods that are more metropolitan and respectable. What if that is to take a century or two? So be it. What are ten or fifteen generations in our millennial history!

A typical instance of "sinification" is to be found in place-names. These, it is well recognized, are of the first importance culturally speaking. Giving names to places is a profound, potent, intimate and often attractive way of taking possession of the world. Anyone who has lived even only briefly in the South Tyrol will have realized this. Imagine what an upset it would be if as we approached the Queen of the Adriatic we came upon signposts indicating

"Venedig", "Venice", "Benisu" and stuck somewhere underneath in small letters "Venezia"; not, moreover, because we Italians want to be good hosts but because a foreign power has imposed this on us. The Chinese entered Tibet and renamed everything, towns, provinces, rivers, mountains, adapting Tibetan to their quite different phonetic system that suffers from considerable limitations. Tibet of course has been covered by a veil of ideograms.

With all these weights and limitations, while the 1960s ran their course, perhaps the Chinese yoke began to weigh a little less heavily on Tibetan necks. Some economic progress had been achieved. With 1965 the Tibetan Autonomous Region had been inaugurated which, at least in theory, was to give official recognition to the many differences, social and cultural, between the mother country and the colony. It must of course be here recorded that the Autonomous Region embraces but a small part of what is effectively Tibet in ethnographic, linguistic and religious terms. Substantial areas inhabited by lamaist Tibetan-speaking populations have been included within the Chinese provinces of Szechwan and Ch'ing-hai. Population data is very uncertain but probably out of some six million Tibetans, 3,800,000 live in the Autonomous Region, the rest in the other provinces. Nor should one entirely forget the lamaist Tibetan – speaking populations in India (Assam, Sikkim, Kashmir, Ladakh), in Bhutan and Nepal.

Slowly the unfortunate Tibetans, who had endured so much, were beginning to get back onto an even keel when another dreadful storm came over the horizon: the Cultural Revolution. It is true that this was monstrous in China too, but its effect in Tibet was maybe even worse, what with the country's isolation, and the strongly chauvinistic Chinese cultural undertow which was allowed free rein and was answerable to nobody. The Cultural Revolution was based on the Maoist notion of "permanent revolution", the need to destroy the old in order to build a new future. Plant certain elementary ideas in the minds of muscle-bound louts with a shortage of grey matter and a total lack of sensitivity, and you will find that even the Uffizi, the Prado and the Louvre will be under threat.

The notorious Red Guard embarked on their activities in Lhasa in August 1966. A month earlier, fanatics had already arrived from the plains bearing with them Mao's new watchword. Shortly afterwards they had established two large bands in the city, who went on to attack each other, it seems. For the most part they were young Chinese working in the new factories in and around Lhasa, but it is said that some Tibetan youths joined these squads. They were nearly all of them extremely young, though some of their leaders were older. Lhasa was turned upside down: the whole place was carpeted with red banners, with red streamers carrying quotations from Mao; then there was a general renaming of streets, squares, intersections, replacing the old names, which had religious connotations, by more "revolutionary" ones (place-names as a method of appropriation!). The Tibetan custom of exchanging white scarves was deemed "reactionary"; the scarves had to be red. Not much harm in that, a relatively innocent manifestation of youthful high-spirits. Then began the trials, the condemned paraded in shame down the streets, the search of houses for "banned" religious artefacts, and the resulting violence done to those found in possession of any.

Once they hit their stride, these bands of youths felt that they were masters in Tibet; holding in one hand Mao's Little Red Book, they would climb on board the tanks and head for the monasteries where they would embark on orgies of destruction. If the few remaining monks did not flee, or worse, if they put up any resistance to the mindless vandals, they ran the risk of losing their lives in grim circumstances. As for the holy images, they were smashed down, trampled upon, defaced, set on fire with the voluptuousness of the fanatical possession. A photograph exists that was taken in secret in a chapel of Norbhu-Lingka after one of these expeditions: the room looks like Buddha's abattoir, arms, heads, haloes, hands, torsos can be seen all piled up. More than pure and simple destruction, it was pathological. This orgy of vandalism continued for months the length and breadth of Tibet. Only a handful of important institutions were saved, those that were garrisoned by the army, which did not share the young hot-heads' ideas. Luckily we may record that among the buildings saved were the Potala, the Jokhang, a part of the Kum-Bum at Gyantse, the monasteries of Sera and Drepung, the monastery of Tashilhumpo, and Shigatse. But the Ramoche in Lhasa is gone, and the strange and picturesque Chagpo-ri, formerly home of the Medical College in Lhasa, is a heap of ruins. The vast holy city of Galden is a pathetic pile of demolished walls, Samye and Mindoling are destroyed, all that remains of Rongphu are some ruins whipped by the elements, the Yumbu Lakhang, Tibet's most ancient building, is a landslide of stones on the hillside, the Palkhor-choide at Gyantse is reduced to a skeleton, all that's left of the monastery of Dung-kar and the shrine of Paju are smashed, fire-licked remnants. For the total destruction of the monastery of Kyangphu and the partial but still very serious destruction of the monastery of Iwang/Yemar, see Roberto Vitali's report on page 229 and photo 62 on p. 230. The list could go on for pages. And it would be one of the sorriest, most shameful lists in the world. It raises the question, how can human beings sink to such depths. It is said that there used to be two thousand holy sites in Tibet – whether monasteries, chapels or shrines; possibly the number is exaggerated, but if barely twenty have survived, as it appears, the proportion is at all events quite appalling. Nine tenths of the testimony to Tibetan civilization are now reduced to dust and embers.[31]

With the 1980s and with the new ideological regime instituted by Deng Xiaoping, the situation in Tibet, as has been said, has improved considerably; there is greater autonomy, there are signs of an economic revival, some measure of religious liberty is being conceded, there are the beginnings of some minimal attention to the artistic inheritance. Furthermore the country is being opened to tourism, with all that this means in terms of contacts and exchanges, of a window on the rest of the world. There has been much talk of the Dalai Lama returning to Lhasa, though it seems that this is not on the cards, not at all events for some considerable time. The Buddhist pope is remaining wisely at Dharamsala, in the north of India, where he is at complete liberty to champion the Tibetan cause both now and in the future.

The 1980s and 1990s

The last two decades of the twentieth century have been a period of slow and general improvement for Tibet, it has to be recognized, especially in comparison with the years of fire and blood of the Cultural Revolution, though there have been plenty of ups and downs, periods of sun and shadow at irregular intervals down the years.

98 *Galden: the great monastery before the Cultural Revolution*

99 Galden: the great monastery after the Cultural Revolution

A formidable witness to the period running from 1959 to 1992 is to be found in Palden Gyatso, a monk of the *Gelug-pa* sect, whose autobiography, *Fire under the Snow* [see Bibliography II] furnishes an account of some thirty years in the various prisons that are scattered about Tibet, suggesting a landscape not unlike the Gulag Archipelago, worthy of the worst eras of Soviet Russia. Palden Gyatso is assuredly a man of great fortitude. He sees but a single star in the sky, the Dalai Lama, and does not give an inch, never once denies his master, though this earns him brutal treatment, even to being tortured with the iniquitous electrical cattle-prod, one of the most diabolical of Chinese inventions.

His writing is always sober, a text in which the author's heroism and that of many of his companions is never stressed or highlighted, indeed it appears almost by stealth, muted, a quality that the reader stumbles upon by chance; and through his account the perfidy of the Chinese comes over all too clearly. At an elementary level they brutalize the Tibetans for being loyal to the Dalai Lama, or for other similar reasons, but then at a more sophisticated and subtle level they try to separate them into many categories, the better to manipulate them to their own advantage.

Ever since 1959 there has been a fundamental classification for separating the

Tibetans into people "of good stock" from "people of evil stock". The former included the landless, hired hands, shepherds and other simple herdsmen, navvies and the like, but it took only the tiniest parcel of land or cattle, the possession of the most run-down artisan's workshop, or the most tenuous connection with the better-off classes or worse still, with the nobility of the time, and the tag "of evil stock", once entered in the official documents, clung to the unfortunate person for ever more, wherever he went. In other words a sort of social racism was instituted, with the creation of a caste who were in favour with the authorities, and a caste execrated by them.

As always happens when a brutal power, and moreover a foreign power, takes control of a people, the human responses are enormously varied. Some, whether out of conviction or calculation, throw in their lot with the occupiers, the foreigners, and collaborate with them fully; the majority try to keep out of the way of the inevitable conflicts that occur if one takes a clearly defined position, and settle into a sorry but convenient bed of compromises, shouting the correct slogans when the need arises, waving the correct banner as required by their "superiors". Finally there are those who resist the regime, most of them silently and covertly, but who on occasions are forced by circumstances to come out and express themselves openly. This can lead to unexplained arrests, or immensely long prison sentences handed down after mock trials. In some cases the drama ends with a death sentence, carried out with a pistol shot in the back of the neck, a frequent event in all Chinese territories, as Amnesty International asserts. Sometimes the victim falls into such despair that he takes his own life.

Palden Gyatso's horizons were as bleak as could be imagined, both because he was classified as ipso facto "of the worst stock" simply for belonging to a family of small landowners, and because he was a monk of the *Gelug-pa* sect, and thus viscerally loyal to the Dalai Lama.

In his book three things stand out. First, the savage, mediaeval harshness with which he was treated. Poor old Cesare Beccaria, the Italian nineteenth-century penologist, what a great pile of additional work would have landed on his plate had he looked at China, and at Tibet in particular! During his early years of imprisonment poor Palden Gyatso was immobilized with metal shackles to his arms and legs. This left him entirely dependent on others at every moment of the day and night, when it was time to eat, drink, go to the toilet. Fortunately, Palden writes, he could always count on the compassion and help of his fellow-prisoners. Indeed, the solidarity among the prisoners, at all moments and in all circumstances, is one of the most moving constants in this terrible journal of tortures.

At one moment the guards noticed that Palden was particularly alert, intelligent, and decided to teach him how to weave mats. Of course the not inconsiderable economic benefit to be derived from this form of craftsmanship, famous in Tibet, was not for the sake of the prisoner, but disappeared into the bureaucratic labyrinth. One thing anyway was certain: it was not possible to weave mats with one's limbs immobilized! Thus the new craft at least freed him from the most painful shackles and from the slavery imposed on him in the eyes of the others.

An equally painful chain of events associated with the account of those years of damnation relates to Palden Gyatso's companions, who were put to death (pistol-shot to the back of the neck) for defying their masters too openly, or who found suicide preferable to the continuation of a life that was too painful and hopeless. Particularly poignant is the story of the monk Nyima ("Light") who contrived to obtain a piece of sharp-edged metal. At bedtime he pulled the covers over his head and in perfect silence slashed a carotid artery in his neck. Nobody realized. In the morning the guards noticed the silhouette of Nyima motionless on his pallet. They pulled back the covers; the corpse of the poor monk lay still in a lake of congealed blood.

Lastly there is a fact that leaves anyone who reads this nightmare account with a particularly painful impression: many of the worst guards in the various prisons surrounding Lhasa – Drapchi, Sangyip and yet others – were Tibetan collaborators, rewarded for their "conversion" by being permitted and even encouraged to persecute the "enemies of the people", those of the "evil stock". And some of the most spiteful persecutors were women, like the notorious Dolkar. The most ruthless and sadistic of the men were equally Tibetan: Paljor and Jampa, for example, who seemed to enjoy torturing Palden Gyatso and others among his companions who were defined as "major criminals", making free use of the electric cattle-prod – a rod rammed down the throat, into the stomach, up the anus (and the vagina in the case of nuns) leaving atrocious burns.

Not to find excuses for the Chinese, but in an effort to understand them in their brutality, it is necessary to bear in mind that their sense of being entrusted with the sacred duty of civilizing the barbarian, making him presentable and conforming to Han ways, freeing him from his superstitions and uncouthness, goes a long way back in their cultural tradition. In such a context any method is licit, given the transcendence and in their view the "nobility" of the goal. In the Tibetans the Chinese found the most repulsive, the least malleable of barbarians, the ones most entrenched in their in their original conceptions of the world, of society, of life; therefore the repression was all the greater, all the more terrible and enraged. From this angle one might detect all too many painful similarities with the work of the missionaries during the early Renaissance, especially in the Americas! They too were capable of the darkest wickednesses perpetrated on the bodies of the natives (maybe by tacitly authorizing the conquistadors to resort to such methods) in order to bring the natives to baptism for the salvation of their souls.

Coercion under a religious impulse has always been the most odious kind in history. The Russians of yore, like the Chinese of today, declared themselves to be atheists: but atheism too can be seen instigating evil, promoting unpardonable cruelty.

For a good decade from 1966 Tibet, along with the rest of the Chinese empire, was caught up in the madness of the Cultural Revolution. "It was past all understanding!" said Palden Gyatso. Even in the prisons there were instances of ritual subversion, that is the inculpation of the top prison governors by junior police officers. The result of this was, paradoxically, a period of greater freedom for the prisoners, even while "outside" the gala festival of the destruction of monasteries, shrines and chapels, the extermination of monks or of layfolk too much attached to their religion was going full swing.

The death of Mao in 1976 raised hopes immensely but in practice led to little change. It was to take the rise of Hu Yaobang to the position of Secretary General of the Chinese Communist Party before there was any real gap in the clouds. His visit to Lhasa in 1980 signalled a pronounced swing towards a more liberal administration of Tibetan affairs.

There now followed some years of authentic openness towards the rest of the world. It was in this period that the Turinese Roberto Vitali was able to visit many religious sites in the centre and south of Tibet and made some surprising discoveries, though he established the complete destruction of the monastery of Kyangphu with all its treasures (some illustrated with photographs in this book, pp. 191 ff.) and the serious damage visited upon that little gem of a monastery, Iwang, which I had visited with Tucci in 1937 (see pp. 220 ff.).

This was also a good moment for another young Turinese, Paolo Oliaro, to make the journey; he was able to proceed on his own, or with one or two chosen companions, to some of the least-known regions of Tibet. The result was a Guide to Tibet which has been a goldmine of information for years. We barely touch on the young of many countries who took advantage of this burst of sunshine in the lowering skies of Chinese oppression and, either on their own or in small groups, made truly astonishing journeys throughout the length and breadth of the country. Particular mention should be made of the young Australian woman, S. Wilby, who crossed almost the entire country on her own, from Lhasa to the westernmost point on the Chang Tang border (described in the December 1987 issue of the *National Geographic Magazine*). Notably too Melvyn Goldstein contrived to spend some months with the nomads of the Chang Tang and gave a minute account of their hard way of life. That was the era when visitors(two Englishmen, Johnson and Moran, for instance) were able to reach Kailasa, and to complete the holy pilgrimage in the area. Later, at an opportune moment, two noted Italian explorers, Olga Amman and Giulia Barletta also reached Kailasa.

Then in 1987, with the arrest of Yulu Dawa Tsering on the charge of disseminating anti-revolutionary propaganda – he had spoken with some foreign visitors – there was a spontaneous anti-Chinese revolt in Lhasa, which exceedingly troubled the authorities and sparked a wave of ruthless repression against the Tibetans and of deep distrust of foreigners. Tourists were still able to visit Tibet, for they brought in valuable hard currency, but only in groups under the close control of Chinese minders. All contact between foreign visitors and the Tibetans was forbidden. Things gradually improved once again, but the moment the cry arose afresh of "Long live free Tibet!" there was a further crackdown. So much so that from the summer of 1989 for more than a year martial law was imposed.

In the 1990s the alternating cycle of relaxation and repression continued, as the police in Lhasa saw fit and as the Tibetans responded to their hated occupiers. The situation was liable to change from month to month, even from week to week, quite unpredictably. Thus it is as well to sniff the air carefully before setting forth.

Meanwhile the campaign to turn Tibetans into Chinese continues on its way like a steamroller, ruthlessly crushing every trace of a thousand-year-old civilization. It is reckoned that in Lhasa now the Chinese outnumber the Tibetans. And of course Chinese is the language spoken by Tibetans with the smallest ambition to make their way in the world; Tibetan has been reduced to the forlorn rank of a local dialect spoken in the remote country areas. Ever more in evidence is writing laid out vertically, ideograms, in place of the elegant phrases spelt out syllabically in the language of Milarepa or Thonmi Sambhota, which goes back fifteen centuries. The school curriculum allows for the odd hour of Tibetan studies, but these are imparted by Chinese teachers whose pronunciation obviously leaves much to be desired.

The architectural subversion of the city of Lhasa is now virtually a *fait accompli*. The characteristic Tibetan houses, with their sturdy stone-built walls that best suit the rigours of the mountain climate have been almost completely replaced by boxlike structures in concrete: the walls are strong but thin, quite unsuitable as protection either against the winter frosts or the summer heat.

In most cases, too, they give Lhasa the look of practically any Chinese city – a planned hideous utilitarian squalor.

One of the most despicable weapons used by the Chinese in their strategy for the cultural genocide of the Tibetans consists in opening red-light districts in the new quarters of Lhasa [32] That's right, you enterprising Tibetan youth: frolic away with your wine and your whores, make with the drugs, that way we'll be shot of your inconvenient presence all the sooner!

One field in which every power that has achieved domination in Tibet has always striven to make itself felt is that of the choice of the new incumbent in a line of abbots who succeed each other by reincarnation. The *trul-ku*, the reincarnated, number (or used to number) many thousands; every important monastery had the ambition to claim one. But the two supreme ones were for centuries the Dalai Lama and the Panchen Lama. We have already defined the two figures in the Tibetan Pantheon (see pp. 127ff., and the Glossary).

In the succession of the Dalai Lama, from the Thirteenth, Thupden Gyatso, 1876–1933, to the Fourteenth, Tenzin Gyatso, 1935– , the Chinese found no way to slip their paw into Tibet's political affairs, because the question had been resolved before they occupied the plateau. With the succession of the Panchen Lama matters proceeded quite differently. The Seventh in the succession, Lobsang Tseten, was born in 1938 and died in 1989. He was what one might call a hesitant, impulsive person. He was educated by Chinese tutors and in his boyhood showed himself to be a willing pawn of Beijing, in the troublesome political game being played between China and Tibet; he applauded the civilizing mission and social activities of the invaders. But in March 1987 the Panchen Lama for the first time and indeed while in Beijing actually spoke up courageously to criticize his Chinese masters' Tibetan policy.

Needless to say his change of position did not go down at all well in Beijing and in the upper echelons of the Chinese Communist Party. In 1989, on the occasion of a visit to Shigatse, the traditional seat of the Panchen Lama, the prelate once again rounded on the Chinese line in the most uncompromising terms: "the price paid by Tibet for development over these years has been too high," he said, "greater than the rewards." Not many days later, on 28 January 1989 the Panchen Lama suddenly met his death. The Chinese authorities spoke of a "heart attack" but the general consensus among Tibetans was that he had been poisoned. With this inconvenient person out of the way, the Chinese expressed their sorrow at the loss of the "great patriot and devoted friend of the Chinese Communist Party".[33]

At the beginning of 1995 the Dalai Lama officially recognized the Tibetan child Ghedun Chökyi Nyima, born in 1989, as the legitimate successor to the deceased Panchen Lama. A few months later, during a raid on the great monastery of Tashilhunpo at Shigatse by the Chinese police, the abbot and some thirty monks were arrested. When the remaining monks recovered from the unpleasant shock they realized that the little Panchen Lama who had been recognized by the Dalai Lama had disappeared. It was immediately said that he would have been taken away to Beijing, willy-nilly along with his relatives. The fact remains that never since 1989 has there been so much as word of the fate of the little *trul-ku*, young and innocent though he is.

The incident of course was quickly known worldwide. The European Parliament, by a resolution dated 18 July 1995 gave notice of its "serious concern at the news of the sequestration of the Tibetan boy Ghedun Chökyi Nyima and his parents by the Chinese authorities". Of course the protest was swept under the carpet, along with so many other complaints emanating from international organizations. A curtain of silence has dropped round the small living *Bodhisattva* that will not readily be penetrated. The Chinese are thick-skinned, enormously so, and impenetrable, not least when "the national interest" is at stake.

Meanwhile a fresh candidate (Chinese this time) has appeared out of the blue to figure as the reincarnation of the deceased Panchen Lama. He is a child of more or less the same age as Ghedun Chökyi Nyima, just as charming, with lively eyes and a ready smile. His name is Gyalchen Norbu. We can count on hearing a great deal about him, and for a long time to come. We shall have at Shigatse an Eighth Panchen Lama brainwashed and manipulated by the Beijing government. Had he been apprised of the political and theological machinations of an Asia country as remote and curious as China, Machiavelli would have been lavish in his applause for those who set up a ploy such as this, in which metaphysics reaches in to play a sly hand of Realpolitik.

What does the future of Tibet look like today? What hope is there for the land of eternal snows, the home of Milarepa and of so many hermit-poets who have left their mark on world literature, among the great seers and visionaries?

Rather little hope, if one views the situation dispassionately.

For any fundamental change in Tibet's situation it would be necessary for a radical transformation to take place on the Far Eastern geo-political horizon, in other words China would have to undergo a true spiritual rebirth of an amply liberal nature.

There is no doubt that in recent years we have witnessed political collapses that were not to be thought of twenty years ago: I am thinking obviously of the dissolution of the Soviet empire. It must be borne in mind, however, that the Soviet organism was vastly more fragile than its Chinese counterpart, especially because it was only partially identified with Russia itself. Besides, there was the silent, underground but potentially powerful opposition of the Orthodox Church.

In China, as has already been suggested, Mao is not to be considered in the same framework as Stalin, Hitler, Mussolini, Franco, Tito and so on; these were historical figures, while Mao was rather the founder of a dynasty, an irresistibly charismatic figure, characteristic in Chinese history, with over two thousand years of idealized life behind it. Dynasties, it must be remembered, are very durable organisms, they last two or three centuries on average. Moreover there is no Church or ideological organization in China capable of challenging or supplanting the Communist party at the appropriate moment. In China there is a total identification between ideology, nationalism, imperialism and the dynasty.

If we read the text of an important document, "Plan for the economic and social development of the Autonomous Region of Tibet, in the Five-Year Plan 1996–2000, and in the longer-term forecast to the year 2010" published by the *Tibet Daily* (the Lhasa daily paper, mostly written in Chinese, of 7 June 1996, and translated into English in the *Tibet Bulletin* at Dharamsala of March–April 1997), it is enough to make the blood run cold.

The plan aims at the total integration of Tibet's economy and its social and cultural life into the Chinese economic and social mould. A clearsighted Darwinian exercise in the management of human resources will tend to result in the many agricultural landowners in the country sorting things out between themselves to achieve a given number of economically viable estates. In the process a huge number of peasants who have failed to enlarge their land-holdings to the minimum size to be commercially productive will be squeezed out and eliminated. Poor things! the reader will at once think. But then he notices that the document regards this as entirely a good thing. The surplus peasants will migrate to the cities which will in the meantime have grown in size and been reorganized, and will furnish precious cheap labour to the small and medium-sized industries just starting up or expanding.

A similar provision is made for the nomads, with an eye to turning them into raisers and producers of beef cattle at a far higher level of production. In Tibet, according to this and other documents, there ought to be some twenty-three million head of cattle. In fact Tibet is to become one of the big centres for meat processing, and thus to feed the entire Chinese population.

Hitherto the Tibetan nomads (see the fine illustrated study by M. Goldstein) have lived in a sort of idyllic harmony with their herds, taking to market only the fully matured animals, and respecting, at any rate in a religious context, that unity between man and beast consecrated in the expression "sentient creatures" (*sem-chen*) that embraces both species. But if the architects of the Plan go about it seriously – and dealing as it does with a colonial report on the Tibetans, there is no reason to expect any reconsiderations or special exemptions – the Tibetan nomads will have to transform themselves into raisers of cattle destined for the slaughterhouse the moment they reach the weight prescribed by law, never mind any question of maturity. Personal rapport between man and beast? What an idea! Those dreamers have to come to terms with the needs of the twenty-first century – or be crushed.

In conclusion: the Tibet Question

Much is spoken about the "Tibet Question". Now that Hollywood has proposed two, possibly three movies in rapid succession based on the tragic – and spectacular – events, of the land of eternal snows, much more will be spoken about it, true and false.[34]

The attitudes towards Tibet and its problems are manifold and often contradictory. The Chinese continue to insist that their political claim to the plateau and its inhabitants has been matured over thousands of years, while many Westerners, in their general ignorance of so exotic a history, allow themselves to be impressed, or remain perplexed and undecided. The tourists who visit Lhasa – and nowadays there are beginning to be quite a few – notice at once the way the guides (Chinese) pay particular attention in showing them certain frescoes in the Potala that feature scenes from seventh-century life, in the era of King Songtsen-gampo. They point a finger emphatically at the panel that shows the arrival of the Chinese Princess Wen Ch'eng in the Tibetan capital, when she came as bride to the King of the plateau; her retinue included a chariot carrying a large image of Buddha, considered to be the very one now venerated in the temple of Johkhang.

This is one of the many historical episodes put forward in support of an age-old claim to a Chinese protectorate over Tibet; scenes follow that ostensibly demonstrate the fealty paid by important lamas in more recent times to the Celestial Court.

Nobody denies these facts, just as nobody will deny that between 1720 and 1912 the Ch'ing dynasty exercised a vestigial form of protectorate over Tibet. The history is right there, a book that anyone may read. But with history, and with time, certain concepts change, as do human sensitivities. In the eighteenth and nineteenth centuries the use of torture, the death penalty, colonial expansion, were patent facts accepted by one and all, whereas today they are an offence to attitudes and susceptibilities that are a great deal more refined and civilized. It might be said that the Chinese have simply been left behind in the evolution of civilized life. If historical precedent could serve to justify the occupation of other people's land, the world would lapse into a terrible and perennial revolution. The British would claim India as their own, along with so many other erstwhile possessions, the French would claim back Algeria and Indo-China, the Japanese would lay claim to Manchuria and Taiwan, the Italians to Eritrea and Somalia, the Russians to Poland, the Greeks would banish the Turks back to Central Asia, and the planet would be in a state of constant warlike upheaval. The Chinese occupation of Tibet forms part of a framework that is no longer relevant to world history – the framework of imperialist conquest and colonial domination can therefore be maintained only by raw might bereft of any legitimacy. And the brutal treatment of the Tibetans by the Chinese often makes one suppose that they are obscurely aware in the depths of their conscience of the substantial evil of the occupation.

The crucial point to consider today is quite another: are the Chinese and Tibetans simply two provincial varieties of the same people or are they to all intents and purposes two distinct peoples? If they are two distinct peoples, as can be readily demonstrated, any form of domination by the one group over the other is quite simply illegal, it is nothing better than a brutal abuse of power. Any right acquired in the past lapses.

As I have tried to make plain in earlier pages, through a long sequence of historical instances, matured over fifteen centuries, Tibetans and Chinese have constituted two entirely distinct and profoundly different peoples for a very long time. I have recorded the four essential moments in the alienation of Tibet from China: 1) the choice of phonetic script in place of ideograms, during the seventh century, a factor that kept the great Chinese philosophy (Confucianism and its schools, Taoism and its offshoots) well away from Tibet, and brought Tibetan culture into a close connection with that of India; 2) the opting for the Indian Buddhist schools of philosophy, rather than for the Chinese schools, at the Council of Lhasa, 792–794; 3) their becoming the heirs of Indian Buddhism after the disappearance of that faith from India during the tenth to twelfth centuries, the period of the Islamic conquest; 4) lastly, the establishment of a wholly autonomous royal-theocratic dominance on the high plateau of Tibet principally by the Fifth Dalai Lama (1617–1682). Anyone inclined to split hairs might bear in mind that the military support on which the Fifth Dalai Lama was able to rely in the establishment of his state was provided not by the Chinese but by their mortal enemies, the Mongols of Gushri Khan.

It would be possible here to observe that the Chinese paradoxically have a far better claim over Japan than over Tibet. The Japanese, after all, adopted their neighbours' ideograms in the fifth century. This led them to develop a civilization deeply imbued with Chinese spiritual substance, and culturally indebted to China in many other fields. Confucianism was actually given precedence as the state philosophy during the Tokugawa era (1600–1868). Their cultural debt to China (which they amply acknowledge) is immense. Their modern language, more than a true Japanese (*Yamato kotoba*), is a Sino-Japanese symbiosis, its various elements virtually inextricable, and which with time keeps drawing closer to Chinese.

In a word, while in the case of Tibet there has been a divergence from China for the past thousand years, in the case of Japan there have been a thousand years of convergence. Of course Japan, being heavily populated, rich and powerful has remained a free sovereign state while Tibet, with its small population, poor and weak as it is, has been enslaved. But there is no denying the paradox.

Thus in theory the Tibetans have the most sacred right to aspire towards a full independence. Even if, at the close of the twentieth century, a dreadful doubt possesses the mind of the observer: no doubt Tibet possesses a culture and civilization that is profoundly original and profoundly different from the Chinese, and yet – for how much longer will this continue to be the case? The brutal labour of Chinese assimilation has been going on now for forty years, subtly, omnivorously and unremittingly and is thus well advanced. Furthermore, one fine day the Dalai Lama will inevitably die. His succession will probably bring to light two candidates for the Fifteenth reincarnation, one of them acceptable to the Tibetan diaspora, the other preferred by the authorities in Beijing. Obviously the one who is going to count up on the plateau will be the Chinese nominee. The new masters will then have their hands not only on the Tibetan body politic but on the nation's very soul.

I should not wish to close this account, begun in 1950 with so much youthful enthusiasm, on so gloomy a note. What can the sincere friends of Tibet do today? Fight for a limited but feasible goal: to obtain the fullest possible autonomy for Tibet. To make the Chinese aware that there is such a thing as world opinion in politics, a pressure for the respecting of the 17-point treaty proposed and signed in 1951. *Le Tibet libre*, like De Gaulle's *le Québec libre*, is perhaps a utopian slogan; but *le Tibet autonome* is not. With this end in mind, let us make our voices heard as loudly as possible!

100 *Seal of the Dalai Lama*

1 G. Tucci: "Tibet" in the series Archaeologia Mundi, Geneva, Nagel, 1973

2 The dates in this and the following sections are rounded up for convenience.

3 According to Tucci: *A Lhasa e oltre*, Rome, 1950, p. 77, the statue does not date back to the Kingdom but would be some centuries more recent.

4 A. MacDonald: " Une lecture . . . Essai sur la formation et l'emploi des mythes politiques dans la religion royale de Srong-bcan sgam-po" in *Etudes tibétaines dédiées à la mémoire de M. Lalou*, Paris, Maisonneuve, 1971, pp. 190–391

5 H. Carrère d'Encausse: *Decline of an Empire*, New York, Newsweek Books, 1979

6 F. Sierksma: *Tibet's Terrifying Deities*, Mouton, The Hague, 1966

7 L. Petech: *Le Civiltà dell' Oriente*, Rome, Casini, 1956, vol. I, p. 1126. On this interesting debate see P. Demiéville: *Le Concile de Lhasa,* Paris, Presses Universitaires de France, 1952.

8 W. D. Shakabpa: *Tibet, a Political History*, Yale University Press, 1967, speaks

bluntly of "hegemonies"; given the prevailing chaos, this seems an exaggeration.

9 Galden, in part because it was a highly visible symbol of the old regime, and partly owing to its distance from Lhasa and thus being less protected, was barbarously destroyed and virtually razed to the ground during the years of the worst anti-religious violence (1966–1976) – see photos 98 and 99.

10 L. Petech, *op. cit.* I, p. 1136

11 D. Snellgrove, H. Richardson: *A Cultural History of Tibet*, London, 1968

12 A similar episode took place almost at the same time in Bhutan: in this case the ploy was to succeed for fully half a century! See M. Aris: *Bhutan*, Warminster, Aris & Phillips, 1979.

13 D. Snellgrove, H. Richardson, *op. cit.*, p. 205

14 G. Tucci: *Tibetan Folk Songs from Gyantse and Western Tibet*, Ascona, Artibus Asiae, 1966, 2nd edition revised and enlarged

15 Yu Dawchyuan: *Love Songs of the Sixth Dalai Lama*, Academia Sinica, Peiping, 1930

16 On this complex and tumultuous period see the very scholarly work of L. Petech: *China and Tibet in the early 18th Century*, Leiden, Brill, 1950 (reissued in 1973 by the Hyperion Press, Westport).

17 "Ah, what a fine appearance of good and holiness at first glance!" exclaimed Father Domenico da Fano in a letter from Lhasa of 3 May 1717. "But now as we begin to penetrate further in, what a sea of superstitions and abominations we discover." See L. Petech: *Il Nuovo Ramusio*, II/1 (Italian Missionaries in Tibet and Nepal); Rome, La Libreria dello Stato, 1952, p. 90

18 Desideri's writings are published in *Il Nuovo Ramusio* II/5, 6, 7 (1954/55/56), edited by L. Petech, as above. And see Bibliography I.

19 E. R. Huc: *Souvenirs d'un voyage en Tartarie, le Tibet et la Chine*, 4 vols., Paris, Plon, 1925 (original edition 1856; many other editions)

20 A great deal has been written about the 1904 expedition. The best and most accessible (albeit from a British standpoint, of course) is to be found in Peter Fleming's *Bayonets to Lhasa*, London, Rupert Hart-Davis, 1961, recently reissued.

21 Charles Bell: *Portrait of the Dalai Lama*, London, Collins, 1946

22 Melvyn C. Goldstein, author of the imposing (898pp.) work, *A History of Modern Tibet, 1913-1951*, (University of California Press, 1989) based himself almost entirely on personal interviews (he lists a good eighty), and on popular comments traceable through various lampoons diligently gleaned from the mouths of the elderly.

23 Ginsburgs & Mathos: *Communist China and Tibet: The first dozen years*, The Hague, Nijhoff, 1964, p. 5

24 For the full text of the seventeen articles see for example S. N. Dhyani: *Contemporary Tibet (its Status in International Law)*, Lucknow, Capital Law House, 1961, p. 139.

25 Franco Calamandrei and Teresa Regard, who visited Tibet late in 1955, came upon calm, serenity, flexible integration of past with present. "Situated in the general framework of the development of China towards socialism, the Tibetan headache becomes a model of how revolutionary tactics and strategy may in the name of progress invoke the very objects that are destined to vanish in the name of progress." The many photographs they took on their visit show us a Tibet still almost unchanged, in which the juxtaposition of lamas and aristocrats with experimental stations for agronomy and animal husbandry, of religious festivals and schools and analytical laboratories, attest the steps towards a well-judged reform. See their *Rompicapo tibetano*, Florence, Parenti, 1959.

26 *Le Tibet et La République populaire de Chine*, Geneva, Commission Internationale de Juristes, 1960

27 D. Howarth (editor): *My Land and My People*, the Autobiography of H. H. the Dalai Lama, Bombay, Asia Publishing House, 1962. This gives a detailed account of those dramatic days.

28 W. D. Shakabpa: *Tibet, a Political History*, p. 320

29 B. R. Burman: *Religion and Politics in Tibet*, New Delhi, Vikas, 1979, pp. 117 and 122

30 See *Le Tibet et la République Populaire de Chine* already cited. See also the *Tibetan Review*, published monthly from New Delhi starting in 1965.

31 In the case of many religious buildings, and civic too (including the famous Yumbu Lakhang) in the 1980s and 1990s, there is evidence of efforts, some of them effective, others merely pathetic, to put in hand restoration with the help of volunteers and dedicated enthusiasts. But such restoration is slow, sporadic and often arbitrary. And the results are generally disappointing. Where are the famous master-craftsmen of former years? And what of the colours which in their time were natural and prepared by the painters themselves, while now the products of the chemical industry are used, and even these are often of inferior quality owing to simple considerations of price.

32 " . . . among the prostitutes of Tibet . . . There are not only monasteries in Lhasa, there are plenty of brothels . . . " Serena Zoli, reviewing *Un' Italiana in Cina del capitalismo Karaoke* by M. P. Baroncelli (Ed. Bietti, 1997) in *Corriere della Sera*, 24 December 1997

33 See C. King: *Tibet, un paese e il suo dramma*, Istituto Tsong Khapa, Pomaia, Pisa, 1996.

34 See *Seven Years in Tibet* directed by J. J. Arnaud, 1997 and *Kundun* ("Presence") directed by Martin Scorsese, 1998.

Glossary

*(The Tibetan name follows in brackets where relevant.
Names that have their own entry in this Glossary are printed in bold.)*

Adi Buddha "The Original Buddha", the supreme, primordial, absolute one, the source of all heavenly beings. The idea had its birth in tenth-century Nepal, and remains prevalent throughout Tibet and elsewhere. According to the various schools, two beings may occupy this highest position:

a *Vajradhara* (Dorje-chang) "He who holds the ***Vajra***" is the Adi Buddha of the reformed schools;

b *Vajrasattva* (Dorje-sempa) "He whose essence is the *Vajra*" is the Adi Buddha of the unreformed schools.

Both are represented in princely attire (jewellery, silken scarves, necklaces, crown); both grasp the *vajra* and *ghanta* (thunderbolt and bell), only the position of their arms and hands differs. Both can appear on their own or in the embrace of their mystic ***shakti***. Other beings – **Samantabhadra, Vairocana, Amitābha** – can hold a similar position to that of the Adi Buddha, depending on different schools.

Akshobhya (Mikyö-pa) One of the five Supreme **Buddhas**

Altan Khan (1507–82). Mongol ruler of notable importance in Tibetan history. In 1578 he met the Abbot Sonam Gyatso at the head of the *Gelug-pa* sect, at Lake Koko-nor, and being impressed by his personality, decided to honour him with the Mongol title of *dalai* ("ocean", with "of wisdom" implied). The title of *Dalai Lama* was retrospectively accorded to the abbot's two predecessors, as a result of which Sonam Gyatso was historically the third Dalai Lama from the start.

Amban Commissioners installed in Lhasa by the Chinese emperors between 1728 and 1912; generally they were two in number, to keep an eye on each other.

Amdo Vast region in north-eastern Tibet that made a notable contribution to the country's culture. Today it is divided between the Chinese provinces of Ch'ing-hai and Kansu, and lies to the north-west of **Kham.**

Amitābha (Öpame) One of the five Supreme **Buddhas**. Considered in certain *Mahayana* Buddhist schools to be the **Adi Buddha.**

Andrade, Antonio de Portuguese missionary who lived at Tsaparang, kingdom of **Guge** in western Tibet, 1625–31.

Arhat (drachompa) Saint who achieved *nirvana*. Ideal of the older form of Buddhism and still venerated in the Buddhist ***Hinayana*** schools. The ***Mahayana*** schools accord greater importance to the ***Bodhisattva***, who merited *nirvana* but renounced it in order to remain in the world, in the cycle of birth and death, so as to help less fortunate souls on their journey towards salvation. Tradition and iconography present the *arhat* mainly in groups of sixteen or eighteen figures, representing them in Buddha's company. Groups of five hundred also exist. Being regarded as ordinary mortals who succeeded in achieving *nirvana*, the *arhat* are always represented with intensely individual characteristics, sometimes verging on the grotesque; their faces often portray common people, artisans, peasants, hermits such as the artists might have encountered them in daily life. There are several sculptured groups of *arhat* in Tibet (as in the monastery of Sera), which generally betray clear Chinese influences. The groups are also portrayed in murals and on religious banners (***tangka***).

Atisha (982–1054). Renowned Bengali Buddhist master, invited to Tibet by the king of Guge, Yeshe-Ö. He arrived in 1042 and stayed until he died. He is to be considered effectively the second founder of Tibetan Buddhism; he radically reformed its theology, its liturgy, its monastic discipline. The ***Kadam-pa*** sect was established by his disciples; this was in its turn reformed by **Tsongkhapa** early in the fifteenth century and gave birth to the ***Gelug-pa*** sect, which retained theocratic power in Tibet until 1959.

Avalokitesvara (Chen-re-zi) ***Bodhisattva*** of the highest order, the very essence of divine love for the living world. The name lends itself to several interpretations, but it is generally accepted to mean "He who looks down", "with compassion" being understood. He is a manifestation of the Supreme Buddha *Amitābha*. The Tibetans see him incarnated in the Dalai Lama. In ancient Buddhist art he is often depicted as fully human, seated or standing, with two arms, wearing the princely adornments of the *Bodhisattvas*. In more recent lamaist art he is depicted with four arms, painted white, and he holds a rosary and a lotus flower in his principal hands. Other common depictions show him with eleven heads and sixteen arms, or with eleven heads and "a thousand arms". The thousand arms generally resolve themselves into a halo with only a summary indication of all those arms and hands. There are countless other forms in which this *Bodhisattva* is depicted in Buddhist iconography (see Getty: *The Gods of Northern Buddhism*). *Avalokitesvara* usually is seen in a triad with ***Manjusri*** and ***Vajrapani***. His cult is also popular in China, where he is known as *Kuanyin*, and in Japan, where he is known as *Kanon*. While in Tibet he is portrayed as a male, in China and Japan he is sexless or has vaguely feminine, maternal connotations. His mantra is the formula *Om mani padme hum*.

Bhrikuti Nepalese princess, thought to be daughter of King Amsuvarman, married to the Tibetan King Songtsen-gampo *c.* 639 A.D. Popular devotion claimed her for the living incarnation of the goddess **Tara** and credited her with bringing the first light of the Buddhist faith to the court of Tibet. She is often represented in art together with the king and his other bride, the Chinese princess Wen-Ch'eng.

Bodhisattva (Changchup-sempa) A saint who has acquired sufficient merit to attain *nirvana*, but who renounces it in order to remain within the cycle of birth and death (*samsara*), in his wish to help all living creatures on their path to salvation. A most transcendental spiritual concept, not unlike the Christian teachings on the Redeemer, it is a distinctive feature of the ***Mahayana*** schools of Buddhism. The term means "He whose essence is Illumination". There are countless *Bodhisattva*s but only a limited group who are venerated and represented iconographically.

They are to be distinguished from Buddhas (who are generally portrayed semi-naked, barely covered by a simple mendicant monk's tunic) by the crown and princely jewellery that adorns them. Certain of them appear of terrifying aspect (*trowo*). The *Bodhisattva*s most frequently to be met with in Tibetan art are: Avalokitesvara, Vajrapani, Manjusri, Maitreya, Samantabhadra, Akasagarbha, Ksitigarbha and Sarvanivarana-vishkambhin – but only the first five still enjoy pre-eminence in iconographic terms.

Buddha (Sengye) "The Illuminated One". The term refers both to the historical Buddha **Sakya-Muni** and to the eternal, heavenly Buddhas who are manifested by those on earth. See Chapter Fifteen for an account of the development of the concept. Buddhas are represented iconographically clad only in the tunic of a mendicant monk, and without adornment. To tell them apart it is necessary to study their gestures and the position of their hands (*mudra*), sometimes the vehicle – animal, flower – and the colours. The historical Buddha Sakya-Muni is normally shown seated, his legs tightly crossed, his left hand on his lap holding a begging bowl while his right hand stretches down to touch the ground, calling it to witness his Illumination.

Buddhas, Five Supreme (Gyalwa-ringa) Five Supreme Buddhas preside over the five great eras of cosmic history (*kalpa*). This concept is typical of *Mahayana* Buddhism. For a long time in the West they were called the Five *Dhyani* Buddhas (Buddhas of Meditation), but it is now recognized that the term is inexact. The Five Supreme Buddhas are constantly represented in Tibetan art (as also in Chinese, Japanese and Korean). One important and beautifully refined group has been described during the visit to the monastery of Kyangphu, and another in the visit to the Great Temple at Gyantse. The group of the *Jina* (Conquerors) usually comprises the following:

Vairocana (Nampar-nangdse): He who illuminates
Akshobhya (Mikyö-pa): The Unmoveable One
Amitābha (Öpame): Infinite Light
Amoghasiddhi (Dönyö-drubpa): Infallible [magic] Power
Ratnasambhava (Rinchen-chungden): Born of a Jewel

The doctrine of the Five Buddhas blends with that of the Three Bodies (*tri-kaya*) and gives rise to a whole series of combinations that at first sight appear to be random but are in fact extremely useful for the drawing up of a plan, a rough and ready mandala with a view to fixing the positions of several beings in the complex Buddhist pantheon, and to identify their iconography. At the apex is the *Dharma-kaya*, the body of law, wherein the Buddhas subsist in spiritual essence and meditation; one step below we find the *Sambogha-kaya*, the body of perfection: this is the level of the *Bodhisattva*s, who mediate between the mortal world and the absolute. Lastly there is the *Nirmana-kaya*, the body of transformation, the mortal bodily form in which Buddha is incarnate as the apostle of every era of history.

If we now combine the Five Supreme Buddhas (and the Five Epochs of the World, *kalpa*) with the Three Bodies, we find the following plan, in which certain beings play a very small role and are seldom encountered while others (those in italics) are frequently met with:

Kalpa	Supreme Buddha	Bodhisattva	Manushi Buddha
I	*Vairocana*	*Samantabhadra* (Kuntu-zangpo) "The wholly good"	Krakucchanda
II	*Akshobhya*	*Vajrapani* (Chanadorje) "He who holds the *Vajra*"	Kanakamuni
III	*Ratnasambhava*	Ratnapani "He who holds the Jewel"	*Dipamkara* (Marmedze)
IV	*Amitābha*	*Avalokitesvara* (Chen-re-zi) "He who looks down [with compassion]"	*Sakya-Muni* (Sakya-thubpa)
V	*Amoghasiddhi*	Visvapani "He who holds the double *Vajra*"	*Maitreya* (Champa)

Lastly, the group of the Five Supreme Buddhas serves as point of reference for a notable series of other pentads (directions of space, colour, elements, etc.) which vary from one school to the next; below is a tabulation that may serve as a general reference:

	Vairocana	Akshobhya	Ratnasambhava	Amitābha	Amoghasiddhi
Space	centre	east	south	west	north
Colour	white	blue	yellow	red	green
Vehicle	lion	elephant	horse	peacock	*garuda* bird
Element	ether	water	earth	fire	air
Mudra	*dharma-chakra*	*bhūmisparsa*	*varada*	*dhyāna*	*abhaya*
Symbol	wheel	thunderbolt	jewel	lotus	double *vajra*
Syllable	*Om*	*Hum*	*Tram*	*Hri*	*Ah*
Family	*moha*	*dvesa*	*cintāmani*	*raga*	*samaya*
Aggregate (*skanda*)	*vijñana* (conscience)	*rūpa* (body)	*vedanā* (sensation)	*samjñā* (perception)	*samskāra* (volition)
Wisdom	of universal law	of the mirror	of equality	of discernment	of fulfilment
Poison	ignorance	hatred	pride	passion	greed
Shakti	*Akasadhat-visvari*	*Locanā*	*Māmakā*	*Pāndari*	*Samayatārā*

Buton-Rimpoche (1290–1364). Abbot of **Shalu** and editor of the first authoritative texts of the ***Kangyur*** and the *Tangyur.*

Capuchin missionaries Present in Lhasa at various times between 1707 and 1745. See Bibliography I: Marchigiani, Cappuccini.

Chagpo-ri "Iron Mountain (*ri*)", name of a steep hill facing the Potala at Lhasa. The picturesque buildings of the Tibetan School of Medicine used to crown the hill, and embodied a number of small but important ancient shrines. The complex had more in common with a mediaeval fort than with a seat of learning. The events of 1959 resulted in the total destruction of everything that had been built over the centuries on this steep, rocky hilltop.

Chakra (Khorlo) "Wheel [of the Law]". One of the most important Buddhist symbols. The wheel's circular movement stands for regularity and thus for law in place of chaos and disorder. It also suggests the cycle of birth and death, to which all living beings are tied in their progress towards *nirvana*. Important temples display the wheel between two gazelles, to record the "Park of the Gazelles" in Varanasi (Benares) where Buddha preached his first sermon.

The wheel also symbolizes the Supreme Buddha Vairocana.

Chamdo Important town in eastern Tibet (pop. *c.* 15,000) built on a tributary of the La-chu which later becomes the Mekong. One of the principal centres in Kham. The most important *Gelug-pa* monastery in the whole of eastern Tibet was built at Chamdo; it was called Champa-ling. Founded in 1437, it was destroyed during the Sino-Tibetan wars.

Chang Tang "The Northern Plains", signifying the vast, inhospitable area of the Tibetan plateau to the north of Lhasa. The plain lies between the chain given the name Transhimalaya by Sven Hedin, and the Kun-lun chain. Its great height, averaging 15,000 feet and more, the cold, the absence of vegetation make the Chang Tang unfit for permanent settlement; only groups of nomads visit it mostly on a seasonal basis.

Chen-re-zi Tibetan name for the *Bodhisattva* **Avalokitesvara.**

Ch'ing-hai or Qinghai See **Koko-nor**

Chorten Known in Sanskrit as a *stupa*, the *chorten* was originally an imitation of the dome-shaped tomb of Buddha. One of the oldest and most famous examples is to be found at Sanchi in Bhopal, northern India. With time numerous regional variations were to be found and the *chorten* was charged with symbolic value. In China it blended with existing structures in the form of towers to give birth to the pagoda, later to be found also in Korea and Japan.

The Tibetan *chorten* has a characteristic shape, as shown on p. 63. All these structures fulfil two fundamental requirements: they are reliquaries (ideally for Buddha's mortal remains, otherwise for different objects considered sacred); and they compose three-dimensional diagrams of the Buddhist universe.

Dalai Lama "Master Ocean [of Wisdom]". The title *Dalai* was first accorded in 1578 by **Altan Khan** to the abbot superior of the *Gelug-pa* sect, who at the time was Sonam Gyatso. The title was then extended retrospectively to his two predecessors. At this moment the line has extended to fourteen Dalai Lamas:

1 Gedun Truppa (1391–1475)
2 Gedun Gyatso (1476–1542)
3 Sonam Gyatso (1543–1588)
4 Yonten Gyatso (1589–1617)
5 Ngawang Losang Gyatso (1618–1682)

6 Tsangyang Gyatso (1683–1706)
7 Kelzang Gyatso (1708–1757)
8 Jampal Gyatso (1758–1804)
9 Lungtok Gyatso (1806–1815)
10 Tsultrim Gyatso (1816–1837)
11 Khedrup Gyatso (1838–1856)
12 Trinley Gyatso (1856–1875)
13 Thubten Gyatso (1876–1933)
14 Tenzin Gyatso (1935–)

Derge "Virtuous place", name of a town in Kham, in eastern Tibet. It is an important cultural centre, and was a small semi-independent principality until recent times. It contained important monasteries of the principal lamaist sects, and was also noted for the craft of metalworking.

Desideri, Ippolito A Jesuit from Pistoia. Born in 1684, he lived in Tibet from 1716 to 1721, and died in 1733. His works are listed in the Bibliography I.

Dhyani Buddha The *Dhyani* Buddhas represent the first stage in the cosmic process of differentiation; they are static, and stand for the thought and order behind the multiple universe. The next stage is the stage of dynamic creation, represented by the *Dhyani Bodhisattvas*. Each *Dhyani* Buddha generates a *Dhyani Bodhisattva*, and each *Dhyani Bodhisattva* creates a universe, a samsaric universe, over which he presides.

Dorje See **Vajra**

Drepung Also known as Depung, one of the three chief monasteries, with Sera and Galden, of the *Gelug-pa* sect, it was founded in 1416 not far from Lhasa. Until 1959 it was home to some nine thousand monks; today it is virtually abandoned, though fortunately neither the buildings nor the works of art have suffered excessively from the recent persecutions.

Dü-kor The Tibetan name for Kalacakra "The Wheel of Time". The name has many references. First, it indicates an important mystical and liturgical system originating in Nepal. Secondly, the texts in which these doctrines are enshrined. Thirdly, as is often the case, the name indicates the god who symbolizes and personifies the scriptures. He is generally shown in an excited state: standing on two legs, he is blue in colour and has anything up to twenty-four arms, each hand grasping some symbolic object. As a rule he is in the company of his *shakti*, coloured yellow or orange. It is often hard to distinguish Dü-kor from Demchog (Samvara).

Five Supreme Buddhas See Buddhas, Five Supreme

Galden Also Ganden, the first and most ancient monastery of the *Gelug-pa* sect, founded in 1409, about twenty miles east of Lhasa. It is the burial place of **Tsongkhapa** and at its apogee was home to some ten thousand monks. Around 1970 it was destroyed but is now being rebuilt.

Garuda (cha-kyung) A mythical bird, the vehicle of Vishnu and now a feature of Tibetan Buddhist iconography. It is often found at the top of the elaborate painted or carved panels serving as background for the statues of various Buddhas. The bird has a hooked beak used to kill snakes, the object of its ferocious hostility.

Gelug-pa The lamaist sect reformed by **Tsongkhapa** in the fourteenth century. Originally the Master's disciples were known as "reformed *Kadam-pa*", but given the sovereign importance the sect accorded to the observance of monastic discipline, they came to be known as *Gelug-pa*, "the Virtuous Ones". They quickly grew in numbers and influence to the point of constituting a true theocratic church. In 1578 their Abbot-general was given the title of Dalai by the Mongol ruler Altan Khan, and in 1642 the Great Fifth Dalai Lama, by virtue of gifts made to him by another Mongol prince, **Gushri Khan**, became a Buddhist Pope whose "ecclesiastical estates stretched from the Pamirs to China and from the Himalayas to Kun-Lun." The *Gelug-pa* are also known as the Yellow Sect, from the colour of their headgear.

Geshe Doctor of divinity. The title was originally used by the monks of the *Kadam-pa* sect, and later was adopted by those of the Sakya and eventually by those of the *Gelug-pa*. A *Geshe* will have passed a significant number of examinations and tests. The title more or less corresponds to the PhD in a British or American university.

Gompá Also Gonpa. A "solitary dwelling", a convent or monastery.

Gön-kang Chapel, normally underground and always dark, in which guardian divinities, whether national or local, are venerated. The entrance is often adorned with the carcass of a yak, stuffed with straw. The chapel will contain masks, ancient weapons and armour; the walls are decorated with paintings of the gods in various terrifying manifestations. (See photos 57 and 72)

Guge Kingdom of western Tibet founded in the ninth century by descendants of the Tibetan royal house. It was for many centuries a most notable centre of Buddhist religion and art. The temples of Tsaparang and Toling have been studied in detail by Tucci (*Indo-Tibetica*, III). The kingdom was visited by the Jesuit Fr d'Andrade, who stayed there from 1624 to 1631. In 1684 the realm devolved upon Lhasa.

Guru Rimpoche See Padma Sambhava

Gushri Khan (1582–1655). Ruler of the Qoshot Mongols, he was at first an enemy and later an ally of the Fifth Dalai Lama, and was to play a major role in Tibetan history. He conquered eastern Tibet (Amdo and Kham), then the central region and part of the western. In 1642 he made a gift of these lands to the "Great Fifth", and this was the origin of the Dalai Lamas' theocratic government of Tibet. From 1642 to 1721 the nation was in practice independent, even if subject to several Mongol incursions. In 1721 the nebulous Chinese protectorate began to take effect, and to continue until 1912.

Gyantse "The Royal Summit", an important locality in Tsang province, west of Lhasa, named after a crag rising suddenly from the plain; from earliest antiquity it was a platform for fortifications. The conspicuous fort (*dzong*) which now crowns the crag dates from the fourteenth century. The town of Gyantse numbers some ten thousand inhabitants. The monastery-city itself (the Palkhor-choide) has been largely destroyed and the monks, who numbered 800 to 1000 have been dispersed. All that remains are the Kum-Bum (the great pagoda), the Tsugla-khang (great temple), and the Labrang (the Abbots' lodging) which is in a sorry state of repair. Today roads connect Gyantse with Lhasa, Shigatse and Yatung.

Hayagriva (Tamdrin) Guardian divinity worshipped by Buddhists from time immemorial. The name means "Horse's Neck", and the god's hair is adorned with one or two small horse's heads. He may originally have been the protector of horses and horse-breeders. He is portrayed in red, a terrifying figure haloed in flame, with a ferocious look in his face. He is known in various guises: single- or double-headed, with four arms, with three heads and four or six arms. Sometimes he is portrayed with ***garuda*** wings, in mystical coition with his ***shakti***, who also displays all the attributes of terror. He is frequently found, especially as a minor, framing figure, in murals or sacred banners (***tangka***). The horse's head normally stands out amid the red hair by being coloured green.

Hinayana (Thepa-chung) The "Small Vehicle", embraces the Buddhist schools faithful to the traditional teachings and rejecting the innovations introduced by followers of the ***Mahayana*** , the "Big Vehicle". The distinction is two thousand years old, and not of Tibet's making. *Hinayana*, or *teravada* ("of the Ancients") Buddhism is found in particular in South Asia, in Sri Lanka, Burma, Thailand and Cambodia. What distinguishes the Small from the Big Vehicle are: a) the rejection of many scriptures deemed late and uncanonical; b) the central position it gives to the historical Buddha, Sakya-Muni; c) the importance it accords to the conception of ***arhat***; d) the small importance it accords to the concept of ***Bodhisattva***, and the complex developments in the theology of the heavenly Buddhas.

Huc Evariste, French Lazarist priest who visited Lhasa, accompanied by Gabet, in 1845/46 and wrote a fascinating account of his journey (Bibliography VI).

Jowo Rimpoche "The Lord Buddha", the name given by Tibetans to central statue of Buddha as a young man wearing a crown, in the Jokhang temple in Lhasa. The statue is covered in gold, pearls and jewels. According to legend it was brought to Lhasa by Princess Wen Ch'eng in the mid-seventh century on her arrival from China as bride of King Songtsen-gampo. Tucci and others have expressed some reservations about the dating of this statue to such a remote era. It is difficult to be entirely sure because the statue is heavily covered in garments and precious ornaments, and the face is frequently given a fresh coat of gilt varnish.

Kadam-pa "Those who follow the Oral Tradition". A lamaist sect reconstituted on the basis of the reforms of **Atisha** (982–1054), whose disciple Domtön was its founder in 1057. The sect's principal monastery is Reting. The *Kadam-pa* tradition, once reformed by Tsongkhapa, was to give rise to the *Gelug-pa* sect.

Kailasa (Kang Rimpoche) Isolated 22,000ft peak rising to the north of the Himalayas not far from Lake Manasarovar. It is sacred to the Buddhists and to the Hindus – for whom it represents Shiva's throne – as also for the devotees of Bon, Tibet's earliest religion. In popular belief the mountain possesses four spectacular springs from which rise the four great rivers of Asia, the Indus, Ganges, Satlej and

Tsangpo/Brahmaputra. In actual fact the four rivers must exclude the Ganges, and rise close to but not directly from this mountain. Kailasa is also identified with Mount **Meru**, the mythical mountain of Buddhist and Hindu cosmology. The walk around the mountain is difficult and dangerous, and is undertaken by many pilgrims from the three faiths as an act of religious sacrifice.

Kalpa One of the five epochs of the world (*kalpa*), each one presided over by a ***Dhyani* Buddha**. Each of these epochs lasts for thousands of years; the number varies from school to school. Three *kalpa*s have now passed, and we are now in the fourth.

Kangyur With **Tangyur** the two basic collections of Tibetan scriptures. *Kangyur* comprises 108 volumes and contains for the most part ancient Indian scriptures in translation. *Tangyur* comprises 225 volumes serves as a commentary to *Kangyur* by Indian and Tibetan writers. The final, definitive organization of this immense depository of scriptures was undertaken by the philosopher and historian Buton-Rimpoche (1290–1364), Abbot of Shalu.

Kargyu-pa or Kaju-pa, "Those who follow the Traditional Scriptures", one of the principal schools of religious thought and one of the seven most important in lamaism.

Karma-pa Tibetan school of thought and religious sect whose genealogy of patriarchs boasts such names as the Indians Naropa and Tilopa, and the Tibetans Marpa, Milarepa and Rechung. It was Rechung who in 1147 founded the mother house of the *Karma-pa* at Gansagon. The sect is considered to be an offshoot of the *Kargyu-pa*. It was probably the first to adopt the principle of reincarnation in order to establish the succession of its abbots. The monastery of Tsur-phu, founded in 1189, is one of its principal centres.

Karuna See **Shakti**

Kata or *Katag*, vaporous white scarves worn round the neck and exchanged between guests and their hosts. The more modest ones are made of cotton, the grander ones of silk. They are also offered votively to the statues of gods. During the Cultural Revolution white was considered a "reactionary" colour and red was substituted.

Kenchira (Sodang) Cylindrical pinnacles in gilt bronze, often a good six foot high, that adorn the façades of major religious buildings. Often printed religious inscriptions, or ones written on strips of paper, will be kept inside them.

Kesar or Gesar of Ling. Name of the most famous hero in Tibetan mythology and title of an epic poem celebrating his feats in several different versions. Evidently a small kingdom of Ling existed from the fourteenth century between the regions of **Kham** and **Amdo**. In fact the epic of Kesar is an echo of that of Caesar, king of Throm, a name that in the last analysis derives from Rum (Byzantium) and hence from Rome. On this fascinating instance of cultural migration see R. A. Stein in Bibliography I.

Kham An important region in eastern Tibet. Today it has been split into the provinces of Qinghai and Sichuan, so its traditional ethnic and cultural unity has been disrupted. Its inhabitants live off their herds rather than off crops; they are known for their stature, taller than that of central Tibetans, and for their proudly independent spirit. During the years of guerrilla warfare they proved a thorn in the side of the Chinese.

Koko-nor (Tso-ngompo) "Blue sea", the Mongol name for a very large lake (4,200 to 6,000 km^2 according to season) lies at an elevation of 10,000 feet, in the north-east corner of the region that is Tibetan in terms of language and ethnology. In the middle there is an island with a temple inhabited by Buddhist hermits. Today it lies within the Chinese province of Ch'ing-hai, named precisely after this lake. Not far from the lake stands one of the most famous Buddhist monasteries, Kum-Bum, founded in 1582 by the Third Dalai Lama on the birthplace of **Tsongkhapa**.

Kublai Khan (1215–1294), grandson of the Mongol emperor Ghengis Khan. He was emperor of a large part of China from 1261. He confirmed the pact with the Abbots of Sakya whereby he sanctioned their government of Tibet and they would afford him assistance by virtue of religion and magic arts, which were held to be of sovereign importance in those days. Kublai Khan confirmed the frontiers of the empire as established during the T'ang dynasty (618–907), and made new annexations. He made two attempts to conquer Japan, in 1271 and 1284. It was during his reign that Marco Polo made a long visit to the imperial court.

Kum-Bum The great pagoda built at Gyantse in the early fifteenth century by Prince Chogyal Rabten. Its height is 109ft and it contains 73 chapels with murals depicting the gods in 26,000 images: the name of the pagoda means "The hundred thousand [images of the saints]". The Kum-Bum was studied in detail by Tucci in 1937 (see *Indo-Tibetica*, IV/1, 2, 3).

There is also a large and important monastery of this name at the birthplace of **Tsongkhapa**, south of Lake Koko-nor in the Chinese province of Qinghai; it was founded in 1577 by the Third Dalai Lama.

Kun-Lun Mountain chain running 1000 miles from the Pamirs to Qinghai, confined on the north by the Tibetan plateau. Its highest peaks rise to 23,000ft. These mountains, far from any cities, are full of mystery and deemed to be home to all manner of mythological figures; they have always excited the imagination in the Far East. Queen Wang-mu's paradise is to be found in these mountains, and the peaches of immortality grow in her garden.

Labrang Administrative centre in a monastery or a monastic city; here the abbots reside.

Lama Foreigners tend to apply this term to all Tibetan, Ladakh, Bhutanese and other religious, but this is vague and inaccurate. The term is complex and indeed varies in its use from one sect to the next. Basically it carries the meaning of "teacher" (cf. *guru*), and a person cannot legitimately assume the title unless he has completed a lengthy training and passed a number of often rather difficult exams. The importance of the *lama* or teacher in any pursuit of intellectual and spiritual improvement is enormous; the master-disciple relationship lies at the core of lamaism. The young monks, and older ones of only modest learning, are known as *trapa*. In the *Gelug-pa* sect the neophytes enter the monastery as seminarists, *rab-chung*, accede later to the style of *getsul*, and may then aspire to become a lama. Those who pursue their studies at an advanced level and pass the necessary exams may assume the title of *geshe*, doctor of divinity. Those appointed to specific tasks or responsibilities need to obtain yet further qualifications.

Lhamoi-latso A more or less circular lake, one mile across, located some 100 miles south-east of Lhasa. In its waters those who have made the greatest spiritual progress are thought to be able to see omens for the future. This is where leaders of the lamaist community come when a Dalai Lama has died and the search is on for the child in whom his spirit is to be reborn.

Some ten miles away there stood an important monastery, Chö-kor-gye, founded by the Second Dalai Lama in 1509 and now reported to be in ruins.

Lhasa Capital of Tibet since the time of King **Songtsen-gampo** (569–649). Originally it was known as Ra-sa, "Land of the Goat" but the more elevating "Land of the Gods" was substituted. The Potala palace was completely reconstructed and adorned with works of art by the Fifth Dalai Lama in the mid-seventeenth century. At the foot of the Potala stands the temple of Jokhang which is crowded with works of art from a number of periods; the principal statue, of the crowned Buddha (Jowo Rimpoche) is supposed to date from the seventh century though the experts are not convinced. Fortunately neither Potala nor Jokhang were seriously damaged during the recent persecutions, though the ancient temple of **Ramoche** suffered hideously, and the School of Medicine, on the **Chagpo-ri** was completely destroyed. The present population of Lhasa has risen above 200,000. The city is linked by road with China, Nepal and India, and by air with Chengdu in Sichuan.

Lokapala (Gyalchen-de-shi) The four legendary kings who protect the directions in space. They almost always are depicted in the entrances to temples, and frequently appear on religious banners (*tangka*). While they are frequently shown as sculptures in China, Korea and Japan, they are seldom encountered in this form in Tibet. Their names are:

Sanskrit	**Tibetan** (pronounced/transcribed)	**Symbols and colours**
Virūdhaka (South)	Pha(g)kyepo/Phags-skyes-po	sword – blue or green
Virūpāksha (West)	Chemishang/sPyan-mi-bzang	*stupa* – red
Vaishravana (North) known also as Kuvera	Namthöse/rNam-thos-sras	banner of victory – yellow
Dhritarāshtra (East)	Yülkor (sung)/Yul-'khor (srung)	lute – white

Mahayana (Thepa-chempo) "The Great Vehicle", the branch of Buddhism cultivated particularly in the northern states of Asia (northern India, Nepal, Kashmir, central Asia, China, Korea, Japan and Tibet). It broke free of ***Hinayana*** in about the first century B.C. It offers a path to salvation for all people, hence the "Great Vehicle"; it accepts later scriptures as canonical; it tends to embrace the cults of local gods met with in the course of its missionary spread, and thrives on a dynamic metaphysical and liturgical development from which it has inherited a dazzling and complex pantheon. In its final phase *mayahana* is identified with ***vajrayana***, which derives its inspiration from the scriptures known under the name of ***Tantra***.

Maitreya (Champa) A celestial being of notable importance throughout the Buddhist world from the earliest times. He is the only *Bodhisattva* known to the *Hinayana* schools of Buddhism, where he is worshipped together with Buddha. In *Mahayana* he holds a pre-eminent position, throughout India, central Asia, China, Korea, Japan and Tibet. He is represented as the great apostle of Buddhism in the future world, in the ***kalpa*** that will succeed the present one. For the moment he dwells in the heaven of Tushita, where certain great and privileged masters, like Asanga, are thought to have been able to visit him and receive from him revelations and an initiation into the doctrines later transcribed in the books of **Tantra**. At the end of the present *kalpa* he will have his Second Coming. Maitreya is not easy to recognize in Buddhist iconography because he is given so many different aspects: he may appear as Buddha, simply dressed as contemplative monk, or as a *Bodhisattva*, crowned and bedecked. Often he is seated in the Western fashion, which makes him clearly identifiable. A legend states that he will appear in the form of a giant, so some of his depictions are on a colossal scale, like the famous one in the tower-shaped temple at **Tashilhumpo**, near Shigatse, where he is shown in a gilt bronze statue standing *c.* 90ft high. Another is located in a little monastery near Samada, on the Gangtok – Gyantse road; if not now destroyed, it stands some 40ft high. There are parts of China where Maitreya is portrayed as a plump, rosy, semi-naked monk, and thus rather easy to mistake for Pu-tai, the god of fortune and wealth.

Manasarovar (Mapham-tso) A vast lake at an elevation of some 15,000ft not far from Mount **Kailasa**; it is held sacred by Buddhists and Hindus alike. The lake affords the most splendid views, and along its shore there used to be several monasteries, now mostly dismantled or destroyed, though some have been rebuilt.

Mandala (Chil-khor) A plan of the universe or of a particular aspect of the universe, described by Tucci as "a spacial syllogism for true mystics". A mandala is essentially an ideal construction: it may be traced in the sand, created by means of coloured powder or flowers on a plain surface, or it may be painted, whether as a mural or on religious banners (*tangka*); it may be created three-dimensionally in sculptures large and small, or in buildings like ***stupa*** and ***chorten***, pagodas, certain temples. Moreover certain towns have been planned on the basis of a mandala – Beijing, Heijo (Nara), Heian (Kyoto), Angkor Thom, for instance. See G. Tucci: *Teoria e pratica del Mandala*, Rome, 1949.

Manjusri (Jampeyan) "The Glorious One", the *Bodhisattva* who incarnates mystical wisdom, the supreme gnosis. His colour is gold or yellow, and his symbols are the book and the sword. His cult is very old and is practised in all areas of ***Mahayana*** Buddhism. Some people hold that he is purely the personification of mystical wisdom, while others believe he is a historical figure who went on to become a deity. **Padma Sambhava** and **Tsongkhapa** are both considered to be living reincarnations of Manjusri; Tsongkhapa in particular is always represented with sword and book, usually laid upon two lotus flowers, their stems held in the hands of the great teacher. The famous shrine on the top of the Chinese Mount Wutai-shan, (Riwo-tsenga in Tibetan) the "Mountain of the Five Terraces", is sacred to Manjusri and a goal for Tibetan pilgrims.

Mendang Walls that run for anything from a few yards to several hundred and divide roads in two down their length. They are covered in sacred inscriptions and are often crowned with turrets similar to ***chorten***. It is normal to leave a *mendang* to one's right as one passes it.

Meru (Ri-rab) According to Indian and Buddhist cosmology this mountain forms the axis of the world. It is frequently identified with 22,000ft Mount **Kailasa** in western Tibet. The four continents are disposed round Mount Meru as follows: to the north, Uttarakuru (Daminyan); to the south, Jambudvīpa (Dzambuling); to the west, Godanīya (Balangchö); and to the east, Videha (Lüphapo). Of these the only real continent is Jambudvīpa, identified with India and the adjacent lands; the other three are mythical, or nebulous.

Milarepa (1040–1123), the greatest poet, mystic and hermit in the religious and literary history of Tibet. He is more fully described in Chapter 12. See also in Bibliography V: Evans-Wentz, W. J., *Tibet's Great Yogi Milarepa* and Chang, G. C. C., *The Hundred Thousand Songs of Milarepa.*

Mudra In Tibetan Buddhist iconography: the ritual position of the hands.

Naropa (*c.* 1016–1100). Renowned Indian ascetic and master of Tantric Buddhism; he came from Bengal but was active in Kashmir and Ladakh. He is patriarch of the ***Kargyu-pa*** sect.

Nechung An official state oracle at the Nechung monastery, less than four miles from Lhasa, whose pronouncements had a supreme value, not least in the search for the new Dalai Lama.

Nima-pa "The Ancients", generic name given to the unreformed sects, and particularly to the followers of **Padma Sambhava**. Also known as the "red sects" owing to the colour of their habits and headgear. The best-known monastery is Mindoling, on the River Tsang-po, south of Lhasa. It was badly damaged, but is now reported to be under reconstruction.

Norbhu-Lingka "Park of Jewels", summer palace of the Dalai Lama since 1755, with pavilions, gardens and ponds. It possessed a valuable art collection, most of it savagely destroyed in 1959. It has been rebuilt and efforts are being made to refurbish the palace within and without.

Padma Sambhava (Pema-chungne) "Born of the Lotus-flower". He is also known as Guru-rimpoche, "Great Precious Master". He was chiefly responsible for introducing Buddhism to Tibet in the eighth century. He was born in Uddyana (today Swat), and was invited to Tibet by King **Tisong-detsen** (755–797), under whose auspices he undertook the construction of the great monastery of **Samye**. According to legend he exterminated the countless demons and monsters who infested Tibet, sparing only those who promised to become champions of the faith

– even as they retained their grim features. Little is known about him as a historical person – he was more a magician and miracle-worker than a saint, it would seem, but he must have been extraordinary, to judge from the influence he had on his contemporaries. There is a most opulently extravagant biography of him, or rather a hagiography, which makes interesting reading for the light it throws on the beliefs and superstitions of his day: it is the *Padma Tanyig* (see Bibliography V, under Toussaint, G. C. for translations).

Padma Sambhava is frequently met in art: he is recognizable from his princely attire and for the characteristic headgear; in his right hand he holds a ***vajra*** (and he appears to have been the first person to introduce the symbol into Tibet), and his left holds a skull-chalice on his lap; resting against his side is a *khatvanga* or spit adorned with human heads and skulls and a double *vajra*. Often he has a *vajra* vertical on the top of his head. Quite often he is accompanied by two wives, Princess Mandarava and Yeshe Chogyal. In Bhutan he is intensely worshipped. In the monastery-fortress of Paro he is celebrated in the spring with a feast at which a portrait painted on cloth and measuring about ninety by one hundred feet is unfurled. In many mystery plays he appears as a masked character. In iconography he is also shown in a number of excitable and terrifying manifestations, mounted on wild beasts. There is no tomb of Padma Sambhava, the legend being that he vanished mysteriously from the world leaving not a trace. (Fig. 97, p. 339 gives a typical representation of him.)

Palkhor-Choide "Eminent circular enclosure of the Faith" is the sacred city of Gyantse with its ring wall across the plain and up along the brow of the hill overlooking it. It used to contain some twenty religious buildings linked to the three sects, *Sakya-pa*, *Shalu-pa*, and *Gelug-pa*, and dates back to the fourteenth century. Today all that remains are the principal temple, the great pagoda of **Kum-Bum**, and the **Labrang**. All else has been razed to the ground; even the rubble has been cleared away, leaving nothing but the bare rock. Once upon a time it was inhabited by eight hundred or a thousand religious; today it is virtually uninhabited.

Panchen Lama Abbot Superior of the great monastery of **Tashilhumpo**, near Shigatse. The name is an abbreviation of *Pandita Chen-po* "Great Sage", the title accorded by the Fifth Dalai Lama in 1650 out of respect for his own master. He is considered to be the reincarnation of the living Buddha **Amitābha**. For the complex relationship between the Panchen Lama and the Dalai Lama see Chapter 7. The system of succession by reincarnation applies to the Panchen Lama as well as to the Dalai Lama. The seven who have held the office to date are:

1. Lobsang Chökyi Gyaltsen (1570–1662)
2. Lobsang Yeshe (1663–1737)
3. Lobsang Palden Yeshe (1738–1780)
4. Lobsang Tenpe Nyima (1782–1853)
5. Losang Palden Chökyi (1855–1882)
6. Lobsang Chökyi Nyima (1883–1937)
7. Lobsang Tseten (1938–1989)

Phags-pa (1235–1280), Abbot Superior of the **Sakya** monastery at the time when this institution was at the height of its power and influence. He enjoyed a warm friendship with Kublai Khan, the Mongol emperor. He invented a style of calligraphy that was widely used for two hundred years.

Phari Town and large fort located at c. 14,000ft at the foot of Mount Chomolhari (23,930ft), to guard the entrance to Tibet from the south. It was destroyed by the British in 1904 and, after being rebuilt, was once more reduced to rubble by the Chinese. Originally known as Phari Dzong, the place is now simply known as Phari: the *dzong*, or citadel, was once the symbol of Tibetan independence, and is no longer mentioned. Given the elevation, the climate is extremely harsh, with cold and wind all the year round. The new motorway connecting Yatung and Gyantse passes through it.

Prajna See **Shakti**

Prajnāpāramitā (Yumchenmo) "The Treatise of the Perfect Gnosis", an esoteric Indian work, one of the most important *sutras* in ***Mahayana*** Buddhism. Versions of varying length exist. The name breaks down into: *prajna*, gnosis, mystical knowledge, *para*, the world beyond, *mita*, arrived – hence "the work that arrives from the world beyond, that arrives at an understanding of the supreme gnosis". From the earliest times the *Prajnāpāramitā* was personified as a woman. In Tibet she frequently appears under her local name of Yumchenmo, often with several heads and arms, but always with one of her principal hands holding a book. In Chapter 11, in the description of Kyangphu monastery there is a description of an outstanding example (later destroyed).

Ramoche "The Great Enclosure", the sanctuary in Lhasa said to have been founded in the seventh century by the Chinese Princess Wen Ch'eng, bride of King Songtsengampo. Today it is badly damaged.

Rinchen-tsangpo (958–1055), an eminent figure in the eleventh-century "Buddhist renaissance". He travelled widely in India and achieved fame as a translator of Sanskrit texts. He founded monasteries in Ladakh and Tibet. One of Tucci's volumes of *Indo-Tibetica* is devoted almost exclusively to Rinchen-tsangpo.

Sakya "Yellow land", one of the principal monasteries, about a hundred miles south of Shigatse. It was founded in 1073 by Könchog Gyalpo. For about a hundred years from 1244 its abbots were charged by the Mongol emperors (who became emperors of China in 1279) with the temporal government of Tibet. With the end of the fourteenth century the abbots lost much of their power, but Sakya continued to be a great cultural centre to our own day. Part of the great shrine has been destroyed in recent times. See Cassinelli and Ekvall, *A Tibetan Principality* in Bibliography III.

Sakya-Muni (Sakya-thubpa) "The Sage from the Sakya sect", the name under which the historical Buddha, who lived in the sixth – fifth centuries B.C. is generally known in Tibet. He is usually portrayed seated tightly cross-legged and wearing a simple monk's tunic. His left hand rests in his lap and holds a begging bowl; his right hand stretches out, palm turned inwards, to touch the ground, so as to call it to witness to his Illumination. There are, however, several other iconographic themes: Buddha as new-born baby, Buddha cutting off his hair as he abandons his worldly existence, Buddha fasting, Buddha "setting the Wheel of the Law spinning", Buddha on his deathbed, surrounded by his disciples, people and animals dramatically showing their grief. See Snellgrove, D. (ed.): *The Image of Buddha* in Bibliography IV.

Sakya Pandita (Kunga Gyaltsen) Fourth abbot of the Sakya monasteries (1182–1251). He made a treaty with the Mongol ruler Geden in 1245 whereby he recognized the Mongols as nominal overlords of Tibet but had himself appointed their viceroy. For more than a century the Sakya abbots reigned over Tibet, several centuries before the Dalai Lamas, from the *Gelug-pa* sect, were to fulfil this function.

Samantabhadra (Kuntu-zangpo) "The entirely and completely Good One", a most important ***Bodhisattva***. The reformed sects see in him the emanation of the Supreme Buddha **Vairocana**. The unreformed sects see in him the emanation of **Adi Buddha**, the original Buddha. When he is shown in this special function he may be readily recognized: he is shown as dark blue, in mystical embrace with his ***shakti***, who is white.

Samsara The fundamental truth of Buddhism is that *samsara*, "the vortex of life", is nothing but empty appearance and illusion, that only the Absolute really exists, and that it is only by identifying oneself with it (becoming Buddha) that one can be liberated from *samsara*.

Samye The oldest shrine in Tibet, founded *c.* 765 by **Padma Sambhava** at the behest of King **Tisong-detsen**. It lies some thirty miles south-east of Lhasa not far from the north bank of River Tsang-po. Its full name signifies "Academy for obtaining the accumulation of changeless meditations". Its layout and general disposition is supposed to follow that of the once-famous although no longer extant Buddhist shrine of Odantapuri in Indian Bihar. A detailed description of Samye is provided by L. A. Waddell in *The Buddhism of Tibet or Lamaism* (see Bibliography III); he mentions the amazing popular legends suggesting that the building of the shrine under the magical guidance of Padma Sambhava was attended by miracles – "humans worked on the site by day, demons by night, so the huge labour made rapid progress". Tucci visited Samye in 1948 and gave his own ample description in *A Lhasa e oltre* (Bibliography VI). Although the abbot has traditionally belonged to the *Sakya-pa* sect, most of the monks come from the unreformed ***Nima-pa***. The shrine was severely damaged during the Cultural Revolution; it is in the process of restoration, but much of its historical and artistic inheritance has been brutally destroyed.

Sera One of the three principal monasteries of the *Gelug-pa* sect, established in 1417 by a disciple of **Tsongkhapa** at the foot of an arid, majestic peak a few miles north of Lhasa. There was a time when it housed five thousand religious. In the early eighteenth century the Jesuit Fr Ippolito **Desideri** was in residence there for a while, and so were Fr Huc and Fr Gabet during their visit in 1845–46 – they have left a detailed description of it. Among the treasures of Sera is a ***vajra*** which used to be carried in procession in Lhasa at the end of each year – it was believed to have arrived at the monastery from India in a miraculous flight. The monastery escaped almost unscathed from the depredations of the Cultural Revolution, and is now coming back to life, albeit on a reduced scale.

Shakti (yum) The spiritual energy of a god personified in a woman, *shakti* is a typical feature of Hindu and Buddhist ***Tantra***. Iconographically, the *shakti* is often shown in mystical coition *(yab-yum)* with her begetter and spouse. The resulting symbolism can be interpreted in a wide number of ways. In every instance the image serves to impress on the minds of the faithful the concept of an intimate, fruitful, final and perfect union between two ideas, two psychic realities, two elements. Frequently the male represents ***karuna***, benevolence, love, while the female represents ***prajna***, gnosis, mystical wisdom. The action thus depicted is meant to unite and intermingle the two spiritual realities just as lovers join their bodies in a blissful conjunction.

Shalu A small monastery, c. fifteen miles east of Shigatse, of notable importance in the religious and cultural history of Tibet. It was founded in 1040 and came to prominence when Abbot Buton (1290–1364), the Aquinas of lamaism, was in charge. Buton wrote a number of books of seminal importance, and was principally responsible for the first authoritative editions of the Indo-Tibetan scriptures, the ***Kangyur*** and the *Tangyur*. Shalu is a monastery of the *Sakya-pa* sect, but achieved a considerable independence within it. Today the buildings and interiors are basically safe even though they suffered from great neglect in recent times; they retain an unusual degree of artistic and historical interest. One of its singular curiosities are its blue tiles, thought to be of Chinese origin.

Sera One of the three principal monasteries of the *Gelug-pa* sect, established in 1417 by a disciple of **Tsongkhapa** at the foot of an arid, majestic peak a few miles north of Lhasa. There was a time when it house five thousand religious. In the early eighteenth century the Jesuit Fr Ippolito **Desideri** was in residence there for a while, and so were Fr Huc and Fr Gabet during their visit in 1845–46 – they have left a detailed description of it. Among the treasures of Sera is a ***vajra*** which used to be carried in procession in Lhasa at the end of each year – it was believed to have arrived at the monastery from India in a miraculous flight. The monastery escaped almost unscathed from the depredations of the Cultural Revolution, and is now coming back to life, albeit on a reduced scale.

Shenrab-Mibo or Tömba-Shenrab, founder of the Bon religion, probably a mythical figure. He originates from the district of Shang-shung. His place in this religion corresponds to that of Gautama Buddha in lamaism. Artists depicted him closely resembling Buddha **Sakya-Muni**.

Shigatse Tibet's second city (*c.* 20,000). It grew up on the banks of the River Tsang-po, at the foot of the local castle (*dzong*), in the fifteenth century and became an agricultural, pastoral and commercial centre, as also a centre of pilgrimage owing to its great *Gelug-pa* monastery of **Tashilhumpo**. It is the residence of the **Panchen Lama**.

Songtsen-gampo (569–649). The greatest of the early Yarlung kings of Tibet, he is the thirty-third ruler in the dynasty but, unlike many of his predecessors, he is an authentically historical figure. He it was who substantially extended the boundaries of the realm he had inherited from his father, reorganized its administration, transferred the capital to Lhasa, and fostered the invention and application of a written language based on an Indian phonetic alphabet in preference to ideograms of Chinese origins, to publish documents and books in Tibetan. He had several wives of whom two, the Nepalese Princess **Bhrikuti** and the Chinese Wen-Ch'eng, are historically pre-eminent: each of these is credited with bringing to Tibet some element of Buddhist religion and iconography. The crowned Buddha (*Jowo*) still venerated in the Jokhang temple at Lhasa, is thought to have arrived with one of these princesses. His date of birth has been much debated, and may have been 569 or 629; we incline to L. Petech's preference for the earlier date. Songtsen-gampo is readily recognized iconographically from the small head of the Supreme Buddha **Amitābha** placed on top of his conical turban – the king is considered to be the reincarnation of the Buddha.

Stupa See **Chorten**

Tabo A considerable tenth-century monastery in the valley of the Spiti, nowadays Indian territory but culturally and linguistically Tibetan. It holds an important collection of sculptures and murals dating from between the eleventh and sixteenth centuries; they constitute one of the principal testimonies to the munificence of the **Guge** kings.

Tangka "Object that is rolled up". Banners generally decorated with religious subjects, although some exist depicting scenes from the epic poem ***Kesar***, and medical subjects. The earliest *tangkas* date back to the twelfth century, and they have continued to be produced right up to recent times, indeed there are still good masters active in Nepal, Bhutan and elsewhere. For technical details on the preparation and painting of the *tangka* see D. P. and J. A. Jackson, *Tibetan Thangka Painting, Methods and Materials*, and L. S. Dagyab, *Tibetan Religious Art*, (Bibliography IV); as also G. Tucci's *Tibetan Painted Scrolls*, which sets out to be a study of the *tangka* only to develop into a broad-ranging encyclopaedia of Tibetan culture, literature and religion. The Jackson text is recommended for a study of techniques. On questions of iconography see also in the Bibliography IV the entries under Getty and Gordon.

Tangyur See **Kangyur**

Tantra Indian scriptures dating from the sixth to eighth centuries A.D., written within a Hindu and a Buddhist framework. Refer to Chapter 15 for greater detail.

Tara (Drolma) Female goddess of Indian origin but adopted by ***Mahayana*** Buddhism from the earliest times and most popular in Tibet and Mongolia, though she has a small cult in China and Japan. Like **Avalokitesvara**, whose companion she is, Tara personifies heavenly love for all living creatures. She is the saviour and redemptrix, somewhat akin to a lamaist Madonna: she may be invoked directly, that is, without the intercession of a lama, which makes her more intimate and familiar than the other goddesses. In some legends she was born from a blue beam of light from the eye of the Supreme Buddha **Amitābha**, according to others, from a teardrop of Avalokitesvara. She is presented in various guises of which the two principal ones are in white and in green (with 21 variations), all of these peaceful and smiling; then there are three Tantric guises in which she is highly agitated – in one she is red (and known under the name of Kurukulla), one in yellow (and known as Bhrikuti) and one in blue (and known as Ekajata). When depicted in five colours she is sometimes considered to be the ***shakti*** of the **Five Supreme Buddhas**. In her various guises Tara is a very popular figure in Tibetan art. For further details see A. Getty, *The Gods of Northern Buddhism*, in the Bibliography IV.

Tarcho (or Darcho), a tall, narrow banner fixed to a pole and covered in sacred formulas and blessings which the wind "recites", wafting sanctity into the surrounding air.

Tashilhumpo One of the principal monasteries of Tibet and fortunately one of those which survived the recent persecutions almost unscathed. It was founded in 1447 by Dedun-dup and almost at once became a major centre of the ***Gelug-pa*** sect. Abbot Lobsang Chökyi Gyaltsen (1570–1662) was the venerated master of the Fifth Dalai Lama, who chose to honour him with the title of **Panchen Lama**. The monastery contains a rich collection of art, including a gigantic statue in gilt bronze, standing some ninety feet high, of the Buddha **Maitreya/Champa**, situated in a special tower-shaped chapel; it is greatly venerated, albeit of little artistic merit. Evidently Tashilhumpo has today reverted to its monastic role even if on a reduced scale.

Third Eye, The The eye of mystic wisdom, depicted in the forehead of heavenly beings in Tantric Buddhism. It is also shown on the masks in sacred mystery plays. Sometimes the eye is shown in large numbers on the hands and other parts of the body. The mule that carries the terrifying goddess **Vajravarahi** is given the third eye on its rump.

As for the book entitled *The Third Eye*, it has its virtues as a work of fiction but as an account of Tibet it is pure fantasy. It has nonetheless hoaxed a large number of readers and still continues to do so. Its author was Cyril Henry Hoskin (1911–1981), who had never set foot in Tibet, and who adopted the pen-name of Lobsang Rampa. (Refer to the article in *Time* Magazine, New York, dated 17 February 1958.)

Thonmi Sambhota Minister of King **Songtsen-gampo**, he lived in the sixth–seventh century. He is traditionally credited with inventing the Tibetan writing system based on the alphabet used in the north of India. Among the many statues in the Potala palace at Lhasa there is one dedicated to him.

Tibet The Tibetans call their country Pö or Pö-yul, and refer to themselves as Pö-pa (the people of Pö). There is a widespread belief that Pö and Bon (the religion) spring from a common etymology that has yet to be traced. It is more likely, however, that the root Bod, Bhut, etc. is to be found in the name Bhutan and Bhutanese tribes from Tibetan stock who live in many of the high valleys of Nepal and India.

The Western name Tibet derives, it would seem, from Arab geographers via Tö-Pö (Upper Pö). For the Chinese, Tibet was Tufan in their oldest documents, until it was displaced by Hsi-Tsang, which could be a corruption of the name Ü-Tsang, the name by which the Tibetans indicate the two chief provinces in their territory: Lhasa (Ü) and Gyantse-Shigatse (Tsang).

Tisong-detsen (755–797). The greatest of the Tibetan kings, he was effectively emperor of the Asiatic highlands, his rule extending from present-day Afghanistan to western China and from Bengal to a great tract of Central Asia. After some hesitation he pronounced Buddhism the official religion in his dominions. He summoned the quiet, scholarly Santirakshita (705–762) and the more ebullient, extrovert **Padma Sambhava** to Tibet to spread the religion. He founded the sanctuary of **Samye** *c.*765, and summoned the Council of Lhasa (792–794), bringing together the leading Buddhist masters of the day, and witnessing the triumph of the Indian masters over the Chinese ones, a crucial turning point in the cultural history of Tibet.

Toling One of the two principal shrines in the ancient kingdom of **Guge** in western Tibet. It dates back to the eleventh century and contains a notable "Mandala Chapel" and "Golden Temple". Today it appears to be little more than a ruin.

Trapa See **Lama**

Trul-ku (or Tul-ku) "Living embodiment", the term Tibetans use to describe a person considered to be a reincarnation of a saint, a great master, a high prelate, or a god. The first *trul-kus* were manifested in the twelfth century among the ***Kargyu-pa*** and the *Sakya-pa* sects; with time the designation became more widespread. It appears that in 1959 there were some five hundred *trul-ku* living in Tibet, Mongolia and other lamaist areas.

Tsang The part of central-southern Tibet that includes the cities of Gyantse and Shigatse. The boundaries of the area have changed a great number of times. The area enjoyed long periods of independence between the late fourteenth and the seventeenth centuries. Tsang, together with the province of Lhasa (Ü) constitute the core of Tibet.

Tsang-po The principal river of Tibet, along whose banks, and those of its tributaries, most of the country's history has unfolded. The river rises in the mountains by Lake **Manasarovar** and first runs for some thousand miles due east, high up in the Himalayas; thence it drops in a series of gorges and carves out a passage through the mountain range to emerge into the plain of Bengal. Where it passes through the gorges it is known as the Dinang; once it reaches the Bengali plain on its way to the Indian Ocean it is called the Brahmaputra ("son of Brahma").

Tsaparang An important monastery thought to have been founded in 978 by **Rinchen-tsangpo**, and now lying in ruins. It was the principal sanctuary in the kingdom of **Guge**. Its numerous chapels and temples contained first-rate sculptures and murals dating from the fourteenth century. There is a minute description of the monastery in *Indo-Tibetica, III*, resulting from G. Tucci's visit.

Tse-pa-me (or Amitayus) A particular aspect of the Supreme Buddha **Amitābha,** he is normally shown seated in the profoundly meditative "adamantine" posture; he has one head, two arms, and in his lap holds in both hands an ornate vase containing the ambrosia of immortality. He is bejewelled and crowned as a ***Bodhisattva.*** His colour is red. His name means "Life without End" . He is frequently portrayed in Tibetan art, being a highly popular figure.

Tsongkhapa (1357–1419) Named Lodrö drapa at his birth near Lake **Koko-nor**, he entered a monastery when still very young and was taught by the masters of the principal schools of the day. The valley in which he was born was known throughout Tibet for the quality of its onions, hence his nickname "he (*pa*) from the land (*kha*) of the onions (*tsong*)" – a name he was always to treasure. He soon came to prominence for his theological texts and his administrative abilities, and proved a tireless lamaist reformer. He founded the monastery of **Galden**, and his disciples founded those of **Sera, Drepung,** and later of **Tashilhumpo**. His sect came to be known as the ***Gelug-pa,*** "the Virtuous", owing to the austerity of its monastic discipline. Eventually it gave birth to the theocratic church whose pontiffs, the Dalai Lamas, ruled Tibet until 1959. Tsongkhapa features a great deal in Tibetan art from the fifteenth century on. He may be readily identified by his russet lama's tunic and the characteristic pointed yellow hood of his sect that he wears on his head. He has the attributes of **Manjusri** – the sword and book – for he is considered to be the *Bodhisattva*'s reincarnation: these objects are generally shown on two lotus flowers that he holds by the stem. He is often depicted, too, in a group of three with his two favourite disciples shown smaller at his feet.

Tun-Huang Chinese town in Kansu, once the terminal point of the Silk Road connecting China with Byzantium and Rome. For many centuries it was a place of prime importance, and as early as 366 A.D. a complex of Buddhist shrines was established in the neighbourhood. For generations the monks would take advantage of caves in a well exposed and completely dry rock wall, painting and sculpting representations of the rich iconography of their faith. Even today 492 caves have been located, many of them still possessing artistic treasures of the Buddhist faith. Early in the twentieth century the Anglo-Hungarian explorer Aurel Stein and the French scholar Paul Pelliot discovered, quite independently of each other, a number of caves in which were sealed up thousands of inscriptions and paintings from the seventh to the ninth centuries, which were of extraordinary artistic and historical interest. Many of these documents have promoted a correct interpretation of Tibetan history – Tun-Huang was in fact a Tibetan possession between 781 and 848.

Ü The name for the province of Lhasa. Traditionally Ü and **Tsang** have fluctuated between rivalry and making a common front against threats from outside.

Vairocana One of the **Five Supreme Buddhas**, and for the *Sakya-pa* sect he is the Original Buddha, occupying a position similar to that of **Adi Buddha.**

Vajra (Dorje) A liturgical object, normally made of metal, that originally symbolized lightning, arrows. It is older than Buddhism. The basic idea of a god whose hand grasps arrows goes back to the earliest antiquity and is to be found the world over, including in the pagan West. Legend has it that Buddha seized arrows from the hands of Indra, Vedic god of the heavens and the clouds. The classic *vajra* consists of two groups of four arrows converging upwards, with a fifth one in the centre – symbolizing the **Five Supreme Buddhas** and every pentad that derives from this. The *vajra* is supposed to have been introduced to Tibet by **Padma Sambhava**. In Tibet, as in Japan and elsewhere, there are numerous legends indicating that *vajras* can fly, cross oceans, locating the prospective sites for a new shrine and so on. (Cf. **Sera**). The notion of the *vajra* as symbol of the thunderbolt and its destructive power was soon combined with the complementary notion of indestructability, hence the symbolism of the diamond. In late Tantric Buddhism the *vajra* went on to acquire a sexual symbolism, becoming the *lingam* (the phallus) of Shiva, or of the phallus in general. The *vajra* is the particular symbol of the Supreme Buddha Akshobhya and of the *Bodhisattva* **Vajrapani**. Many of the gods have one attributed to them as a secondary symbol. There exists also a double *vajra*, cruciform, which is the particular symbol of the Supreme Buddha Amoghasiddhi, as also of other, minor luminaries in the Tibetan Buddhist pantheon.

Vajrabhairava (Dorje Chi-che) The god has nine faces, of which the middle one is that of a bull, and thirty-four arms; his two principal hands hold a dagger and a skull-goblet filled with entrails; his diadem consists of skulls and he wears necklaces made of severed human heads, of human bones and of snakes; his phallus is bejewelled. Terrifying though he looks, Vajrabhairava is in fact a benign deity, and his aspect serves to banish evil, not to express it. As an active, beneficent Guardian he is known as "Conqueror of Death".

Vajrapani (Chanadorje) "He who grasps the *vajra*", name by which a *Bodhisattva* is known who has been highly popular since time immemorial; he is to be found on the reliefs at Gandhara at the dawn of the Common Era. He represents the embattled aspect of the guardians of the Faith, and is generally portrayed or sculpted in an attitude of excitability and wrath. He is often to be seen with **Manjusri** and **Avalokitesvara**.

Vajravarahi (Dorje-pamo) "The Adamantine Sow", she is protector-goddess for the Tantric schools of Buddhism, and is a particular form of Marici, "Beam of Light", goddess of Dawn. A. Getty (*The Gods of Northern Buddhism*) suggests that the animal on which Marici rode was a bear (possibly related to the constellations of the Greater and Lesser Bear) but then developed in India, where the bear is unfamiliar, into a boar or sow. Vajravarahi is reincarnated as Palden Lhamo in the person of the Abbess of Samding.

Vajrayana (Dorje-thepa) "Adamantine Vehicle", the latest and most perfect development of ***Mahayana***. It is the vehicle of Tantric Buddhism that came to perfection particularly in Bengal during the fifth to the tenth centuries, and thence became known in Tibet.

Yab-yum "Father-Mother", the mystical coition of two gods or of a Buddha with his ***shakti***. It is the characteristic manifestation of the fantasy demonstrated by Tantric

Buddhism in creating brazen and indeed scandalous symbols that are nonetheless deeply significant and thus hugely effective.

Yama (Shinje) God of death, king of the underworld. He is represented in a terrifying aspect, coloured blue-black, with the head of a wild yak; he is mounted on a rabid bull that is in the process of sexually assaulting an unfortunate body lying under him; in his right hand he holds a skeleton for a sceptre, and in his left a noose for catching his human prey; he wears a necklace of severed heads and a crown of skulls; he is decked out in all kinds of jewels and serpents, and his phallus is completely erect. Often he is accompanied by his sister-bride Yami, a dishevelled woman undergoing a powerful orgasm; in her hand she holds a skull-chalice brimful of blood. Yama is also portrayed in a less ferocious guise as the god who upholds the "Wheel of Life".

Yamantaka (Dorje-chi-che) "He who defeats Yama", thus the conqueror of Death. A guardian divinity especially for the *Gelug-pa*. Yamantaka is also regarded as an aspect of **Vajrabhairava**.

Yamdrok-tso The lake "of the upper pastures", indeed it is a remarkably beautiful complex of lakes in the barren mountains south of the River Tsang-po, on the road between Gyantse and Lhasa.

The important monastery of Samding (for years a ruin but now partially rebuilt) occupies a beautiful site on the western shore of the lake. It was founded in the late seventeenth century by Tinle-Tsomo, a highly respected abbot of the unreformed (red) sect. It was one of the few Tibetan monasteries ruled by an abbess, who incarnated the guardian spirit **Vajravarahi**; each abbess succeeded by reincarnation. (An account is given in L. A. Waddell, *The Buddhism of Tibet or Lamaism*, Bibliography III.)

Yumbu-lagang The oldest building in Tibet, it dates back to earlier than 850. It stood in the Yarlung valley and served as temple and fort. During the Cultural Revolution the Red Guards tore it down fanatically, but it has now been rebuilt.

Bibliography

1. HISTORICAL AND GENERAL

Amar Kaur, J. S., *Himalayan Triangle. A Historical Survey of British India's Relations with Tibet, Sikkim and Bhutan, 1865–1950*, London, British Library, 1988

Bacot, J., *Introduction à l'histoire du Tibet*, Société Asiatique, Paris, 1962

Barraux, R., *Histoire des Dalai Lamas. Quatorze reflets sur le Lac des Visions*, Paris, Albin Michel, 1993

Beckwith, C. I., *The Tibetan Empire of Central Asia*, Princeton University Press, 1993

Bell, C., *Tibet, Past and Present*, Oxford University Press, 1924; reprinted 1968

Bell, C., *Portrait of the Dalai Lama*, [Life of the Thirteenth Dalai Lama], London, Collins, 1946

Daffinà, P. (ed.), *Indo-Sino-Tibetica: studi in onore di Luciano Petech*, Rome, Bardi, 1990

Demiéville, P., *Le Concile de Lhasa (792–794)*, Paris, Presses Universitaires de France, 1952

Deshayes, L., *Histoire du Tibet*, Paris, Fayard, 1997

Desideri, I., *Il Nuovo Ramusio, i missionari italiani nel Tibet e nel Nepal*, ed. L. Petech; II. 5, 6, 7 [these three Parts embrace all Desideri's writings on Tibet and his voyages], Rome, Ismeo, 1954–1956

Desideri, I., *An Account of Tibet* (ed. F. De Filippi), London, Routledge, 1937

Fleming, P., *With Bayonets to Lhasa*, London, Rupert Hart-Davis, 1961

Goldstein, M.C., *A History of Modern Tibet, 1913-1951: the Demise of the Lamaist State*, Berkeley, University of California Press, 1989

Haarh, E., *The Yar-lung Dynasty*, Copenhagen, Gad, 1969

Hoffmann, H., *Tibet. A Handbook*, Indiana University Press, 1973

Landon, P., *Lhasa*, (2 vol.), London, 1905

MacGregor, J., *Tibet, a Chronicle of Exploration*, London, Routledge & Kegan Paul, 1970

Marchigiani, Cappuccini, *Il Nuovo Ramusio, i missionari italiani nel Tibet e nel Nepal*, ed. L. Petech; I. 1–4 [these four Parts embrace all the Capuchin Friars' writings on Tibet and Nepal], Rome, Ismeo, 1952–1954

Norbu, T.J. and Turnbull, C., *Tibet*, London, Chatto & Windus, 1969, Penguin, 1976

Peissel, M., *Mustang, royaume tibétain interdit*, Geneva, Olizane, 1988

Pelliot, P., *Histoire ancienne du Tibet*, Paris, 1961

Petech, L., *China and Tibet in the early 18th century*, Leyden, Brill, 1950, Westport, Hyperion, 1973

Petech, L., *Aristocracy and Government in Tibet (1728–1959)*, Rome, Ismeo, 1973

Richardson, H., *Tibet and its History*, Oxford University Press, 1962; rev. ed. Boulder, Shambala, 1984

Richardson, H., *High Peaks, Pure Earth, Collected Writings on Tibetan History and Culture*, London, Serindia, 1998

Roerich, G. N., *The Blue Annals of gShon-nu-dpal (1439–1481)*, (2 vol.) Calcutta, 1949–1953, New Delhi, 1958

Schulemann, G., *Geschichte der Dalai Lamas*, Leipzig, 1958

Shakabpa, W. D., *Tibet, a Political History*, Yale University Press, 1967, 1973

Shen, T. and Liu, S., *Tibet and the Tibetans*, Stanford University Press, 1953, New York, 1973
Siiger, H., *The Lepchas. Culture and Religion of a Himalayan People*, (2 vol.) Copenhagen, The National Museum of Denmark, 1967
Snellgrove, D. L. and Richardson, H., *A Cultural History of Tibet*, London and New York, 1968, Boulder, Prajna, 1980
Smith, W. W. jr, *Tibetan Nation, A History of Tibetan Nationalism and Sino-Tibetan Relations*, Westview Press, 1996
Stein, R. A., *Tibetan Civilization*, London, Faber & Faber, 1972
Tucci, G., *Le tombe dei re tibetani*, Rome, Ismeo, 1950
Tucci, G., *Tibet, paese delle nevi*, Novara, De Agostini, 1967
Tucci, G., *Tibet* (Archaeologia Mundi series), Geneva, Nagel, 1973
Waddell, L. A., *Lhasa and its Mysteries*, London, 1906
Wylie, T. V., *The Geography of Tibet according to the Dzam-gling-rgyas-bshad*, Rome, Ismeo, 1962
Younghusband, P., *India and Tibet*, London, John Murray, 1910

II. CURRENT AFFAIRS

[Given that Tibet remains a live issue, the entries are coded as (PB=Pro-Beijing) and (PFT= Pro-Free-Tibet); entries with no coding are attempting to be impartial.]

Amnesty International, *People's Republic of China: Recent Reports on Political Prisoners and Prisoners of Conscience in Tibet*, London, 1991, with subsequent editions (PFT)
Andrugtsang, Gompo Tashi, *Four Rivers, Six Ranges: Reminiscences of the Resistance Movement in Tibet*, Dharamsala, 1973 (PFT)
Avedon, J. F., *In Exile from the Land of Snows*, New York, A.A.Knopf, 1984 (PFT)
Burman, B. R., *Religion and Politics in Tibet*, New Delhi, Vikas, 1979
Calamandrei, F. and Régard, T., *Rompicapo tibetano*, Florence, Parenti, 1959 (PB)
Dalai Lama, Fourteenth, *My Land and My People*, London, 1962 (PFT)
Dhyani, S. N., *Contemporary Tibet, its Status in International Law*, Lucknow, 1961
Donnet, P. A., *Tibet, mort ou vif*, Paris, Gallimard, 1990 (PFT)
Epstein, I., *Tibet Transformed*, Beijing, New World Press, 1983 (PB)
Ford, R.W., *Captured in Tibet*, London, 1957 (PFT)
Gelder, S. and R., *The Timely Rain, Travels in New Tibet*, London, Hutchinson, 1964 (PB)
Ginsburgs, G., and Mathos, M., *Communist China and Tibet, the First Dozen Years*, The Hague, Nijhoff, 1964
Gold, P., *Tibetan Reflections, 1959–1984*, Boston, Wisdom Publications, 1984 (PFT)
Goldstein, M. et al., *The Struggle for Modern Tibet: the Autobiography of Tashi Tsering*, London, Sharpe, 1997 (PFT)
Goldstein, M., *The Snow Lion and the Dragon; China, Tibet and the Dalai Lama*, Berkeley, University of California, 1997 (PFT)
Han Suyin, *Lhasa, étoile-fleur*, Paris, Stock, 1976 (PB)
Harrer, H., *Return to Tibet*, London, Weidenfeld & Nicolson, 1984 (PFT)
Karan, P. P., *The Changing Face of Tibet: the Impact of Chinese Communist Ideology on the Landscape*, University Press of Kentucky, 1976

Lehmann, P. H. and Ullal, J., *Tibet, das stille Drama auf dem Dach der Erde*, Hamburg, GEO, 1981 (PFT)

Li, T. T., *The Historical Status of Tibet*, New York, Columbia University Press, 1956 (PB)

Marazzi, A., *Tibetani in Svizzera. Analisi di una distanza culturale*, Milan, 1975

Moraes, F., *The Revolt in Tibet*, New York, Macmillan, 1960

Norbu, D., *Tibet, the Road Ahead*, New Delhi, HarperCollins India, 1997 (PFT)

Nowak, M., *Tibetan Refugees: Youth and the Generation of Meaning*, Rutgers University Press, 1984

Palden Gyatso, *Fire under the Snow*, London, Harvill, 1997 (PFT)

Patt, D., *A Strange Liberation: Tibetan Lives in Chinese Hands*, Ithaca, Snow Lion, 1996 (PFT)

Peissel, M., *Les Cavaliers du Kham*, Paris, 1973 (PFT)

Schwartz, R. D., *Circle of Protest: Political Ritual in the Tibetan Uprising*, London, Hurst, 1994 (PFT)

Strong, A. L., *Tibetan Interviews*, Beijing, New World Press, 1959 (PB)

Strong, A. L., *When Serfs Stood up in Tibet*, Beijing, New World Press, 1965 (PB)

Taring, R. D., *Daughter of Tibet*, London, John Murray, 1970 (PFT)

Tsering Shakya, *The Dragon in the Land of Snows. A History of Modern Tibet since 1947*, London, Pimlico, 1999 (PFT)

United Nations Commission on Human Rights, *Tibet, the Facts*, *Report prepared by the Buddhist Scientific Association*, Dharamsala, 1990 (PFT)

Van, Grasdorff, G., *Panchen Lama, otage de Pékin*, Paris, Ramsay, 1997 (PFT)

Van Walt Van Praag, M. C., *The Status of Tibet: History, Rights and Prospects in International Law*, Boulder (Col), Westview Press, 1987 (PFT)

Verni, P., *Dalai Lama, Biografia autorizzata*, Milan, Jaca Book, 1990 (PFT)

Various authors, *Tibet and the People's Republic of China*, Geneva, Commission Internationale de Juristes, 1960

Various authors, *Concerning the Question of Tibet*, Beijing, Foreign Languages Press, 1987 (PB)

III. RELIGION

Aris, M., *Hidden Treasures and Secret Lives. A Study of Pemalingpa (1450–1521) and the Sixth Dalai Lama (1683–1706)*, London, Kegan Paul, 1989

Bell, C., *The Religion of Tibet*, Oxford University Press, 1931, 1968

Beyer, S., *The Cult of Tara*, Berkeley, University of California Press, 1973

Blondeau, A. M., "Les Religions du Tibet" in Puech, H.C., *Histoire des Religions*, Paris, Gallimard, 1970

Cassinelli, C. W. and Ekvall, R. B., *A Tibetan Principality. The Political System of Sa sKya (Sakya)*, Ithaca, Cornell University Press, 1969

Dalai Lama, Fourteenth, *Freedom in Exile*, London, Hodder & Stoughton, 1990

Dalai Lama, Fourteenth, *My Tibet*, London, Thames & Hudson, 1990

Dalai Lama, Fourteenth, *Awakening the Mind, Lightening the Heart*, San Francisco, Harper, 1995

Dalai Lama, Fourteenth, *The Way to Freedom*, London, Thorsons, 1997

Dalai Lama, Fourteenth, *The Joy of Living and Dying in Peace*, London, Thorsons, 1997

Grünwedel, A., *Mythologie des Buddhismus in Tibet und der Mongolei*, Leipzig, 1970, Osnabrück, 1990
Guenther, H. V., *The Jewel Ornament of Liberation by Gampo-pa*, London, 1959
Guenther, H. V., *The Life and Teaching of Naropa*, Oxford, 1963
Gyurme, D. and Kapstein, M., *The Nyigma School of Tibetan Buddhism*, Boston, Wisdom, 1991
Hoffmann, H., *The Religions of Tibet*, London, Allen & Unwin, 1961
Karmay, S., *A Treasury of Good Sayings. A Tibetan History of Bon*, London University Press, 1972
Karmay, S., *The Great Perfection (rzogs chen), a Philosophical and Meditative Teaching in Tibetan Buddhism*, Leiden, Brill, 1988
Kvaerne, P., *The Bon Religion of Tibet*, London, Serindia, 1995
Manca, N. (ed.), *Monachesimo tibetano in dialogo*, Rome, AVE, 1995
Nebesky-Wojkowitz, R. de, *Oracles and Demons of Tibet*, Oxford University Press, 1956
Nebesky-Wojkowitz, R. de, *Tibetan Religious Dances,* The Hague, 1976
Obermiller, E., *History of Buddhism by Bu-ston*, Heidelberg, 1931, Tokyo, 1964
Snellgrove, D. L., *Buddhist Himalaya,* Oxford, 1957
Snellgrove, D. L., *The Hevajra Tantra*, Oxford, 1961
Snellgrove, D. L., *Himalayan Pilgrimage*, Oxford, 1961
Snellgrove, D. L., *Nine Ways of Bon*, London, 1967
Snellgrove, D. L., *Four Lamas of Dolpo*, Oxford, 1967–68
Snellgrove, D. L., *Indo-Tibetan Buddhism*, London, Serindia, 1987
Thurman, R., (ed.), *The Life and Teachings of Tsong Khapa*, Dharamsala, LTWA, 1993
Toscano, G., The Tibetan works of Ippolito Desideri translated into Italian: *T'o-ran(g)s (Dawn), Snyin(g)-po (The Essence of Christian Doctrine), 'Byun(g) Kun(g)s (The Origins of Living Creatures and All Things),* Rome, Ismeo, 1981, 1982, 1984
Tucci, G., *Teoria e prattica del Mandala*, Rome, 1949
Tucci, G., *The Religions of Tibet*, London, Routledge, 1970
Tucci, G. and Heissig, W., *Les religions du Tibet et de la Mongolie,* Paris, Payot, 1973
Tucci, G., "Buddhism" in *Encyclopaedia Britannica,* 15th edition, 1974
Waddell, L.A., *The Buddhism of Tibet or Lamaism*, London 1883, 1971

IV. TIBETAN ART AND ICONOGRAPHY

Beguin, G., *Les Peintures du Bouddhisme tibétain*, Paris, 1995
Bhattacharyya, B., *The Indian Buddhist Iconography*, Oxford, 1924, Calcutta, Mukhopadhyay, 1968
Chakravarti, S., *A Catalogue of the Tibetan Thankas in the Indian Museum*, Calcutta, 1980
Chayer, A., *Art et archéologie du Tibet*, Paris, Picard, 1994
Clark, W. E., *Two Lamaist Pantheons*, Cambridge (MA), Harvard University Press, 1937
Dagyab, L. S., *Tibetan Religious Art*, Wiesbaden, Harrassowitz, 1977
De Malmann, M. T., *Introduction à l'iconographie du tantrisme bouddhique*, Paris, Adrien-Maisonneuve, 1975
Eracle, J., (Musée d'Ethnographie de Genève), *Thanka de l'Himalaya, images de sagesse*, Ivrea, Priuli & Verlucca, 1993

Fisher, R. E., *Art of Tibet*, London, Thames & Hudson, 1997
Gerner, M., *Architectures de l'Himalaya*, Geneva, Del Court, 1988
Getty, A., *The Gods of Northern Buddhism*, Oxford University Press, 1928, Tokyo, Tuttle, 1962
Goepper, R., and Poncar, I., *Alchi: Ladakh's Hidden Buddhist Sanctuary*, London, Serindia, 1996
Gordon, A. K., *The Iconography of Tibetan Lamaism*, New York, Columbia University Press, 1939, Tokyo, Tuttle, 1959
Gordon, A. K., *Tibetan Religious Art*, New York, Columbia University Press, 1952, Paragon, 1963
Handa, O. C., *Buddhist Monasteries in Himachal Pradesh*, London, Sangam, 1988
Heller, Amy, *Tibetan Art*, London, Antique Collectors
Henss, Michael, *Tibet, die Kulturdenkmäler*, Zurich, Atlantis, 1981
Jackson, D. P. and J. A., *Tibetan Thangka Painting, Methods and Materials*, London, Serindia, 1984
Jackson, D. P., *A History of Tibetan Painting*, Vienna, 1996
Karmay, H., *Early Sino-Tibetan Art*, Warminster, Aris & Phillips, 1975
Karmay, S. G., *Secret Visions of the Fifth Dalai Lama*, London, Serindia, 1988
Klimburger-Salter, D. (et al.), *Tabo, a Lamp for the Kingdom*, Milan, Skira, 1997
Lauf, D. I., *Tibetan Sacred Art*, London, Shambala, 1976
Lo Bue, E. and Ricca, F., *Gyantse Revisited*, Florence, Le Lettere, 1990
Mortari Vergara, P., and Beguin, G. (ed.), *Dimore umane, santuari divini: origini, sviluppo e diffusione dell' architettura tibetana*, Rome, Il Bagatto, 1987
Ngor, T., *Tibetan Mandalas in the Ngor Collection*, Tokyo, Kodansha, 1981
Olshak, B. C., *Mystic Art of Ancient Tibet*, New York, 1973
Olson, E., *Catalogue of the Tibetan Collections in the Newark Museum*, Newark, 1950
Pal, P., *The Art of Tibet*, New York, 1969
Pal, P., *Lamaist Art, the Aesthetics of Harmony*, Boston, 1970
Pal, P., *Art of Tibet: A Catalogue of the Los Angeles County Museum of Art Collection*, Los Angeles, University of California Press, 1983
Pal, P., *Tibetan Paintings: The Study of Tibetan Thankas, 11th–19th Centuries,* London, Sotheby, 1984
Rhie, M. and Thurman, R.A.F., *Wisdom and Compassion, the Sacred Art of Tibet*, New York, Abrams, 1991
Ricca, F. and Lo Bue, E., *The Great Stupa of Gyantse*, London, Serindia, 1993
Roerich, G., *Tibetan Paintings*, Paris, Geuthner, 1925
Schmid, T., *The Cotton-clad Mila*, Stockholm, 1958
Schmid, T., *The Eighty-five Siddhas,* Stockholm, 1958
Schroeder, U. von, *Indo-Tibetan Bronzes*, Hong Kong, Visual Dharma, 1981
Seckel, D., *Kunst der Buddhismus*, Baden Baden, 1962
Sierksma, M., *Tibet's Terrifying Deities*, The Hague, Mouton, 1966
Singh, M., *Himalayan Art*, London, Macmillan, 1968
Snellgrove, D., *The Image of Buddha*, Tokyo, Kodansha, 1980
Tucci, G., *Indo-Tibetica*, Rome, Reale Accademia d'Italia, 1932–1941
Tucci, G., *Tibetan Painted Scrolls*, Rome, Libreria dello Stato, 1949

Various authors, *Dieux et demons de l'Himalaya: Art du Bouddhisme lamaique*, Paris, Catalogue of Exhibition at Grand Palais, 1977

Vitali, R., *Early Temples of Central Tibet*, London, Serindia, 1989

V. TIBETAN LITERATURE

Bacot, J., *Trois mystères tibétains: Tchrimekunden, Djroazanmo, Nansal,* Paris, Bossard, 1921, l'Asiatique, 1987

Bacot, J., *Le Poète tibétain Milarepa*, Paris, Bossard, 1925

Bacot, J., "La Conversion du chasseur" in *Etudes d'orientalisme publiées à la mémoire de R. Linossier, I*, Paris, Leroux, 1932

Bacot, J., *La Vie de Marpa, le "Traducteur"*, Paris, Bouddhica I/VII, 1937

Bacot, J., *Zugiñima*, Paris, Cahiers de la Société asiatique, XIV, 1957

Bosson, J. E., *Treasury of Phoristic Jewels: the Subhasitaratnanidhi of Sa Skya Pandita*, Bloomington, Indiana University Press, 1969

Chang, G. C. C., *The Hundred Thousand Songs of Milarepa*, Boulder (CO), Shambala 1962

David-Neel, A. and Lama Yongden, *La Vie surhumaine de Guesar de Lan*, Paris, 1931

Dessaussoy, D., *Le Fou divin Drukpa Kunley, yogi tantrique du XVIe siècle*, Paris, Albin Michel, 1982

Evans-Wentz, W. J., *The Tibetan Book of the Dead*, Oxford University Press, 1927

Evans-Wentz, W. J., *Tibet's Great Yogi Milarepa: a Biography from the Tibetan*, Oxford University Press, 1928

Evans-Wentz, W. J., *Tibetan Yoga and Secret Doctrine*, Oxford University Press, 1935

Evans-Wentz, W. J., *The Tibetan Book of the Great Liberation*, London, 1954

Ferrari, A., *Mk'en brtse's Guide to the Holy Places of Central Tibet*, Rome, Serie Orientale XVI, 1958

Fromaget, A., *Océan de pure mélodie: Vie et chant du Sixième Dalai Lama du Tibet*, Paris, Dervy, 1995

Gordon, A. K., *Tibetan Tales*, London, 1953

Helffer, M., *Les Chants dans l'épopée tibétaine de Ge-sar d'après le livre de la course de cheval*, Geneva, Droz, 1977

Laufer, B., *Der Roman einer tibetischen Königin*, Leipzig, 1911

Ma Gcig (Orofino, C., ed.), *Canti spirituali*, Milan, Adelphi, 1995

Stein, R.A., *L'épopée tibétaine de Gesar dans sa version lamaique de Ling*, Paris, Presses Universitaires de France, 1956

Stein, R.A., *Vie et chants de 'Brug-pa Kun-legs, le Yogin*, Paris, Maisonneuve, 1972

Toussaint, G. C., *The Life and Liberation of Padma Sambhava*, Emeryville (CA), Dharma, 1978

Tucci, G., *Il Libro tibetano dei morti*, Milan, Bocca, 1949

Tucci, G., *Tibetan Folksongs*, Ascona, Artibus Asiae, 1966

Van Heurck, P., *Chants attribués à Tsang Yang Gyatso, Sixième Dalai Lama*, Rikon-Zurich, Opuscula tibetana XVI, Tibet Institut, 1984

Vostrikov, A. I., *Tibetan Historical Literature*, Calcutta, Indian Studies, 1970

Yu, D., *Love Songs of the Sixth Dalai Lama*, Beijing, Academia Sinica Monographs A/5, 1930

VI. TRAVEL, EXPLORATION, ETHNOLOGY AND SOCIOLOGY

Amman, O. and Barletta, G., *Tibet sconosciuto: Kailas, la montagna più sacro del mondo*, Como, Dadò, 1996

Arnold, P., *Avec les lamas tibétains*, Paris, Arthème Fayard, 1970

Aziz, B. N., *Tibetan Frontier Families: Reflections of Three Generations from D'ong-ri*, New Delhi, 1978

Bacot, J., *Le Tibet revolté*, Paris, Hachette, 1912

Bell, C., *The People of Tibet*, Oxford, Clarendon Press, 1928, 1968

Berry, S., *A Stranger in Tibet: the Adventures of a Wandering Zen Monk*, Tokyo, Kodansha International, 1989

Carrasco, P., *Land and Polity in Tibet*, Seattle, 1959

Chapman, F. S., *Lhasa, the Holy City*, London, Chatto & Windus, 1938, Sutton, 1984

Dargyay, E. K., *Tibetan Village Communities: Structure and Change*, Warminster, Aris & Phillips, 1980

Das, S. C., *Journey to Lhasa and Central Tibet*, 1904, New Delhi, 1970

David-Neel, A., *Voyage d'une Parisienne à Lhasa*, Paris, Plon, 1927

David-Neel, A., *Le Journal de voyage (1918–1940)*, Paris, Plon, 1976

David-Neel, A., *Magic and Mystery in Tibet*, London, Abacus, 1977

Duncan, M. H., *Harvest Festival Dramas of Tibet*, Hong Kong, Orient, 1955

Duncan, M. H., *Customs and Superstitions of Tibet*, London, Mitre, 1964

Ekvall, R. B., *Religious Observances in Tibet: Patterns and Function*, Chicago, 1964

Goldstein, M. C. and Breall, C. M., *Nomads of Western Tibet: the Survival of a Way of Life*, Hong Kong, Odyssey, 1990

Hadfield, C. and J., *A Winter in Tibet*, London, Impact, 1988

Harrer, H., *Seven Years in Tibet*, London, Hart-Davis, 1954

Harrer, H., *Tibet is my Country: the Autobiography of Thubten Norbu, Brother of the Dalai Lama, as Told to H. Harrer*, London, Hart-Davis, 1960

Harrer, H., *Return to Tibet*, London, Weidenfeld & Nicolson, 1984

Hedin, S., *Trans-Himalaya*, London, 1909–13

Huc, E. R., *Souvenirs d'un voyage en Tartarie, le Tibet et la Chine*, 1856, Paris, Plon, 1925

Johnson, R. and Moran, K., *Kailas, on Pilgrimage to the Sacred Mountain of Tibet*, London, Thames & Hudson, 1989

Kawaguchi, E., *Three Years in Tibet*, Madras, 1909, 1979

Khsla, G. D., *Himalayan Circuit: A Journey to the Inner Himalayas*, London, Macmillan, 1956

Kimura, H., *Japanese Agent in Tibet*, London, Serindia, 1991

Kingdon Ward, F., *The Land of the Blue Poppy*, London, 1913, 1973

Kingdon Ward, F., *Plant-hunting on the Edge of the World*, London, 1930, 1974

Kingdon Ward, F., *A Plant-hunter in Tibet*, London, Cape, 1937

MacDonald, D., *The Land of the Lama*, London, 1928

Migot, A., *Tibetan Marches*, London, 1955

Norbu, N., *Viaggio nella cultura dei nomadi tibetani*, Arcidosso, Shang-Shung, 1990

Pallis, M., *Peaks and Lamas*, London, Cassell, 1948

Pallis, M., *The Way and the Mountain*, London, Peter Owen, 1960

Pemba, T., *Young Days in Tibet*, London, Cape, 1957

Rock, J., *Lamas, Princes and Brigands: Joseph Rock's Photographs of the Tibetan*

Borderlands of China, New York, China Institute of America, 1992
Sis, V., and Vanis, J., *Der Weg nach Lhasa*, Prague, Artia, 1956
Swami Pranavananda, *Exploration in Tibet*, University of Calcutta, 1950
Teichman, E., *Travels of a Consular Officer in Eastern Tibet*, Cambridge, 1921
Tucci, G. and Ghersi, E., *Cronaca della missione scientifica Tucci nel Tibet occidentale 1933*, Rome, Reale Accademia d'Italia, 1934
Tucci, G., *Santi e briganti nel Tibet ignoto*, Milan, Hoepli, 1937, 1981
Tucci, G., *A Lhasa e oltre*, Rome, 1952, Newton Compton, 1980
Verni, P. and Sevegnani, V., *Tibet: le danze rituali dei Lama*, Florence, Nardini, 1990
Verni, P., *Mustang, ultimo Tibet*, Milan, Corbaccio, 1997
Wilby, S., "Nomad's Lands: a Journey through Tibet" in *The National Geographic Magazine*, Washington, D.C., 1987

VII MISCELLANEOUS WORKS

Bishop, P., *The Myth of Shangri-la: Tibet, Travel Writing and the Western Creation of Sacred Landscape*, London, Athlone, 1989
Bonavia, D. and Bartlett, M., *Tibet* (photographs of), New York, Vendome Press, 1981
Born, F., *Le Tibet d'Alexandra David-Neel* (photographs), Paris, Plon, 1980
Brauen, H., *Harrers Impressionen aus Tibet*, Innsbruck, Pinguin, 1974
Cardelli, C., *Tra Valli e picchi*, Milan, Bayer, 1995
Fujita, H., *The World of Tibetan Buddhism* (photographs), Tokyo, 1981
Govinda, L. G., *Tibet in Pictures*, Berkeley, Dharma, 1979
Gyurme, D. and Meyer, F., *Tibetan Medical Paintings: Illustrations of the "Blue Beryl" Treatise of Sangye Gyatso (1635–1705)*, London, Serindia, 1992
Huntingdon, J. C., *The Phur-pa, Tibetan Ritual Daggers*, Ascona, Artibus Asiae, 1975
Jest, C., *Dolpo, Communautés de langue tibétaine du Nepal*, Paris, Centre national de recherche scientifique, 1975
Kling, K., *Tibet, terre du ciel* (photographs), Paris, Chêne, 1984
Lhalungpa, L. P., *Tibet, the Sacred Realm: Photographs, 1880–1950*, Philadelphia, Aperture, 1983
Müller, C. C. and Raunig, W., *Der Weg zum Dach der Welt*, Innsbruck, Pinguin
Poncar, J., *Tor zum Himmel, Tibet* (photographs), Cologne
Rechung Rimpoche, *Tibetan Medicine*, London, Wellcome Institute, 1973
Richardson, H., *Ceremonies of the Lhasa Year*, London, Serindia, 1993
Tung, R. J., *A Portrait of Lost Tibet* (photographs), London, Thames & Hudson, 1980
Vandor, I., *Bouddhisme tibétain, les traditions musicales*, Paris, Buchet Chastel, 1976
Waterfall, A. C., *The Postal History of Tibet*, London, Pall Mall Stamp Co., 1981
Willis, J. (ed.), *Feminine Ground: Essays on Women in Tibet*, Ithaca, Snow Lion, 1989
Various authors, *The Potala Palace of Tibet*, Shanghai, People's Publishing House, 1982

VIII BIBLIOGRAPHIES

Kuloy, H. K. and Imaeda, Y., *Bibliography of Tibetan Studies*, Narita, Naritasan Shinshoji, 1986
Lindegger, P. and Kung, R., *Sachkatalog der Sekundärliteratur am Tibet-Institut*, Rikon/Zurich, 1981
Yakushi, Y., *Catalogue of Himalayan Literature*, Tokyo, Hakusuisha, 1984

IX GUIDEBOOKS

Batchelor, S., *The Tibet Guide*, London, Wisdom, 1987

Booz, E. B., *A Guide to Tibet*, London, Collins, 1982, Berkeley (CA), Lonely Planet, 1986

Buckley, M. and Strauss, R., *Tibet, a Travel Survival Kit*, Berkeley (CA), Lonely Planet, 1986

Chan, V., *Tibet Handbook*, Chico (CA), 1994

Keilhauer, A. and P., *Ladakh und Zanskar*, Cologne, Du Mont, 1982

McCue, G., *Trekking in Tibet: a Traveller's Guide*, Seattle, The Mountaineers, 1991

Majupuria, T. C. and I., *Tibet, a Guide to the Land of Fascination*, Bangkok, Tecpress Service, 1988

Oliaro, P., *Guida al Tibet*, Turin, Centro Documentazione Alpina, 1987

Raineri, M. C. and Crespi, E., *Tibet, Viaggio nella "Terra proibita"*, Bologna, Calderini, 1988

Schettler, M. and G., *Kashmir, Ladakh and Zanskar*, Berkeley (CA), Lonely Planet, 1985

Somare, G. and Vigorelli, L., *Tibet*, Milan, CLUP, 1988

X RECORDED TIBETAN MUSIC

UNESCO Musical Anthology of the Orient, 9, 10,11, *The Music of Tibetan Buddhism*, Kassel, Bärenreiter, 30/L 2009/11

Note: For the works of "Lobsang Rampa" see Glossary under "Third Eye".

Index

Bold type indicates a Glossary entry. *Italics* indicates an illustration